Spirit-Filled
Scripture Study Guide

Spirit-Filled
Scripture Study Guide

Special Thanks To:

My wife, Trina

My Son, Aaron and his wife Errin Cody; their daughters, Avery Jane and Macy Claire; their son, Jude Aaron.

My daughter, Alicia and her husband Caleb; their sons, Jaiden Mark, Gavin Luke, Landon James, and Dylan Paul; their daughter, Hadley Marie.

My parents, Pastor B.B. and Velma Hankins, who are now in Heaven with the Lord.

My wife's parents, Rev. William and Ginger Behrman.

SAMPLE:

II TIMOTHY 2:15 Study to shew thyself approved unto God, a workman that needeth not to be ashamed, rightly dividing the word of truth.

> *(AMP)* Study and be eager and do your utmost to present yourself to God approved (tested by trial), a workman who has no cause to be ashamed, correctly analyzing and accurately dividing – rightly handling and skillfully teaching – the Word of Truth.
>
> *(TLB)* Work hard so God can say to you, "Well done." Be a good workman, one who does not need to be ashamed when God examines your work. Know what his Word says and means.
>
> *(NIV)* Do your best to present yourself to God as one approved, a workman who does not need to be ashamed and who correctly handles the word of truth.

The whole Bible is not about faith,
*but the **whole Bible** does have the capacity*
*to **produce faith** for whatever you need*
*to **receive from God.***

~Mark Hankins
11:23
THE LANGUAGE OF FAITH

REFERENCES
Old Testament Scriptures 11
New Testament Scriptures 12

TRANSLATION ABBREVIATIONS 18

RIGHTEOUSNESS
Reference List 27
Scriptures 29

REDEMPTION
Reference List 51
Scriptures 53

FAITH
Reference List 133
Scriptures 135

HOLY SPIRIT
Reference List 177
Scriptures 179

**AUTHORITY
OF THE BELIEVER**
Reference List 197
Scriptures 199

PRAYER
Reference List 225
Scriptures 227

DIVINE HEALING
Reference List 267
Scriptures 269

FINANCES
Reference List 291
Scriptures 293

LOVE
Reference List 315
Scriptures 317

JOY
Reference List 335
Scriptures 337

PEACE
Reference List 347
Scriptures 349

ETERNAL LIFE
Reference List 359
Scriptures 361

SIGNS & WONDERS
Reference List 407
Scriptures 409

TOPICAL REFERENCE 415

BIBLIOGRAPHY 419

RESOURCES 428

Old Testament

GENESIS

2:8 293
2:10 293
2:12 293
8:22 293
13:2 293
21:6 337

EXODUS

15:25, 26 269
23:25 269

NUMBERS

14:28 135

DEUTERONOMY

7:15 269
8:18 293
14:22 293
14:23 293
26:8, 9 294
28:21-65 270

JOSHUA

1:8 . . . . 135, 294
6:16, 20 135

II SAMUEL

6:14 339

I CHRONICLES

29:3 294
29:12 295
29:26 295
29:28 295

II CHRONICLES

9:20 295
9:27 295
20:20 295
26:5 296

NEHEMIAH

8:10 339

JOB

5:22 337
8:6 296
8:7 296
8:21 339
36:11 296

PSALM

1:1 135
1:2 136
1:3 136
2:4 337
4:7 340
4:8 349
5:11, 12 338
22:1 63
22:6 63
22:7 63
22:8 63
22:9 64
22:10 64
22:11 64
22:12 64
22:13 64
22:14 64
22:15 65
22:16 65
22:17 65
22:18 65
23:1 296
30:2 272
32:11 338
33:6 136
33:9 136
34:9 297
34:10 297
35:27 297
37:4 227
42:11 272
55:22 227
66:12 297
68:3, 4 339
71:7 409
88:4 65
88:5 65
88:6 65
88:7 66
88:8 66
88:10 66
88:11 66
88:12 66
88:16 67

PSALM

89:15 . . . . 46, 340
89:16 . . . . 47, 340
89:17 349
89:18 349
89:34 136
91:1-6, 10 273
100:2 227
100:4 227
103:2, 3 274
105:37 297
107:20 274
110:2 199
112:1-3 47
112:2 298
112:3 298
115:14 298
115:15 298
119:89 137
119:90 137
119:97 137
119:130 137
119:148 137
119:162 338
119:165 349
126:1-3 340
138:2 137
147:14 298

PROVERBS

3:5 137
3:6 137
3:9, 10 298
4:20, 21 138
4:20-22 274
4:22 138
4:23 138
4:24 138
6:2 138
8:20 298
8:21 298
10:11 138
10:22 299
10:24 47
11:24, 25 299
12:6 139
12:13 139

12:14 139
12:18 . . . . 139, 274
12:25 139
13:3 139
13:22 299
14:3 140
15:4 140
15:6 300
15:15 341
15:23 . . . . 140, 341
16:21 140
16:23 140
16:24 140
17:22 . . . . 274, 341
18:7 140
18:20 141
18:21 141
21:23 141
22:4 300
22:17 141
22:18 141
22:19 142
28:1 47

ECCLESIASTES
11:1-6 300

ISAIAH
1:19 300
8:18 409
12:3 341
26:3 349
28:11 . . . . 179, 227
28:12 . . . . 227, 349
32:17 . . . . 48, 350
32:20 301
43:25, 26 48
43:26 228
48:18 350
53:3-5 . . . . 53, 275
53:5 . . . . 53, 350
53:7 54
53:10 54
53:11 54
53:12 54
54:13 350
54:14 48

54:17 48
55:10 142
55:11 142
60:17 301
61:7 301

JEREMIAH
1:12 142
15:16 338
30:17 275
33:3 228
33:6 275

DANIEL
4:2, 3 409

JONAH
2:2 62
2:4 62
2:6 62

HABAKKUK
3:17-19 337

MALACHI
3:10 301
4:2 . . . . 49, 276

New Testament

MATTHEW
6:25-33 351
6:32 . . . . 302, 351
6:33 . . . . 302, 351
7:7 228
7:8 228
7:11 . . . . 229, 303
7:24 143
7:25 143
7:26 144
7:27 144
8:2, 3 276
8:13 144
8:16, 17 276
8:17 58
9:28 144
9:29 145

9:34, 35 277
12:40 62
14:30 145
14:31 145
17:20 145
18:18 . . . . 199, 229
18:19 230
21:21, 22 146
23:23 303
24:35 146
27:46 63

MARK
5:25-34 . . . . 147, 277
6:5, 6 147
9:23 148
10:46-52 148
11:14 148
11:22 148
11:23 149
11:24 . . . . 149, 230
11:25 231
16:17 . . . . . 199, 278, 409
16:18 . . . . . . 200, 279, 409

LUKE
1:37 . . . . 150, 279
1:38 . . . . 150, 279
1:45 . . . . 151, 279
4:18 179
4:19 179
5:5 . . . . 151, 279
5:15 151
5:15-20 280
5:16-20 151
6:38 304
10:19 . . . . 200, 280
12:31, 32 304
13:11-13, 16 280
16:9-12 304
17:5, 6 152
17:14 . . . . 152, 281
17:15 . . . . 152, 281
18:8 152
22:31, 32 152

JOHN
1:4 361

1:16 110
3:15 361
3:16 361
3:36 361
4:10 362
4:14 362
4:49, 50 . . . . 153, 282
5:21 363
5:24 . . . . 94, 363
5:25 364
5:26 364
5:39 364
5:40 364
6:33 365
6:35 365
6:40 365
6:47 365
6:48 365
6:51 366
6:53 . . . . 95, 366
6:54 . . . . 95, 366
6:56 . . . . 96, 366
6:57 367
6:63 367
6:68 367
7:38 . . . . 179, 367
8:12 368
10:10 368
10:28 369
11:25 369
11:40 . . . . 153, 282
12:31, 32 73
12:50 369
13:34 317
13:35 317
14:6 369
14:12 . . . . 200, 409
14:12-14 282
14:15 180
14:16 180
14:17 180
14:19 370
14:20 370
14:27 352
15:4, 5 . . . . 120, 282

15:7 . . . . 153, 231
16:13 180
16:14 181
16:15 181
16:23 232
16:24 . . . . 232, 341
16:33 353
17:2 370
17:3 370
17:23 317
20:27 154
20:29 154
20:30 410
20:30, 31 370
21:25 410

ACTS

1:8 181
2:4 181
2:13 182
2:15 182
2:16 182
2:17, 18 182
2:22 410
2:24 60
2:27 61
2:28 371
2:31 61
2:33 61
2:43 410
3:15 371
3:16 283
4:24 232
4:29 . . . . 233, 410
4:30 . . . . 233, 410
4:31 . . . . 183, 234
4:32 234
5:12 410
5:20 371
7:55, 56 183
8:5-8 410
8:13 411
8:15-17 184
9:17 184
9:32-35 283
10:38 283

10:44-47 184
11:14, 15 185
11:18 372
13:2-4 185
13:33, 34 68
13:46 372
13:48 373
13:52 . . . . 185, 341
14:7-10 284
15:28 185
16:25 234
17:25 373
19:6 186
19:11, 12 411
27:25 154

ROMANS

1:16, 17 . . . . 29, 155
1:17 . . . . 29, 373
2:28, 29 156
3:4 156
3:21 83
3:21, 22 30
3:22 84
3:24 . . . . 31, 84
3:25 . . . . 31, 85
3:26 . . . . 32, 86
3:27 . . . . 33, 87
4:16 157
4:17 . . . . 157, 373
4:18 157
4:19 158
4:20 158
4:21 158
4:25 . . . . 33, 56
5:1 . . . . 33, 112, 353
5:2 . . . . 33, 113
5:5 318
5:6 59
5:8 60
5:9 60
5:10 . . . . 100, 373
5:11 . . . . 101, 374
5:17 . . . . 34, 102, 201, 375
5:18 376
5:21 377

6:4 . . . . 87, 377
6:5 88
6:6 89
6:7 90
6:8 . . . . 91, 378
6:11 . . . . 91, 379
6:14 . . . . 34, 92
6:17, 18 35
6:23 380
7:9 380
7:10 380
8:1 . . . . 35, 92
8:2 . . . . 93, 284, 380
8:6 381
8:10 . . . . 94, 381
8:11 . . . . . . 186, 284, 381
8:13 382
8:14 187
8:16 . . . . 124, 187
8:17 125
8:26 . . . . 187, 235
8:27 . . . . 188, 235
8:28 236
8:30 36
8:32 109
8:33, 34 36
8:34 127
8:37 122
8:38 123
8:39 123
10:2 37
10:3 37
10:4 37
10:5 38
10:6 38
10:7 38
10:8 . . . . 38, 159
10:9, 10 38
10:9 159
10:10 159
10:17 160
12:3 160
11:29 188
12:9, 10 319
13:10 319

14:9 126
14:17 . . . . 39, 342
14:18 342
15:19 411

I CORINTHIANS

1:5 105
1:7 106
1:8 106
1:9 106
1:30 . . . . 39, 107
2:4, 5 411
2:9 188
2:10 189
2:11 189
2:12 189
2:13 189
2:14 189
2:16 117
3:16 190
3:21 110
5:17 117
6:13, 15, 19, 20 285
6:17 121
6:19 190
12:7 191
12:9 191
12:10 191
12:11 191
12:27 121
13:4-8 320
14:1 322
14:2 236
14:4 236
14:14 237
14:15 237
14:33 354
15:45 382
15:57 103

II CORINTHIANS

2:14 103
2:16 383
3:4, 5 104
3:6 383
3:17 191
3:18 191

4:10 383
4:11 383
4:12 384
4:13 160
4:18 160
5:4 384
5:7 161
5:14 74
5:17 117
5:19 74
5:21 . . . . 39, 55
6:14, 15 122
6:16 192
8:9 . . . . 59, 304
9:6 305
9:7 305
9:8 306
9:9 307
9:10 307
9:11 308
10:4 201
10:5 202
12:12 412
13:4 384

GALATIANS

2:19 385
2:20 . . . . 75, 285, 385
3:5 412
3:9 308
3:13 . . . . 58, 269, 309
3:14 309
3:21 385
3:29 125
4:4, 5 124
4:6 124
4:7 124
5:6 322
5:22 322
5:23 323
5:24 323
5:25 385
6:7-10 310
6:8 385
6:14 76
6:15 76

EPHESIANS

1:3 107
1:4, 5 40
1:6 . . . . 40, 108
1:7 99
1:8 108
1:11 108
1:16, 17 . . . . 202, 238
1:18 . . . . 203, 239
1:19-20 . . . . 205, 240
1:19-21 . . . . . . 72, 207, 242
1:21 . . . . 72, 207, 242
1:22 . . . . 208, 243
1:23 . . . . 209, 244
2:1 386
2:4, 5 . . . . . . 82, 210, 386
2:6 . . . . 83, 210
2:10 120
2:18 . . . . 40, 113
3:12 41
3:14 . . . . 211, 245
3:15 . . . . 211, 245
3:16 . . . . . . 192, 211, 245
3:17 . . . . 213, 247
3:18 . . . . 213, 247
3:19 . . . . 214, 248
3:20 . . . . 215, 249
3:21 . . . . 216, 250
4:9, 10 62
4:18 387
4:23 41
4:24 . . . . 41, 118
4:27 . . . . 216, 285
4:31 323
4:32 334
5:18 192
5:19 193
5:30 121
6:10 216
6:11 217
6:12 217
6:13 218
6:14 219
6:15 219
6:16 . . . . 161, 219
6:18 250

PHILIPPIANS

1:6 193
1:11 111
1:21 387
1:25 342
2:9 219
2:10 220
2:13 . . . . 193, 285
2:16 387
3:9 42
4:4 342
4:6 . . . . 251, 354
4:7 . . . . . . 117, 252, 355
4:13 104
4:15 310
4:16 310
4:17 310
4:18 311
4:19 . . . . 110, 311

COLOSSIANS

1:9 252
1:10 253
1:11 254
1:12 . . . . 97, 255, 285
1:13 . . . . 97, 256, 286
1:14 . . . . 98, 257, 286
1:18 388
1:21 42
1:22 43
2:3 109
2:9, 10 78
2:11 79
2:12 80
2:13 . . . . 80, 388
2:14 80
2:15 . . . . 68, 220
2:20 77
3:1 81
3:3 78
3:4 388
3:9, 10 119
3:14 324
3:16 257

I THESSALONIANS

1:5 412
3:12 325
4:9 326
4:10 326
5:10 389
5:23 194

II THESSALONIANS

1:3 161
3:16 356

I TIMOTHY

1:16 389
2:1 258
2:2 258
2:3 258
2:4 259
2:5 127
2:6 57
2:8 259
3:16 67
4:8 312
6:12 . . . . 162, 389
6:13 389
6:17-19 312
6:19 390

II TIMOTHY

1:1 390
1:7 116
1:10 391
1:14 194
2:24 327
2:25 327
2:26 329
3:16 162
3:17 162

TITUS

1:2 391
2:14 57
3:5 43
3:7 392

PHILEMON

6 111

HEBREWS

1:9 343
2:4 412

2:9 57
2:14, 15 . . . . 70, 221
3:1 162
4:3 163
4:12 392
4:14 . . . . 128, 163
4:16 128
6:17 163
6:18 164
7:2 312
7:5 313
7:8 313
7:22 . . . . 128, 164
7:25 127
8:6 127
9:12 72
9:24 126
9:26 56
10:1, 2 . . . . 43, 114
10:12 114
10:14 . . . . 44, 115
10:16 115
10:17 115
10:19 . . . . 44, 115
10:20 393
10:22 . . . . 45, 116
10:38 393
11:1 165
11:3 166
11:6 166
11:11 . . . . 167, 343
11:30 167
12:1 167
12:2 167
12:9 393
13:5 168
13:6 168
13:8 277
13:15 259
13:20, 21 112

JAMES
1:2 343
1:3 344
1:5 . . . . 169, 260
1:6 . . . . 169, 260

1:7 . . . . 169, 260
1:21 169
1:22 169
1:23 170
1:24 170
1:25 170
2:14 171
2:17 171
2:20-22 172
4:7 . . . . 222, 286
5:13-18 260
5:15, 16 287
5:16 45

I PETER
1:3 393
1:5 194
1:8 344
1:23 394
1:25 172
2:9 125
2:24 . . . . 59, 287, 395
2:25 129
3:4 172
3:7 395
3:10 172
3:8-12 329
3:12 . . . . 46, 262
3:18 . . . . 67, 395
4:6 396
4:8 331
5:7 . . . . 262, 356
5:8 . . . . 223, 287
5:9 . . . . 223, 287

II PETER
1:3, 4 109
1:4 396

I JOHN
1:1 396
1:2 397
1:9 46
2:1 129
2:10 331
3:8 288
3:9 397
3:14 398

3:15 398
3:18 331
4:4 195
4:7 . . . . 332, 399
4:8 332
4:9 399
4:16 332
4:17 121
5:1 399
5:4 . . . . 99, 173, 399
5:11, 12 . . . . 96, 400
5:13 400
5:14 263
5:15 263
5:18 401
5:20 401

III JOHN
2 . . . . 288, 313

JUDE
20 264
21 333

REVELATION
1:5 . . . . 68, 401
1:6 126
1:18 401
2:7 401
3:5 402
7:17 402
12:11 173
13:8 402
17:8 402
20:12 402
20:15 403
21:6 403
21:27 403
22:1 403
22:2 404
22:14 404
22:17 404
22:19 404

Scriptures are King James Version unless otherwise marked. Translations used in the text are identified by the abbreviations as noted below. Appreciation is expressed to the publishers for permission to reprint selections from the following translations of the Bible.

Abbrev Bible   The Abbreviated Bible.

ABPS   *The Holy Bible Containing the Old and New Testaments: An Improved Edition.* American Baptist Publication Society.

ABV   *The New Testament of Our Lord and Savior, Jesus Christ.* American Bible Union Version.

Adams   Adams, Jay E. *The New Testament in Everyday English.*

Alf.   Alford, Henry. *The New Testament for English Readers.*

AMP   *The Amplified Bible.*

HT Ander   Anderson, H.T. *A Translation of the New Testament.*

ASV   *American Standard Version.*

Authentic   Schonfield, Hugh. *The Authentic New Testament.*

Barclay   Barclay, William. *The New Testament, A New Translation.*

Bart. & Pet.   Barrlett, Edward and Peters, John. *Scriptures Hebrew and Christian.*

Barth   Barth, Markus. *Anchor Bible.*

Basic   *The Bible in Basic English.*

Baxter   Baxter, Richard. *A Paraphrase of the New Testament with Notes.*

Beck   Beck, William. *The Holy Bible in the Language of Today.*

Berk.   Verkuyl, Gerrit. *The Holy Bible, The Berkeley Version in Modern English.*

N. Berk.   Verkuyl, Gerrit. The Holy Bible, *The New Berkeley Version in Modern English.*

Bird, R.	Bird, Robert. *Paul of Tarsus.*
Black.	Blackwelder, Boyce. *Letters from Paul, An Exegetical Translation.*
Book	*The Book of Books, A Translation of the New Testament Complete and Unabridged.*
Bruce	Bruce, F.F. *The Letters of Paul, An Expanded Paraphrase.*
Campbell	Campbell, Alexander. *The Sacred Writings of the Apostles and Evangelists of Jesus Christ.*
Carpenter	Carpenter, S.C. *A Paraphrase of Ephesians.*
Carpenter	Carpenter, S.C. *Selections from Romans and the Letter to the Philippians.*
Cent.	Montgomery, Helen Barrett. *Centenary Translation of the New Testament.*
Clem.	Clemenston, Edgar Lewis. *The New Testament A Translation.*
Comp.	*The Companion Bible.*
Conc.	*Concordant Literal New Testament, Sixth Edition.*
Condon	Condon, Kevin. *The Alba House New Testament.*
Conf.	*Confraternity Version New Testament.*
Conq.	Conquest, J.T. *The Holy Bible Containing then Old and New Testaments.*
Cony.	Conybeare, W.J. *The Epistles of Paul.*
Cornish	Cornish, Gerald Warre. *Saint Paul from the Trenches.*
Cress.	Cressman, A. *Good News for the World.*
Crickmer	Crickmer, William Burton. *The Greek Testament Englished.*
Cunn.	Cunnington, E.E. *The New Covenant.*
Deaf	*The New Testament English Version the Deaf.*

Dist.   *The Distilled Bible / New Testament.*

Dodd.   Doddridge, P. *The Family Expositor: or a Paraphrase and Version of The New Testament.*

Deane   Deane, Anthony C. *St. Paul and His Letters.*

Douay   *Douay Rheims Version of the Holy Bible.*

Eadie   Eadie, John. *Translation of Buchanan's Latin Psalms into English Verse.*

Este   Estes, Chester. *The Better Version of the New Testament.*

Fenton   Fenton, Ferrar. *The Holy Bible in Modern English.*

Fides   Regan, Mary Perkins. *The Fides Translation.*

GNB   *Good News Bible. The Bible in Today's English Version.*

Gspd.   Goodspeed, Edgar J. *The New Testament, An American Translation.*

Godbey   Godbey, W.B. *Translation of the New Testament.*

Hammond   Hammond, H. *A Paraphrase and Annotations upon All the Books of the New Testament, Second Edition.*

Hanson   Hanson, J.W. *The New Covenant.*

Har.   Harrison, R.K. *The Psalms for Today: A New Translation from the Hebrew into Current English.*

Hayford   Hayford, Jack W. *Spirit-Filled Life Bible.*

Hoerber   Hoerber, Robert G. *St. Paul's Shorter Letters.*

Hudson   Hudson, James T. *The Pauline Epistles, Their Meaning and Message.*

Jer.   *The Jerusalem Bible.*

Johnson   Johnson, Ben Campbell. *Matthew and Mark, A Rational Paraphrase of The New Testament.*

Johnson Johnson, Ben Campbell. *The Heart of Paul, A Rational Paraphrase of The New Testament.*

Jordan Jordan, Clarence. *The Cotton Patch Version of Paul's Epistles.*

JPS The Jewish Publication Society of America. *The Holy Scriptures, A New Translation.*

K. & L. Kleist, James A. and Lilly, Joseph L. *The New Testament Rendered from The Original Greek with Explanatory Notes.*

Kling. Klingensmith, Don J. *The New Testament in Everyday English.*

Knox Knox, Ronald. *The Old Testament Newly Translated from the Latin Vulgate.*

Knox Knox, Ronald. *The New Testament of Our Lord and Savior Jesus Christ, A New Translation.*

Lamsa Lamsa, George M. *The Holy Bible from Ancient Eastern Manuscripts.*

Lau. Laubach, Frank C. *The Inspired Letters in Clearest English.*

Lesser Lesser, Isaac. *Twenty-Four Books of the Holy Scriptures.*

Letters *Letters to Street Christians by Two Brothers from Berkeley.*

Lovett Lovett, C.S. *Lovett's Lights on First John.*

Lovett Lovett, C.S. *Lovett's Lights on Galatians, Ephesians, Philippians, Colossians, 1 & 2 Thessalonians with Rephrased Text.*

MacK. MacKnight, James. *A New Literal Translation from the Original Greek of All the Apostolical Epistles.*

Mar. Marshall, Alfred. *The Interlinear Greek-English New Testament.*

Masoretic O.T. *The Holy Scriptures According to the Masoretic Text: A New Translation.*

McFadyen McFadyen, John Edgar. *The Message of the Psalmists.*

Merrick Merrick, James. *A Version or Paraphrase of the Psalms.*

Message	Peterson, Eugene. *The Message//Remix, The Bible in Contemporary Language.*
Mof.	Moffat, James. *The New Testament Containing the Old and New Testaments.*
NAB	*New American Bible.*
NASB	*New American Standard Bible.*
NEB	*New English Bible.*
NEV	*New English Version of the Holy Bible.*
NIV	*New International Version of the Holy Bible.*
New Life	Ledyard, Gleason. *The New Life Testament.*
Noli	Noli, Fan. S. *The New Testament of Our Lord and Savior Jesus Christ.*
Norlie	Norlie Norlie, Olaf M. *Norlie's Simplified New Testament in Plain English — For Today's Readers.*
Phil.	Phillips, J.B. *The New Testament in Modern English.*
Pilcher	Pilcher, Charles Venn. *The Epistle of St. Paul to the Romans.*
Pl. English	Williams, Charles Kingsley. *The New Testament, A New Translation in Plain English.*
Quaker	Purver, Anthony. *Quaker Bible.*
Richert	Richert, Ernest L. *Freedom Dynamics.*
Rieu	Rieu, E.V. *The Acts of the Apostles.*
Rieu	Rieu, E.V. *The Four Gospels.*
River.	Ballentine, William G. *The Riverside New Testament.*
Roth.	Rotherham, J.B. *The Emphasized Bible.*
Roth 2	Rotherham, J.B. *The New Testament: Critically Emphasized, Second Edition.*

RSV   *Revised Standard Version*

SEB   *The Simple English Bible.*

Sept.   Brenton, Charles Lee. *The Septuagint Version of the Old Testament.*

Sanday &   Sanday and Headlam. *Romans in I.C.C.*
Headlam

Sharpe   Sharpe, Samuel. *The Hebrew Scriptures, Vol. II.*

Sharpe   Sharpe, Samuel. *The New Testament, Translated from Griebach's Text.*

Shuttle.   Shuttleworth, Philip Nicholas. *Paraphrastic Translation of the Apostolical Epistles.*

Smith, J.M   Smith J.M. and Goodspeed, E.J. *The Complete Bible, An American Translation.*

Smith, J.   Smith, Julia. *The Holy Bible Translated Literally from the Original Tongues.*

Spencer   Spencer, Francis. *The New Testament of Our Lord and Saviour Jesus Christ.*

Spur.   Spurrell, Helen. *A Translation of the Old Testament Scriptures from the Original Hebrew.*

Stanley   Stanley, Arthur. *The Epistles of St. Paul to the Corinthians, Second Edition.*

Stevens   Stevens, George Barker. *The Epistles of Paul in Modern English.*

Stevens   Stevens, George Barker. *The Messages of the Apostles.*

Swann   Swann, George. *New Testament of Our Lord and Savior, Jesus Christ.*

Syriac   Murdock, James. *The Syriac New Testament.*

Taylor   Taylor, John. *A Paraphrase with Notes on the Epistle to the Romans.*

TLB   Taylor, Ken. *The Living Bible.*

Torah   *The Torah: The Five Books of Moses.*

Trans.   *The Translator's New Testament.*

20th C. 1	*The Twentieth Century New Testament.*
20th C.R.	*The Twentieth Century New Testament, Revised Edition.*
Tomanek	Tomanek, James L. *The New Testament of Our Lord and Savior Jesus Anointed.*
Wade	Wade, G.W. *The Documents of the New Testament.*
Wand	Wand, J.W.C. The New Testament Letters.
Way	Way, Arthur S. *The Letters of St. Paul to the Seven Churches and Three Friends with the Letter to the Hebrews.*
Weekes	Weekes, Robert D. *The New Dispensation Translated from the Greek.*
Weym.	Weymouth, Richard Francis. *The New Testament.*
Wms.	Williams, Charles G. *The New Testament.*
Wood	Wood, C.T. *The Life, Letters and Religion of St. Paul.*
Worrell	Worrell, A.S. *The Worrell New Testament.*
Wuest	Wuest, Kenneth S. *The New Testament, An Expanded Translation.*
Young	Young, Arthur. *Young's Literal Translation of the Holy Bible.*

God would not make an "unrighteous" new creature. He already had an unrighteous old creature. As a new creature **IN CHRIST** you have been made the righteousness of God **IN HIM.**

Mark Hankins
TAKING YOUR PLACE IN CHRIST

PSALM
89:15 46
89:16 47
112:1-3 47

PROVERBS
10:24 47
28:1 47

ISAIAH
32:17 48
43:25, 26 48
54:14 48
54:17 48

MALACHI
4:2 49

ROMANS
1:16, 17 29
3:21, 22 30
3:24 31
3:25 31
3:26 32
3:27 33
4:25 33
5:1,2 33
5:17 34
6:14 34
6:17, 18 35
8:1 35
8:30 36
8:33, 34 36
10:2 37
10:3 37
10:4 37
10:5 38
10:6 38
10:7 38
10:8 38
10:9, 10 38
14:17 39

I CORINTHIANS
1:30 39

II CORINTHIANS
5:21 39

EPHESIANS
1:4, 5 40
1:6 40
2:18 40
3:12 41
4:23 41
4:24 41

PHILIPPIANS
3:9 42

COLOSSIANS
1:21 42
1:22 43

TITUS
3:5 43

HEBREWS
10:1, 2 43
10:14 44
10:19 44
10:22 45

JAMES
5:16 45

I PETER
3:12 46

I JOHN
1:9 46

God has made us 100% righteous **IN CHRIST.** You cannot be 25, 50, 75, or 90% righteous— **IN CHRIST** you have been made 100% righteous.

Mark Hankins
Taking Your Place In Christ

ROMANS 1:16, 17 For I am not ashamed of the gospel of Christ: for it is the power of God unto salvation to every one that believeth; to the Jew first, and also to the Greek. For therein is the righteousness of God revealed from faith to faith: as it is written, The just shall live by faith.

(Johnson) I am confident that the good news will release God's dynamic energy which makes all persons whole.

(Richert) In the meantime, I am pleased to present in writing the substance of my message which will reveal the Master's dynamic method rendering safe and sound all who subscribe to it.

(Way) In the Glad-tidings there is no feature of which I am ashamed. It is the means through which God exerts His power for the salvation of everyone who puts faith in the Message...God's gift of righteousness is revealed in it, lifting men from one step of faith to another. This is the import of that passage of Scripture, which says, "It is from the soil of faith that the righteous shall grow up into real life."

(Pilcher) For I am not ashamed of the Gospel. I have witnessed its divine power to free men from the bondage of sin, if only they will surrender themselves to Jesus Christ in loyal acceptance and trust...For in this Gospel, the righteousness of God is revealed in a system connected from first to last with faith...

(GNB) I have complete confidence in the gospel; it is God's power to save all who believe... For the gospel reveals how God puts people right with himself: it is through faith from beginning to end...

(Noli) I am proud of the Gospel of Christ. It is a message of divine power. It brings salvation to every believer...It reveals that divine righteousness comes from faith and faith only.

(Hayman) ...it being God's own weapon of might...The means of becoming righteous before God is being revealed in it, springing out of, leading up to faith, as Scripture says, "Now the righteous who is so by faith shall have life."

(Lovett) ...It is a power which emanates from God and saves all who believe in it... It reveals God's way of making men as righteous as Himself. It is a process which, from beginning to end, is entirely by faith. As the Scripture says, "He who receives his life by faith is made right with God."

(Stevens) The gospel, I say, can save men, for in it a way is revealed in which sinful men may be accepted before God and may stand in his presence approved and forgiven. Faith is the condition - the procuring cause, on the human side, of this acceptance - and also its result...

(20th C. 1) For in it, there is a revelation of a righteousness which comes from God, the result of faith and leading to faith; as Scripture says - "Those who stand right with God will find Life as the result of faith."

(Deaf) The Good News shows how God makes people right with Himself. God's way of making people right begins and ends with faith...

ROMANS 1:16, 17 (Wms.) For in the good news, God's Way of man's right standing with Him is uncovered, the Way of faith that leads to greater faith...

(Weym.) For in the Good News a righteousness which comes from God is being revealed, depending on faith and tending to produce faith...

(Wade) ...a right standing with God, granted by Him in consequence of rudimentary faith, and resulting in a more developed faith...

(Trans.) ...the beginning and the end of the process by which God puts men right with himself is faith...

(NIV) ...a righteousness that is by faith from first to last...

(Phil.) I see in it God's plan for imparting righteousness to men...

See faith p. 155

ROMANS 3:21, 22 But now the righteousness of God without the law is manifested, being witnessed by the law and the prophets; Even the righteousness of God which is by faith of Jesus Christ unto all and upon all them that believe; for there is no difference...

(Carpenter) But what has happened now is that, outside the Law, apart from all question of injunction and prohibition, a wholly new kind of righteousness has been revealed to a wondering world. It does not say, "How many commandments have you kept?" Answer, "All, or nearly all." "Very good; go up top." It says something much more marvelous and much more divine than that. It says, "Do you pledge yourself solely and utterly to Christ?" ...The longed for words "Not Guilty" are heard by those who are His, who stand in a true relation towards Him. He strikes off their fetters, He breaks the prison doors, He lifts them to the happy level where they hear the emancipating verdict, "Prisoner at the Bar, you may go free."

(Way) But now we have a new revelation - the offer of God's gift of righteousness quite independently of obedience to the Mosaic Law...This righteousness of God's bestowal is attained through trust in Jesus the Messiah, and is vouchsafed only to those who believe in Him.

(Wms.) But now God's way of giving men right standing with Himself has come to light; a way without connection with the law...God's own way of giving men right standing with Himself is through faith in Jesus Christ...

(Weym.) But now a righteousness coming from God has been brought to light apart from any Law...a righteousness coming from God...

(Hayman) But as facts now stand, our view opens upon a righteousness God-given, notresting on law...I mean, a righteousness God-given, through faith in Jesus Christ; in which are included and to which are entitled all believers alike, without distinction.

ROMANS 3:21, 22 (Black.) ...God's kind of righteousness stands manifested apart from law [of any kind]...Indeed God's kind of righteousness is through faith in Jesus Christ. It is effective for all who are trusting [in him].

> *(Phil.)* ...it is a righteousness imparted to, and operating in, all who have faith in Jesus Christ.

ROMANS 3:24 Being justified freely by his grace through the redemption that is in Christ Jesus:

> *(Barclay)* And all can enter into a right relationship with God as a free gift, by means of his grace, through the act of deliverance which happened in Jesus Christ.
>
> *(Lovett)* God's method of justification is to give men His righteousness as a free gift. It is possible for Him to offer it completely by grace since it comes through the redemptive death of Christ Jesus.
>
> *(Wade)* Such, by His gratuitous Favour, stand right with Him through the redemption which was effected in Christ Jesus...
>
> *(Trans.)* They are freely put right with Him by His grace, through the act of liberation effected by Christ Jesus.
>
> *(Beck)* They are justified freely by grace, through the ransom Christ Jesus paid to free them.
>
> *(Wms.)* ...but anybody may have right standing with God as a free gift of His undeserved favor, through the ransom provided in Christ Jesus.
>
> *(Authentic)* ...freely exonerated through the discharge of liability by Christ Jesus.

See redemption p. 84

ROMANS 3:25 Whom God hath set forth to be a propitiation through faith in his blood, to declare his righteousness for the remission of sins that are past, through the forbearance of God;

> *(AMP)* Whom God put forward (before the eyes of all) as a mercy seat and propitiation by His blood (the cleansing and life-giving sacrifice of atonement and reconciliation, to be received) through faith. This was to show God's righteousness, because in His divine forbearance He had passed over and ignored former sins without punishment.
>
> *(20th C. 1)* For God placed him before the world, to be, by his sacrifice of himself, a means of reconciliation through faith...
>
> *(Cent.)* For God openly set him forth for himself as an offering of atonement through faith, by means of his-blood, in order to show forth his righteousness...
>
> *(Phil.)* God has appointed him as the means of propitiation, a propitiation accomplished by the shedding of his blood, to be received and made effective in ourselves by faith...

ROMANS 3:25 (Way) God ordained Him from of old to be the atonement for a world's sin. The essence of this atonement consisted in the shedding of His blood: the channel whereby we profit by it is faith in Him: the effect is a new revelation of God's justice. He suspended judgment on the sins of that former period, the period of His forbearance...

(Richert) Also, by causing Jesus to pay the death penalty for all men's failure retroactively, the Majesty reveals the highest judicial integrity...He did not foreclose on human delinquency long ago.

(Lovett) God offered Jesus as a public sacrifice that His shed blood might cleanse us from our sins when we put our faith in Him. At the same time, this act vindicated His justice. The sacrifice of Jesus clearly showed why God, in His forbearance, was able to overlook the sins of men in the past.

(Hudson) Him God has [publicly] set forth as annulling sin through his bloody death, [which annulment takes effect in us] through faith. This was to give an exhibition of his righteousness [necessary] because, in his forbearance, God had overlooked sins committed previously...

(Carpenter) But our Lord, by His sacrifice, has made for us a way into the pardoning grace of God. His was a truly spiritual sacrifice. His blood, shed on the Cross, is the red seal of it. There is the true Mercy-Seat. And the power of faith is such that by faith a man can unite himself with the divine Victim, and in that union enter into the blessed state of at-one-ment with the Father.

(NEB) For God designed him to be the means of expiating sin by his sacrificial death, effective through faith. God meant by this to demonstrate his justice, 26 because in his forbearance he had overlooked the sins of the past—to demonstrate his justice now in the present, showing that he is himself just and also justifies any man who puts his faith in Jesus.

(Adams) Whom God publicly provided (by the shedding of His blood) as an appeasing sacrifice to be appropriated by faith. He did this to demonstrate His righteousness because, in His tolerance, He had passed by sins committed previously...

ROMANS 3:26 To declare, I say, at this time his righteousness: that he might be just, and the justifier of him which believeth in Jesus.

(Fenton) ...and to display His righteousness at this present time, so that He might be righteous Himself, and make the believer in Jesus righteous as well.

(Wood) ...so that He is at once righteous, and yet can accept and justify sinful men...

(20th C. 1) ...in order that he might be righteous, and make those who have faith in Jesus stand right with himself.

(Beck) Now He wanted to show His righteousness, to be righteous Himself and make righteous anyone who believes in Jesus.

ROMANS 3:26 (Worrell) ...for the manifestation of His righteousness in the present time, to the end that He may be righteous, even when declaring righteous him who has faith in Jesus.

(Basic) ..to make clear his righteousness now, so that he might himself be upright, and give righteousness to him who has faith in Jesus.

ROMANS 3:27 Where is boasting then? It is excluded. By what law? of works? Nay: but by the law of faith.

(AMP) Then what becomes of [our] pride and [our] boasting? It is excluded (banished, ruled out entirely). On what principle? [On the principle] of doing good deeds? No, but on the principle of faith.

(Message) So where does that leave our proud Jewish insider claims and counterclaims? Canceled? Yes, canceled. What we've learned is this: God does not respond to what we do; we respond to what God does.

ROMANS 4:25 Who was delivered for our offences, and was raised again for our justification.

(AMP) Who was betrayed and put to death because of our misdeeds and was raised to secure our justification (our acquittal), [making our account balance and absolving us from all guilt before God].

(Message) The sacrificed Jesus made us fit for God, set us right with God.

(Letters) Jesus, the One who died because we are so rotten and was raised from the dead to make us truly good.

(ASV) Who was delivered up for our trespasses, and was raised again for our justification.

(Weym.) Who was delivered up because of our offenses, and was raised to life for our acquittal because of our justification.

See redemption p. 56

ROMANS 5:1-2 Therefore being justified by faith, we have peace with God through our Lord Jesus Christ: By whom also we have access by faith into this grace wherein we stand, and rejoice in hope of the glory of God.

(AMP) Therefore, since we are justified (acquitted, declared righteous, and given a right standing with God) through faith, let us [grasp the fact that we] have [the peace of reconciliation to hold and to enjoy] peace with God through our Lord Jesus Christ (the Messiah, the Anointed One). Through Him also we have [our] access (entrance, introduction) by faith into this grace (state of God's favor) in which we [firmly and safely] stand. And let us rejoice and exult in our hope of experiencing and enjoying the glory of God.

ROMANS 5:1-2 (TLB) So now, since we have been made right in God's sight by faith in his promises, we can have real peace with him because of what Jesus Christ our Lord has done for us. For because of our faith, he has brought us into this place of highest privilege where we now stand, and we confidently and joyfully look forward to actually becoming all that God has had in mind for us to be.

> *(Weym.)* …through whom also, as the result of faith, we have obtained an introduction into that state of favour with God in which we stand, and we exult in hope of some day sharing in God's glory.

> *(Mof.)* Through him we have to access to this grace where we have our standing, and triumph in the hope of God's glory.

> *(Jordan)* Through him we also got an open door into this favored position we hold, and we get "status" from the confidence we receive from God's greatness.

ROMANS 5:17 For if by one man's offence death reigned by one; much more they which receive abundance of grace and of the gift of righteousness shall reign in life by one, Jesus Christ.

> *(Conc.)* For if the reign of death was established by the one man (Adam), through the sin of him alone far more shall the reign of life be established in those who receive the overflowing fullness of the free gift of righteousness by the one man Jesus Christ.

> *(Cent.)* For if through the transgression of the one, death reigned as king through the one...

> *(Beck)* If one man by his sin made death a king...

> *(Knox)* And if death began its reign through one man, owing to one man's fault...

> *(TLB)* The sin of this one man, Adam, caused death to be king over all.

> *(Gspd.)* …all the more will those who receive God's overflowing mercy and gift of uprightness live and reign through the one individual Jesus Christ.

> *(Wms.)* …to a much greater degree will those who continue to receive the overflow of His unmerited favor and His gift of right standing with Himself, reign in real life through one, Jesus Christ.

> *See redemption p. 102; authority of the believer p. 201; eternal life p. 375*

ROMANS 6:14 For sin shall not have dominion over you: for ye are not under the law, but under grace.

> *(Pilcher)* Sin shall not dominate you, because you are not under the dispensation of the Law, which would control you by external commands, but under a dispensation of God's loving kindness and grace, which inspires you from within to right living.

> *(Richert)* Also, there is no further cause for a guilt complex as though you were still under the Law.

ROMANS 6:14 (Wade) ...for Sin is no longer to exercise mastery over you; for you are not under the constraint of Law but are recipients of Divine Favour.

> *(20th C.R.)* For sin shall not lord it over you. You are living under the reign, not of Law, but of Love.
>
> *(Roth.)* For sin over you shall not have lordship, for ye are not under law, but under favour.
>
> *(Knox)* Sin will not be able to play the master over you any longer...
>
> *(Barclay)* ...will no longer hold sway over your life...
>
> *See redemption p. 92*

ROMANS 6:17, 18 But God be thanked, that ye were the servants of sin, but ye have obeyed from the heart that form of doctrine which was delivered you. Being then made free from sin, ye became the servants of righteousness.

> *(Stevens)* Your obedience and service to sin are things of the past...When you thus broke away from bondage to sin, you entered a bondage to righteousness...
>
> *(Way)* Thank God! your thraldom to sin is a thing of the past: you have rendered allegiance - from the heart you have rendered it - to the New Teaching, the mold into which you have let your nature be run.
>
> *(Weym.)* But thanks be to God that though you were once in thraldom to Sin, you have now yielded a hearty obedience to that system of truth in which you have been instructed.
>
> *(Hudson)* ...you became obedient from the heart to the regulative force of the teaching you were taught...
>
> *(Roth. 2)* ...ye rendered obedience out of the heart unto that mold of teaching into which ye were delivered up...
>
> *(Dodd.)* ...the model of doctrine into which ye were delivered as into a mold...
>
> *(Pilcher)* So, being freed from sin's slavery, you have become willing slaves of righteousness.
>
> *(TLB)* And now you are free from your old master, sin; and you have become slaves to your new master, righteousness.
>
> *(Bruce)* You have been emancipated from sin's ownership; you have become "enslaved" to righteousness.
>
> *(RSV, NIV)* ...slaves of righteousness.

ROMANS 8:1 There is therefore now no condemnation to them which are in Christ Jesus, who walk not after the flesh, but after the Spirit.

> *(Way)* No sentence of condemnation, therefore, can lie against those whose life is a union with the Messiah, with Jesus.
>
> *(Phil.)* No condemnation now hangs over the head of those who are "in" Christ Jesus.
>
> *(Sanday & Headlam)* This being so, no verdict of "Guilty" goes forth any longer against the Christian. He lives in closest union with Christ.

ROMANS 8:1 (Barclay) We can therefore say that there is now no condemnation for those whose life is one with the life of Christ.

(Jordan) There is, then, no charge outstanding against those who are in (wedlock to) Jesus Christ.

(Johnson) Now there is no accusing voice nagging those who are united to Jesus Christ...

(Wms.) ...no condemnation at all for those who are in union with...

(Wuest) ...not even one bit of condemnation...

(Pl. Eng.) ...no sentence of "Guilty"...

(Pilcher) ...those who are spiritually united with Christ...

(MacK.) ...engrafted on Christ Jesus...

See redemption p. 92

ROMANS 8:30 Moreover whom he did predestinate, them he also called: and whom he called, them he also justified: and whom he justified, them he also glorified.

(Richert) First, God identifies us as his own, then introduces us to our privileges and responsibilities, further he makes us viable and competent, and ultimately grants us his divine splendor.

(Way) And to us whom so He called He gave righteousness: and us, to whom He has given righteousness, He has crowned with glory too.

(Basic) ...and to those to whom he gave righteousness, in the same way he gave glory.

(New Life) ...Then He shared His shining greatness with those He made right with Himself.

(Phil.) ...he made them righteous in his sight and then lifted them to the splendor of life as his own sons.

(AMP) ...and those whom He justified, He also glorified - raising them to a heavenly dignity and condition (state of being).

(Lovett) ...He also justified them, making them as righteous as Jesus. Beyond that He glorified them, making them partakers of Christ's glory.

(Wms.) ...and those whom He calls He brings into right standing with Himself...

(Lau.) ...He gave His own glory to those whose charges He cleared.

ROMANS 8:33, 34 Who shall lay anything to the charge of God's elect? It is God that justifieth. Who is he that condemneth? It is Christ that died, yea rather, that is risen again, who is even at the right hand of God, who also maketh intercession for us.

(GNB) Who will accuse God's chosen people? God himself declares them not guilty!

ROMANS 8:33, 34 (Carpenter) Let the accuser launch his charges. They will fall harmless to the ground. The Judge of all the world has set our feet upon the way of righteousness. There is no other court that can reverse that verdict...[Christ] is now seated at the right hand of the Majesty on high. It is His voice which says all the time, "Father, remember those for whom I died." That precious Death, that mighty Resurrection, that glorious Ascension, that Good Shepherd pleading at the right hand of God, that marvelous series of creative acts, has forged a union that cannot be broken.

(Way) ...God saith I am righteous - who dares condemn me to death?

(Wms.) It is God who declared them in right standing...

(Beck) ...It is God who makes us righteous.

See redemption p. 127

ROMANS 10:2 For I bear them record that they have a zeal of God, but not according to knowledge.

(Lovett) From personal experience, I can testify to their ardent zeal for Him. Unfortunately, however, their enthusiasm is misdirected since it is not based on true spiritual knowledge.

(Richert) Oh, many are zealous in a religious way. Unfortunately, their zeal is not matched with understanding the ways of the Almighty.

(Hudson) For I bear them witness that they have a zeal for God, but [a zeal] not [informed] by accurate knowledge.

ROMANS 10:3 For they being ignorant of God's righteousness, and going about to establish their own righteousness, have not submitted themselves unto the righteousness of God.

(Lovett) Failing to understand God's merciful way of making men righteous, they set up a program for making themselves righteous. In doing so, they missed the way of salvation.

(Richert) Ignoring his way to worthiness they insisted on a do-it-yourself approach.

(Jordan) Not understanding God's program, and trying to set up one of their own, they didn't yield to God's program.

(Jer.) Failing to recognize the righteousness that comes from God, they tried to promote their own idea of it, instead of submitting to the righteousness of God.

ROMANS 10:4 For Christ is the end of the law for righteousness to every one that believeth.

(Lovett) What they failed to understand was that everything the Law demanded was summed up in Christ and that the legal program came to an end when He appeared.

ROMANS 10:5 For Moses describeth the righteousness which is of the law, That the man which doeth those things shall live by them.

> *(TLB)* For Moses wrote that if a person could be perfectly good and hold out against temptation all his life and never sin once, only then could he be pardoned and saved.

ROMANS 10:6 But the righteousness which is of faith speaketh on this wise, Say not in thine heart, Who shall ascend into heaven? (that is, to bring Christ down from above;)

> *(Richert)* Becoming acceptable to God by trust is not based on accomplishing some impossible feat like storming heaven to bring God's Son down to us...

ROMANS 10:7 Or, Who shall descend into the deep? (that is, to bring up Christ again from the dead.)

> *(AMP)* Or who will descend into the abyss? that is, to bring Christ up from the dead [as if we could be saved by our own efforts].

ROMANS 10:8 But what saith it? The word is nigh thee, even in thy mouth, and in thy heart: that is, the word of faith, which we preach;

> *(Johnson)* Look for the answer nearer by, even in your mouth and in the center of your being. I refer to the message of faith which I am preaching.
> *(MacEvilly)* [paraphrase]...the matter is neither difficult nor remote from thee, it is in thy mouth and in thy heart; by acts of both one and the other, that is, by internal acts of faith, and by the external profession of the same....The whole gospel which we preach is reduced to this narrow compass.
> *(Phil.)* For the secret is very near you, in your own heart, in your own mouth. It is the secret of faith, which is the burden of our preaching,

ROMANS 10:9, 10 That if thou shalt confess with thy mouth the Lord Jesus, and shalt believe in thine heart that God raised him from the dead, thou shalt be saved. For with the heart man believeth unto righteousness; and with the mouth confession is made unto salvation.

> *(AMP)* Because if you acknowledge and confess with your lips that Jesus is Lord and in your heart believe (adhere to, trust in, and rely on the truth) that God raised Him from the dead, you will be saved. For with the heart a person believes (adheres to, trusts in, and relies on Christ) and so is justified (declared righteous, acceptable to God), and with the mouth he confesses (declares openly and speaks out freely his faith) and confirms [his] salvation.
> *(Lovett)* If then your lips testify to the fact that Jesus is Lord, because your heart truly believes that God raised Him from the dead, you will be saved. For it is the task of the heart to believe God's offer of righteousness through faith, and the task of the lips to affirm that His offer of salvation has been accepted.

ROMANS 10:9, 10 (Phil.) If you openly admit by your own mouth that Jesus Christ is the Lord, and if you believe in your own heart that God raised him from the dead, you will be saved.

(Message) With your whole being you embrace God setting things right, and then you say it, right out loud: "God has set everything right between him and me!"

(Weym.) For with the heart men believe and obtain righteousness, and with the mouth they make confession and obtain salvation.

(TLB) For it is by believing in his heart that a man becomes right with God...

(Basic) For with the heart man has faith to get righteousness...

See faith p. 159

ROMANS 14:17 For the kingdom of God is not meat and drink; but righteousness, and peace, and joy in the Holy Ghost.

(Way) The Kingdom of God is not a matter of eating and drinking: it is righteousness, heart peace, and joy in the presence of the Holy Spirit.

(Knox) The kingdom of God is not a matter of eating or drinking this or that; it means rightness of heart, finding our peace and our joy in the Holy Spirit.

See joy p. 342

I CORINTHIANS 1:30 But of him are ye in Christ Jesus, who of God is made unto us wisdom, and righteousness, and sanctification, and redemption.

(Way) ...our means of right-standing....

(Trans.)...It is God who has restored us in him....

(GNB) ...by Him we are put right with God.

(Wood) ...real righteousness imparted to us.

II CORINTHIANS 5:21 For he hath made him to be sin for us, who knew no sin; that we might be made the righteousness of God in him.

(GNB) Christ was without sin, but for our sake God made him share our sin in order that in union with him we might share the righteousness of God.

(Way) Jesus knew not sin, yet God made him to be the World's Sin for our sakes, that we, whose sin he had thus assumed, might become, by our union with him, the very righteousness of God.

(Black.) ...in our behalf God identified him with everything in the whole realm of sin in order that by trusting him we might become [recipients of] God's kind of righteousness.

(Wms.) ...so that through union with Him we might come into right standing with God.

(Cony.) ...changed into the righteousness of God in Christ.

(Wood) Think of it: Christ the sinless was made the personification of sin for us, in order that in union with Him we might become the very righteousness of God.

II CORINTHIANS 5:21 (Trans.) ...God made him to be sin itself on our behalf...

(Jer.) For our sake God made the sinless one into sin...

(NEB) ...God made him one with the sinfulness of men...

See redemption p. 55

EPHESIANS 1:4, 5 According as he hath chosen us in him before the foundation of the world, that we should be holy and without blame before him in love: Having predestinated us unto the adoption of children by Jesus Christ to himself, according to the good pleasure of his will.

(AMP) Even as [in His love] He chose us [actually picked us out for Himself as His own] in Christ before the foundation of the world, that we should be holy (consecrated and set apart for Him) and blameless in His sight, even above reproach, before Him in love. For He foreordained us (destined us, planned in love for us) to be adopted (revealed) as His own children through Jesus Christ, in accordance with the purpose of His will [because it pleased Him and was His kind intent].

(TLB) ...he decided then to make us holy in his eyes, without a single fault—we who stand before him covered with his love. His unchanging plan has always been to adopt us into his own family by sending Jesus Christ to die for us. And he did this because he wanted to!

(20th C. 1) For in the person of Christ he chose us for himself before the creation of the world, intending that we might be holy and blameless in his sight, living in a spirit of love.

(Carpenter) Our footsteps tread the earth, but we are of the company of heaven. In Christ two Natures and two states of life are joined...He has lifted us to the divine level where God is.

(RSV) He destined us in love to be his sons through Jesus Christ, according to the purpose of his will...

EPHESIANS 1:6 To the praise of the glory of his grace, wherein he hath made us accepted in the beloved.

(Knox) ...he has taken us into his favour in the person of his beloved Son.

See redemption p. 108

EPHESIANS 2:18 For through him we both have access by one Spirit unto the Father.

(Kling.) For by him we both have a way in by one Spirit to the Father.

(Way) For through Him have we, both we and you, united in one Spirit, admission to the presence of the Father.

(Trans.) It is through him that both of us, in one Spirit, are able* to go right into the Father's presence. (*Greek — technical term for the right of approach to persons in high office.)

EPHESIANS 2:18 (Stevens) His salvation for all brings them together as sons of a common Father with unrestricted access to His presence.

See redemption p. 113

EPHESIANS 3:12 In whom we have boldness and access with confidence by the faith of him.

(Authentic) In Him, by faith in Him, we enter God's presence boldly and confidently.

(Trans.) In union with him and through faith in him we may confidently draw near to God and speak to him freely.

(Hayman) In whom we have consciousness of privilege and free access in the confidence of that faith of which He is the object.

(GNB) In union with Christ and through our faith in him we have the boldness to go into God's presence with all confidence.

(TLB) Now we can come fearlessly right into God's presence, assured of his glad welcome...

(Bruce) ...we have our free birthright and our right of access, and full confidence to exercise it.

(Lovett) ...we not only have free access to God, but can feel perfectly at ease in His presence.

(Johnson) Through Christ, who is the key of God's eternal purpose, we have a confident audience with the Father through our trust in him.

(Berk.) ...in whom by faith in Him we enjoy the confidence of unreserved approach.

(Knox) ...who gives us all our confidence, bids us come forward, emboldened by our faith in him.

(Roth.) In whom we have our freedom of speech...

(Kling.) ...a confident way in...

(Barclay) ...we can enter God's royal presence with no fear and in perfect trust.

EPHESIANS 4:23 And be renewed in the spirit of your mind.

(AMP) And be constantly renewed in the spirit of your mind [having a fresh mental and spiritual attitude].

(TLB) Now your attitudes and thoughts must all be constantly changing for the better.

(Gspd.) You must adopt a new attitude of mind...

EPHESIANS 4:24 And that ye put on the new man, which after God is created in righteousness and true holiness.

(AMP) And put on the new nature (the regenerate self) created in God's image

(Godlike) in true righteousness and holiness.

(Fenton) ...the New Man, the one created God-like in righteousness and holiness...

EPHESIANS 4:24 (Berk.) ...put on the new nature that is created in God's likeness in genuine righteousness and holiness.

(Johnson) Discover new ways of expressing your new, unique personhood in Christ, ways which are in harmony with who you really are...

(Cress.) ...you have stopped being the person you used to be...

(Lovett) ...old nature and its evil products...

(Adams) ...put on the new person that you are...

(Weym.) ...clothe yourselves with that new and better self which has been created to resemble God in the righteousness and holiness which come from the truth.

(Way) ...that you must clothe yourselves in the new humanity that has been created in God's image, in a state of righteousness and holiness born of the Truth.

(Wuest) And that you have put on once for all the new self...

(Lau.) And you must put on the fresh dress of your new nature...

(NEB) ...put on the new nature of God's creating...

(Basic) And put on the new man, to which God has given life...

(Wms.) ...the new self which has been created in the likeness of God...

(20th C. R.) ...clothe yourselves in that new nature...

(Godbey) ...who has been created in harmony with God...

(HT Ander) ...put on the new man which is created according to the will of God...

(Carpenter) ...Above all, the new life is the real life, the life that is the life indeed.

PHILIPPIANS 3:9 And be found in him, not having mine own righteousness, which is of the law, but that which is through the faith of Christ, the righteousness which is of God by faith.

(TLB) And become one with him, no longer counting on being saved by being good enough or by obeying God's laws, but by trusting Christ to save me; for God's way of making us right with himself depends on faith—counting on Christ alone.

(Message) I didn't want some petty, inferior brand of righteousness that comes from keeping a list of rules when I could get the robust kind that comes from trusting Christ—God's righteousness.

COLOSSIANS 1:21 And you, that were sometime alienated and enemies in your mind by wicked works, yet now hath he reconciled.

(AMP) And although you at one time were estranged and alienated from Him and were of hostile attitude of mind in your wicked activities.

COLOSSIANS 1:22 In the body of his flesh through death, to present you holy and unblameable and unreproveable in his sight.

>*(AMP)* Yet now, has [Christ, the Messiah] reconciled [you to God] in the body of His flesh through death, in order to present you holy and faultless and irreproachable in His [the Father's] presence.
>
>*(Roth)* ...to present you holy and blameless and unaccusable before him...
>
>*(NEB)* ...so that he may present you before himself as dedicated men, without blemish and innocent in his sight.
>
>*(Basic)* ...so that you might be holy and without sin and free from all evil before him...
>
>*(Johnson)* ...He intends for you to be complete, guiltless, and free of negative judgment in your relation to him.
>
>*(Message)* ...whole and holy in his presence.
>
>*(Jordan)* ...dedicated, clean and above reproach.

TITUS 3:5 Not by works of righteousness which we have done, but according to his mercy he saved us, by the washing of regeneration, and renewing of the Holy Ghost.

>*(Message)* But when God, our kind and loving Savior God, stepped in, he saved us from all that. It was all his doing; we had nothing to do with it. He gave us a good bath, and we came out of it new people, washed inside and out by the Holy Spirit.
>
>*(AMP)* He saved us, not because of any works of righteousness that we had done, but because of His own pity and mercy, by [the] cleansing [bath] of the new birth (regeneration) and renewing of the Holy Spirit.

HEBREWS 10:1, 2 For the law having a shadow of good things to come, and not the very image of the things, can never with those sacrifices which they offered year by year continually make the comers thereunto perfect. For then would they not have ceased to be offered? because that the worshippers once purged should have had no more conscience of sins.

>*(Barclay)* The Jewish law was no more than a shadow of the good things which are to come; you will not find in it the true expression of these realities. By going on making the same sacrifices which are offered year after year forever, the law can never perfect those who are trying to find the way into God's presence. If these sacrifices could have done this, they would obviously have ceased to be offered, because the worshipper would have been once and for all cleansed, and would no longer be haunted by the sense of sin.
>
>*(Weym.)* ...give complete freedom from sin to those who draw near...the consciences of the worshippers - who in that case would now have been cleansed once for all - would no longer be burdened with sins?
>
>*(Trans.)* ...the worshippers would have been purified once and for all and would no longer have a sense of guilt.

HEBREWS 10:1, 2 (Lovett) ...People whose consciences have been cleansed don't feel guilty any more, and have no further need of sacrifices.

(Jordan) For once you get a congregation genuinely forgiven of its sins, it no longer has a guilty conscience about them.

(Knox) ...There would be no guilt left to reproach the consciences of those who come to worship...

(AMP) ...they would no longer have any guilt or consciousness of sin.

See redemption p. 114

HEBREWS 10:14 For by one offering he hath perfected for ever them that are sanctified.

(Weym.) For by a single offering, He has forever completed the blessing for those whom He is setting free from sin.

(Lau.) So with that one sacrifice He made us holy and brought us into perfect union with God.

(Barclay) For by one sacrifice, valid forever, he enabled men to enter into perfect communion with God.

(Pl. Eng.) ...he has for all time brought into perfect union with God those who are made holy.

(Gspd.) ...he has forever qualified those who are purified from sin to approach God.

See redemption p. 115

HEBREWS 10:19 Having therefore, brethren, boldness to enter into the holiest by the blood of Jesus.

(Stevens) Since, now, the immediate presence of God, the most holy place of the upper sanctuary, has been made accessible to us...

(Lovett) And so then, my brothers, because of the blood of Jesus, let us go boldly right into the holiest place of all, the very presence of God.

(Cunn.) Having therefore, brethren, boldness to use the entrance into the Holy of Holies in the blood of Jesus...

(TLB) ...now we may walk right into the very Holy of Holies where God is, because of the blood of Jesus.

(NEB) ...the blood of Jesus makes us free to enter boldly...

(Cent.) ...we have a cheerful confidence, brothers, to enter into the Holiest...

(Fenton) ...having free entry into the interior of the Holies through the blood of Jesus, an open and living pathway...

(Roth.) Having therefore, brethren, freedom of speech for the entrance through the Holy Place by the blood of Jesus...

See redemption p. 115

HEBREWS 10:22 Let us draw near with a true heart in full assurance of faith, having our hearts sprinkled from an evil conscience, and our bodies washed with pure water.

(Dodd.) ...let us not stand at a distance as if God were inaccessible; but, on the contrary, let us draw near with a sincere and affectionate heart, in the full assurance of faith, supported by such considerations as these, which may well embolden us...to make our approach unto him in the most cheerful expectation of his blessing.

(Lovett) ...let us, as members of His family, exercise our right of access and press closer and closer to the Father. But we must come with childlike faith and the unshakable assurance that He is eager to receive us...

(Weym.) ...let us draw near with sincerity and unfaltering faith, having had our hearts sprinkled, once for all, from consciences oppressed with sin...

(Berk.) ...let us draw near with honest hearts and with unqualified assurance of faith...

(AMP) Let us all come forward and draw near with true (honest and sincere) hearts in unqualified assurance and absolute conviction engendered by faith, [that is, by that leading of the entire human personality on God in absolute trust and confidence in His power, wisdom and goodness,]...

(Mof.) ...sprinkled clean from a bad conscience...

(Wade) ...in the fulness of conviction which faith creates...

(Smith, J. M.) ...in sincerity of heart and with perfect faith...

(Wms., Gspd.) ...with our hearts cleansed from the sense of sin...

(Jordan) ...Let's cleanse our hearts from any unworthy feeling...

See redemption p. 116

JAMES 5:16 Confess your faults one to another, and pray one for another, that ye may be healed. The effectual fervent prayer of a righteous man availeth much.

(Weym.) ...The heartfelt supplication of a righteous man exerts a mighty influence.

(AMP) ...makes tremendous power available - dynamic in its working.

(Trans.) The good man's prayer is very powerful because God is at work in it.

(Fenton) ...Very powerfully productive is the prayer of a righteous man.

(TLB) ...The earnest prayer of a righteous man has great power and wonderful results.

(NIV) ...The prayer of a righteous man is powerful and effective.

(Adams) ...The petition of a righteous person has very powerful effects.

(Authentic) ...the heartfelt petition of an upright man has great force.

(Swann) ...The energetic supplications of a righteous one prevails greatly.

(Godbey) ...the inward working prayer of a righteous man avails much.

(Roth. 2) ...Much avails a righteous man's supplication, working inwardly.

(Noli) ...the prayer of a righteous man has tremendous power.

(New Life) ...The prayer from the heart of a man right with God has much power.

JAMES 5:16 (Stevens) ...secures great blessing from God.
(**Cress.**) ...big things can be done.

I PETER 3:12 For the eyes of the Lord are over the righteous, and his ears are open unto their prayers; but the face of the Lord is against them that do evil.
(**Norlie**) For the Lord's eyes rest on the righteous and His ears listen to their prayers...
(**Knox**) On the upright, the Lord's eye ever looks favourably...
(**Wuest**) ...the Lord's eyes are directed in a favorable attitude towards the righteous...
See prayer p. 262

I JOHN 1:9 If we confess our sins, he is faithful and just to forgive us our sins and to cleanse us from all unrighteousness.
(**AMP**) If we (freely) admit that we have sinned and confess our sins, He is faithful and just (true to His own nature and promises) and will forgive our sins (dismiss our lawlessness) and continually cleanse us from all unrighteousness - everything not in conformity to His will in purpose, thought and action.
(**Basic**) If we say openly that we have done wrong, he is upright and true to his word, giving us forgiveness of sins and making us clean from all evil.
(**Wade**) If we acknowledge our sins, God is faithful to His promises, and righteous in His nature, so that He forgives us our sins, and purifies us from unrighteousness of every kind.
(**K. & L.**) If we openly confess our sins, God, true to his promises and just, forgives us our sins and cleanses us from every stain of iniquity.
(**Lovett**) If we confess our sins, then true to His Word, He is faithful to forgive us.
(**Jordan**) If we honestly face up to our sins, he is so fair and straight that he will put our sins behind him and will rid us of every bad habit.

PSALM 89:15 Blessed is the people that know the joyful sound: they shall walk, Oh Lord, in the light of thy countenance.
(**Mof.**) Happy is the people who know thy festal songs, who live within the sunshine of thy favour!
(**Knox**) Happy is the people that know well the shout of praise, that lives, Lord, in the smile of thy protection!
(**Young**) O the happiness of the people knowing the shout, O Jehovah, in the light of Thy face they walk habitually.
(**Masoretic O.T.**) ...the joyful shout...
(**GNB**) How happy are the people who worship you with songs...
(**Norlie**) ...who go about radiant with Your presence.
See joy p. 340

PSALM 89:16 In thy name shall they rejoice all the day: and in thy righteousness shall they be exalted.

>*(Fenton)* In Your Name they can laugh all the day...
>*(NEB)* ...thy righteousness shall lift them up.
>*See joy p. 340*

PSALM 112:1-3 Praise ye the Lord. Blessed is the man that feareth the Lord, that delighteth greatly in his commandments. His seed shall be mighty upon earth: the generation of the upright shall be blessed. Wealth and riches shall be in his house: and his righteousness endureth for ever.

>*(AMP)* Praise the Lord! (Hallelujah!) Blessed (happy, fortunate, to be envied) is the man who fears (reveres and worships) the Lord, who delights greatly in His commandments. His (spiritual) offspring shall be mighty upon earth; the generation of the upright shall be blessed. Prosperity and welfare are in his house, and his righteousness endures forever.
>*(Basic)* A store of wealth will be in his house...
>*(TLB)* He himself shall be wealthy...
>*(Knox)* There is affluence and prosperity in his household...

PROVERBS 10:24 The fear of the wicked, it shall come upon him: but the desire of the righteous shall be granted.

>*(TLB)* The wicked man's fears will all come true, and so will the good man's hopes.
>*(RSV)* When the tempest passes, the wicked is no more, but the righteous is established forever.
>*(Mof.)* ...a good man's repose will last forever.
>*(Basic)* ...the upright man will get his desire.
>*(Jer.)* ...what the virtuous desires comes to him as a present.

PROVERBS 28:1 The wicked flee when no man pursueth: but the righteous are bold as a lion.

>*(ABPS)* The wicked flee, when no one pursues; But the righteous are bold as the young lion.
>*(Berk.)* The wicked flee when there is no one pursuing, but the righteous are as fearless as a young lion.
>*(Roth.)* The lawless fleeth when no man pursueth, but the righteous like a lion are confident.
>*(Masoretic O.T.)* The wicked flee when no man pursueth; but the righteous are secure as a young lion.
>*(Basic)* The evil man goes running away when no man is after him, but the upright are without fear, like the lion.

ISAIAH 32:17 And the work of righteousness shall be peace; and the effect of righteousness quietness and assurance for ever.

(AMP) And the effect of righteousness will be peace [internal and external], and the result of righteousness will be quietness and confident trust forever.

(Mof.) ...and justice brings us welfare, honesty renders us secure...

(TLB) And out of justice, peace. Quietness and confidence will reign forever more.

(Jer.) ...integrity will bring peace, justice give lasting security.

(Basic) ...and the effect of an upright rule will be to take away fear for ever.

See peace p. 350

ISAIAH 43:25, 26 I, even I, am he that blotteth out thy transgressions for mine own sake, and will not remember thy sins. Put me in remembrance: let us plead together: declare thou, that thou mayest be justified...

(Roth.) I am he that is ready to wipe out thy transgressions for my own sake, - and thy sins not remember. Put me in mind, let us enter into judgment at once, recount thou that thou mayest be justified.

(Mof.) Yet it is I who (for my own sake) blot out your ill deeds, I put your sins out of my mind; recall to me, in your defense, a single item proving you innocent!

(NEB) I alone, I am He, who for his own sake wipes out your transgressions, who will remember your sins no more.

(ASV) ...set thou forth thy cause, that thou mayest be justified.

(Smith, J.M.) Recall the matter to me, and let us argue it out together; recount it, that you may be proved in the right!

(NAB) Would you have me remember, have us come to trial? Speak up, prove your innocence!

(TLB) Oh, remind me of this promise of forgiveness, for we must talk about your sins. Plead your case for my forgiving you.

ISAIAH 54:14 In righteousness shalt thou be established: thou shalt be far from oppression; for thou shalt not fear: and from terror, for it shall not come near thee.

(AMP) You shall establish yourself in righteousness (rightness, in conformity with God's will and order): you shall be far from even the thought of oppression or destruction, for you shall not fear, and from terror, for it shall not come near you.

ISAIAH 54:17 No weapon that is formed against thee shall prosper; and every tongue that shall rise against thee in judgment thou shalt condemn. This is the heritage of the servants of the Lord, and their righteousness is of me, saith the Lord.

(Jer.) Such will be the lot of the servants of Yahweh, the triumphs I award them...

ISAIAH 54:17 (AMP) But no weapon that is formed against you shall prosper, and every tongue that shall rise against you in judgment you shall show to be in the wrong. This [peace, righteousness, security, triumph over opposition] is the heritage of the servants of the Lord [those in whom the ideal Servant of the Lord is reproduced]; this is the righteousness or the vindication which they obtain from Me [this is that which I impart to them as their justification], says the Lord.

> *(Young)* This is the inheritance of the servants of Jehovah, And their righteousness from me, an affirmation of Jehovah!
>
> *(Mof.)* ...Such is the lot of the Eternal's servants; thus, the Eternal promises, do I maintain their cause.
>
> *(NEB)* ...their vindication comes from me...

MALACHI 4:2 But unto you that fear my name shall the Sun of righteousness arise with healing in his wings; and ye shall go forth, and grow up as calves of the stall.

> *(Berk.)* But for you, who revere My name, the sun of righteousness will arise with healing in its beams, and you will go forth and leap like calves from the stall.
>
> *(Jer.)* ...with healing in its rays; you will leap like calves going out to pasture.
>
> *(RSV)* ...shall go forth leaping like calves from the stall.
>
> *(Sept.)* ...and you shall go forth and leap for joy like young bullocks loosed from yokes.
>
> *(Roth.)* ...And ye shall come forth and leap for joy like calves let loose from the stall...
>
> *See divine healing p. 276*

God sees you
IN CHRIST,
but you must see yourself
IN HIM.
You look a whole lot better
IN CHRIST
than you do outside
of Him.

Mark Hankins
Taking Your Place In Christ

PSALM

22:1 63
22:6 63
22:7 63
22:8 63
22:9 64
22:10 64
22:11 64
22:12 64
22:13 64
22:14 64
22:15 65
22:16 65
22:17 65
22:18 65
88:4 65
88:5 65
88:6 65
88:7 66
88:8 66
88:10 66
88:11 66
88:12 66
88:16 67

ISAIAH

53:3 53
53:4 53
53:5 53
53:7 54
53:10 54
53:11 54
53:12 54

JONAH

2:2 62
2:4 62
2:6 62

MATTHEW

8:17 58
12:40 62
27:46 63

JOHN

1:16 110
5:24 94
6:53 95
6:54 95

6:56 96
12:31, 32 73
15:4, 5 120

ACTS

2:24 60
2:27 61
2:31 61
2:33 61
13:33, 34 68

ROMANS

3:21 83
3:22 84
3:24 84
3:25 85
3:26 86
3:27 87
4:25 56
5:1 112
5:2 113
5:6 59
5:8 60
5:9 60
5:10 100
5:11 101
5:17 102
6:4 87
6:5 88
6:6 89
6:7 90
6:8 91
6:11 91
6:14 92
8:1 92
8:2 93
8:10 94
8:16 124
8:17 125
8:32 109
8:34 127
8:37 122
8:38 123
8:39 123
14:9 126

I CORINTHIANS

1:5 105

1:7 106
1:8 106
1:9 106
1:30 107
2:16 117
3:21 110
5:17 117
6:17 121
12:27 121
15:57 103

II CORINTHIANS

2:14 103
3:4, 5 104
5:14 74
5:17 117
5:19 74
5:21 55
6:14, 15 122
8:9 59

GALATIANS

2:20 75
3:13 58
3:29 125
4:4, 5 124
4:6 124
4:7 124
6:14 76
6:15 76

EPHESIANS

1:3 107
1:6 108
1:7 99
1:8 108
1:11 108
1:19-21 72
2:4, 5 82
2:6 83
2:10 120
2:18 113
4:9, 10 62
4:24 118
5:30 121

PHILIPPIANS

1:11 111
4:7 117

COLOSSIANS
4:13 104
4:19 110

COLOSSIANS
1:12 97
1:13 97
1:14 98
2:3 109
2:9, 10 78
2:11 79
2:12 80
2:13 80
2:14 80
2:15 68
2:20 77
3:1 81
3:3 78
3:9, 10 119

I TIMOTHY
2:5 127
2:6 57
3:16 67

II TIMOTHY
1:7 116

TITUS
2:14 57

PHILEMON
6 111

HEBREWS
2:9 57
2:14, 15 70
4:14 128
4:16 128
7:22 128
7:25 127
8:6 127
9:12 72
9:24 126
9:26 56
10:1, 2 114
10:12 114
10:14 115
10:16 115
10:17 115
10:19 115
10:22 116

13:20, 21 112

I PETER
2:9 125
2:24 59
2:25 129
3:18 67

II PETER
1:3, 4 109

I JOHN
2:1 129
4:17 121
5:4 99
5:11, 12 96

REVELATION
1:5 68
1:6 126

ISAIAH 53:3 He is despised and rejected of men; a man of sorrows, and acquainted with grief; and we hid as it were our faces from him; he was despised, and we esteemed him not.

    (Spur.) ...deserted of men...

    (Basic) 52:14...his face was so changed by disease as to be unlike that of a man. 53:3.. he was a man of sorrows, marked by disease.

    (Leeser) ...a man of pains, and acquainted with disease...

    (Masoretic O.T.) ...a man of pains, and acquainted with disease.

    (Roth., ABV) ...Man of pains and familiar with sickness...

ISAIAH 53:4 Surely he hath borne our griefs, and carried our sorrows: yet we did esteem him stricken, smitten of God, and afflicted.

    (Spur.) ...hath upborne...

    (Basic) But it was our pain he took, and our diseases were put on him: while to us he seemed as one diseased, on whom God's punishment had come.

    (Leeser) But only our diseases did He bear Himself, and our pains He carried.

    (NEB) Yet on himself he bore our sufferings, our torments he endured, while we counted him smitten by God, struck down by disease and misery.

    (Masoretic O.T.) Surely our diseases he did bear, and our pains he carried...

    (ABV) ...wounded for our rebellions...

    (Smith, J.M.) Yet it was our pains that he bore, our sorrow that he carried...

    (Roth.) Yet surely our sicknesses he carried. And as for our pains, he bare the burden of them...

ISAIAH 53:5 But he was wounded for our transgressions, he was bruised for our iniquities: the chastisement of our peace was upon him; and with his stripes we are healed.

    (Spur.) ...by His union with us we are healed...

    (Leeser) ...through His bruises was healing granted to us.

    (Knox) ...on him the punishment fell that brought us peace...

    (AMP) ...the chastisement [needful to obtain] peace and well-being for us was upon Him, and with the stripes [that wounded] Him we are healed and made whole.

    (Young) ...by his bruise there is healing to us.

    (GNB) ...We are healed by the punishment he suffered, made whole by the blows he received.

    (NEB) ...the chastisement he bore is health for us...

    (ABV) ...He was treated violently...

    (Mof.) ...the blows that fell to him have brought us healing.

    (Roth.) ...by his stripes there is healing for us.

See divine healing p. 275; peace p. 350

ISAIAH 53:7 He was oppressed, and he was afflicted, yet he opened not his mouth: he is brought as a lamb to the slaughter, and as a sheep before her shearers is dumb, so he openeth not his mouth.

> *(Young)* It hath been exacted, and he hath answered...
> *(Spur.)* It was exacted, and He was made answerable...
> *(Quaker)* ...exacted upon Him.

ISAIAH 53:10 Yet it pleased the Lord to bruise him; he hath put him to grief; when thou shalt make his soul an offering for sin, he shall see his seed, and he shall prolong his days, and the pleasure of the Lord shall prosper in his hand.

> *(Young)* And Jehovah hath delighted to bruise him, He hath made him sick...
> *(ABV)* Yet it pleased Jehovah to crush Him with grievous sickness, (With the purpose that) if He were to make Himself an offering for guilt, He would see (His) seed, He would prolong His days. And the pleasure of Jehovah would prosper to His hand.
> *(Leeser)* But the Lord was pleased to crush Him through disease...
> *(Mof.)* But the Eternal chose to vindicate his servant, rescuing his life from anguish; he let him prosper to the full, in a posterity with life prolonged.
> *(Masoretic O.T.)* Yet it pleased the Lord to crush him by disease...
> *(Spur.)* Yet it pleased Jehovah to crush Him under my travail...gave His soul...
> *(Fides)* He was offered because it was His own will, and He opened not His mouth.

ISAIAH 53:11 He shall see of the travail of his soul, and shall be satisfied: by his knowledge shall my righteous servant justify many; for he shall bear their iniquities.

> *(ABV)* In consequence of the anguish of His soul, He would experience satisfaction. By His knowledge will my servant bring righteousness to many and their iniquities He will bear.
> *(Masoretic O.T.)* Of the travail of his soul, he shall see to the full, even My servant, Who by his knowledge did justify the Righteous One to the many, And their iniquities he did bear.
> *(Basic)* ...made clear his righteousness before men...

ISAIAH 53:12 Therefore will I divide him a portion with the great, and he shall divide the spoil with the strong; because he hath poured out his soul unto death: and he was numbered with the transgressors; and he bare the sin of many, and made intercession for the transgressors.

> *(ABV)* And let Himself be numbered with the rebellious...
> *(Mof.)* Therefore shall he win victory, he shall succeed triumphantly, since he has shed his lifeblood, and let himself be numbered among rebels, bearing the great world's sins, and interposing for rebellious men.

ISAIAH 53:12 (Smith, J.M.) ...and with the strong shall he share the spoil...

(Jer.) ...letting himself be taken for a sinner...

(GNB) ...He willingly gave his life and shared the fate of evil men. He took the place of many sinners...

(Young) ...he exposed to death his soul...

(Basic) ...taking on himself the sins of the people...

(Spur.) ...apportion to Him the many...In whose stead He poured forth His soul unto death.

II CORINTHIANS 5:21 For he hath made him to be sin for us, who knew no sin; that we might be made the righteousness of God in him.

(Jer.) For our sake God made the sinless one into sin...

(Worrell) Him Who knew no sin He made to be sin on our behalf, that we may become God's righteousness in Him.

(N. Berk.) ...made sin on our behalf, so that in Him we might share the righteousness of God.

(Letters) The Father took the Son, who never had any evil in Him, and laid the evil of the universe on Him.

(Black.) ...in our behalf God identified him with everything in the whole realm of sin in order that by trusting him we might become [recipients of] God's kind of righteousness.

(Way) ...on purpose to render righteousness attainable to us...

(Wood) Think of it: Christ the sinless was made the personification of sin for us...

(Cony.) ...changed into the righteousness of God in Christ.

(Way) Jesus knew not sin; Yet God made Him to be the world's sin for our sakes...

(Wms.) ...so that through union with Him we might come into right standing with God.

(GNB) ...God made him share our sin in order that in union with him we might share the righteousness of God.

(Knox) ...God made him into sin for us, so that in him we might be turned into the holiness of God.

(NEB) ...God made him one with the sinfulness of men...

(Wade) Him Who had no acquaintance with sin God for our sakes treated as an embodiment of Sin, in order that we, on our part, might become, through union with Him, an embodiment of the Righteousness that God desires.

(TLB) For God took the sinless Christ and poured into him our sins. Then, in exchange, he poured God's goodness into us!

See righteousness p. 39

HEBREWS 9:26 For then must he often have suffered since the foundation of the world: but now once in the end of the world hath he appeared to put away sin by the sacrifice of himself.

(Hayford) ...to do away with sin by His personal sacrifice.

(Berk.) ...to eliminate sin by His self-sacrifice.

(Conq.) ...end of the types...

(Adams) ...appeared once, and once only, at the end of the ages to set aside sin by sacrificing Himself.

(Barclay) ...to wipe out sin...

(Gspd.) ...to put an end to sin...

(Weym., River.) ...to do away with sin...

(20th C. R.) ...to abolish sin...

(Knox) ...annulling our sin...

(Cent.) ...the destruction of sin...

(Jordan) But now at this high point of history, he has come on the scene and nullified sin by his one complete sacrifice.

ROMANS 4:25 Who was delivered for our offences, and was raised again for our justification.

(Hudson) ...who was given up to death because of our trespasses, and raised from the dead because our justification had been effected.

(AMP) Who was betrayed and put to death because of our misdeeds and was raised to secure our justification (our acquittal), [making our account balance and absolving us from all guilt before God].

(Message) The sacrificed Jesus made us fit for God, set us right with God.

(Letters) Jesus, the One who died because we are so rotten and was raised from the dead to make us truly good.

(Weym.) Who was surrendered to death because of the offenses we had committed...

(Berk.) ...who was handed over on account of our misdeeds and was raised for our justification.

(Roth.) ...raised to make righteousness possible for us...

(Richert) As our Stand-in he paid the death penalty due us by law for our crimes. And as our Agent; he was restored to life, making us accepted as though we were as deserving as he!

(Mar.) Who was delivered because of the offences of us and was raised because of the justification.

(Roth.) ...on account of our offences...on account of the declaring us righteous.

(NASB) ...because of our transgressions...because of our justification.

(N. Berk.) ...put to death on account of our misdeeds and was raised on account of our justification.

(Conc.) ...because of our justifying.

(Fenton) ...was betrayed through our sins, and raised through our righteousness.

ROMANS 4:25 (Young) ...who was delivered up because of our offences, and was raised up because of our being declared righteous.

See righteousness p. 33

TITUS 2:14 Who gave himself for us, that he might redeem us from all iniquity, and purify unto himself a peculiar people, zealous of good works.

(20th C. 1) ...he gave himself on our behalf, to deliver us from all wickedness, and to purify for himself a People who should be peculiarly his own and eager to do good.

(Barclay) ...to liberate us from all wickedness...

(Gspd.) ...to free us...

(Weym.) ...to purchase our freedom from all iniquity...a people who should be His own...

(K. & L.) ...from every kind of iniquity...

(Way) ...Full of enthusiasm for good deeds.

(Jordan) ...that he might cut us loose from every evil habit...

(Basic) ...a people clean in heart and on fire with good works.

(Worrell) ...a special people...

(Hayman) ...That He might redeem us from all depravity...

(Phil.) ...to release us from every kind of lawlessness...

I TIMOTHY 2:6 Who gave himself a ransom for all, to be testified in due time.

(Pl. Eng.) ...who gave himself as the price of freedom for all men; of this truth witness was to be given at the proper time...

(Adams) ...gave Himself as a ransom payment for all sorts of persons...

(Trans.) He gave himself to set all men free...

(20th C. 1) ...who gave himself as a ransom on behalf of all men...

(Way) ...it was for all men...

HEBREWS 2:9 But we see Jesus, who was made a little lower than the angels for the suffering of death, crowned with glory and honour; that he by the grace of God should taste death for every man.

(Hudson) ...to drain death's bitter cup for every man.

(Cress.) ...He did this so that He could die for every person.

(Way) But we do see the archetype of the New Humanity, Jesus...

(Knox) ...in God's gracious will, in tasting death he should stand for us all.

(NEB) ...so that, by God's gracious will, in tasting death, He should stand for us all.

(K. & L.) ...experience the throes of death...

(Letters) ...that death could be the death all of us deserved...

(Hayman) ...He, on behalf of every man, might taste of death.

GALATIANS 3:13 Christ hath redeemed us from the curse of the law, being made a curse for us: for it is written, Cursed is every one that hangeth on a tree.

(Berk.) Christ has bought us free from the curse of the Law...

(Noli) ...by becoming a curse for us...

(Black.) ...by taking the curse upon himself in our behalf...

(Deaf) ...The law put a curse on us. But Christ took away that curse. He changed places with us. Christ put himself under that curse...

(Hayman) Christ it was, who redeemed us from the curse of the law, by receiving our curse on His own person.

(Way) From that curse, which is of the essence of the Law, we Jews have been ransomed only by Messiah...

(Trans.) Christ ransomed us from the curse of the Law by taking that curse upon himself for our sakes...

(Wand) Now, Christ bought us off the curse of the Law at the cost of being accursed for our sakes...

(Weym.) Christ purchased our freedom...

(20th C.R.) Christ ransomed us from the curse pronounced in the Law...

(GNB) ...the curse that the Law brings...

(Barclay) ...by taking the curse upon himself for our sakes...

(Beck.) Christ paid the price to free us...

(Gspd.) ...by taking our curse upon himself...

See divine healing p. 269; finances p. 309

MATTHEW 8:17 That it might be fulfilled which was spoken by Esaias the prophet, saying, Himself took our infirmities and bare our sicknesses.

(Noli) He took up our infirmities, and carried away our sicknesses.

(NEB) He took away our illnesses and lifted our diseases from us.

(Cress.) ...he took away the things that made us weak, He took away the things that made us sick...

(Norlie) ...He took our infirmities upon Himself, and took away our diseases.

(AMP) ...He Himself took [in order to carry away] our weaknesses and infirmities and bore away our diseases.

(Trans.) ...He took away our illnesses and carried away our diseases.

(Jer.) He took our sicknesses away and carried our diseases for us.

(Mof.) ...He took away our sicknesses and our diseases he removed.

(New Life) ...He took on Himself our sickness and carried away our diseases.

(Gspd., NASV, N. Berk.) ...carried away our diseases.

I PETER 2:24 Who his own self bare our sins in his own body on the tree, that we, being dead to sins, should live unto righteousness: by whose stripes ye were healed.

> *(Adams)* ...so that by dying to sins we might live to righteousness...
>
> *(NEB)* In his own person he carried our sins...
>
> *(Pl. Eng.)* ...that we might die to sins and live again in righteousness...
>
> *(Mof.)* ...that we might break with sin and live the good life...
>
> *(20th C.R.)* ...His bruising was your healing.
>
> *(Wuest)* ...by means of whose bleeding stripe* (singular), you were healed.
>
> *(FSB, Godbey)* ...by whose stripe you are healed.
>
> *(Alf.)* ...by whose stripe ye were healed.
>
> *See divine healing p. 287; eternal life p. 395*

See divine healing p. 287; eternal life p. 395

II CORINTHIANS 8:9 For ye know the grace of our Lord Jesus Christ, that, though he was rich, yet for your sakes he became poor, that ye through his poverty might be rich.

> *(Johnson)* You know the unconditional love of our Lord Jesus Christ; he had all the wealth of God and he became a pauper so that through his poverty we could become wealthy.
>
> *(Cress.)* ...Because he became poor, you can become rich.
>
> *(Bart. & Pet.)* ...He beggared Himself...
>
> *(Wood)* ...we might gain riches through His poverty.
>
> *(Weekes)* For ye know the generosity...
>
> *(Weym.)* ...the condescending goodness...
>
> *(Basic)* ...though he had wealth, he became poor on your account, so that through his need, you might have wealth.
>
> *(Wuest)* ...by means of His poverty you might be made wealthy.
>
> *(AMP)* ...enriched — abundantly supplied.
>
> *See finances p. 304*

See finances p. 304

ROMANS 5:6 For when we were yet without strength, in due time Christ died for the ungodly.

> *(Hayman)* ...came timely to the rescue by dying for the ungodly.
>
> *(Richert)* ...died in our place while we were still unworthy and corrupt.
>
> *(Phil.)* ...it was while we were powerless to help ourselves that Christ died for sinful men.
>
> *(Jordan)* ...Christ died for people who couldn't care less for a loving God.
>
> *(Weekes)* For while we were yet powerless, Christ in due time died in behalf of the ungodly.
>
> *(TLB)* When we were utterly helpless with no way of escape, Christ came at just the right time and died for us sinners who had no use for him.

ROMANS 5:8 But God commendeth his love toward us, in that, while we were yet sinners, Christ died for us.

> *(Phil.)* Yet the proof of God's amazing love is this...
>
> *(Basic)* ...God has made clear his love to us...
>
> *(20th C.R.)* But God puts his love for us beyond doubt by the fact that Christ died on our behalf, while we were still sinners.
>
> *(Jordan)* ...while we were still sinful trash...
>
> *(Richert)* ...died in our place, while we were still virtually criminals.
>
> *(Hayman)* But what enhances God's love toward us is Christ's dying for us while yet sinners.

ROMANS 5:9 Much more then, being now justified by his blood, we shall be saved from wrath through him.

> *(Barclay)* Already, here and now, we have been put into a right relationship with God through the death of Jesus.
>
> *(Lau.)* We are now right with God through the blood of Christ...
>
> *(N. Berk.)* ...declared righteous by His blood...
>
> *(20th C.R.)* ...now that by his sacrifice of himself we stand right with God...
>
> *(Jordan)* So now that we have been taken on board by his sacrifice...
>
> *(Beck)* Now that His blood has made us righteous...
>
> *(Basic)* ...if we now have righteousness by his blood...
>
> *(Weekes)* ...having now been made righteous by means of his blood...
>
> *(Richert)* And while Jesus paid our death penalty, which provides the basis for our being regarded as worthy...

ACTS 2:24 Whom God hath raised up, having loosed the pains of death: because it was not possible that he should be holden of it.

> *(Fenton)* Whom God has raised up, having liberated from the agonies of Death; because it was not possible that He should be mastered by him.
>
> *(Berk.)* ...Him God raised up by unfastening the cords of death...
>
> *(NAB)* God freed him from death's bitter pangs, however, and raised him up again...
>
> *(Conq.)* ...loosed the bands of death...
>
> *(Jer.)* ...but God raised him to life, freeing him from the pangs of Hades; for it was impossible for him to be held in its power.
>
> *(N. Berk.)* Him God raised up by setting Him free from the pangs of death; for He could not be held in its grip.
>
> *(Wms.)* But God raised Him up by loosing Him from the pangs of death, since it was impossible for Him to be held by the power of death.
>
> *(Adams)* ...releasing Him from the agonies of death...

ACTS 2:24 (Weym.) But God has raised Him to life, ending the pangs of death. It was not possible for Him to be held fast by death.

> *(NIV)* ...freeing him from the agony of death, because it was impossible for death to keep its hold on him.
>
> *(Pl. Eng.)* ...having loosed the birth-pains of death...
>
> *(Roth.)* Whom God raised up, loosing the pangs of death...
>
> *(Cunn.)* ...whom God raised, relieving the birth-pangs of Death...
>
> *(Mar.)* ...whom God raised up loosening the pangs of death...
>
> *(Knox)* ...releasing him from the pangs of death; it was impossible that death should have the mastery over him.
>
> *(Conf.)* ...having loosed the sorrows of hell, because it was not possible that he should be held fast by it.
>
> *(Douay)* ...having loosed the sorrows of hell...
>
> *(HT Ander)* ...it was not possible for Him to be held in subjection to it.
>
> *(Baxter)* ...held and conquered by it.

ACTS 2:27 Because thou wilt not leave my soul in hell, neither wilt thou suffer thine Holy One to see corruption.

> *(AMP)* For You will not abandon my soul, leaving it helpless in Hades (the state of departed spirits)...
>
> *(Weym.)* For Thou wilt not leave me in the grave...
>
> *(N. Berk.)* ...Thou wilt not abandon my soul to the realm of the dead...
>
> *(Roth.)* ...thou wilt not abandon my soul unto hades...
>
> *(Trans.)* ...you will not abandon my soul to Hades...
>
> *(Mar.)* ...for not thou wilt abandon the soul of Me in hades...

ACTS 2:31 He seeing this before spake of the resurrection of Christ, that his soul was not left in hell, neither his flesh did see corruption.

> *(Weym.)* ...He was not left forsaken in the Unseen World, nor did His body undergo decay.
>
> *(Roth.)* ...neither was he abandoned unto hades...
>
> *(Fenton)* ...that He was neither left in the land of spirits, nor did His body see corruption.

ACTS 2:33 Therefore being by the right hand of God exalted, and having received of the Father the promise of the Holy Ghost, he hath shed forth this, which ye now see and hear.

> *(NAB)* Exalted at God's right hand, he first received the promised Holy Spirit from the Father, then poured this Spirit out on us. This is what you now see and hear.

EPHESIANS 4:9,10 Now that he ascended, what is it but that he also descended first into the lower parts of the earth? He that descended is the same also that ascended up far above all heavens, that he might fill all things.

> *(20th C.R.)* Now surely this 'going up' must imply that he had already gone down into the world beneath. He who went down is the same as he who went up — up beyond the highest Heaven, for it is his aim to fill the whole universe with his presence.
> *(Weekes)* ...the under regions of the earth...that he might make all things complete.*
> (*fill up all things)
> *(Syriac)* ...that he might fulfill all things.
> *(Cress.)* ...he did this so he would be everywhere.
> *(Lovett)* ...first descended to this spiritual underworld.
> *(Wood)* ...impart His fullness to all things.
> *(HT Ander)* ...descended into the lower earthly regions.
> *(Deane)* ...both descended into the realm of the dead and ascended into heaven.

MATTHEW 12:40 For as Jonas was three days and nights in the whale's belly; so shall the Son of man be three days and three nights in the heart of the earth.

> *(GNB)* In the same way that Jonah spent three days and nights in the big fish, so will the Son of Man spend three days and nights in the depths of the earth.
> *(Wade)* ...in the bosom of the earth...

JONAH 2:2 And said, I cried by reason of mine affliction unto the Lord, and he heard me; out of the belly of hell cried I, and thou heardest my voice.

> *(GNB)* From deep in the world of the dead I cried for help, and you heard me.
> *(Basic)* ...out of the deepest underworld I sent up a cry, and you gave ear to my voice.
> *(Berk.)* ...From the innermost part (or, womb) of Sheol I cried for help...
> *(Spur.)* ...out of the womb of Hades...
> *(NAB)* ...from the belly of the fish Jonah said this prayer to the Lord...
> *(Masoretic O.T.)* ...Out of the belly of the netherworld cried I...

JONAH 2:4 Then I said, I am cast out of thy sight; yet I will look again toward thy holy temple.

> *(GNB)* I thought I had been banished from your presence and would never see your holy Temple again.

JONAH 2:6 I went down to the bottoms of the mountains; the earth with her bars was about me for ever: yet hast thou brought up my life from corruption, O Lord my God.

> *(GNB)* I went down to the very roots of the mountains, into the land whose gates lock shut forever. But you, O Lord my God, brought me back from the depths alive.

JONAH 2:6 (Roth) ...Then didst thou bring up — out of the pit — my life...

> *(Basic)* ...You have taken up my life from the underworld, O Lord my God.
>
> *(Spur.)* ...great abyss encompassed me...am expelled from Thy presence...
>
> *(Masoretic O.T.)* Yet hast Thou brought up my life from the pit...
>
> *(NAB)* ...the bars of the netherworld were closing behind me forever, But you brought up my life from the pit...
>
> *(Spur.)* ...roots of the mountains...The earth with her bars shot by me continually...

MATTHEW 27:46 And about the ninth hour Jesus cried with a loud voice, saying, Eli, Eli, lama sabachthani? that is to say, My God, my God, why hast thou forsaken me?

> *(SEB)* ...My God, my God, why did you abandon me?
>
> *(Basic)* ...My God, my God, why are you turned away from me?
>
> *(Jordan)* ...O my God, O my God, why have you left me here?

PSALM 22:1 My God, my God, why hast thou forsaken me? why art thou so far from helping me, and from the words of my roaring?

> *(Har.)* My God, my God, why have You abandoned me?
>
> *(NEB)* ...and art so far from saving me, from heeding my groans?
>
> *(TLB)* ...Why do you refuse to help me or even to listen to my groans?
>
> *(Mof.)* ...Why do my cries of anguish bring no help?

PSALM 22:6 But I am a worm, and no man; a reproach of men, and despised of the people.

> *(Smith)* But I am a worm and not a man, A shame to mankind, and despised of the people.
>
> *(Har.)* For my part I am a worm, and not a human being; insulted by men, despised by society.
>
> *(Knox)* But I, poor worm, have no manhood left; I am a by-word to all, the laughing-stock of the rabble.
>
> *(Jer.)* ...scorn of mankind, jest of the people...

PSALM 22:7 All they that see me laugh me to scorn: they shoot out the lip, they shake the head, saying...

> *(RSV)* All who see me mock at me...
>
> *(NEB)* ...jeer at me...
>
> *(Mof.)* ...they toss their heads and sneer...

PSALM 22:8 He trusted on the Lord that he would deliver him: let him deliver him, seeing he delighted in him.

> *(ASV)* Commit thyself unto Jehovah; let him deliver him: Let him rescue him, seeing he delighteth in him.

PSALM 22:8 (NAB) He relied on the Lord; let him deliver him, let him rescue him, if he loves him.

PSALM 22:9 But thou art he that took me out of the womb: thou didst make me hope when I was upon my mother's breasts.
> *(Smith, J.M.)* Yet thou didst bring me forth from the womb; thou didst give me security on my mother's breast.
> *(NAB)* You have been my guide since I was first formed...

PSALM 22:10 I was cast upon thee from the womb: thou art my God from my mother's belly.
> *(ASV)* I was cast upon thee from the womb; Thou art my God since my mother bare me.
> *(Knox)* From the hour of my birth, thou art my guardian; since I left my mother's womb, thou art my God!
> *(Har.)* I was thrown on Your care from birth...

PSALM 22:11 Be not far from me, for trouble is near; for there is none to help.
> *(Knox)* Do not leave me now, when trouble is close at hand; stand near, when I have none to help me.

PSALM 22:12 Many bulls have compassed me: strong bulls of Bashan have beset me round.
> *(Mof.)* A brutal horde besets me, fierce bulls of Bashan hem me in...
> *(Knox)* My enemies ring me round, packed close as a herd of oxen...
> *(TLB)* I am surrounded by fearsome enemies...

PSALM 22:13 They gaped upon me with their mouths, as a ravening and a roaring lion.
> *(Roth.)* They have opened wide against me their mouth, a lion rending and roaring.
> *(Har.)* ...opened their mouths at me like a voracious, roaring lion.

PSALM 22:14 I am poured out like water, and all my bones are out of joint: my heart is like wax; it is melted in the midst of my bowels.
> *(Spur.)* I am weak like water, And all My bones are disjointed...
> *(Knox)* I am spent as spilt water, all my bones out of joint, my heart turned to molten wax within me...
> *(Mof.)* ...my strength is weak as water, all my limbs give way...
> *(Har.)* My energy drains away from me like water, and all my bones are dislocated...
> *(Jer.)* I am like water draining away...
> *(ASV)* ...My heart is like wax; It is melted within me.

PSALM 22:15 My strength is dried up like a potsherd; and my tongue cleaveth to my jaws; and thou hast brought me into the dust of death.

> *(Young)* Dried up as an earthen vessel is my power...
> *(Basic)* My throat is dry like a broken vessel...
> *(Har.)* ...and my tongue sticks to my palate...
> *(Roth.)* ...And in the dust of death wilt thou lay me.
> *(Knox)* ...thou hast laid me in the dust, to die.

PSALM 22:16 For dogs have compassed me: the assembly of the wicked have enclosed me: they pierced my hands and my feet.

> *(Roth.)* For dogs have surrounded me, an assembly of evil doers have encircled me...
> *(TLB)* The enemy, this gang of evil men, circles me like a pack of dogs...
> *(NEB)* ...and they have hacked off my hands and my feet.

PSALM 22:17 I may tell all my bones: they look and stare upon me.

> *(Spur.)* As if they would number all My bones, they gaze at Me, they stare at Me.
> *(Knox)* ...they stand there watching me, gazing at me in triumph.
> *(NEB)* I tell my tale of misery, while they look on and gloat.

PSALM 22:18 They part my garments among them, and cast lots upon my vesture.

> *(Smith, J.M.)* They distribute my garments among them, and over my robe they cast lots.
> *(TLB)* They divide my clothes among themselves by a toss of the dice.

PSALM 88:4 I am counted with them that go down into the pit: I am as a man that hath no strength...

> *(Knox)* ...a man past all help...

PSALM 88:5 Free among the dead, like the slain that lie in the grave, whom thou rememberest no more: and they are cut off from thy hand.

> *(Hanson)* ...numbered with those who descend...
> *(Knox)* ...there among the lordless dead.
> *(Basic)* My soul is among the dead, like those in the underworld, to whom you give no more thought; for they are cut off from your care.

PSALM 88:6 Thou hast laid me in the lowest pit, in darkness, in the deeps.

> *(Jer.)* You have plunged me to the bottom of the Pit, to its darkest, deepest place...
> *(Masoretic O.T.)* In the nethermost pit...

PSALM 88:6 (Hanson) ...to a darkened place in the depths.

(Mof.) In the nethermost pit thou hast placed me, in abysses dark and deep...

(NAB) You have plunged me into the bottom of the pit, into the dark abyss.

(McFadyen) Thou hast set me at the bottom of the underworld, among the shadows deep and dark.

(Quaker) Thou hast put me into a pit of the lower and dark places into the depths.

(Eadie) ...confined in dangerous deep.

PSALM 88:7 Thy wrath lieth hard upon me, and thou hast afflicted me with all thy waves. Selah.

(Jer.) ...weighted down by your anger, drowned beneath your waves.

(Mof.) ...thy wrath lies heavy upon me, thy waves all overwhelm me.

(Eadie) Thou buriest me in gloomy night, and pressest me laid low and causest all the billows of Thy wrath o'er me to flow.

PSALM 88:8 Thou hast put away mine acquaintance far from me; thou hast made me an abomination unto them: I am shut up, and I cannot come forth.

(Knox) ...I lie in a prison whence there is no escape...

(Mof.) ...I cannot escape from my prison...

(McFadyen) ...I am as a prisoner, unable to go out.

(Quaker) ...I am shut up, I cannot get out.

PSALM 88:10 Wilt thou shew wonders to the dead? shall the dead arise and praise thee? Selah.

(Sharpe) Will departed spirits arise to praise thee?

(Merrick) Shall regions that exclude the day, Thy miracles to view display. And pale oblivion confines drear, the records of Thy justice hear?

(Hanson) Can you do a wonder for the dead?...

PSALM 88:11 Shall thy lovingkindness be declared in the grave? or thy faithfulness in destruction?

(Mof.) ...thy faithfulness within the world below?

(Sharpe) ...will thy kindness be declared in the tomb? Or thy faithfulness in the pit of destruction?

PSALM 88:12 Shall thy wonders be known in the dark? and thy righteousness in the land of forgetfulness?

(Hanson) Can your wonder be perceived in the darkness, your triumph in the land of oblivion?

PSALM 88:16 Thy fierce wrath goeth over me; thy terrors have cut me off.

(NEB) Thy burning fury has swept over me, thy onslaughts have put me to silence...

(Davies) ...the streams of Thy wrath...

(McFadyen) Thy terrors are upon me, they have robbed me of my senses. Thy fierce and awful anger, like a surging flood continually round about me, has swept me into destruction.

(Merrick) Beneath Thy heavy hand I groan, woes heaped on woes come rolling on and o'er me hang, ordained by Thee. Tremendous as a swelling sea...

I TIMOTHY 3:16 And without controversy great is the mystery of godliness: God was manifest in the flesh, justified in the Spirit, seen of angels, preached unto the Gentiles, believed on in the world, received up into glory.

(Barclay) No one can deny the greatness of the truth of our religion, the truth which only a disciple can understand...

(20th C.R.) Yes, and confessedly the deep truths of our religion are wonderful...proved righteous in spirit...

(Trans.) ...He was revealed in a human body...

(Weekes) ...He, who was manifested in bodily form, was made righteous in spirit, was observed by angels, was proclaimed among the nations...

(Knox) ...justification won in the realm of the Spirit; a vision seen by angels...

(Beck) ...became righteous in spirit...

(Young, River.) ...declared righteous in spirit...

(Phil.) ...was considered righteous in the Spirit...

(HT Ander) ...justified in spirit...

I PETER 3:18 For Christ also hath once suffered for sins, the just for the unjust, that he might bring us to God, being put to death in the flesh, but quickened by the Spirit.

(Barclay) ...he died to open the way to God for you. He underwent physical death, but in his spirit he was brought to life...

(Wuest) ...that He might provide you with an entree into the presence of God having in fact, been put to death with respect to the flesh [His human body], but made alive with respect to the spirit [His human spirit]...

(Mar.) ...being put to death on the one hand in the flesh, quickened on the other in the spirit...

(20th C.R.) ...His body died, but his Spirit rose to new Life.

(Norlie) ...put to death in His body, but He was made alive again in His Spirit.

(Godbey) ...quickened in spirit. (footnote: His own human spirit)

(Beck) ...made alive in His spirit.

(Jer.) In the body he was put to death, in the spirit he was raised to life...

I PETER 3:18 (Knox) ...but endowed with fresh life in his spirit, [19]and it was in his spirit that he went and preached to the spirits who lay in prison...

>*(RSV, ASV, NASV, Alf., Young, Weym., AMP)* ...made alive in the spirit.
>
>*(Cress.)* ...spirit had new life.
>
>*(Hayman)* ...but again brought to life in the spirit.
>
>*(HT Ander)* ...made alive in spirit.
>
>*(FSB, Bart. & Pet.)* ...endued with life in the spirit.
>
>*See eternal life p. 395*

ACTS 13:33, 34 God hath fulfilled the same unto us their children, in that he hath raised up Jesus again; as it is also written in the second psalm, Thou art my Son, this day have I begotten thee. And as concerning that he raised him up from the dead, now no more to return to corruption, he said on this wise, I will give you the sure mercies of David.

>*(20th C. 1)* ...This day thou hast been born to me.
>
>*(New Life)* ...I have given you Life today.
>
>*(N. Berk.)* But that He raised Him from the dead, never to return to decay, He has expressed this way...
>
>*(Berk.)* ...today I have generated Thee.
>
>*(Lovett)* ...for I have sired You this very day!

REVELATION 1:5 And from Jesus Christ, who is the faithful witness, and the first begotten of the dead, and the prince of the kings of the earth. Unto him that loved us, and washed us from our sins in his own blood...

>*(Godbey)* ...To the one loving us with divine love...
>
>*(Weym.)* ...the first of the dead to be born to life...
>
>*(Wade)* ...the First of the dead to be born into renewed Life...
>
>*(Noli)* ...the pioneer of the resurrection...
>
>*(20th C. 1)* ...the First of the Dead to be born again...
>
>*See eternal life p. 401*

COLOSSIANS 2:15 And having spoiled principalities and powers, he made a shew of them openly, triumphing over them in it.

>*(20th C.R.)* He rid himself of all the Powers of Evil, and held them up to open contempt when he celebrated his triumph over them on the cross!
>
>*(Barclay)* On the cross he stripped the demonic powers and authorities of their power, and made a public spectacle of them, as if they had been captives in a victor's triumphal procession.

COLOSSIANS 2:15 (Way) He stripped away from Himself all trammels of 'Principalities and Powers': He paraded them unsparingly, as He haled them in the Triumph of the Cross.

(Cony.) And He disarmed the Principalities and the Powers [which fought against Him], and put them to open shame, leading them captive in the triumph of Christ.

(Phil.) And then, having drawn the sting of all the powers ranged against us, he exposed them, shattered, empty and defeated, in his final glorious triumphant act!

(Hayman) ...having spoiled the orders of the rebel hierarchy, He paraded then in open triumph gained over them by the cross.

(Deane) He set himself, and us, free from all the spirit-powers of evil; on the Cross he put them to open shame and triumphed over them.

(Bart. & Pet.) ...boldly, triumphing over them on the cross.

(Quaker) ...putting off as if clothes with them.

(Hammond) By means also of His death, He hath divested the evil spirits of their power, thrown them out of their temples...

(Weym.) And the hostile princes and rulers He stripped off from Himself, and boldly displayed them as His conquests, when by the Cross He triumphed over them.

(Trans.) There *Christ stripped** the demonic rulers and authorities of their power over him, and in his own triumph made a public show of them.

> *"en auto" may mean "in him" or "in it" (the cross)
>
> ** The verb translated "stripped," used for the stripping off of clothes, may denote an action done by oneself or by someone else.

(Wand) ...he stripped away like a cast-off garment every demonic Rule and Authority and made a public exhibition of them...

(Noli) He despoiled the infernal dominions and realms. He dragged their rulers as captives in procession, and through his cross he led us all to triumph.

(Lau.) And He tore the swords from the hands of all the spirit rulers and the powers in the spirit world.

(Alf.) ...in him.

(Douay, Conq.) ...in himself.

(Berk.) ...and, disarming the princes and authorities, He publicly exposed them to disgrace as He personally triumphed over them.

(Pl. Eng.) He disarmed all powers and authorities, and made them a public show, and dragged them behind Him in the victory-march of Christ.

(NAB) Thus did God disarm the principalities and powers. He made a public show of them and, leading them off captive, triumphed in the person of Christ.

(Johnson) And by his resurrection, Christ demonstrated the emptiness of every earthly power when God acts. You have this kind of triumph in life because of your relation to God through Christ.

COLOSSIANS 2:15 (Cress.) He won the victory over powers and rulers. He showed that they had no power at all.

> *(Lovett)* He openly displayed Jesus' triumph over Satan, disarming him and his entire band of spirits down to the last demon.
>
> *(Adams)* Disarming rulers and authorities, God publicly exposed them, triumphing over them in Him.
>
> *See authority of the believer p. 220*

See authority of the believer p. 220

HEBREWS 2:14,15 Forasmuch then as the children are partakers of flesh and blood, he also himself likewise took part of the same; that through death he might destroy him that had the power of death, that is, the devil; And deliver them who through fear of death were all their lifetime subject to bondage.

> *(Jer.)* ...so that by his death, he could take away all the power of the devil...
>
> *(Jordan)* ...he might break the grip of the one who controls death...
>
> *(Wuest)* ...He might render inoperative the one having the dominion of death, that is, the devil, and effect the release of those...
>
> *(Weekes)* ...he might put an end to him who possesseth the lordship of death...
>
> *(Norlie)* ...who has the power of death...
>
> *(Alf.)* ...he might destroy him that hath the power of death...
>
> *(Cent.)* ...he might render powerless him...
>
> *(River.)* ...he might defeat him...
>
> *(Wand)* ...He might frustrate...
>
> *(Godbey)* ...he might set at nought him who has the power of death...
>
> *(Cony.)* ...He might destroy the lord of death, that is, the Devil...
>
> *(Phil.)* ...so that by going through death as a man...
>
> *(Roth.)* ...He might paralyse him...
>
> *(Wms.)* ...He by His death might put a stop to the power of him who has the power of death, that is, the devil.
>
> *(Authentic)* ...He might put out of commission him who wields the power of death, namely the Devil...
>
> *(Wade)* ...He might reduce to impotence him who has in Death the instrument of his sway, that is the Devil...
>
> *(Way)* He did this, that he might be able to die, and by his death might annihilate the power of him who sways the sceptre of death's terrors—that is, the devil—and so might transfer into a new existence those who through the haunting dread of death were all their lifetime bowed beneath a yoke of veritable slavery.
>
> *(Pl. Eng.)* ...by death he might bring to nothing the lord of death, that is, the devil, and might set free from slavery all those that all their lives had lived in fear of death.

HEBREWS 2:14,15 (Knox) ...he would depose the prince of death...he would deliver those multitudes who lived all the while as slaves, made over to the fear of death.

(Gspd.) ...he might dethrone the lord of death, the devil, and free from their slavery men who had always lived in fear of death.

(Hayman) ...in order through death to disable him that held the empire of death...

(Smith, J. M.) ...that by his death he might dethrone the lord of death, the devil...

(AMP) ...that by [going through] death He might bring to nought and make of no effect him who had the power of death...And also that He might deliver and completely set free all those who through the [haunting] fear of death were held in bondage throughout the whole course of their lives.

(20th C.R.) ...that by his death he might render powerless him whose power lies in death—that is the Devil—and might in this way deliver all those who, from fear of death, had all their lives been living in slavery.

(Noli) ...for he wanted through his own death to overthrow the devil who has the power of death...

(Berk.) ...so that by means of His death He might neutralize the one who wields the power of death, namely the devil...

(NAB) ...that by his death he might rob the devil, the prince of death, of his power...

(Hudson) ...him who rules in the sphere of death, that is, the devil...

(Lovett) For it was only by dying as a MAN that He could cancel the power of the devil, who rules the realm of death.

(Weym.) ...He might render powerless him who had authority over death, that is, the Devil, and might set at liberty all those...

(Basic) ...he took a body himself and became like them; so that by his death he might put an end to him who had the power of death, that is to say, the Evil One; And let those who all their lives were in chains because of their fear of death, go free.

(Lau.) ...He died as we die, so that He might destroy the devil, who is the king of death. He set us free from death. We need no longer be slaves to the fear of death.

(Mof.) ...he might crush him who wields the power of death (that is to say, the devil) and release from thraldom those who lay under a life-long fear of death.

(TLB) ...for only as a human being could he die and in dying break the power of the devil who had the power of death. Only in that way could He deliver those...

(NASB) ...He might render powerless...

(Hammond) ...might frustrate and make void the devil's desire (which was to keep men forever under the power of death).

See authority of the believer p. 221

HEBREWS 9:12 Neither by the blood of goats and calves, but by his own blood he entered in once into the holy place, having obtained eternal redemption for us.

> *(AMP)* He went once for all into the [Holy of] Holies [of heaven], not by virtue of the blood of goats and calves [by which to make reconciliation between God and man], but His own blood, having found and secured a complete redemption (an everlasting release for us).

> *(Quaker)* ...by His own blood entered once into the sanctuary and got everlasting redemption.

> *(Cent.)* ...not taking the blood of goats and oxen, but his own blood and entered...

> *(Weym.)* ...taking with Him not the blood of goats and calves, but His own blood...

> *(Gspd.)* ...taking with him no blood of goats and calves, but his own, and secured our permanent deliverance.

> *(Jer.)* ...taking with him not the blood of goats and bull calves, but his own blood...

> *(Noli)* ...not with the blood of goats and calves, but with His own blood, and achieved our eternal redemption.

> *(20th C.R.)* ...with his own blood; and having secured our permanent deliverance...

> *(Trans.)* ...with his own blood, and has secured eternal deliverance for us.

> *(N. Berk.)* ...not with the blood of goats and calves, but with His own blood He entered...

> *(Wms.)* ...with His own blood...

> *(Barclay)* ...he secured eternal deliverance for us.

> *(Pl. Eng.)* ...and so he won an everlasting deliverance.

> *(Norlie)* ...and won for us eternal redemption.

EPHESIANS 1:19-21 And what is the exceeding greatness of his power to us-ward who believe, according to the working of his mighty power, Which he wrought in Christ, when he raised him from the dead, and set him at his own right hand in the heavenly places, Far above all principality and power, and might, and dominion, and every name that is named, not only in this world, but also in that which is to come...

> *(N. Berk.)* ...how overwhelmingly great is His power...

> *(AMP)* ...His power in and for us who believe...

> *(NEB)* ...and how vast the resources of his power open to us who trust in him.

> *(Basic)* ...And how unlimited is his power to us who have faith...

> *(Wuest)* ...the superabounding greatness of His inherent power to us who are believing ones as measured by the operative energy of the manifested strength of His might...

> *(Noli)* ...and how immeasurable is his power in us who believe in Him...

> *(Hayman)* ...what the overwhelming greatness of His power exerted on us who believe, as measured by that energy of omnipotence put forth in Christ when He raised Him from the dead...

> *(Carpenter)* Calculate, if you can, the gigantic power behind all this...

EPHESIANS 1:19-21 (Weym.) ...the transcendent greatness of His power in us believers, as seen in the working of His infinite might, when He displayed it in Christ...

(Fenton) ...the exceeding greatness of His power in us believers, through His mighty energy, which energized in Christ...

(Wade) ...and how transcendently great is His power manifested in us who have faith. That power in us is due to the same exercise of His Mighty Sovereignty as was displayed in the instance of the Christ...

(Beck) ...the vast resources of His power working in us who believe. It is the same mighty power with which He worked in Christ, raised him from the dead...

(Authentic) ...indicated by the operation of the mighty force God employed in the case of Christ in raising Him from the dead...

(Jordan) May you experience the incredible outburst of his power in us who rely on his might and his abundant energy. This same energy working in Christ raised him from the dead and gave him spiritual victory and authority over every ruler...

(Cent.) ...the surpassing greatness of his might in us who believe, as seen in the energy of that resistless might which he exercised in raising Christ from the dead, and in seating him at his right hand in the heavenly heights...

(Trans.) ...and the limitless scope of his power at work in us once we believe in him. This is that same stupendous power which he exerted when he raised Christ from death and enthroned him at his right hand in the supernatural world.

(GNB) ...and how very great is his power at work in us who believe. This power working in us is the same as the mighty strength which he used when he raised Christ from death and seated him at his right side in the heavenly world.

(Wms.) ...measured by His tremendously mighty power...far above every other government, authority, power, and dominion, yea, far above every other title that can be conferred...

(Barclay) ...that power demonstrated in the action of the mighty strength which was operative in the case of Christ. There he gave him a place far above all spiritual powers, above every ruler and authority and power and lord, above every possible title of honour...

(Lau.) I pray that you may realize that His power in us who believe, is great beyond measure. It is the same mighty power that worked in Christ. By that power God raised Him from the dead and had Him sit at His right hand in heaven. There Jesus sits above all rulers, above all authority, above all power, above all lords...

See authority of the believer p. 205, 207; prayer p. 240, 242

JOHN 12:31, 32 Now is the judgment of this world: now shall the prince of this world be castout. And I, if I be lifted up from the earth, will draw all men unto me.

JOHN 12:31, 32 (TLB) The time of judgment for the world has come—and the time when Satan, the prince of this world, shall be cast out. And when I am lifted up [on the cross], I will draw every one to me.

(AMP) Now the judgment (crisis) of this world is coming on [sentence is now being passed on this world]. Now the ruler (evil genius, prince) of this world shall be cast out (expelled). And I, if and when I am lifted up from the earth [on the cross], will draw and attract all men [Gentiles as well as Jews] to Myself.

(Message) At this moment the world is in crisis. Now Satan, the ruler of this world, will be thrown out. And I, as I am lifted up from the earth, will attract everyone to me and gather them around me.

II CORINTHIANS 5:14 For the love of Christ constraineth us; because we thus judge, that if one died for all, then were all dead...

(Cress.) We believe that one man died for all people. So it is as if they all died.

(Wood) ...with whom we all died...

(Beck) The love of Christ compels us because we're convinced one died for all and so all have died.

(Weym.) For the love of Christ overmasters us, since we are convinced of this, that One died for all, hence they all died.

(Mof.) For I am controlled by the love of Christ, convinced that as One has died for all, then all have died.

(GNB) We are ruled by the love of Christ, now that we recognize that one man died for everyone, which means that they all share in his death.

(Way) ...to this conclusion have we come—One died for the sake of all: in Him then did all die.

(Knox) ...if one man died on behalf of all, then all thereby became dead men.

(Cony.) ...if one died for all, then all died [in Him].

(Jordan) In a sense, then, we all died when He died for all.

(Lau.) We know that Christ died for all of us. So our old self died with Him.

(Hayman) ...if on behalf of all One died, then in Him all died.

(Fenton) ...the love of Christ sustains us, deciding us, that One died for all, therefore all died...

(Bird, R.) The love of Jesus compels me to speak, for I consider that Jesus, having died for all, it is as if all men had died to sin.

II CORINTHIANS 5:19 To wit, that God was in Christ, reconciling the world unto himself, not imputing their trespasses unto them; and hath committed unto us the word of reconciliation.

II CORINTHIANS 5:19 (AMP) It was God [personally present] in Christ, reconciling and restoring the world to favor with Himself, not counting up and holding against [men] their trespasses [but cancelling them], and committing to us the message of reconciliation [of the restoration to favor].

(Barclay) The fact is that God was acting in Christ to turn the world's enmity to himself into friendship, that he was not holding men's sins against them, and that he placed upon us the privilege of taking to men who are hostile to him this offer of his friendship.

(Wand) That ministry is based on the fact that God was in Christ reconciling the world to Himself, wiping out the debit balance of our transgressions and setting His reconciliation to the credit of our account.

(TLB) For God was in Christ, restoring the world to himself, no longer counting men's sins against them but blotting them out. This is the wonderful message he has given us to tell others.

(Jordan) God was in Christ, hugging the world to himself. He no longer keeps track of men's sins, and has planted in us his concern for getting together.

(Hayman) ...lodging in us the message of that reconciliation.

(Deane) This is the gift of God; who has become man's friend through the work of Christ...

GALATIANS 2:20 I am crucified with Christ: nevertheless I live; yet not I, but Christ liveth in me: and the life which I now live in the flesh I live by the faith of the Son of God, who loved me, and gave himself for me.

(Noli) I have been crucified with Christ. Now it is not my old self, but Christ Himself who lives in me.

(Cress.) I died when Christ died on a cross. I do not live now, but Christ lives in me.

(Jer.) I have been crucified with Christ, and I live now not with my own life but with the life of Christ who lives in me. The life I now live in this body I live in faith: faith in the Son of God who loved me and who sacrificed himself for my sake.

(Barclay) I have been crucified with Christ. My own life is dead; it is Christ who lives in me. True, my physical life goes on, but its mainspring is faith in the Son of God...

(Lau.) ...Christ took me to the cross with Him, and I died there with Him.

(Way) Yes, I have shared Messiah's crucifixion. I am living indeed, but it is not I that live, it is Messiah whose life is in me.

(Mar.) With Christ I have been co-crucified...

(Weym., Cent., 20th C.R., AMP, TLB, N. Berk., Wms., Wade, Pl. Eng., Worrell, Alf., Mof., Fenton, Gspd., ASV, NASB, RSV, NEB, NIV) I have been crucified with Christ.

(Young, Wuest, Cunn.) ...with Christ I have been crucified...

(Conc., Roth.) With Christ, have I been crucified...

GALATIANS 2:20 (Wand) I have been actually crucified with Christ...

(Beck) I was crucified with Christ...

(Deane) ...it is faith in Christ which gives life, and my life is mystically united to his...

(Abbrev. Bible) I was crucified with Christ so that he might live in me...

(Dist.) I consider myself as having died and now enjoying a second existence, which is simply Jesus using my body.

See divine healing p. 285; eternal life p. 385

GALATIANS 6:14 But God forbid that I should glory, save in the cross of our Lord Jesus Christ, by whom the world is crucified unto me, and I unto the world.

(Cress.) ...the things of the world have become dead to me, and I have become dead to the world.

(Way) But never be it mine to boast of aught save of the Cross of our Lord, of Jesus the Messiah, by whose death the world has died on that cross to me, and I have died to the world.

(Lau.) ...On His cross the world died to me and I died to the world.

(Norlie) ...on it the world has been crucified to me, and I have been crucified to the world.

(Bruce) But far be it from me to boast about anything except the cross of our head Jesus Christ: that cross forms a permanent barrier (to erect a fence) between the world and me, and between me and the world.

(N. Berk., 20th C.R., AMP, Mar., Berk.) ...through whom the world has been crucified to me.

(Barclay, Mof., Gspd., Godbey, Black., Authentic, Cent., Conc., Wms., Pl. Eng., RSV, NASB, NIV) ...the world has been crucified to me...

(Roth., Alf., ASV, Young) ...hath been crucified...

(Deane) ...I am dead to worldly fame.

GALATIANS 6:15 For in Christ Jesus neither circumcision availeth any thing, nor uncircumcision, but a new creature.

(AMP) ...a new creation [the result of a new birth and a new nature in Christ Jesus, the Messiah].

(Cress.) ...must become a new person.

(Adams) ...what counts is a new creation.

(Trans.) Whether a man is circumcised or uncircumcised does not matter; what matters is that he can be created anew.

(Way) Circumcision is nothing; uncircumcision is nothing: the creation of a new nature in us is everything.

(Wade) For neither circumcision nor uncircumcision is of any importance, but only a newlycreated nature.

GALATIANS 6:15 (Barclay) ...What matters is the creating of the man all over again.

(Lau.) ...It is the new birth that means everything.

(Wand) ...The one thing of importance is that we should be created afresh in a new order of existence.

(GNB) ...what does matter is being a new creature.

(Phil.) ...but the power of new birth.

COLOSSIANS 2:20 Wherefore if ye be dead with Christ from the rudiments of the world, why, as though living in the world, are ye subject to ordinances?

(NAB) If with Christ you have died to cosmic forces...

(Hudson) If you died with Christ and left behind the elemental world spirits...

(Wood) You are dead with Christ to the principles which govern the world of men.

(Knox) If, by dying with Christ, you have parted company with worldly principles...

(Barclay) Your death with Christ means that the world's rudimentary teaching has nothing more to do with you. Why then go on living as if your life was dominated by the world?

(AMP) If then you have died with Christ to material ways of looking at things and have escaped from the world's crude and elemental notions and teachings of externalism, why do you live as if you still belong to the world?

(N. Berk.) If with Christ you have become dead to the elementary principles of the world, why allow regulations to be imposed on you as if you were living under the world's control?

(Conq.) ...principles of the world.

(Way) If, by your share in Messiah's death, you are severed from the rudimentary teachings of externalism...

(Cony.) If, then, when you died with Christ, you put away the childish lessons of outward things...

(Norlie) If you have died with Christ, to worldly ways of looking at things...

(GNB) You have died with Christ and are set free from the ruling spirits of the universe...

(Trans.) You died with Christ...

(Lau., New Life, and Beck) ...you have died...

(Conc.) If, then, you died together with Christ...

(Young) If, then, ye did die with Christ...

(Roth.) If ye have died, together with Christ...

(Weym., Conf., Authentic, Gspd., NASB) If you have died with Christ...

(Wuest) In view of the fact that you died with Christ...

(TLB) Since you died, as it were, with Christ...

(20th C.R.) Since, with Christ, you became dead...

COLOSSIANS 2:20 (NEB) Did you not die with Christ and pass beyond reach of the elemental spirits of the universe?

(Phil.) ...why, as if you were still part and parcel of this world-wide system...

(Deane) With Christ you died, so to speak, to the "elementals," the unseen worldly spirits.

COLOSSIANS 3:3 For ye are dead, and your life is hid with Christ in God.

(Black.) For you died [in your identification with his death], and your life [which is the result of his resurrection], is hidden with Christ in God.

(NAB) After all, you have died!

(Deaf) Your old sinful self has died...

(Johnson) In a sense you have already passed away, and your life is already firmly united with Christ in God.

(Wood) ...with whom your life is bound up.

(Barclay) For you died to this world, and now you have entered with Christ into the secret life of God.

(Way) You have died to things of earth, and your real life now has been hidden, by its union with Messiah, in the being of God.

(Wade) ...you died to the world, and your real Life, ever since, has been, together with the Christ, hidden from human sight in union with God.

(TLB) You should have as little desire for this world as a dead person does...

(Knox) ...you have undergone death...

(Beck., Wand., Trans., Authentic, N. Berk., Gspd., Wms., Conf., Norlie, Weym., Jer., AMP, GNB, NASB, Berk.) ...you have died...

(20th C.R., Wuest, Mof., Conc., Fenton, Lau., NIV) For you died...

(Alf., Mar., Worrell, Cunn, ASV) For ye died...

(Jordan) For you all died...

(Young) ...for ye did die...

(Roth.) For ye have died...

COLOSSIANS 2:9, 10 For in him dwelleth all the fulness of the Godhead bodily. And ye are complete in him, which is the head of all principality and power...

(Barclay) ...He is supreme over every demonic power and authority.

(Norlie) And you have come to fullness of life through union with Him, who is the fountainhead of all authority and power.

(Hudson) ...for in him the full content of God's nature has its permanent embodied home...

(Berk.) ...and in Him, who is the head of all princedom and authority, you are enjoying fulness of life.

(Cress.) Christ has everything God has. And you, too, have everything when you are in him.

COLOSSIANS 2:9, 10 (Lovett) When you received the person of Christ, you were joined to the same fullness! Therefore, your own spiritual makeup is now full, you are complete in Christ, the fountain from which all authority and power proceeds.

(Wood) In Him, incarnate I say, resides the fulness of deity, and in union with Him you can attain your full development.

(Wms.) For it is in Him that all the fullness of Deity continues to live embodied, and through union with Him you too are filled with it. He is the Head of all principalities and dominions.

(20th C.R.) For the Godhead in all its fulness dwells in Christ in a bodily form.

(Gspd.) For it is in him that all the fulness of God's nature lives embodied, and in union with him you too are filled with it.

(Way) For it is in Him that all the "Plentitude of the Godhead" has its corporeal home. Nay more, by union with Him you too are filled with that Plentitude...

(Trans.) For in him, that is in his body, God in all his completeness dwells; and in union with him, who is the head over every spiritual ruler and authority, you too come to perfection.

(GNB) For the full content of divine nature lives in Christ...and you have been given full life in union with him. He is supreme over every spiritual ruler and authority.

(N. Berk.) ...and in Him, who is the head of all rule and authority, you are enjoying fullness of life.

(AMP) ...[in Christ you too are filled with the Godhead—Father, Son and Holy Spirit—and reach full spiritual stature]...

(TLB) So you have everything when you have Christ, and you are filled with God through your union with Christ...

COLOSSIANS 2:11 In whom also ye are circumcised with the circumcision made without hands, in putting off the body of the sins of the flesh by the circumcision of Christ.

(Black.) ...by the spiritual circumcision wrought by Christ in liberating you from [the domination of] the old nature.

(Trans.) When you became one with him, your lower nature was stripped away. That was like being circumcised in Christ's way, and it was a spiritual, not a physical, operation.

(GNB) ...the circumcision made by Christ, which consists of being freed from the power of this sinful self.

(Weym.) ...you threw off your sinful nature in the circumcision of Christ...

(Norlie) When you became united to Him, you became circumcised with a circumcision not made by hand. In the circumcision of Christ, you were set free from your sinful nature.

COLOSSIANS 2:12 Buried with Him in baptism, wherein also ye are risen with him through the faith of the operation of God, who hath raised him from the dead.

> *(Jordan)* ...and with him you have been raised by the inner working of faith in the might of God, who raised Him from the dead.
>
> *(Lovett)* You received the death of Christ, that is, once you were baptized into Him, His death became yours as surely as though you had shared His tomb...you also have His resurrection life working in you.
>
> *(Trans.)* When you were baptized, you were buried with him and, in union with him, you were raised again because you believed that God who raised him from the dead really had the power to do it.
>
> *(Authentic)* ...In Him equally you have been raised up by the faith in God who raised him from the dead.
>
> *(20th C.R.)* ...in baptism you were also raised to Life with him...
>
> *(Hayman)* With Him in baptism you were buried, with Him therein raised again, through your faith in the divine energy put forth by God's raising Him from the dead.
>
> *(Knox)* ...you, by baptism, have been united with his burial, united, too, with his resurrection, through your faith in that exercise of power by which God raised him from the dead.
>
> *(Wood)* ...in baptism you were brought into real union with His death and resurrection.

COLOSSIANS 2:13 And you, being dead in your sins and the uncircumcision of your flesh, hath he quickened together with him, having forgiven you all trespasses.

> *(Berk.)* ...you He made to live jointly with Himself...
>
> *(Wood)* ...God gave you life with Christ.
>
> *(Phil.)* You, who were spiritually dead because of your sins & your uncircumcision (that is, the fact that you were outside the Law), God has now made to share in the very life of Christ!
>
> *(Knox)* And in giving life to him, he gave life to you too, when you lay dead in your sins...
>
> *(Way)* ...you God thrilled with that same new life of Jesus.
>
> *(GNB)* You were at one time spiritually dead...
>
> *(20th C.R.)* ...to you God gave Life in giving life to Christ!
>
> *(Cony.)* ...and you, also...God raised to share His life.
>
> *(Mar.)* ...he co-quickened you with him...
>
> *See eternal life p. 388*

COLOSSIANS 2:14 Blotting out the handwriting of ordinances that was against us, which was contrary to us, and took it out of the way, nailing it to the cross.

> *(Adams)* ...erasing the handwritten certificate of indebtedness with its requirements that stood against us...

COLOSSIANS 2:14(Trans.) He cancelled the bond which required us to keep the law's demands. There it was, condemning us at every point, but he took it right away and nailed it to the cross.

(Lau.) God crossed out the whole debt against us in His account books. He no longer counted the laws that we had broken. He nailed the account book to the cross and closed the account.

(Pl. Eng.) ...he destroyed the record of the debts standing against us, and its rules and regulations; he nailed it to the cross, and he put it out of sight.

COLOSSIANS 3:1 If ye then be risen with Christ, seek those things which are above, where Christ sitteth on the right hand of God.

(Deane) ...your thoughts must be fixed on the things of heaven...

(NAB) Since you have been raised up in company with Christ, set your heart on what pertains to higher realms where Christ is seated at God's right hand.

(Johnson) If indeed you have experienced God's resurrection power, then live a resurrection life.

(Cress.) Were you raised from death with Christ? Then try to get the things which are in heaven.

(Lovett) ...shift your ambitions to heaven...your master reigns there — that's the place to invest...

(Barclay) If then you have been raised to life with Christ, your heart must be set on the great realities of that heavenly sphere, where Christ is seated at the right hand of God. Your constant concern must be with heavenly realities, not with worldly trivialities.

(AMP) If then you have been raised with Christ [to a new life, thus sharing His resurrection from the dead], aim at and seek the [rich, eternal treasures] that are above, where Christ is, seated at the right hand of God.

(NEB) Were you not raised to life with Christ? Then aspire to the realm above, where Christ is, seated at the right hand of God.

(Mof., NIV) Since, then, you have been raised with Christ...

(20th C.R.) Since, therefore, you were raised to Life with the Christ...

(Pl. Eng.) Since then, you were raised with Christ...

(Wand) Since then you have risen with Christ...

(Jer.) Since you have been brought back to true life with Christ...

(Wuest) In view of the fact, therefore, that you were raised with Christ...

(NASB, Trans., Norlie, Authentic, New Life, N. Berk., Lau.) ...you have been raised...

(Beck, Deaf) ...you were raised...

(GNB) You have been raised to life...

(Young, Gspd., Worrell) ...ye were raised with...

COLOSSIANS 3:1 (Alf., ASV) ...ye were raised together with Christ...

    (Roth) ...ye have been raised together with the Christ...

    (Weym.) ...you have risen with Christ...

    (Mar.) ...ye were co-raised with Christ...

    (Cony.) ...you were made partakers of Christ's resurrection...

    (Phil.) ...reach out for the highest gifts of Heaven, where Christ reigns in power.

EPHESIANS 2:4, 5 But God, who is rich in mercy, for his great love wherewith he loved us, Even when we were dead in sins, hath quickened us together with Christ, (by grace ye are saved;).

    (20th C.R.) Yet God, in his abundant compassion, and because of the great love with which he loved us, gave Life to us in giving life to the Christ, even though at that time we were dead because of our offences.

    (GNB) But God's mercy is so abundant, and his love for us is so great, that while we were spiritually dead in our disobedience he brought us to life with Christ.

    (K. & L.) ...was moved by the intense love with which he loved us...he made us live with the life of Christ...

    (Jordan) ...God in his overflowing sympathy and great love breathed the same new life into us as into Christ.

    (Noli) ...out of his excessive love for us...

    (AMP) ...Because of and in order to satisfy the great and wonderful and intense love with which He loved us...He gave us the very life of Christ Himself, the same new life with which He quickened Him.

    (Berk.) ...alive in unison with Christ...

    (Wood) ...gave us new life with Christ...

    (Way) Even when in trespasses we lay dead, Thrilled us with the same new life wherewith He quickened our Messiah.—By free grace alone have ye obtained salvation!

    (Knox) Our sins had made dead men of us, and he, in giving life to Christ, gave life to us too...

    (Cony.) ...called us to share the life of Christ...

    (Godbey) ...created life in us in Christ...

    (Weekes, Basic, Phil.) ...gave us life together with Christ...

    (Carpenter) ...He quickened us with the risen life of Christ...

    (Abbrev. Bible) ...gave us life by uniting us with Christ...

    (Wade) ...spiritually dead...spiritually alive...

    (Mar., Young) ...(by grace ye are having been saved)...

    (Lau., Wand, New Life) ...we have been saved.

    (Cunn., Weym., NASB, NIV, Conf., Wade, 20th C. 1, 20th C.R., Godbey, Wms., Norlie, Pl. Eng., N. Berk., Trans., Mof., GNB, Jer., Gspd.) ...you have been saved.

EPHESIANS 2:4, 5 (ASV) ...have ye been saved.
See authority of the believer p. 210; eternal life p. 386

EPHESIANS 2:6 And hath raised us up together, and made us sit together in heavenly places in Christ Jesus.

(NAB) Both with and in Christ Jesus, he raised us up and gave us a place in the heavens.

(Johnson) ...we ourselves now exercise an authority like that which Christ has in the presence of God.

(Cress.) God raised us from death with Christ Jesus and gave us a place to sit with him in heaven.

(Wood) ...in the heavenly sphere in Christ.

(20th C.R.) And through our union with Christ Jesus, God raised us to life with him, and also caused us to sit with him on high.

(GNB) In our union with Christ Jesus he raised us up with him to rule with him in the heavenly world.

(K. & L.) Together with Christ Jesus and in him, he raised us up and enthroned us in the heavenly realm.

(Way) And with Him He raised us from the death-sleep, And with Him throned us in the high heavens, By virtue of our union with Messiah Jesus.

(Knox) ...raised us up too, enthroned us too above the heavens, in Christ Jesus.

(Wms.) And He raised us with Him and through union with Christ Jesus He made us sit down with Him in the heavenly realm.

(Barclay) Because of our union with Christ Jesus he raised us from spiritual death, and gave us a seat with him in the heavenly places.

(Cornish) God raised us out of it all with Christ, and He sat us down on the right hand of power with Him and gave us dominion...

(Bird, R.) ...raising up life in us with Him, to sit in Heavenly Places.

(Carpenter) We found ourselves not only risen from death but in Christ, in Christ who is in Heaven, and therefore in the heavenly realm ourselves.
See authority of the believer p. 210

ROMANS 3:21 But now the righteousness of God without the law is manifested, being witnessed by the law and the prophets.

(Fenton) ...a Divine righteousness...

(Black.) ...God's kind of righteousness...

(Wood) ...show His righteousness undimmed.

(Wms.) But now God's way of giving men right standing with Himself has come to light; a way without connection with the law...

ROMANS 3:21 (Weym.) But now a righteousness coming from God has been brought to light...

(20th C.R.) But now, quite apart from Law, there stands revealed a righteousness which comes from God, to which the Law and the Prophets bear witness.

(20th C. 1) ...there stands revealed a righteousness which comes from God...

(GNB) But now God's way of putting people right with himself has been revealed. It has nothing to do with law...

(Trans.) ...God's way of putting men right with himself has been revealed and it is quite independent of law.

(Carpenter) ...a wholly new kind of righteousness has been revealed to a wondering world.

(Hayman) But as facts now stand, our view opens upon a righteousness God-given, not resting on law, though with the Law and the Prophets to attest it...

ROMANS 3:22 Even the righteousness of God which is by faith of Jesus Christ unto all and upon all them that believe: for there is no difference.

(Fenton) ...a Divine righteousness by means of a Faith from Jesus Christ, to all believers...

(Adams) ...that is channeled through faith in Jesus.

(Black.) Indeed God's kind of righteousness is through faith in Jesus Christ. It is effective for all who are trusting [in him].

(Wood) ...God's righteousness is communicated to all without distinction, through faith in Christ.

(Wms.) ...God's own way of giving men right standing with Himself is through faith in Jesus Christ...

(Weym.) ...a righteousness coming from God...

(20th C.R.) ...a righteousness which comes from God through faith in Jesus Christ, and is for all, without distinction, who believe in him.

(20th C. 1) It is a righteousness which comes from God through faith in Jesus Christ...

(Trans.) ...it is God's own way of putting men right with himself through faith in Jesus Christ ...

(GNB) God puts people right through their faith in Jesus Christ. God does this to all who believe in Christ.

(Way) This righteousness of God's bestowal is attained through trust in Jesus the Messiah, and is vouchsafed only to those who believe in Him.

(Phil.) ...it is a righteousness imparted to, and operating in, all who have faith in Jesus Christ.

(Lau.) ..Every person who has faith in Jesus Christ is forgiven and made right with God...

(Weekes) ...God's righteousness...

ROMANS 3:24 Being justified freely by his grace through the redemption that is in Christ Jesus...

(Hudson) ...through the deliverance [effected] in Christ Jesus.

ROMANS 3:24 (Cress.) ...Christ Jesus paid for them and set them free.

(20th C. 1) ...are being set right with him through the deliverance which is in Christ Jesus.

(GNB) But by the free gift of God's grace all are put right with him through Christ Jesus, who sets them free.

(Trans.) They are freely put right with Him by His grace, through the act of liberation effected by Christ Jesus.

(Weekes) ...who are made righteous, as a free gift, by His loving-favor, through the redemption that is by Christ Jesus...

(N. Berk.) We are justified freely by His grace through the ransom that Christ Jesus provided.

(Roth.) Being declared righteous freely by his favour through the redemption that is in Christ Jesus...

(Pl. Eng.) ...they are delivered without price by the grace of God through the liberation made in Jesus Christ.

(Gspd.) ...by his mercy they are made upright for nothing, by the deliverance secured through Christ Jesus.

(Beck) They are justified freely by grace, through the ransom Christ Jesus paid to free them.

(Wade) Such, by His gratuitous Favour, stand right with Him through the redemption which was effected in Christ Jesus...

(Authentic) ...freely exonerated through the discharge of liability by Christ Jesus.

See righteousness p. 31

ROMANS 3:25 Whom God hath set forth to be a propitiation through faith in his blood, to declare his righteousness for the remission of sins that are past, through the forbearance of God;

(AMP) Whom God put forward (before the eyes of all) as a mercy seat and propitiation by His blood (the cleansing and life-giving sacrifice of atonement and reconciliation, to be received) through faith. This was to show God's righteousness, because in His divine forbearance He had passed over and ignored former sins without punishment.

(20th C. 1) For God placed him before the world, to be, by his sacrifice of himself, a means of reconciliation through faith...

(Cent.) For God openly set him forth for himself as an offering of atonement through faith, by means of his-blood, in order to show forth his righteousness...

(Phil.) God has appointed him as the means of propitiation, a propitiation accomplished by the shedding of his blood, to be received and made effective in ourselves by faith...

(Way) God ordained Him from of old to be the atonement for a world's sin. The essence of this atonement consisted in the shedding of His blood: the channel whereby we profit by it is faith in Him: the effect is a new revelation of God's justice. He suspended judgment on the sins of that former period, the period of His forbearance...

ROMANS 3:25 (Richert) Also, by causing Jesus to pay the death penalty for all men's failure retroactively, the Majesty reveals the highest judicial integrity…He did not foreclose on human delinquency long ago.

(Lovett) God offered Jesus as a public sacrifice that His shed blood might cleanse us from our sins when we put our faith in Him. At the same time, this act vindicated His justice. The sacrifice of Jesus clearly showed why God, in His forbearance, was able to overlook the sins of men in the past.

(Hudson) Him God has [publicly] set forth as annulling sin through his bloody death, [which annulment takes effect in us] through faith. This was to give an exhibition of his righteousness [necessary] because, in his forbearance, God had overlooked sins committed previously…

(Carpenter) But our Lord, by His sacrifice, has made for us a way into the pardoning grace of God. His was a truly spiritual sacrifice. His blood, shed on the Cross, is the red seal of it. There is the true Mercy-Seat. And the power of faith is such that by faith a man can unite himself with the divine Victim, and in that union enter into the blessed state of at-one-ment with the Father.

(NEB) For God designed him to be the means of expiating sin by his sacrificial death, effective through faith. God meant by this to demonstrate his justice, 26 because in his forbearance he had overlooked the sins of the past—to demonstrate his justice now in the present, showing that he is himself just and also justifies any man who puts his faith in Jesus.

(Adams) Whom God publicly provided (by the shedding of His blood) as an appeasing sacrifice to be appropriated by faith. He did this to demonstrate His righteousness because, in His tolerance, He had passed by sins committed previously…

ROMANS 3:26 To declare, I say, at this time his righteousness: that he might be just, and the justifier of him which believeth in Jesus.

(Fenton) …and to display His righteousness at this present time, so that He might be righteous Himself, and make the believer in Jesus righteous as well.

(Wood) …so that He is at once righteous, and yet can accept and justify sinful men…

(20th C. 1) …in order that he might be righteous, and make those who have faith in Jesus stand right with himself.

(Beck) Now He wanted to show His righteousness, to be righteous Himself and make righteous anyone who believes in Jesus.

(Worrell) …for the manifestation of His righteousness in the present time, to the end that He may be righteous, even when declaring righteous him who has faith in Jesus.

(Basic) ..to make clear his righteousness now, so that he might himself be upright, and give righteousness to him who has faith in Jesus.

ROMANS 3:27 Where is boasting then? It is excluded. By what law? of works? Nay: but by the law of faith.

(AMP) Then what becomes of [our] pride and [our] boasting? It is excluded (banished, ruled out entirely). On what principle? [On the principle] of doing good deeds? No, but on the principle of faith.

(Message) So where does that leave our proud Jewish insider claims and counterclaims? Canceled? Yes, canceled. What we've learned is this: God does not respond to what we do; we respond to what God does.

ROMANS 6:4 Therefore we are buried with him by baptism into death: that like as Christ was raised up from the dead by the glory of the Father, even so we also should walk in newness of life.

(Hudson) ...so we might [be raised from a life of sin now dead and buried and] have our being in a new realm of life.

(Cress.) So we were buried when he was buried because we were baptized into his death.

(Letters) Aren't you hip to the fact that when the Spirit identified us with Jesus the Messiah, He identified us with His death?

(Mof.) Our baptism in his death made us share his burial, so that, as Christ was raised from the dead by the glory of the Father, we too might live and move in the new sphere of Life.

(TLB) Your old sin-loving nature was buried with Him by baptism when He died, and when God the Father, with glorious power, brought him back to life again, you were given his wonderful new life to enjoy.

(Wade) Therefore we, sharing His Death through our baptismal immersion, were with Him laid in the grave, in order that, as Christ was raised to Life from among the dead, through His Father's glorious Power, we, too, might pursue our course in the possession of fresh Life.

(Jer.) ...in other words, when we were baptized we went into the tomb with him and joined him in death...

(Lau.) ...just as He was raised from the dead through the Father's glory, we too are to live a new kind of life like His.

(Wuest) ...thus also we by means of a new life imparted may order our behavior.

(20th C.R.) ...so we, also, may live a new Life.

(Trans.) ...his being raised from the dead by the Father's glorious* act means a new way of life for us. (*The primary meaning of the word "doxa" is brightness, radiance, splendor in a physical sense. Thus "glory" in the New Testament signifies God's active and radiant presence in all His majesty, splendor and sublimity.)

(Carpenter) ...it was a descent with Christ into the grave...

ROMANS 6:4 (Hayman) So then, through this reception into His death by baptism, we were with Him buried; in order that, as Christ was through the Majesty Eternal raised from out of the dead, so our course also should lie in newness of life.

See eternal life p. 377

ROMANS 6:5 For if we have been planted together in the likeness of his death, we shall be also in the likeness of his resurrection.

(Johnson) Since we have participated in his death, we will also participate in the new life his resurrection releases.

(Roth.) For if we have come to be grown together in the likeness of his death...

(Cress.) Have we shared with Christ and died as he died? Then we shall share with him by rising from death as he arose.

(Wood) ...it is a real death to our old self and sin.

(Hammond) ...thereby have been grafted into Christ, that we are become the same tree with Him, partaking of the same juice with the same root (...the lively resemblance and portraiture of His resurrection).

(Wade) For if we have become one with Him (as a graft becomes one with a treestock) through an experience corresponding to His Death, we must equally be one with Him through an experience corresponding to His Resurrection also.

(Authentic) For if we have become identified with the manner of His death, surely we shall be with His resurrection also.

(Jordan) For if we have been fellow plants in the garden of his death, we shall also be fellow plants in the garden of his risen life.

(Way) For if, by having died like Him, we have entered into living union with Him, most certainly we shall not be less so in consequence of having risen with Him.

(Wms.) For if we have grown into fellowship with Him by sharing a death like His, surely we shall share a resurrection life like His.

(Norlie) For if we were united with Him, as it were, by sharing His death, then we shall share His resurrection also and live with Him!

(Trans.) For if we have been identified with him in a death like his, we shall also be identified with him in a resurrection like his.

(N. Berk.) For if we have been united with him in a death like his, then the same must be true of our resurrection with him.

(TLB) For you have become a part of him, and so you died with him, so to speak, when he died; and now you share his new life, and shall rise as he did.

(Taylor, J.; 1754 paraphrase) For as the twig, by being first dead to the old trunk, whence it is cut off, is grafted into a new stock, and receives from it a new Life, and, in union with it grows up into a fruitful tree, so we Gentiles have in baptism been grafted into Christ and vitally united to Him.

ROMANS 6:5 (Carpenter) ...the glory of the Father touches us, and we are raised to a new and better life.

(Bart. & Pet.) For so surely as we have become united with the likeness of His death...

ROMANS 6:6 Knowing this, that our old man is crucified with him, that the body of sin might be destroyed, that henceforth we should not serve sin.

(Wade) ...our original humanity was nailed to the cross with Him.

(Berk.) ...aware of this, that our old self has been jointly crucified with Him, so that the sin controlled body might be devitalized and we no longer be slaves of sin.

(Hudson) ...that sin's control of the body might be rendered null...

(Johnson) ...so that we are no longer controlled by old habits and attitudes.

(Hayman) ...keeping in view the fact that our earlier self was crucified with Him...

(Bart. & Pet.) ...the body ruled by sin...

(Conq.) ...been crucified as he was...

(Cress.) ...The old person we used to be was nailed to the cross with him...

(Bruce) ...our old inherited self was crucified with Him, so that the material with which sin had to operate might be put out of operation...

(Adams) ...we might no longer serve sin as its slaves.

(Richert) ...our former evil identities have been executed, so to speak. Our old rebel selves were exterminated and that leaves us no further role to perform as offenders. We were linked with the Divine Representative in death.

(Way) This we recognise, that our former self was nailed to His cross with Him, so that that body which was the instrument of sin might be made impotent for evil, so that we could not any longer be slaves of sin.

(Weym.) This we know—that our old self was nailed to the cross with Him, in order that our sinful nature might be deprived of its power, so that we should no longer be the slaves of sin.

(20th C.R.) We recognize the truth that our old self was crucified with Christ, in order that the body, the stronghold of Sin, might be rendered powerless, so that we should no longer be slaves to Sin.

(20th C. 1) For we must recognize the fact that our old self was crucified with Christ, in order that our body may cease to be under the tyranny of Sin, so that we may no longer be slaves to Sin.

(Trans.) This we know, that our former self was crucified with him in order that our sinful self might be destroyed and that we might no longer be slaves to sin.

(Phil.) Let us never forget that our old selves died with him on the cross that the tyranny of sin over us might be broken...

(GNB) And we know that our old being has been put to death with Christ on his cross, in order that the power of the sinful self might be destroyed...

ROMANS 6:6 (Wms.) ...our former self was crucified with Him, to make our body that is liable to sin inactive, so that we might not a moment longer continue to be slaves to sin.

(Roth.) Of this taking note—that our old man was crucified together with him...

(Basic) Being conscious that our old man was put to death on the cross with him...

(AMP) ...our old (unrenewed) self was nailed to the cross with Him in order that [our] body [which is the instrument] of sin might be made ineffective and inactive for evil...

(N. Berk.) ...being aware of this, that our old self was crucified with Him...

(Jordan) ...so that the sinful nature may be wiped out, and we no longer need be addicted to sin.

(New Life) ...our old sinful self, was nailed to the cross with Christ...

(Lau.) Our old self was nailed to the cross with Him...

(Beck) ...our old self was nailed with Him to the cross...

(Jer.) ...our former selves have been crucified with him...

(Mof.) ...our old self has been crucified with him...

(Fenton, NEB) ...has been crucified...

(Norlie) ... our old sinful self was crucified with Christ...

(Gspd., Wade, Cent., NAS, NIV) ... our old self was crucified...

(Mar., Black., Young, Cunn., Cony., ASV) ...was crucified...

(Noli) ...our old nature was crucified...

(Knox) ...our former nature has been crucified with him...

(TLB) Your old evil desires were nailed to the cross with him...

ROMANS 6:7 For he that is dead is freed from sin.

(Roth.) A man who has died to his sin is delivered from his sin and made righteous.

(Wade) ...has expiated his crime and becomes technically a righteous being.

(Adams) ...freed from sin by justification.

(Way) You know, the man who has died is incapable of sinning, as much so as if he were perfectly righteous.

(Weym.) ...for he who has paid the penalty of death stands absolved from his sin.

(20th C.R.) For the man who has died has been pronounced righteous and released from Sin.

(20th C. 1) For those who have become dead to sin are released from its power.

(Phil.) ...for a dead man can safely be said to be immune to the power of sin.

(Wms.) For when a man is dead, he is freed from the claims of sin.

(N. Berk.) For a corpse is considered guiltless of sin.

(Richert) His dying settled the death penalty.

(Hayman) ...for the dead to sin is enfranchised from its power.

ROMANS 6:8 Now if we be dead with Christ, we believe that we shall also live with him.

(Black.) Now in view of the fact that we died with Christ...

(Johnson) ..and since we have died (as it were) with Christ, we believe that we have also come alive through the new principle of life he revealed.

(Way) Well, if we have died along with Messiah (and have so been accounted righteous), we have a right to believe that we shall also share His new life.

(Weym.) But, seeing that we have died with Christ, we believe that we shall also live with Him...

(20th C.R.) And our belief is, that as we have shared Christ's Death, we shall also share his Life.

(Phil.) And if we were dead men with him we can believe that we shall also be men newly alive with him.

(TLB) And since your old sin-loving nature "died" with Christ, we know that you will share his new life.

(Cony.) Now, if we have shared the death of Christ, we believe that we shall also share His life.

(Mof.) We believe that as we have died with Christ...

(AMP) Now if we have died with Christ...

See eternal life p. 378

ROMANS 6:11 Likewise reckon ye also yourselves to be dead indeed unto sin, but alive unto God through Jesus Christ our Lord.

(Deaf) 10...he died to defeat the power of sin one time—enough for all time... 11In the same way, you should see yourselves as being dead to the power of sin. And see yourselves as being alive for God through Christ Jesus.

(Richert) Because you are vitally connected to Jesus, God's appointed Minister who now directs our lives in all dimensions.

(Way) 10In respect of His death, He passed by dying, once for all, out of the sphere of sin; but, in respect of His new life, He is in living relation to God. 11In the same manner you also are to account yourselves to be, in relation to sin, dead men; but in relation to God, living men, whose life is absorbed in the life of the Messiah, Jesus.

(Basic) Even so see yourselves as dead to sin...

(Weym.) In the same way you also must regard yourselves as dead in relation to sin, but as alive in relation to God, because you are in Christ Jesus.

(Wade) So you, too, must count yourselves dead men who have finished with Sin, yet fully alive to serve God in union with Christ Jesus.

(N. Berk.) Similarly let us consider ourselves as actually dead to sin...

(Authentic) And so you no less can count yourselves dead so far as sin is concerned, but alive to God in Christ Jesus.

ROMANS 6:11 (New Life) ...Think of yourselves as dead to the power of sin. But now you have new life because of Jesus Christ our Lord...

    (Knox) And you, too, must think of yourselves as dead to sin...

    (Wuest) ...be constantly counting upon the fact...

    (Norlie) ...you have been restored to life again...

    (Gspd.) ...through union with Christ Jesus.

    (NASB) ...in Christ Jesus.

See eternal life p. 379

ROMANS 6:14 For sin shall not have dominion over you: for ye are not under the law, but under grace.

    (Berk.) Sin shall not be your master...

    (Deaf) Sin will not be your master...

    (Cress.) ...God's blessing rules over you.

    (Adams) Sin must not be your lord and master...

    (Wood) Sin shall not be tyrant over you...

    (Roth.) But sin over you shall not have lordship, for ye are not under law but under favour.

    (Wade) ...for Sin is no longer to exercise mastery over you; for you are not under the constraint of Law but are the recipients of Divine Favour.

    (20th C.R.) For Sin shall not lord it over you. You are living under the reign, not of Law, but of Love.

    (20th C. 1) For Sin shall have no power over you...

    (Knox) Sin will not be able to play the master over you any longer...

    (Barclay) ...will no longer hold sway over your life...

    (Jer.) ...will no longer dominate your life...

    (River.) ...shall not be king over you...

    (Cony.) ...shall not have the mastery over you...

    (NEB, Trans.) ...shall no longer be your master...

    (NASB) ... shall not be master over you...

    (Jordan, Hudson) Sin shall not lord it over you...

    (Conc.) For Sin shall not be lording it over you...

    (Mar.) ...Sin for you shall not lord it over...

See righteousness p. 34

ROMANS 8:1 There is therefore now no condemnation to them which are in Christ Jesus, who walk not after the flesh, but after the Spirit.

    (Berk.) ...and behave in no flesh-governed way but in a spiritual way.

    (Johnson) Now there is no accusing voice nagging those who are united to Jesus Christ...

    (Roth.) ...no sentence of punishment...

ROMANS 8:1 (Richert) There is no condemning Law in force to defeat us now that we are identified with Jesus.

(20th C.R.) There is, therefore, now no condemnation for those who are in union with Christ Jesus.

(Jordan) There is, then, no charge outstanding against those who are in (wedlock to) Jesus Christ.

(Phil.) No condemnation now hangs over the head of those who are "in" Christ Jesus.

(Barclay) We can therefore say that there is now no condemnation for those whose life is one with the life of Christ.

(Way) No sentence of condemnation, therefore, can lie against those whose life is a union with the Messiah, with Jesus.

(Wms.) ...no condemnation at all for those who are in union with...

(Pl. Eng.) ...no sentence of "Guilty"...

(Norlie) ...no death sentence hanging over those who are in Christ Jesus.

(Mof.) ...no doom now for those...

(Bird, R.) There is no blame to them that are in Jesus...

See righteousness p. 35

ROMANS 8:2 For the law of the Spirit of life in Christ Jesus hath made me free from the law of sin and death.

(Black.) For the principle* of the Spirit of life in Christ Jesus has liberated you from the principle* of sin and death. (*force of action)

(Johnson) The new principle of life which Christ revealed...

(Adams) ...since the Spirit's law of life in Christ Jesus has freed you from sin's law and death.

(Wood) ...because spiritual life is found in union with Christ and has set them free from the sway of sin and death.

(N. Berk.) ...for the life-giving principles of the Spirit have freed you in Christ Jesus from the control of the principles of sin and death.

(Berk., Knox) The spiritual principle of life has set me free, in Christ Jesus, from the principle of sin and of death.

(Phil.) For the new spiritual principle of life "in" Christ Jesus lifts me out of the old vicious circle of sin and death.

(Way) For the law of the Spirit, which breathes a life absorbed into that of the Messiah Jesus, has emancipated me—the erewhile thrall—from the law of sin, of death.

(Trans.) For the principle of spiritual life in Christ Jesus has liberated me from the principle of sin and death.

(Mof.) ...the law of the Spirit brings the life which is in Christ Jesus, and that law has set me free from the law of sin and death.

ROMANS 8:2 (Weekes) For the law of the spirit of the Life that is through Christ Jesus...

(GNB) For the law of the Spirit, which brings us life in union with Christ Jesus, has set me free from the law of sin and death.

(20th C.R.) For through your union with Christ Jesus...

(AMP) ...the law of our new being...

See divine healing p. 284; eternal life p. 380

ROMANS 8:10 And if Christ be in you, the body is dead because of sin; but the Spirit is life because of righteousness.

(Black.) ...death is inevitable for the body because of sin...

(Hudson) ...[your] spirit...is a living thing because of [being integrated into Christ's] righteousness.

(Johnson) ...your spirit is truly free to direct your life.

(Richert) ...Your old evil-oriented self is now defunct and the living Spirit within sensitizes you to what is right and good.

(Wms.) But if Christ lives in you, although your bodies must die because of sin, your spirits are now enjoying life because of right standing with God.

(20th C. 1) ...but if Christ is within you, then, though the body is dead as a consequence of sin, the spirit is full of Life as a consequence of righteousness.

(Weym.) ...though your body must die because of sin, yet your spirit has Life because of righteousness.

(Wade) ...though your body is no better than a corpse on account of the infection of Sin, your Spirit is endued with Life because of the power of Righteousness.

(Cony.) ...yet your spirit is life, because of righteousness [which dwells within it]...

(Cent.) ...your spirit is full of life because of righteousness.

(Trans.) ...your spirit is alive because you have been made right with God.

(Pl. Eng.) ...your spirit is a living thing because of righteousness.

(Beck) ...your spirits are alive because you are righteous.

(Way) ...your spirit is instinct with life through the power of righteousness.

See eternal life p. 381

JOHN 5:24 Verily, verily, I say unto you, he that heareth my word, and believeth on him that sent me, hath everlasting life, and shall not come into condemnation; but is passed from death unto life.

(Deaf) ...He has already left death and has entered into life.

(Barclay) I tell you, and it is true, if a man listens to my message and believes in him who sent me, he already has eternal life. He is no longer on the way to judgment; he has already crossed the boundary between death and life.

JOHN 5:24 (Basic) ...The man whose ears are open to my word and who has faith in him who sent me, has eternal life.

> *(Gspd.)* ...possesses eternal life, and will not come into judgment, but has already passed out of death into life.
>
> *(Alf.)* ...shall not come into condemnation: but is passed from death unto life.
>
> *(Jordan)* ...has spiritual life...has transferred from the death region to the life region.
>
> *(20th C. R.)* ...has already passed out of Death into Life.
>
> *(20th C. 1)* ...have enduring Life...have already passed out of Death into Life.
>
> *(Weym.)* ...has the Life of the Ages...but has passed over out of death into Life.
>
> *(Knox)* ...enjoys eternal life...he has passed over already from death to life.
>
> *(Wade)* ...has Eternal Life ..has already passed over from spiritual Death into spiritual Life.
>
> *(Mof.)* ...he has already passed from death across to life.
>
> *(NIV)* ...he has crossed over from death to life.
>
> *(Young)* ...out of the death to the life.
>
> *(NEB)* ...has hold of eternal life...
>
> *(Roth.)* ...life age-abiding...
>
> *(N. Berk.)* ...he comes under no sentence but has passed over from death into life.
>
> *(AMP)* ...has (possesses now) eternal life...he has already passed over out of death into life.
>
> *(TLB)* ...will never be damned for his sins...
>
> *See eternal life p. 363*

JOHN 6:53 Then Jesus said unto them, Verily, Verily, I say unto you, Except ye eat the flesh of the Son of man, and drink his blood, ye have no life in you.

> *(Deaf)* ...you don't have real life in you.
>
> *(Berk.)* ...you have no inner life.
>
> *(TLB)* ...Unless you eat the flesh of the Messiah and drink his blood, you cannot have eternal life within you.
>
> *(Wade)* ...you lack within you true Life.
>
> *(Fenton)* ...you do not possess life in yourselves.
>
> *(Mof.)* ...you have no life within you.
>
> *(Jordan)* ...you'll have no inner life.
>
> *See eternal life p. 366*

JOHN 6:54 Whoso eateth my flesh, and drinketh my blood, hath eternal life; and I will raise him up at the last day.

> *(AMP)* ...has (possesses now) eternal life...
>
> *(Wms.)* ...already possesses eternal life...
>
> *(Knox)* ...enjoys eternal life.

JOHN 6:54 (Weym.) ...the Life of the Ages...
    (Mof., NEB, Barclay) ...possesses eternal life...
    (Roth.) ...life age-abiding...
    (Jordan) ...has spiritual life...
    (20th C. 1) ...enduring Life...
        See eternal life p. 366

JOHN 6:56 He that eateth my flesh, and drinketh my blood, dwelleth in me, and I in him.
    (20th C. 1) Those who take my flesh for their food, and drink my blood, are always in union with me, and I with them.
    (Wade) He that feeds on my Flesh and drinks my Blood remains in union with me and I in union with him.
    (Phil.) The man who eats my body and drinks my blood shares my life and I share his.
    (Wms.) Whoever continues to eat my flesh and drink my blood continues to live in union with me and I in union with him.
    (Weym.) ...remains in union with me, and I remain in union with him.
        See eternal life p. 366

I JOHN 5:11, 12 And this is the record, that God hath given to us eternal life, and this life is in his Son. He that hath the Son hath life; and he that hath not the Son of God hath not life.
    (Conq.) ...hath this life...
    (Fenton) And this is the evidence—that God has granted to us eternal life; and the same life that exists in His Son. The possessor of the Son possesses that life; whoever does not possess the Son of God does not possess that life.
    (Wade) ...God has given us Eternal Life, and it is in His Son that this life is to be found. He who possesses the Son possesses this Life. He who does not possess the Son of God does not possess this Life.
    (NEB) ...God has given us eternal life, and that this life is found in his Son. He who possesses the Son has life indeed; he who does not possess the Son of God has not that life.
    (Barclay) ...God gave us eternal life, and that his Son is the source of this life.
    (Jordan) ...God gave us spiritual life...
    (Authentic) He who possesses the Son possesses Life. He who does not possess the Son of God does not possess Life.
    (Syriac) Every one that taketh hold of the Son, taketh hold of life...
    (Young) ...this—the life—is in His Son...
    (Lau.) ...this eternal life...this eternal life.
    (Knox) ...he is lifeless, who has no hold of the Son of God.
    (AMP, Trans., N. Berk.) ...that life...that life.
        See eternal life p. 400

COLOSSIANS 1:12 Giving thanks unto the Father, which hath made us meet to be partakers of the inheritance of the saints in light.

(Fenton) ...Who brought us into the partnership of the inheritance...

(NAB) ...for having made you worthy...

(Deaf) ...He has made you able to have the things he prepared for you...

(Hudson) ...fit for your share of the inheritance which God's people have in the Light.

(Cress.) ...made us ready to have a part in what God's people have where all is light.

(Barclay) We pray that you will be ever grateful to the Father, who has made you fit to receive a share in the possession which he promised to his dedicated people in the realm of light.

(Wand) ...who has made it possible for you to claim your share of the inheritance with the Saints in the Kingdom of Light.

(N. Berk.) ...who has qualifled you for your share in the inheritance of the saints in the light.

(Pl. Eng.) ...who has made us ready to take possession of our portion...

(Weym.) ...who has made us fit to receive our share...

(Roth.) ...the Father that hath made you sufficient for your share...

(Cent.) ...fit to receive our share of the heritage...

(TLB) ...to share all the wonderful things that belong to those who live in the kingdom of light.

(Godbey) ...who has made us worthy...

(Wms.) ...who has qualified you to share the lot...

(Noli) ...he enabled us to share the inheritance of the saints who live in the light.

(Trans.) ...fit to take your place...

See prayer p. 255; divine healing p. 285

COLOSSIANS 1:13 Who hath delivered us from the power of darkness, and hath translated us into the kingdom of his dear Son.

(Cress.) ...saved us out of the kingdom where it is dark...

(Adams) ...brought us instead into the empire...

(Barclay) It was he who rescued us from the grip of the power of darkness, and transferred us to the Kingdom of his dear Son.

(Gspd.) He has rescued us from the dominion of darkness, and has transferred us into the realm of his dear Son...

(Wand) It was He who rescued us out of the power of darkness and established us as citizens in the Kingdom of His beloved Son...

(N. Berk.) He has rescued us from the domain of darkness, and has transferred us into the kingdom of His Beloved Son.

(Pl. Eng.) He has freed us from the power of darkness and carried us away into the kingdom of his beloved Son.

COLOSSIANS 1:13 (Weym.) It is God who has delivered us out of the dominion of darkness, and has transferred us into the Kingdom...

(Cent.) For he has delivered us out of the dominion of the darkness, and transplanted us into the kingdom of his dear Son...

(TLB) For he has rescued us out of the darkness and gloom of Satan's kingdom and brought us into the kingdom of his dear Son...

(Cony.) For He has delivered us from the dominion of darkness, and transplanted us into the kingdom of his beloved Son...

(Jordan) It was the Father who sprang us from the jailhouse of darkness, and turned us loose in the new world of his beloved Son...

(Wuest) ...who delivered us out of the tyrannical rule of the darkness and transferred us into the kingdom of the Son of his love.

(Basic) ...Who has made us free from the power of evil and given us a place in the kingdom of the Son of his love.

(AMP) The Father has delivered and drawn us to Himself out of the control and dominion of darkness and has transferred us into the kingdom of the Son of His love.

(20th C. R.) For God has rescued us from the tyranny of Darkness, and has removed us into the Kingdom of his Son, who is the embodiment of His love...

(Mof.) ...rescuing us...

See prayer p. 256; divine healing p. 286

COLOSSIANS 1:14 In whom we have redemption through his blood, even the forgiveness of sins.

(Wms.) ...by whom we possess the ransom from captivity...

(Hudson) ...in whom we enjoy deliverance [from that darkness]...

(Barclay) It is through this Son that we have received the liberation which comes when sins are forgiven.

(Gspd.) ...by whom we have been ransomed from captivity.

(Wand) ...through whom we enjoy redemption and remission of sins.

(Pl. Eng.) ...in whom we have our deliverance, that is, forgiveness of sins.

(Weym.) ...in whom we have our redemption...

(TLB) ...Who bought our freedom with his blood and forgave us all our sins.

(Cony.) ...in whom we have our redemption...

(20th C. R.) ...and through whom we have found deliverance in the forgiveness of our sins.

(Way) In whom we have our ransoming, The remission of our sins.

(Roth.) ...the remission of our sins...

(Beck) ...who paid the ransom to forgive our sins and set us free.

(Trans.) And the Son forgave our sins and set us free.

(Conf.) ...in whom we have our redemption, the remission of our sins.

COLOSSIANS 1:14 (Godbey) ...the remission of sins...
See prayer p. 257; divine healing p. 286

EPHESIANS 1:7 In whom we have redemption through his blood, the forgiveness of sins, according to the riches of his grace.

(Berk.) In Him and through His blood we enjoy redemption...

(Barclay) It is in and through Christ and the sacrifice of his life that we have been liberated, a liberation which means the forgiveness of sins.

(Jordan) For it was by this One's supreme sacrifice that we got our "emancipation," the forgiveness for the mess we made of things.

(K. & L.) In him we have our redemption through his blood, the remission of our transgressions.

(Way) For in His person we have, through the shedding of His blood, the true Redemption...

(Wms.) It is through union with Him that we have redemption by His blood...

(Gspd.) It is through union with him and through his blood that we have been delivered and our offenses forgiven...

(20th C. 1) For by union with Christ...

(Berk., Knox) ...we enjoy redemption...

(Mof.) ...we enjoy our redemption...

(Cony.) ...we have our redemption...

(Cent., Pl. Eng.) ...we have deliverance...

(Weym.) ...we have our deliverance...

(Jer.) ...we gain our freedom...

(Berk) ...who bought us with His blood to forgive our sins and set us free.

(Roth.) ...the remission of our offences.

(Young, Godbey, Weekes, Conf.) ...remission...

(Barth) ...through the shedding of His blood we possess freedom in Him.

I JOHN 5:4 For whatsoever is born of God overcometh the world: and this is the victory that overcometh the world, even our faith.

(Deaf) ...every person that is a child of God has the power to win against the world.

(Adams) ...since whoever has been born of God defeats the world. And this is what defeats the world: our faith.

(20th C. R.) ...because all that has received the new Life from God conquers the world. And this is the power that has conquered the world—our faith!

(20th C. 1) ...all that has derived its Life from God masters the world. This is the power that has mastered the world—our faith!

(Wand) ...all God's children conquer the world. The means by which we conquer the world is our faith.

I JOHN 5:4 (NEB) ...every child of God is victor over the godless world. The victory that defeats the world is our faith.

> *(GNB)* ...because every child of God is able to defeat the world. And we win the victory over the world by means of our faith.
>
> *(Gspd.)* ...every child of God is victorious over the world. The victory that has triumphed over the world is our faith.
>
> *(Barclay)* ...to be a child of God is to be victorious over the world, and the victory which conquers the world is our faith.
>
> *(Phil.)* ...for God's "heredity" within us will always conquer the world outside us. In fact, this faith of ours is the only way in which the world has been conquered.
>
> *(Wuest)* ...is constantly coming off victorious over the world. And this is the victory that has come off victorious over the world, our faith.
>
> *(Godbey)* ...everything which has been born of God conquers the world: and this is the victory which has conquered the world, our faith.
>
> *(Mof.)* Our faith, that is the conquest which conquers the world. Who is the world's conqueror but he who believes that Jesus is the Son of God?
>
> *(N. Berk.)* ...this is the victory that triumphs over the world, the faith that we have. Who is the world's victor...?
>
> *(Weym.)* ...the victorious principle which has overcome the world is our faith.
>
> *See faith p. 173; eternal life p. 399*

ROMANS 5:10 For if, when we were enemies, we were reconciled to God by the death of his Son, much more, being reconciled, we shall be saved by his life.

> *(Johnson)* If Christ through his death created a truce between us and God when we were acting like God's enemies, now that we are at peace won't he make us whole through his life?
>
> *(Cress.)* ...his life will save us.
>
> *(Richert)* ...by restoring life to His Son, He assures us we are safe and sound...
>
> *(Wood)* If His death reconciled us to God while we were His enemies, much more will His life in us save us now that we are reconciled.
>
> *(Barclay)* It was the death of his Son which restored us to friendship with God, even when we were hostile to him. And, if that is so, now that we are God's friends, how much surer we can be that we will be saved by his continuing life!
>
> *(Knox)* ...reconciled to him, we are surer than ever of finding salvation in his Son's life.
>
> *(Way)* ...for, if, while we were still God's enemies, peace was made between us and Him by means of the death of His Son, much more may we expect, now that this peace has been made, that in the life of His Son we shall find shelter from all future wrath.
>
> *(Jordan)* For if, while we were rebels, we were won over to God through his Son's death, how much more, having been won over, shall we be saved in his life.

ROMANS 5:10 (AMP) ...we shall be saved (daily delivered from sin's dominion) through His [resurrection] life.

(Conq.) ...by His being raised from the dead.

(20th C. R.) ...shall we be saved by virtue of Christ's Life.

(Syriac) ...how much more shall we, in his reconciliation, life (or, be saved) by his life?

(Cony.) ...being already reconciled, shall we be saved by sharing in His life...

(20th C. 1) ...by sharing Christ's Life.

(Gspd.) ...through sharing in his life!

(Wade) ...through sharing His Life!

(Cent.) ...saved in his life.

(Wuest) ...by the life He possesses.

(Norlie) ...by His life in us.

(Young) ...saved in his life.

(Weekes) ...by means of his life.

See eternal life p. 373

ROMANS 5:11 And not only so, but we also joy in God through our Lord Jesus Christ, by whom we have now received the atonement.

(Barclay) And this is not merely a future hope. Here and now we can take a legitimate and joyful pride in our relationship with God, made possible through the work of our Lord Jesus Christ, for by him we have been made friends with God.

(Way) Nay, we have more than a sense of security: we even exult in a new life in God, which has come through our Lord Jesus the Messiah, from whose hands we have received this our charter of peace.

(Jordan) And on top of all this, we get "status" with God through our Lord Jesus Christ, by whom we have now been won over.

(Mof.) Not only so, but we triumph in God through our Lord Jesus Christ, by whom we now enjoy our reconciliation.

(N. Berk.) ...we also exult in God through our Lord Jesus Christ...

(Roth.) ...even boasting in God...

(Black.) ...we are jubilant continually...

(Johnson) So we are not only glad about the future, but at this very moment we are happy because God has made us one with himself through Jesus Christ.

(Conq.) ...by His being raised from the dead.

(Hayman) Nay, our state is not one of bare safety, but of positive triumph in God through Jesus Christ.

See eternal life p. 374

ROMANS 5:17 For if by one man's offence death reigned by one; much more they which receive abundance of grace and of the gift of righteousness shall reign in life by one, Jesus Christ.

(Lovett) Since it is true that death established its reign through one man because of his sin...

(Richert) Following Adam's representative offense, all men had to submit to death as he did...Then we come under the new life as purchased by our Agent Jesus.

(Cress.) ...People who take that gift will live and rule.

(Wood) If the result of the one man's sin could be such widespread death, much more must it be true that Christ's righteousness will bring to men life in the Kingdom of God.

(Weym.) For if, through the transgression of the one individual, Death made use of the one individual to seize the sovereignty, all the more shall those who receive God's overflowing grace and gift of righteousness reign as kings in Life through the one individual, Jesus Christ.

(Way) If, in consequence of that single first transgression, death became king of men's lives, through the one man's demerit, all this will be far more than compensated when those who receive the measureless wealth of God's grace and God's gift of righteousness shall be kings in the New Life, through the merit of the One, Jesus the Messiah.

(Beck) If one man by his sin made death a king, we, on whom God has poured His love and His gift of righteousness, are all the more certain the one Jesus Christ makes us live and be kings.

(Wand) If then by one man's transgression all became the subjects of death, much more shall those who receive the bounty of God and the gift of righteousness through the Unique Person Jesus Christ become the lords of life.

(Lau.) That one man, Adam, when he sinned, put all men under the rule of death. But that other Man, Jesus Christ, makes men right with God so that they shall live and rule like kings. This He does for all who accept God's rich forgiving love and His free gift.

(AMP) ...those who receive (God's) overflowing grace (unmerited favor) and the free gift of righteousness (putting them into right standing with Himself) reign as kings in life...

(Phil.) ...men by their acceptance of his more than sufficient grace and righteousness should live all their lives like kings!

(Wms.) ...the overflow of His unmerited favor and His gift of right standing with Himself, reign in real life...

(Pl. Eng., N. Berk., Cent., Wuest) ...in life will reign as kings...

(Smith, J.M.) ...God's overflowing mercy...

(Young) ...the death did reign...

(Barclay) ...because of what the one man Jesus Christ has done.

(Knox) ...which bids men enjoy a reign of life...

See authority of the believer p. 201; righteousness p. 34; eternal life p. 375

I CORINTHIANS 15:57 But thanks be to God, which giveth us the victory through our Lord Jesus Christ.

(Basic) But praise be to God who gives us strength to overcome through our Lord Jesus Christ.

(Wand) But thanks be to God, who through our Lord Jesus Christ, has bestowed on us the victory over both.

(Noli) But give thanks to God. He granted us victory through our Lord Jesus Christ.

(Mof.) The victory is ours, thank God!

(AMP) ...who gives us the victory—making us conquerors...

(Way) ...who is ever giving us the victory...

(Authentic) ...who has given us victory...

(Douay) ...hath given us the victory...

(Godbey) ...our victory...

II CORINTHIANS 2:14 Now thanks be unto God which always causeth us to triumph in Christ, and maketh manifest the savor of his knowledge by us in every place.

(Cress.) ...Christ leads us to victory every time.

(Barclay) Thanks be to God, for he always gives us a place as sharers in the victory procession of Christ, and, just as at such an earthly triumph, the perfume of incense fills the streets, so God through us has displayed in every place the fragrance of the knowledge of himself.

(New Life) We thank God for the power Christ has given us. He leads us and makes us win in everything.

(Basic) But praise be to God who makes us strong to overcome in Christ, and makes clear through us in every place the value of the knowledge of him.

(Mof.) Wherever I go, thank God, he makes my life a constant pageant of triumph in Christ, diffusing the perfume of his knowledge everywhere by me.

(Way) ...thank God, it is He who everywhere leads me, leads me in Messiah's triumph procession. By me He wafts abroad through every land the knowledge of Jesus, the incense of His triumphal march.

(N. Berk.) ...who invariably leads us on triumphantly in Christ and evidences through us in every place the fragrance that results from knowing Him.

(Lau.) Thank God, Who is giving us victory after victory...

(Wms.) ...He always leads me in His triumphal train, through union with Christ, and everywhere through me keeps spreading the perfume of the knowledge of Him.

(Deane) ...God...makes me...a censer-bearer in a procession of triumph...

(Weym.) ...who in Christ ever heads our triumphal procession, and by our hands waves in every place that sweet incense, the knowledge of Him.

II CORINTHIANS 2:14 (Cony.) ...who leads me on from place to place in the train of his triumph, to celebrate his victory over the enemies of Christ.

> *(20th C. R.)* ...who, through our union with the Christ, leads us in one continual triumph, and uses us to spread the sweet odour of the knowledge of him in every place.

> *(Wand)* ...my journey turned out to be a triumphal procession everywhere. (God made it so through Christ.)

PHILIPPIANS 4:13 I can do all things through Christ which strengtheneth me.

> *(Black.)* Through him who constantly empowers me, I have strength for anything [which I may encounter].

> *(NAB)* In him who is the source of my strength I have strength for everything.

> *(Hudson)* In him who fills me with power I have strength for anything.

> *(Johnson)* I can do everything I need to do because Christ is the energizing center of my life.

> *(Cress.)* ...can do all things because Christ gives me strength.

> *(Lovett)* There is no situation which can overwhelm me now.

> *(Way)* I am equal to every lot, through the help of Him who gives me inward strength.

> *(Mof.)* ...in Him who strengthens me, I am able for anything.

> *(20th C. R.)* I can do everything in the strength of him who makes me strong!

> *(Weym., NEB)* I have strength for anything through Him who gives me power.

> *(Basic)* I am able to do all things through him who gives me strength.

> *(Baxter)* Christ will strengthen me for all that He calls me to.

> *(Smith, J. M.)* I can do anything through him who gives me strength.

> *(N. Berk.)* I have strength for every situation through Him who empowers me.

> *(Barclay)* He who fills me with his dynamic power has made me able to cope with any situation.

> *(Godbey)* I can do all things through him who fills me up with dynamite.

> *(AMP)* I have strength for all things in Christ Who empowers me [I am ready for anything and equal to anything through Him Who infuses inner strength into me; I am self-sufficient in Christ's sufficiency].

> *(Wade)* I am capable of anything and everything in union with Him Who endows me with Power.

> *(Jer.)* There is nothing I cannot master with the help of the One who gives me strength.

> *(Roth.)* I have might for all things in him that empowereth me.

> *(Wuest)* I am strong for all things in the One who constantly infuses strength in me.

II CORINTHIANS 3:4, 5 And such trust have we through Christ to God-ward: Not that we are sufficient of ourselves to think any thing as of ourselves; but our sufficiency is of God.

II CORINTHIANS 3:4, 5 (Noli) I have complete confidence in God through Christ. I do not mean that I am qualified of myself to claim anything as originating with me. My qualification comes from God.

(Basic) And this is the certain faith which we have in God through Christ...our power comes from God.

(K. & L.) Not that we are competent of ourselves to take credit for anything as originating from us. Really our competency is from God. He it is who has made us competent ministers of a new covenant...

(Phil.) Not that we are in any way confident of our own resources—our ability comes from God.

(Cony.) ...not thinking myself sufficient to gain wisdom by my own reasonings, as if it came from myself, but drawing my sufficiency from God.

(AMP) ...our power and ability and sufficiency are from God.

(Knox) ...our ability comes from God.

(Mof.) ...my qualifications come from God.

(Beck) ...God gives us our ability.

(NAB) This great confidence in God is ours, through Christ.

(Deaf) It is God who makes us able...

(Cress.) God makes us able to do it.

(Wood) All of our sufficiency comes from God, who has made us capable of ministering.

(Hayman) This then shows the sort of confidence we have through Christ towards God. Not that we are qualified to ascribe anything of ours to ourselves as the source of it...

I CORINTHIANS 1:5 That in every thing ye are enriched by him, in all utterance, and in all knowledge...

(Hayman) In Him indeed you are highly gifted in everything—all discourse, all discernment being yours; thus confirming the impression made by my testimony to Jesus Christ among you.

(Mof.) ...in him you have received a wealth of all blessing, full power to speak of your faith and full insight into its meaning...

(20th C. R.) For through union with him you were enriched in every way—in your power to preach, and in your knowledge of the Truth...

(Wms.) ...because you have in everything been richly blessed through union with Him, with perfect expression and fullness of knowledge.

(Way) You have been endowed with a wealth of inspired utterance, with a wealth of spiritual illumination.

(Barclay) For through your union with him your lives have been enriched in everything, with the result that you are equipped with every kind of knowledge and with complete ability to communicate it.

I CORINTHIANS 1:5 (Weekes) ...in every way ye have been made rich through him...
(Wade) ...with all kinds of inspired Utterance and every variety of spiritual Knowledge....
(Black.) ...with eloquence of speech and depth of insight.

I CORINTHIANS 1:7 So that ye come behind in no gift; waiting for the coming of our Lord Jesus Christ...
(Mof.) Thus you lack no spiritual endowment.
(20th C. R.) And thus there is no gift in which you are deficient...
(Barclay) The result is that there is no spiritual gift which you do not possess, while you eagerly await the time when our Lord Jesus Christ will again burst upon the stage of history.
(New Life) You have the gifts of the Holy Spirit that you need...
(NEB) There is indeed no single gift you lack...
(Jer.) ...you will not be without any gifts of the Spirit...

I CORINTHIANS 1:8 Who shall also confirm you unto the end, that ye may be blameless in the day of our Lord Jesus Christ.
(Trans.) He will also make you firm to the end with no accusation against you in the Day of our Lord Jesus Christ.
(20th C. R.) ...God Himself will strengthen you.
(Jordan) Indeed, he will stand by you, come what may.

I CORINTHIANS 1:9 God is faithful, by whom ye were called unto the fellowship of his Son Jesus Christ our Lord.
(New Life) God is faithful. He chose you to be joined together with His Son...
(20th C. R.) God will not fail you, and it is he who called you into communion with his Son, Jesus Christ, our Lord.
(Barclay) You can rely on God by whom you were called to share the life of his Son, Jesus Christ, our Lord.
(NEB) It is God himself who called you to share in the life of his Son...
(Knox) The God, who has called you into the fellowship of his Son, Jesus Christ our Lord, is faithful to his promise.
(Weym.) God is ever true to His promises...
(N. Berk.) ...the companionship of His Son...
(Deaf) ...to share life with his Son...
(Hudson) God is to be relied on. He called you to share [the glory of] his Son Jesus Christ our Lord.
(Johnson) You can depend utterly and completely on God who invited you into a relationship with his Son, Jesus Christ our Lord.

I CORINTHIANS 1:30 But of him are ye in Christ Jesus, who of God is made unto us wisdom, and righteousness, and sanctification, and redemption...

(Way) And so, not from man, but from God do you draw your life in Messiah—Jesus—in Jesus who became for us God-given wisdom, our righteousness, our consecration, our ransom!

(Wms.) So you owe it all to Him through union with Christ Jesus, whom God has made our wisdom, our means of right standing, our consecration, and our redemption.

(Hayman) ...the incarnation for us of God-given wisdom, as well as righteousness, sanctification and redemption.

(Bart. & Pet.) But His creation are ye in Christ Jesus...

(Trans.) It is by his act that you are in Christ Jesus and it is God who has made him our wisdom. It is God who has restored us in him, made us his people and set us free.

(Noli) God is the source of your life, your wisdom, your consecration, and your redemption in Jesus Christ.

(GNB) But God has brought you into union with Christ Jesus, and God has made Christ to be our wisdom. By him we are put right with God; we become God's holy people and are set free.

(NAB) God it is who has given you life in Christ Jesus...

(Deaf) It is God that has made you part of Christ Jesus...

(Johnson) But God himself has placed you in a relationship with Christ who is our source for everything.

(Wood) ...real righteousness imparted to us, power to progress, and a redemption as from slavery.

(Authentic) But you are His offspring in Christ Jesus, who was begotten to be wisdom to us from God.

(New Life) God Himself, made the way so you can have new life through Christ Jesus...

(Wade) It is from Him that you—you, I say—derive your spiritual Life through union with Christ Jesus...

(Lau.) It was God who gave us the new life we have in Christ Jesus...

(River.) ...wisdom from God and righteousness and holiness and deliverance.

(Barclay) ...our liberation.

(AMP) But it is from Him that you have your life in Christ Jesus,...

EPHESIANS 1:3 Blessed be the God and Father of our Lord Jesus Christ, who hath blessed us with all spiritual blessings in heavenly places in Christ.

(Conq.) ...among heavenly beings...

(GNB) Let us give thanks to the God and Father of our Lord Jesus Christ! For in our union with Christ he has blessed us by giving us every spiritual blessing in the heavenly world.

EPHESIANS 1:3 (Barclay) Praise to the God and Father of our Lord Jesus Christ, for he in the heavenly places has blessed us with every spiritual blessing, because our life is bound up with the life of Christ.

(20th C. 1) Praise be to the God and Father of Jesus Christ, our Lord, who, through our union with Christ, bestowed upon us from on high every spiritual blessing.

(Norlie) ...who has blessed us in Christ with every spiritual blessing that heaven itself enjoys.

(Trans.) ...who in Christ has blessed us with every spiritual blessing from the supernatural world.

(Lau.) ...and Christ has blessed us with heaven's every blessing.

(Jer.) ...with all the spiritual blessings of heaven in Christ.

EPHESIANS 1:6 To the praise of the glory of his grace, wherein he hath made us accepted in the beloved.

(Roth.) Unto the praise of the glory of his favour wherewith he favoured us in the Beloved One...

(Knox) Thus he would manifest the splendour of that grace by which he has taken us into his favour in the person of his beloved Son.

(N. Berk.) ...for the praise of His glorious grace with which He has freely favored us in union with the Beloved.

See righteousness p. 40

EPHESIANS 1:8 Wherein he hath abounded toward us in all wisdom and prudence;

(Berk.) ...which He poured out on us with the gift of greatest wisdom and insight.

(Roth.) According to the riches of his favour which he made to superabound towards us.

(Knox) So rich is God's grace, that has overflowed upon us in a full stream of wisdom and discernment, to make known to us the hidden purpose of his will.

(Carpenter) The heavens were opened, and all the gifts of God descended, abounding and cascading on us, wisdom to know that which had been unknowable.

EPHESIANS 1:11 In whom also we have obtained an inheritance, being predestinated according to the purpose of him who worketh all things after the counsel of his own will...

(Adams) ...operating everything in agreement with the counsel of His will...

(Cony.) ...in whom we also receive the portion of our lot, having been predestined thereto according to His purpose, whose working makes all fulfil the counsel of His own will...

(GNB) ...God chose us to be his own people in union with Christ because of his own purpose, based on what he had decided from the very beginning.

(Carpenter) ...we are the inheritors of what Christ has done...We are the earthly property of which His human Incarnation has made Him King.

COLOSSIANS 2:3 In whom are hid all the treasures of wisdom and knowledge.

(TLB) In him lie hidden all the mighty, untapped treasures of wisdom and knowledge.

(GNB) He is the key that opens all the hidden treasures of God's wisdom and knowledge.

(20th C. 1) For all God's treasures of wisdom and knowledge are to be found stored up in Christ.

(Jordan) For in him, still unexplored...

(Shuttle.) ...brought to a perfect knowledge of the immense wisdom of the divine arrangements and of the great mystery of the Eternal God namely, of the Father, and of the Lord Jesus Christ, in whom are stored all the secret treasures of wisdom and knowledge.

II PETER 1:3, 4 According as his divine power hath given unto us all things that pertain unto life and godliness, through the knowledge of him that hath called us to glory and virtue: Whereby are given unto us exceeding great and precious promises: that by these ye might be partakers of the divine nature, having escaped the corruption that is in the world through lust.

(Jordan) Through his divine power and through the knowledge of him who has invited us because of the goodness of his own heart, he has loaded us up with all we need for the good life. In so doing he has dealt us in on some wonderful offers that are out of this world.

(Weym.) It is by means of these that He has granted us His precious and wondrous promises, in order that through them you may, one and all, become sharers in the very nature of God, having completely escaped the corruption which exists in the world through earthly cravings.

(New Life) ...Through these promises you can have God's own life in you...

(NEB) ...through them you may escape the corruption with which lust has infected the world, and come to share in the very being of God.

(Lau.) ...God also gave us His divine nature.

ROMANS 8:32 He that spared not his own Son, but delivered him up for us all, how shall he not with him also freely give us all things?

(NEB) He did not spare his own Son, but gave him up for us all; and with this gift how can he fail to lavish upon us all he has to give?

(Richert) And Jesus returned to life so that he could personally guarantee to us every benefit of his gracious act.

(Jordan) 31If God is rootin' for us, who can win over us? 32If he didn't hold back his own Son, but put him in the game for us all, won't he even more gladly in addition to his Son, equip us with all we need to win the game?

(Jer.) Since God did not spare his own Son, but gave him up to benefit us all, we may be certain, after such a gift, that he will not refuse anything he can give.

ROMANS 8:32 (Knox) ...and must not that gift be accompanied by the gift of all else?

(K. & L.) ...how can he fail to grant us all other blessings with him?

(Wand) 31...who or what can possibly be against us? 32...grant us every other conceivable good.

I CORINTHIANS 3:21 Therefore let no man glory in men. For all things are yours.

(Black.) Actually everything belongs to you.

(TLB) ...For God has already given you everything you need.

(Gspd.) For it all belongs to you...all of it belongs to you.

(K. & L.) ...All things belong to you...

(Weym., Noli) ...everything belongs to you.

JOHN 1:16 And of his fulness have all we received, and grace for grace.

(Fenton) So out of His fulness we were all supplied, with gift heaped upon gift.

(Barclay) ...out of the Word's complete perfection we have all received, and to us there has come wave upon wave of grace.

PHILIPPIANS 4:19 But my God shall supply all your need according to his riches in glory by Christ Jesus.

(Hudson) And my God, on the scale of his wealth, will fully supply in Christ Jesus your every need in [heaven's] glory.

(Lovett) ...out of the fantastic treasures amassed in Christ...

(Jer.) In return my God will fulfill all your needs, in Christ Jesus, as lavishly as only God can.

(N. Berk.) And my God will fully supply all your needs according to His abundant wealth so glorious in Christ Jesus.

(Wade) And every need of yours my God will satisfy in Glory through Christ Jesus (as His inexhaustible resources enable Him to do).

(TLB) And it is he who will supply all your needs from his riches in glory, because of what Christ Jesus has done for us.

(Way) And God, my God, shall fill up the measure of all your need, with an abundance limited only by His own riches, shall supply it by His glorious presence in the person of Messiah Jesus.

(20th C. R.) ...fully satisfy your every need, through your union with Christ Jesus.

(NEB) And my God will supply all your wants out of the magnificence of his riches in Christ Jesus.

(AMP) ...will liberally supply (fill to the full) your every need...

(Deane) And the God in whom I trust will of His heavenly wealth supply all your needs.

PHILIPPIANS 4:19 (Abbrev. Bible) And my God will supply your wants in the riches which are in Christ.

See finances p. 311

PHILIPPIANS 1:11 Being filled with the fruits of righteousness, which are by Jesus Christ, unto the glory and praise of God.

(Way) ...full harvest of righteousness...

(Black.) ...being filled with the fruit which righteousness yields...

(Lovett) Then you will reap the full harvest that follows a life lived for Jesus Christ.

(Adams) ...that grows through Jesus Christ...

(Wade) ...richly laden with the Harvest of righteousness...

(Mof.) ...your life all covered with that harvest of righteousness which Jesus Christ produces, to the glory and the praise of God.

(20th C. R.) ...bearing a rich harvest of that righteousness which comes through Jesus Christ...

PHILEMON 6 That the communication of thy faith may become effectual by the acknowledging of every good thing which is in you in Christ Jesus.

(Fenton) ...so that your energetic unity in the Faith may advance into a recognition of every benefit there is for us in Christ.

(Way) ...as you impart your faith to others, it may grow into a living force whereby men may recognize all the good that is in you.

(Lau.) I pray that everyone who meets you may catch your faith and learn from you how wonderful it is to live in Christ.

(NEB) My prayer is that your fellowship with us in our common faith may deepen the understanding of all the blessings that our union with Christ brings us.

(Basic) That the faith which you have in common with them may be working with power, in the knowledge of every good thing in you, for Christ.

(GNB) My prayer is that our fellowship with you as believers will bring about a deeper understanding of every blessing which we have in our life in union with Christ.

(Pl. Eng.) I pray that your fellowship in faith may greatly increase your knowledge of every good thing that is ours in Christ.

(AMP) ...full recognition and appreciation and understanding and precise knowledge of every good [thing] that is ours in [our identification with] Christ Jesus...

(Wand) ...to realize all the benefits that flow from our Christian profession.

(Syriac) ...in the knowledge of all the good things ye possess in Jesus the Messiah.

(TLB) ...as you share your faith with others it will grip their lives too, as they see the wealth of good things in you that come from Christ Jesus.

(Authentic) ...securing knowledge of every good thing that is ours in Christ.

PHILEMON 6 (Hayman) ...may work in thee a recognition...

    (Comp.) ...may have a vivid sense of every good thing in you which is in Christ Jesus...

HEBREWS 13:20, 21 Now the God of peace, that brought again from the dead our Lord Jesus, that great shepherd of the sheep, through the blood of the everlasting covenant, Make you perfect in every good work to do his will, working in you that which is wellpleasing in his sight, through Jesus Christ; to whom be glory for ever and ever. Amen.

    (Hammond) ...enabling and exciting in you...

    (Wms.) May God, who gives us peace, who brought back from the dead our Lord Jesus, who through the blood by which He ratified the everlasting covenant, is now the Great Shepherd of the sheep, perfectly fit you to do His will, He Himself, through Jesus Christ, accomplishing through you what is pleasing to Him.

    (20th C. R.) May God, the source of all peace, who brought back from the dead him who, by virtue of the blood that rendered valid the unchangeable Covenant, is the Great Shepherd of God's Sheep, Jesus, our Lord...

    (Weym.) ...fully equip you with every grace that you may need for the doing of His will...

    (Mar.) ...may he adjust you in every good thing...

    (Way) ...who by the Blood that sealed the eternal Covenant brought up from among the dead the Great Shepherd of His sheep, even our Lord Jesus, make you perfect in all that is good, so that you may do His will. May He bring to pass in you the performance of what is well-pleasing in His sight, through the agency of Jesus the Messiah...

    (Lau.) ...He sealed the eternal agreement between God and man with His own blood...

    (Hayman) ...effecting in you what He Himself delights in...

ROMANS 5:1 Therefore being justified by faith, we have peace with God through our Lord Jesus Christ.

    (Berk.) Since, then, we are made righteous through faith, let us enjoy peace with God through our Lord Jesus Christ.

    (Hudson) ...let us enjoy the peace with God which is ours through Our Lord Jesus Christ.

    (20th C. R.) Therefore, having been pronounced righteous as the result of faith, let us enjoy peace with God, through Jesus Christ, our Lord.

    (Wms.) Since we have been given right standing with God through faith, then let us continue enjoying peace with God...

    (Young) Having been declared righteous, then, by faith...

    (Weekes) Being therefore made righteous from faith...

    (GNB) Now that we have been put right with God through faith...

    (Lau.) We are made right with God by our faith...

    (Mof.) ...let us enjoy the peace we have with God...

ROMANS 5:1 (Cent.) ...let us continue to enjoy the peace we have with God...

(AMP) Therefore, since we are justified (acquitted, declared righteous, and given a right standing with God) through faith, let us [grasp the fact that we] have [the peace of reconciliation to hold and to enjoy, peace with God through our Lord Jesus Christ the Messiah, the Anointed One.]

(Hayman) So then having by means of faith made righteousness ours, we have peace with God...

ROMANS 5:2 By whom also we have access by faith into this grace wherein we stand, and rejoice in hope of the glory of God.

(Berk.) ...by whom we also obtain through faith entrance to this grace in which we stand firm...

(Hudson) 2It was through him, that we were piloted too into [this state of God's] favor in which we have our berth...3Nor [should we exult] merely [in our brilliant prospects]. Let us also exult in our [present] troubles.

(Cress.) Because we believe, Christ has brought us to the place where God blesses us. We are in that place now.

(Weym.) ...through whom also, as the result of faith, we have obtained an introduction into that state of favour with God in which we stand, and we exult in hope of some day sharing in God's glory.

(Mof.) Through him we have got access to this grace where we have our standing, and triumph in the hope of God's glory.

(Way) Through Him, too, we have been introduced by this door of faith into the favour of God in which we have so firm a footing: yes, and we are exulting in the hope of something higher yet, the glory of God's presence.

(Jordan) Through him we also got an open door into this favored position we hold, and we get "status" from the confidence we receive from God's greatness.

(20th C. R.) ...we have obtained admission to that place in God's favour in which we now stand.

(Wms.) ...in which we safely stand...

(Gspd.) ...the favor of God that we now enjoy...

(K. & L.) ...this state of grace in which we now abide...

(Weekes) ...this loving-favour...

EPHESIANS 2:18 For through him we both have access by one Spirit unto the Father.

(Hudson) ...we...actually enjoy our access to the Father through him.

(Cress.) Because of what Christ has done.

(Lovett) ...have direct access...

EPHESIANS 2:18 (Barclay) ...for through him, we both possess the right of access through the one Spirit to the Father.

> *(Way)* For through Him have we, both we and you, united in one Spirit, Admission to the presence of the Father.
>
> *(Trans.)* It is through him that both of us, in one Spirit, are able* to go right into the Father's presence. (*Greek—technical term for the right of approach to persons in high office.)
>
> *(Stevens)* In his death for our entire race, he has healed the old division and has united Jew and Gentile; his common salvation brings them together as sons of a common Father.
>
> *See righteousness p. 40*

HEBREWS 10:1, 2 For the law having a shadow of good things to come, and not the very image of the things, can never with those sacrifices, which they offered year by year continually make the comers thereunto perfect. For then would they not have ceased to be offered? because that the worshippers once purged should have had no more conscience of sins.

> *(NAB)* ...would have had no sin on the conscience.
>
> *(Barclay)* The Jewish law was no more than a shadow of the good things which are to come; you will not find in it the true expression of these realities. By going on making the same sacrifices which are offered year after year for ever, the law can never perfect those who aretrying to find the way into God's presence. If these sacrifices could have done this, they wouldobviously have ceased to be offered, because the worshipper would have been once and for all cleansed, and would no longer be haunted by the sense of sin.
>
> *(Weym.)* ...give complete freedom from sin to those who draw near...the consciences of the worshippers—who in that case would now have been cleansed once for all—would no longer be burdened with sins?
>
> *(Jordan)* For once you get a congregation genuinely forgiven of its sins, it no longer has a guilty conscience about them.
>
> *(AMP)* ...they would no longer have any guilt or consciousness of sin.
>
> *(Knox)* ...There would be no guilt left to reproach the consciences of those who come to worship...
>
> *(K. & L.)* ...would no longer have the least consciousness of sin.
>
> *(Trans.)* ...the worshippers would have been purified once and for all and would no longer have a sense of guilt.
>
> *See righteousness p. 43*

HEBREWS 10:12 But this man, after he had offered one sacrifice for sins for ever, sat down on the right hand of God.

> *(Way)* But He, after offering for sin one sacrifice which shall ever avail, sat down, His work accomplished, at the right hand of God.

HEBREWS 10:12 (Barclay) ...a sacrifice which is effective for ever...

(Norlie) But He offered one sacrifice, good for ever, and then took His seat at the right hand of God.

(Jordan) But this minister made one final sweep of sin by his supreme sacrifice and then took his place by God's side at his right arm.

HEBREWS 10:14 For by one offering he hath perfected for ever them that are sanctified.

(Weym.) For by a single offering He has for ever completed the blessing for those whom He is setting free from sin.

(Lau.) So with that one sacrifice He made us holy and brought us into perfect union with God.

(Barclay) For by one sacrifice, valid for ever, he enabled men to enter into perfect communion with God.

(Gspd.) ...he has forever qualified those who are purified from sin to approach God.

(Way) ...He has for ever perfectly cleansed those who, from age to age, become His consecrated ones.

(Pl. Eng.) ...he has for all time brought into perfect union with God those who are made holy.

See righteousness p. 44

HEBREWS 10:16 This is the covenant that I will make with them after those days, said the Lord, I will put my laws into their hearts, and in their minds will I write them.

(Jordan) "This constitution which I shall draw up for them—the time will come," says the Lord...

(Knox) ...I will implant my laws in their hearts, engrave them in their innermost thoughts.

(Noli) ...I will impress my laws into their hearts, and I will inscribe them upon their minds.

(ASV) ...I will put my laws on their heart, and upon their mind also will I write them.

HEBREWS 10:17 And their sins and iniquities will I remember no more.

(Wms.) I will never, never any more recall their sins and deeds of wrong.

(Noli) I will forget their sins and trespasses forever.

HEBREWS 10:19 Having therefore, brethren, boldness to enter into the holiest by the blood of Jesus...

(Fenton) 19... having free entry into the interior of the Holies through the blood of Jesus, 20 an open and living pathway...

(Lovett) ...let us go boldly right into the holiest place of all, the very presence of God.

(Cunn.) Having therefore, brethren, boldness to use the entrance into the Holy of Holies in the blood of Jesus.

HEBREWS 10:19 (K. & L.) ...we have confident access to the Holy Place, thanks to the blood of Jesus...

> *(Way)* ...we can confidently plead our claim for access, by right of Jesus' blood, into that Holiest Place.
>
> *(TLB)* ...now we may walk right into the very Holy of Holies where God is, because of the blood of Jesus.
>
> *(NEB)* ...the blood of Jesus makes us free to enter boldly...
>
> *(Cent.)* ...we have a cheerful confidence, brothers, to enter into the Holiest...
>
> *(Syriac)* ...by the blood of Jesus, and by a way of life.
>
> *See righteousness p. 44*

HEBREWS 10:22 Let us draw near with a true heart in full assurance of faith, having our hearts sprinkled from an evil conscience, and our bodies washed with pure water.

> *(Way)* ...let us draw near with a sincere heart, in fulness of faith, having our hearts sprinkled with the blood which cleanses all guilt from the conscience...
>
> *(Weym.)* ...let us draw near with sincerity and unfaltering faith, having had our hearts sprinkled, once for all, from consciences oppressed with sin...
>
> *(Jordan)* Let's cleanse our hearts from any unworthy feeling...
>
> *(Wade)* ...in the fulness of conviction which faith creates...
>
> *(Wms., Gspd.)* ...with our hearts cleansed from the sense of sin...
>
> *(20th C. R.)* ...with our hearts purified by the sprinkled blood from all consciousness of wrong...
>
> *(ASV)* ...in fullness of faith...
>
> *(Berk.)* ...let us draw near with honest hearts and with unqualified assurance of faith...
>
> *(Lovett)* ...exercise our right of access and press closer and closer to the Father.
>
> *See righteousness p. 45*

II TIMOTHY 1:7 For God hath not given us the spirit of fear; but of power, and of love, and of a sound mind.

> *(NAB)* The Spirit God has given us is no cowardly spirit, but rather one that makes us strong, loving, and wise.
>
> *(Conq.)* ...courage...
>
> *(Wms.)* For the Spirit that God has given us does not impart timidity but power and love and self-control.
>
> *(GNB)* For the Spirit that God has given us does not make us timid; instead, his Spirit fills us.
>
> *(New Life)* ...He gave us a spirit of power and of love and of a good mind.
>
> *(Norlie)* ...of power and love and wise discretion.
>
> *(AMP)* ...of calm and well-balanced mind and discipline and self-control.
>
> *(Smith, J.M.)* ...a spirit not of timidity but of power, love, and self-discipline.

PHILIPPIANS 4:7 And the peace of God, which passeth all understanding, shall keep your hearts and minds through Christ Jesus.

(Hudson) And God's peace, which excels [and that] any wit [of man can devise], shall, in Christ Jesus, guard your hearts and your thoughts...

(Lovett) God's peace, which operates beyond the range of human understanding, will protect your feelings and thought life in Christ.

(Wood) ...peace of God, which surpasses any conception we have...

(Wms.) Then, through your union with Christ Jesus, the peace of God, that surpasses all human thought, will keep guard over your hearts and thoughts.

(Way) And so the peace that God gives, the peace that transcends all conception, shall be the fortress-warder of your hearts, of all your thoughts, in this your life in Messiah Jesus.

(Barclay) And God's peace, which is beyond both our understanding and our contriving, will stand guard over your hearts and minds, because your life is linked for ever with the life of Christ Jesus.

(Authentic) God's peace, which towers above* all reasoning, will stand guard over your minds and thoughts in Christ Jesus. (*like a dominating and protective fortress)

(Weym.) ...a garrison to guard your hearts and minds in union with Christ Jesus.

See prayer p. 252; peace p. 355

I CORINTHIANS 2:16 For who hath known the mind of the Lord, that he may instruct him? But we have the mind of Christ.

(20th C. R.) ...We, however, have the very mind of Christ.

(Wade) ...But we share the mind of Christ.

II CORINTHIANS 5:17 Therefore if any man be in Christ, he is a new creature: old things are passed away; behold, all things are become new.

(Adams) ...brand new things have come into being.

(20th C. R.) Therefore, if any one is in union with Christ, he is a new being! His old life has passed away; a new life has begun!

(AMP) Therefore if any person is [ingrafted] in Christ, (the Messiah) he is a new creation (a new creature altogether); the old [previous moral and spiritual condition] has passed away. Behold, the fresh and new has come!

(TLB) When someone becomes a Christian, he becomes a brand new person inside. He is not the same any more. A new life has begun!

(Wade) So if anyone becomes united to Christ, he is a fresh Creation; the original conditions have passed away; mark! they have been replaced by new conditions.

(NEB) When anyone is united to Christ, there is a new world; the old order has gone, and a new order has already begun.

II CORINTHIANS 5:17 (Cony.) Whosoever, then, is in Christ, is a new creation; his old being has passed away, and behold, all has become new.

    (Wms.) So if anybody is in union with Christ, he is the work of a new creation; the old condition has passed away, a new condition has come.

    (GNB) When anyone is joined to Christ, he is a new being...

    (Way) Whoso hath passed into that New Life of Messiah, He is created anew: The old life has passed away; Lo, it has become new!

    (Lau.) If a man is in Christ, he is created new. The man he was has passed away, and, behold, a new man has been created!

    (Noli) For everyone who is united with Christ has become a new man...

    (Phil.) ...he becomes a new person altogether—the past is finished and gone, everything has become fresh and new.

    (Weym.) ...the old state of things has passed away; a new state of things has come into existence.

    (Beck) ...he is a new being...

    (Shuttle.) ...the deadliness of our former condition is passed away...

    (Deane) ...and the true Christian is not merely a man altered but a man re-made...

    (Stanley) If anyone has entered into fellowship with Christ, a new world has at once opened upon him, an old world has passed away.

EPHESIANS 4:24 And that ye put on the new man, which after God is created in righteousness and true holiness.

    (AMP) And put on the new nature (the regenerate self) created in God's image, [Godlike] in true righteousness and holiness.

    (Fenton) ...the New Man, the one created God-like in righteousness and holiness...

    (Berk.) ...put on the new nature that is created in God's likeness in genuine righteousness and holiness.

    (Johnson) Discover new ways of expressing your new, unique personhood in Christ, ways which are in harmony with who you really are...

    (Cress.) Be a new person. That new person has been made like God. He does what is right and he is holy because he knows the truth.

    (Lovett) ...old nature and its evil products...

    (Adams) ...put on the new person that you are.

    (Weym.) ...clothe yourselves with that new and better self which has been created to resemble God in the righteousness and holiness which come from the truth.

    (Way) ...that you must clothe yourselves in the new humanity that has been created in God's image, in a state of righteousness and holiness born of the Truth.

    (Wuest) And that you have put on once for all the new self...

EPHESIANS 4:24 (Lau.) And you must put on the fresh dress of your new nature...

(NEB) ...put on the new nature of God's creating...

(Basic) And put on the new man, to which God has given life...

(Wms.) ...the new self which has been created in the likeness of God...

(20th C. R.) ...clothe yourselves in that new nature...

(Godbey) ...who has been created in harmony with God...

(HT Ander) ...put on the new man which is created according to the will of God...

(Carpenter) ...Above all, the new life is the real life, the life that is the life indeed.

COLOSSIANS 3:9, 10 Lie not one to another, seeing ye have put off the old man with his deeds; and have put on the new man, which is renewed in knowledge after the image of him that created him.

(Noli) For you are through with your old self and your old practices. Now you have begun life as a new man, recreated in wisdom after the image of the Creator.

(Gspd.) For you have stripped off your old self with its ways and have put on that new self newly made in the likeness of its Creator, to know him fully.

(AMP) ...you have stripped off the old (unregenerate) self with its evil practices, and have clothed yourselves with the new [spiritual self], which is [ever in the process of being] renewed and remolded into [fuller and more perfect knowledge upon] knowledge, after the image (the likeness) of Him Who created it.

(Hayman) Lie not one to another, you who stripped yourselves of the former man with his practices, you who put on the new man, who is being remolded towards higher knowledge on the lines of his Creator.

(Deane) ...which continually will come nearer to the pattern of him who created it.

(Adams) ... renewed in such a way as to produce full knowledge that is in keeping with the image of his Creator.

(Fenton) ... and put on the new, that is renewed in knowledge — the very picture of its Creator...

(Berk.) ...Having stripped off the old nature with its practices, & having put on the new self...

(Weym.) ...you have stripped off the old self with its doings, and have clothed yourselves with the new self...

(NEB) ... you have discarded the old nature with its deeds and have put on the new nature...

(Mof.) ...you have stripped off the old nature with its practices, and put on the new nature...

(20th C. R.) ...and clothe yourselves with that new self, which, as it gains in knowledge, is being constantly renewed in resemblance to him who made it.

(Way) ...and have clothed yourselves with the new, which is ever rising through higher developments into perfect knowledge, is being moulded into the likeness of Him who created it.

COLOSSIANS 3:9, 10 (GNB) ...and have put on the new self. This is the new being which God, its Creator, is constantly renewing in his own image...

(Wand) ...and put on the new, in which the image of its Creator is always being renewed and perfected as our knowledge of Him increases.

EPHESIANS 2:10 For we are His workmanship, created in Christ Jesus unto good works, which God hath before ordained that we should walk in them.

(Berk.) ...for we are His formation, created as we are in Christ Jesus for good works, which God previously prepared for us to enjoy life in them.

(Johnson) ...we are God's artistry, his creative work produced by our relationship to Christ...

(Conq.) ...before provided...

(Way) Nay, but His handiwork are we, who in Messiah Jesus' person have been re-created that we may do good deeds — a path which God has made ready for us, That our feet may walk therein.

(Jer.) We are God's work of art, created in Christ Jesus to live the good life as from the beginning He had meant us to live it.

(AMP) For we are God's (own) handiwork (His workmanship), recreated in Christ Jesus, (born anew) that we may do those good works which God predestined (planned beforehand) for us, (taking paths which He prepared ahead of time) that we should walk in them — living the good life which He prearranged and made ready for us to live.

(Wade) For His handiwork are we, created anew through union with Christ Jesus, for the accomplishment of such good works as God, in His designs, has made ready in advance to be the sphere wherein we are to pursue our activities.

(Norlie) We are created anew in Christ Jesus...

(Lau.) He made us all over new. We were born again in Christ...

(Mar.) For of Him we are a product...

(20th C. R.) ...created, by our union with Christ Jesus, for the good actions in doing which God had prearranged that we should spend our lives.

(Cent.) ...for we are his handiwork, created in Christ Jesus for good deeds, which God predestined us to make our daily way of life.

(Deane) What we are is what God has made us, through our union with Christ...

(Baxter) For we ourselves are God's work new made by regeneration which planted us into Christ.

JOHN 15:4, 5 Abide in me, and I in you. As the branch cannot bear fruit of itself, except it abide in the vine; no more can ye, except ye abide in me. I am the vine; ye are the branches: he that abideth in me, and I in him, the same bringeth forth much fruit: for without me, ye can do nothing.

JOHN 15:4, 5 (New Life) Get your life from Me and I will live in you. No branch can give fruit by itself. It has to get life from the vine. You are able to give fruit only when you have life from Me. I am the Vine and you are the branches. Get your life from Me.

(Phil.) You must go on growing in me and I will grow in you. For just as the branch cannot bear any fruit unless it shares the life of the vine, so you can produce nothing unless you go on growing in me. I am the vine itself; you are the branches. It is the man who shares my life and whose life I share who proves fruitful. For the plain fact is that apart from me you can do nothing at all.

(Wuest) Maintain a living communion with me, and I with you. Just as the branch is unable to be bearing fruit from itself as a source unless it remains in a living union with the vine, so neither you, unless you maintain a living communion with me...He who maintains a living communion with me and I with him...

(20th C. R.) ...he that remains united to me, while I remain united to him — he bears fruit plentifully...

(Wms.) ...Whoever remains in union with me and I in union with him will bear abundant fruit, because you cannot do anything cut off from union with me.

(Authentic) ...apart from Me, you are powerless.

(Quaker) ...remain in Me and let Me in you...

See divine healing p. 282

I CORINTHIANS 6:17 But he that is joined unto the Lord is one spirit.

(Wms.) But the man who is in union with the Lord is spiritually one with Him.

(Fenton) But the union with the Lord is one spirit.

(20th C. 1) ...a man who is united with the Lord is one with him in spirit.

(Weym.) But he who is in union with the Master is one with Him in spirit.

(TLB) But if you give yourself to the Lord, you and Christ are joined together as one person.

(Authentic) But he who unites himself with the Master forms a single spirit.

I CORINTHIANS 12:27 Now ye are the body of Christ, and members in particular.

(Phil.) ...and individually, you are members of him.

(Adams) Now you are Christ's body and each member is a part of it.

EPHESIANS 5:30 For we are members of his body, of his flesh, and of his bones.

(NEB) ...it is his body, of which we are living parts.

I JOHN 4:17 Herein is our love made perfect, that we may have boldness in the day of judgment: because as He is, so are we in this world.

(Cress.) ...We are like Christ in this world.

I JOHN 4:17 (Weym.) ...just what He is, we also are in the world.

    (20th C.R.) ...what Christ is that we also are in this world.

    (Jer.) ...even in this world we have become as he is.

    (Norlie) ...we are like Him, while we are yet in this world.

    (Phil.) ...for we realize that our life in this world is actually his life lived in us.

    (Adams) ...whatever He is, we also are in this world.

    (GNB) ...our life in this world is the same as Christ's.

    (Hay.) ...exactly as Christ is, are we also in this world.

II CORINTHIANS 6:14, 15 Be ye not unequally yoked together with unbelievers: for what fellowship hath righteousness with unrighteousness? And what communion hath light with darkness? And what concord hath Christ with Belial? Or what part hath he that believeth with an infidel?

    (Wms.) Stop forming intimate and inconsistent relations with unbelievers.

    (NEB) Do not unite yourselves with unbelievers; they are no fit mates for you.

    (Way) Do not contract mismated alliances with unbelievers...

    (Jordan) Don't get hitched up with non-Christians.

    (New Life) How can Christ get along with the devil? How can one who has put his trust in Christ get along with one who has not put his trust in Christ?

    (MacK.) Become not discordantly yoked with infidels...

    (Berk.) ...what common ground is there between righteousness and lawlessness or what association between light and darkness? Or what harmony between Christ and Belial, or what partnership between a believer and an unbeliever?

    (Johnson) My dear friends, please don't enter into binding contracts (like marriage) with non-Christians. How can that work for you? Do people in a right relationship with God have the same goals as those who have not made this crucial choice?

ROMANS 8:37 Nay, in all these things we are more than conquerors through him that loved us.

    (Black.) ...we are winning an overwhelming victory...

    (Johnson) No, in all these circumstances we may live triumphantly through Christ's love.

    (Richert) Listen! In all things Jesus our great Leader has established us as invincible champions through His amazing provision for us.

    (Noli) No, we are going to overcome all these trials and march to victory through God who loved us.

    (Wms.) And yet in all these things we keep on gloriously conquering through Him who loved us.

    (NEB) ...and yet, in spite of all, overwhelming victory is ours through him who loved us.

    (Jordan) ...we come out on top everytime through him who set his heart on us.

ROMANS 8:37 (Trans.) ...we are triumphantly victorious...

(Lau.) ...we shall have victory and more than victory...

(Way) Yet, amidst all of this, we are the victors—Ay, more than victors, in the might of Him who hath loved us!

(TLB) But despite all this, overwhelming victory is ours through Christ who loved us enough to die for us.

(Wuest) But in these things, all of them, we are coming off constantly with more than the victory through the One who loved us.

(20th C.R.) ...we more than conquer...

(Phil.) ...we win an overwhelming victory...

(GNB) ...we have complete victory...

(NASB) ...we overwhelmingly conquer...

(Mar.) ...we overconquer...

ROMANS 8:38 For I am persuaded, that neither death, nor life, nor angels, nor principalities, nor powers, nor things present, nor things to come...

(Deaf) ...not ruling spirits, nothing now or nothing in the future, no powers, nothing above us, nothing below us, or anything else in the whole world.

(Johnson) I am utterly convinced that nothing in death, nor any circumstance of life, nor good or evil spiritual forces...

(Noli) For I am absolutely sure that neither death, nor life, nor angels, nor devils, nor dominions, nor present, nor future...

(Wms.) For I have full assurance...

(NEB) For I am convinced that there is nothing in death or life, in the realm of spirits or superhuman powers...

(Jordan) For I am absolutely convinced that neither death nor life nor angels nor rulers nor the present nor the future nor force nor mountain nor valley nor anything else in the universe...

(Trans.) ...neither angels nor demonic powers, nothing present, nothing to come, no supernatural forces...

(Lau.) ...nor even the princes of the dark spirit world...

(Weym.) ...nor the forces of nature...

ROMANS 8:39 Nor height, nor depth, nor any other creature, shall be able to separate us from the love of God, which is in Christ Jesus our Lord.

(Noli) ...nor sky, nor abyss, nor any other power of the universe...

(Trans.) ...neither spirits of the sky nor spirits of the abyss, nothing in the whole universe...

GALATIANS 4:4, 5 But when the fulness of the time was come, God sent forth his Son, made of a woman, made under the law, To redeem them that were under the law, that we might receive the adoption of sons.

> *(TLB)* To buy freedom for us who were slaves to the law so that he could adopt us as his very own sons.
>
> *(Way)* ...that He might ransom from captivity all those who were under the hand of the Law, that we might thus receive at His hands the charter of our sonship.
>
> *(NEB)* ...to purchase freedom for the subjects of the law, in order that we might attain the status of sons.
>
> *(Barclay)* ...it was his purpose that the time of slavery should end and the time of sonship begin.
>
> *(Trans.)* ...in order that we might receive the full status of sons.
>
> *(Mof.)* ...that we might get our sonship.
>
> *(NIV)* ...that we might receive the full rights of sons.

GALATIANS 4:6 And because ye are sons, God hath sent forth the Spirit of his Son into your hearts, crying, Abba, Father.

> *(Wood)* Our sonship is now proved by the Spirit within us, which makes us cry, "Abba, Father."
>
> *(TLB)* And because we are his sons God has sent the Spirit of his Son into our hearts, so now we can rightly speak of God as our dear Father.
>
> *(Cent.)* ...crying, "Dear, dear Father!"
>
> *(Deane)* ...so that instinctively you address God as your Father.

GALATIANS 4:7 Wherefore thou art no more a servant, but a son; and if a son, then an heir of God through Christ.

> *(TLB)* Now we are no longer slaves, but God's own sons. And since we are His sons, everything He has belongs to us, for that is the way God planned.
>
> *(Knox)* ...and because thou art a son, thou hast the son's right of inheritance.
>
> *(Deaf)* ...God will give you the things He promised because you are His child.
>
> *(Baxter)* But you are sons, under a Fatherly government...
>
> *(Wood)* ...and because we are God's Sons, we inherit His promises.

ROMANS 8:16 The Spirit itself beareth witness with our spirit, that we are the children of God.

> *(20th C.R.)* The Spirit himself unites with our spirits in bearing witness to our being God's children.
>
> *(Wood)* We are conscious of the Divine Spirit moving in our spirit, to assure us that we are children of God.

ROMANS 8:16 (Hayman) The Spirit itself confirms the witness of our own spirit...
See Holy Spirit p. 187

ROMANS 8:17 And if children, then heirs; heirs of God, and joint-heirs with Christ; if so be that we suffer with him, that we may be also glorified together.

(Cress.) If we are his children, God will give us what he has.

(Basic) And if we are children, we have a right to a part in the heritage; a part in the things of God, together with Christ.

(TLB) ...for all God gives to his Son Jesus is now ours too...

(Knox) ...heirs of God, sharing the inheritance of Christ.

(Syriac) ...participators of the inheritance of Jesus Messiah.

(Hayman) ...Christ's own co-heirs...

GALATIANS 3:29 And if ye be Christ's, then are ye Abraham's seed, and heirs according to the promise.

(Black.) ...you are heirs of everything included in the promise.

(NAB) ...you are the descendants of Abraham, which means you inherit all that was promised.

(Johnson) ...you are the offspring of Abraham and participate in God's legacy to him.

(Wood) And as Christ is Abraham's seed, you are in Him the inheritors of the promises.

(New Life) If you belong to Christ, then you have become the true children of Abraham. What God promised to him is now yours.

(TLB) And now that we are Christ's we are the true descendants of Abraham, and all of God's promises to him belong to us.

(Barclay) If you are Christ's, then you are descendants of Abraham, with the right to possess all that God promised him.

(Lau.) ...you are heirs of the promise God made to him.

(Knox) ...the promised inheritance is yours.

I PETER 2:9 But ye are a chosen generation, a royal priesthood, an holy nation, a peculiar people; that ye should shew forth the praises of him who hath called you out of darkness into his marvelous light.

(Fenton) ...a people for action...

(Jordan) But you all are a special breed, a noble clergy, a different race, a show-stock people, so that you might demonstrate the virtues of the One who called you out of darkness into his dazzling light. The former nobodies are now God's somebodies; the outcast are now included in the family.

(Godbey) But you are an elect race, a royal priesthood, a holy nation, a people unto conquest...

I PETER 2:9 (Weym.) But you are a chosen race, a priesthood of kingly lineage, a holy nation, a people belonging specially to God...

(NEB) ...a people claimed by God for his own, to proclaim the triumphs of him who has called you out of darkness into his marvelous light.

REVELATION 1:6 And hath made us kings and priests unto God and his Father; to him be glory and dominion for ever and ever. Amen.

(Berk.) ...and has made us into royalty, into priests of God...

(Adams) ...made us an empire.

(Pl. Eng.) To him that loves us and has loosed us from our sins by his life's blood, and has made us to be a kingdom, priests to his God and Father...

(Jer.) ...and made us a line of kings, priests to serve his God and Father...

(Young) ...and did make us kings and priests...

(Authentic) ...and has given us kingship as priests...

ROMANS 14:9 For to this end Christ both died, and rose, and revived, that he might be Lord both of the dead and living.

(Richert) In fact, he appointed Jesus to experience both death and recovery of life.

(20th C.R.) The very purpose for which Christ died and came back to life was this—that he might be Lord over both the dead and the living.

(NEB) This is why Christ died and came to life again, to establish his lordship over dead and living.

(Weym.) For this was the purpose of Christ's dying and coming to life—namely...

(Wuest) ...that He might exercise lordship...

(Roth.) ...he might have lordship...

(Authentic) ...that He might have jurisdiction over...

(Wade) ...Christ died and came to Life again, that He might exercise lordship...

HEBREWS 9:24 For Christ is not entered into the holy places made with hands, which are the figures of the true; but into heaven itself, now to appear in the presence of God for us.

(Cent.) For it was not into a Sanctuary made by hands, a mere type of the reality, that Christ entered, but He entered into heaven itself, now to appear in the very presence of God on our behalf.

(Trans.) ...where he now appears in God's presence on our behalf.

(Conf.) ...to appear now before the face of God on our behalf...

(20th C. R., Weym., Mof., Worrell) ...on our behalf.

(ASV) ...to appear before the face of God for us.

HEBREWS 9:24 (Baxter) For it was not to officiate in a Tabernacle made by man that Christ became our High Priest, but it was to officiate by continued intercession for us in the Heavens, in the Presence of God's Glory, of which the other was but a type.

I TIMOTHY 2:5 For there is one God, and one mediator between God and men, the man Christ Jesus.

> *(Beck)* ...One who brings God and men together...
> *(Jordan)* For God is one, and there is one connecting link between God and man— the Man Christ Jesus.
> *(Berk.)* ...and one go-between of God and of men...

HEBREWS 7:25 Wherefore he is able also to save them to the uttermost that come unto God by him, seeing he ever liveth to make intercession for them.

> *(Mof.)* Hence for all time he is able to save those who approach God through him, since he is always living to intercede on their behalf.
> *(Wand)* He can save to the utmost limit of completeness...
> *(20th C. 1)* ...he is able to be, in every sense, the Saviour of those who come to God through him...
> *(Authentic)* ...to save absolutely...
> *(Lau.)* ...He always lives in heaven and is praying for them.

ROMANS 8:34 Who is he that condemneth? It is Christ that died, yea rather, that is risen again, who is even at the right hand of God, who also maketh intercession for us.

> *(NEB)* ...who is at God's right hand, and indeed pleads our cause.
> *(Lau.)* ...it is He who pleads for us.
> *(Berk.)* ...who also pleads on our behalf.
> *(Richert)* Since the Almighty himself declares us innocent, obviously no one else can declare us guilty.

See righteousness p. 36

HEBREWS 8:6 But now hath he obtained a more excellent ministry, by how much also he is the mediator of a better covenant, which was established upon better promises.

> *(Mof.)* As it is, however, the divine service he has obtained is superior, owing to the fact that he mediates a superior covenant, enacted with superior promises.
> *(Jordan)* ...he is the author of a more vital commitment, or constitution...
> *(Noli)* ...he is the dispenser of a superior New Testament, based on nobler promises from heaven.

HEBREWS 7:22 By so much more was Jesus made a surety of a better testament.

    (Mof.) And this makes Jesus surety for a superior covenant.

    (NIV, GNB, NASB, NAB) ...the guarantee...

    (Noli) ...Jesus became the eternal guarantee...

    (Weym.) ...so much the more also is the Covenant of which Jesus has become the guarantor, a better covenant.

    (Gspd.) ...the agreement which he guarantees is better than the old one.

    (Cent.) And by so much Jesus becomes the guarantor of a better covenant.

    (Phil.) And he is, by virtue of this fact, himself the living guarantee of a "better" agreement.

    (GNB) This difference, then, also makes Jesus the guarantee of a better covenant.

    (Wms.) ...so much the more Jesus has become the guarantee of a better covenant.

    (Norlie) This makes Jesus a guarantee of a much better covenant.

    (AMP) In keeping with [the oath's greater strength and force], Jesus has become the Guarantee of (stronger) agreement [a more excellent and more advantageous covenant].

    (Pl. Eng.) Therefore the bond which Jesus makes sure is a better bond.

    (Lovett) ...the living guarantee...

        See faith p. 164

HEBREWS 4:14 Seeing then that we have a great high priest, that is passed into the heavens, Jesus the Son of God, let us hold fast our profession.

    (Cent.) ...let us hold fast our confession of faith.

    (Pl. Eng.) ...let us hold fast to the declaration of our faith.

    (N. Berk.) ...let us hold firmly to our confession.

    (Barclay) ...we must never lose our grip of the faith we have publicly professed.

    (Cony., Conf.) ...let us hold fast our confession.

    (Mof.) ...let us hold fast to our confession.

    (AMP) ...let us hold fast our confession [of faith in Him].

    (Fenton) ...let us cling to this confession...

    (Bart. & Pet.) ...let us cling to our confession.

        See faith p. 163

HEBREWS 4:16 Let us therefore come boldly unto the throne of grace, that we may obtain mercy, and find grace to help in time of need.

    (Mof.) So let us approach the throne of grace with confidence...

    (Bart. & Pet.) ...draw near with boldness...

    (Roth.) Let us then be approaching with freedom of speech unto the throne of favour...

    (Lau.) So we dare to come to God's throne with confidence...

    (20th C. 1) ...Let us go up boldly to the Throne of Mercy...

HEBREWS 4:16 (Barclay) We must then fearlessly and confidently come to the throne of grace, and then we will find mercy and grace to help us in every situation when we need them.

(Fenton) Let us go, therefore, with freedom to the throne of the Giver, so that we may receive mercy; and we shall find a perfectly supporting gift.

(Jordan) ...having every assurance that we shall both find and be given all the mercy and inner strength we need for any situation.

I JOHN 2:1 My little children, these things write I unto you, that ye sin not. And if any man sin, we have an advocate with the Father, Jesus Christ the righteous...

(Barclay) ...we have one to plead our cause with the Father, I mean Jesus Christ—and he is good.

(Jordan) ...if a person does go wrong, we have a fair-minded lawyer, Jesus Christ, to represent us before the Father.

(Weekes) ...we have a Helper near the Father—Jesus Christ—a Righteous One.

(Adams) ...an Advocate Who stands face to face with the Father...

(Pl. Eng.) ...we have a Friend with the Father...

(Berk.) ...we have a Counsel for defense in the Father's presence...

(Wms.) ...if anyone ever sins, we have One who pleads our cause with the Father, Jesus Christ, One who is righteous.

(NEB) ...we have one to plead our cause with the Father, Jesus Christ, and he is just.

(NIV) ...one who speaks to the Father in our defense—Jesus Christ, the Righteous One.

(Noli) ...our defender...

I PETER 2:25 For ye were as sheep going astray; but are now returned unto the Shepherd and Bishop of your souls.

(Jordan) For you all were wandering aimlessly like sheep, but now you have been corralled by the Shepherd and Overseer of your hearts.

(Weym.) ...the Shepherd and Protector of your souls.

(Knox) ...who keeps watch over your souls.

(Mof.) ...the Shepherd and Guardian of your souls.

Anytime God wants to
change someone's life,
He always touches
THEIR MOUTH.

Mark Hankins
11:23 - The Language of Faith

FAITH moves God. **FAITH** moves mountains. **FAITH** won't move anything until it moves <u>YOU</u>. The first part of you that your **FAITH** will move is <u>your mouth.</u> God is a **FAITH** God.

Mark Hankins
11:23: THE LANGUAGE OF FAITH

NUMBERS
14:28 135
JOSHUA
1:8 135
6:16, 20 135
PSALM
1:1 135
1:2 136
1:3 136
33:6 136
33:9 136
89:34 136
119:89 137
119:90 137
119:97 137
119:130 137
119:148 137
138:2 137
PROVERBS
3:5 137
3:6 137
4:20, 21 138
4:22 138
4:23 138
4:24 138
6:2 138
10:11 138
12:6 139
12:13 139
12:14 139
12:18 139
12:25 139
13:3 139
14:3 140
15:4 140
15:23 140
16:21 140
16:23 140
16:24 140
18:7 140
18:20 141
18:21 141
21:23 141
22:17 141
22:18 141

22:19 142
ISAIAH
55:10 142
55:11 142
JEREMIAH
1:12 142
MATTHEW
7:24 143
7:25 143
7:26 144
7:27 144
8:13 144
9:28 144
9:29 145
14:30 145
14:31 145
17:20 145
21:21, 22 146
24:35 146
MARK
5:25-34 147
6:5, 6 147
9:23 148
10:46-52 148
11:14 148
11:22 148
11:23 149
11:24 149
LUKE
1:37 150
1:38 150
1:45 151
5:5 151
5:15 151
5:16-20 151
17:5, 6 152
17:14 152
17:15 152
18:8 152
22:31, 32 152
JOHN
4:49, 50 153
11:40 153
15:7 153
20:27 154

20:29 154
ACTS
27:25 154
ROMANS
1:16, 17 155
2:28, 29 156
3:4 156
4:16 157
4:17 157
4:18 157
4:19 158
4:20 158
4:21 158
10:8 159
10:9 159
10:10 159
10:17 160
12:3 160
II CORINTHIANS
4:13 160
4:18 160
5:7 161
EPHESIANS
6:16 161
II THESSALONIANS
1:3 161
I TIMOTHY
6:12 162
II TIMOTHY
3:16 162
3:17 162
HEBREWS
3:1 162
4:3 163
4:14 163
6:17 163
6:18 164
7:22 164
11:1 165
11:3 166
11:6 166
11:11 167
11:30 167
12:1, 2 167

HEBREWS
13:5 168
13:6 168

JAMES
1:5 169
1:6 169
1:7 169
1:21 169
1:22 169
1:23 170
1:24 170
1:25 170
2:14 171
2:17 171
2:20-22 172

I PETER
1:25 172
3:4 172
3:10 172

I JOHN
5:4 173

REVELATION
12:11 173

NUMBERS 14:28 Say unto them, As truly as I live, saith the Lord, as ye have spoken in mine ears, so will I do to you...

> *(Knox)* Tell them this, As I am a living God, the Lord says, the very words you have used in my hearing shall come true.

> *(Smith, J.M.)* ...I will do to you just as I have heard you say.

> *(Jer.)* Say to them, As I live—it is Yahweh who speaks—I will deal with you according to the very words you have used in my hearing.

JOSHUA 1:8 This book of the law shall not depart out of thy mouth; but thou shalt meditate therein day and night, that thou mayest observe to do according to all that is written therein: for then thou shalt make thy way prosperous, and then thou shalt have good success.

> *(Mof.)* This law-book you shall never cease to have on your lips; you must pore over it day and night, that you may be mindful to carry out all that is written in it, for so shall you make your way prosperous, so shall you succeed.

> *(Roth.)* ...then thou must talk to thyself therein day and night...

> *(NAB)* ...Recite it by day and by night...

> *(Knox)* The law thou hast in writing must govern every utterance of thine; night and day thou must ponder over it, so as to carry out all the terms of it faithfully; so wilt thou guide thy steps truly and prosper.

> *(AMP)* ...then you shall deal wisely and have good success.

> *(Jer.)* Have the book of this Law always on your lips...

> *(Basic)* Let this book of the law be ever on your lips and in your thoughts day and night, so that you may keep with care everything in it; then a blessing will be on all your way, and you will do well.

> *(Young)* ...then thou dost cause thy way to prosper, and then thou dost act wisely.
> See finances p. 294.

JOSHUA 6:16, 20 And it came to pass at the seventh time, when the priests blew with the trumpets, Joshua said unto the people, Shout; for the Lord hath given you the city. So the people shouted when the priests blew with the trumpets; and it came to pass, when the people heard the sound of the trumpet, and the people shouted with a great shout, that the wall fell down flat, so that the people went up into the city, every man straight before him, and they took the city.

> *(Beck)* ...the people shouted very loudly.

PSALM 1:1 Blessed is the man that walketh not in the counsel of the ungodly, nor standeth in the way of sinners, nor sitteth in the seat of the scornful.

> *(Young)* O the happiness of that one, who...

PSALM 1:1 (Norlie) The man is happy who does not follow the advice of the wicked; who does not loiter in the way taken by sinners, nor resides in the dwelling of the disdainful.

(Message) How well God must like you—you don't hang out at Sin Saloon, you don't slink along Dead-End Road, you don't go to Smart-Mouth College.

PSALM 1:2 But his delight is in the law of the Lord; and in his law doth he meditate day and night.

(Smith, J.M.) ...in his law does he study day and night.

(Norlie) But whose greatest pleasure is in the law of the Lord, so that day and night he recites this law to himself.

(Mof.) ...[he] finds his joy in the Eternal's law, poring over it day and night.

(Jer.) ...but finds his pleasure in the law of Yahweh, and murmurs his law day and night.

(Roth.) ...and in his law doth he talk with himself day and night.

(Message) Instead you thrill to God's Word, you chew on Scripture day and night.

PSALM 1:3 And he shall be like a tree planted by the rivers of water, that bringeth forth his fruit in his season; his leaf also shall not wither; and whatsoever he doeth shall prosper.

(Beck) ...He succeeds in everything he does.

(Basic) ...he will do well in all his undertakings.

(Smith, J.M.) And whatsoever he does he brings to success.

(GNB) ...They succeed in everything they do.

PSALM 33:6 By the word of the Lord were the heavens made; and all the host of them by the breath of his mouth.

(GNB) The Lord created the heavens by his command, the sun, moon, and stars by his spoken word.

(Mof.) The heavens were made at the Eternal's order, and all their host at his mere word.

PSALM 33:9 For he spake, and it was done; he commanded, and it stood fast.

(GNB) When he spoke, the world was created; at his command everything appeared.

(Beck) He spoke and it was, He ordered and it came into being.

PSALM 89:34 My covenant will I not break, nor alter the thing that is gone out of my lips.

(GNB) I will not break my covenant with him or take back even one promise I made him.

(NAB) ...the promise of my lips I will not alter.

(Beck) I will not violate My covenant or break My promise.

(TLB) ...I will not take back one word of what I said.

PSALM 119:89 For ever, O Lord, thy word is settled in heaven.

    (Knox) Lord, the word thou hast spoken stands ever unchanged in heaven.

    (Smith, J.M.) Forever, O Lord, Thy word stands fast in the heavens.

PSALM 119:90 Thy faithfulness is unto all generations: thou hast established the earth, and it abideth.

    (Knox) Loyal to his promise, age after age, is he who made the enduring earth.

PSALM 119:97 O how love I thy law! it is my meditation all the day.

    (Mof.) ...I muse upon it all day long.

PSALM 119:130 The entrance of thy words giveth light; it giveth understanding unto the simple.

    (Beck) Your word is a door that lets in light...

    (NAB) The revelation of your words sheds light, giving understanding to the simple.

PSALM 119:148 Mine eyes prevent the night watches, that I might meditate in thy word.

    (Mof.) I waken through the night to muse upon thy word.

PSALM 138:2 I will worship toward the holy temple, and praise thy name for thy lovingkindness and for thy truth: for thou hast magnified thy word above all thy name.

    (Leeser) ...thou has magnified above all thy name thy promise.

    (Beck) ...I thank Your name because You are kind and faithful, and have made Your name and Your promise greater than everything.

PROVERBS 3:5 Trust in the Lord with all thine heart; and lean not unto thine own understanding.

    (Jer.) Trust wholeheartedly in Yahweh, put no faith in your own perception.

    (Leeser) ...and upon thy own understanding do not rely.

    (Basic) ...not looking to your reason for support.

    (NAB) Trust in the Lord with all your heart, on your own intelligence rely not.

    (RSV) Trust in the Lord with all your heart, and do not rely on your own insight...

    (Mof.) Rely with all your heart on the Eternal, and never lean on your own insight...

PROVERBS 3:6 In all thy ways acknowledge him, and he shall direct thy paths.

    (Mof.) ...have mind of him wherever you may go, and he will clear the road for you.

    (AMP) In all your ways know, recognize, and acknowledge Him, and He will direct and make straight and plain your paths.

PROVERBS 4:20, 21 My son, attend to my words; incline thine ear unto my sayings. Let them not depart from thine eyes; keep them in the midst of thine heart.

> *(Knox)* ...let a man master them (my words)...
> *(TLB)* ...let them penetrate deep within your heart.

See divine healing p. 274

PROVERBS 4:22 For they are life unto those that find them, and health to all their flesh.

> *(Knox)* ...they will bring life and healing to his whole being.
> *(Leeser)* ...and to all his body a healing.
> *(Roth.)* ...to every part of one's flesh they bring healing.

PROVERBS 4:23 Keep thy heart with all diligence; for out of it are the issues of life.

> *(AMP)* ...out of it flow the springs of life.
> *(Douay)* With all watchfulness keep thy heart, because life issueth out from it.
> *(Mof.)* Guard above all things, guard your inner self, for so you live and prosper...

PROVERBS 4:24 Put away from thee a froward mouth, and perverse lips put far from thee.

> *(ASV)* Put away from thee a wayward mouth...
> *(Mof.)* ...bar out all talk of evil, and banish wayward words.
> *(NEB)* Keep your mouth from crooked speech and your lips from deceitful talk.

PROVERBS 6:2 Thou art snared with the words of thy mouth, thou art taken with the words of thy mouth.

> *(Basic)* You are taken as in a net by the words of your mouth, the sayings of your lips have overcome you.

PROVERBS 10:11 The mouth of a righteous man is a well of life: but violence covereth the mouth of the wicked.

> *(Douay)* ...a vein of life...
> *(GNB)* ...but a wicked man's words hide a violent nature...
> *(Mof.)* The talk of good men is a life-giving fountain: the talk of bad men overflows with harm.
> *(NEB)* The words of good men are a fountain of life; the wicked are choked by their own violence.
> *(Basic)* ...the mouth of the evildoer is a bitter cup.

PROVERBS 12:6 The words of the wicked are to lie in wait for blood: but the mouth of the upright shall deliver them.

(NEB) The wicked are destroyed by their own words; the words of the good man are his salvation.

PROVERBS 12:13 The wicked is snared by the transgression of his lips: but the just shall come out of trouble.

(Jer.) His own lips are to blame when the wicked man is entrapped...

PROVERBS 12:14 A man shall be satisfied with good by the fruit of his mouth: and the recompense of a man's hands shall be rendered unto him.

(Jer.) When a man is filled with good things, it is the fruit of his own words...

(Sept.) ...the recompense of his lips shall be given to him.

(GNB) Your reward depends on what you say and what you do...

(AMP) From the fruit of his words a man shall be satisfied with good...

(Mof.) A man reaps the result of all his words...

PROVERBS 12:18 There is that speaketh like the piercings of a sword: but the tongue of the wise is health.

(Mof.) A reckless tongue wounds like a sword, but there is healing power in thoughtful words.

(GNB) Thoughtless words can wound as deeply as any sword, but wisely spoken words can heal.

(Basic) There are some whose uncontrolled talk is like the wounds of a sword, but the tongue of the wise makes one well again.

See divine healing p. 274

PROVERBS 12:25 Heaviness in the heart of man maketh it stoop: but a good word maketh it glad.

(Sept.) A terrible word troubles the heart of a righteous man...

PROVERBS 13:3 He that keepeth his mouth keepeth his life: but he that openeth wide his lips shall have destruction.

(Beck) Watch your mouth and you'll protect your life...

(NAB) He who guards his mouth protects his life; to open wide one's lips brings downfall.

(GNB) Be careful what you say and protect your life. A careless talker destroys himself.

(Douay) ...he that hath no guard on his speech shall meet with evils.

(Mof.) He guards his life who guards his lips...

PROVERBS 14:3 In the mouth of the foolish is a rod of pride: but the lips of the wise shall preserve them.

> *(Mof.)* ...men of sense are safe with what they say.

PROVERBS 15:4 A wholesome tongue is a tree of life: but perverseness therein is a breach in the spirit.

> *(Basic)* A comforting tongue is a tree of life, but a twisted tongue is a crushing of the spirit.
> *(ASV)* ...a breaking of the spirit.

PROVERBS 15:23 A man hath joy by the answer of his mouth: and a word spoken in due season, how good is it!

> *(Basic)* ...a word at the right time, how good it is!
> *(Beck)* ...how fine is something said at the right time.
> *(Douay)* ...a word in due time is best.
> *(Fenton)* A man can please by the word of his mouth, For how sweet is an opportune word!
> *See joy 341.*

PROVERBS 16:21 The wise in heart shall be called prudent: and the sweetness of the lips increaseth learning.

> *(Douay)* ...he that is sweet in words shall attain to greater things.

PROVERBS 16:23 The heart of the wise teacheth his mouth, and addeth learning to his lips.
> *(Sept.)* The heart of the wise will discern the things which proceed from his own mouth, and on his lips he will wear knowledge.

PROVERBS 16:24 Pleasant words are as a honeycomb, sweet to the soul, and health to the bones.

> *(Douay)* Well ordered words...
> *(NAB)* ...healthful to the body.
> *(Basic)* ...new life to the bones.

PROVERBS 18:7 A fool's mouth is his destruction, and his lips are the snare of his soul.
> *(Jer.)* The mouth of the fool works his own ruin, his lips are a snare for his own life.
> *(Knox)* From his own words his (the fool's) undoing comes, from his own lips the snare.
> *(Sept.)* The lips of a fool bring him into troubles, and his bold mouth calls for death. A fool's mouth is ruin to him...
> *(NEB)* The stupid man's tongue is his undoing; his lips put his life in jeopardy.

PROVERBS 18:20 A man's belly shall be satisfied with the fruit of his mouth; and with the increase of his lips shall he be filled.

> *(Douay)* ...the offspring of his lips shall fill him.
>
> *(Jer.)* When a man's stomach is full, it is the fruit of his own mouth, it is the yield of his lips that fills him.
>
> *(GNB)* You will have to live with the consequences of everything you say.
>
> *(AMP)* ...with the consequence of his words he must be satisfied [whether good or evil].
>
> *(Mof.)* A man must answer for his utterances, and take the consequences of his word.

PROVERBS 18:21 Death and life are in the power of the tongue: and they that love it shall eat the fruit thereof.

> *(Jer.)* Death and life are in the gift of the tongue, those who indulge it must eat the fruit it yields.
>
> *(GNB)* What you say can preserve life or destroy it; so you must accept the consequences of your words.
>
> *(Mof.)* Death and life are determined by the tongue...
>
> *(Knox)* Of life and death, the tongue holds the keys...

PROVERBS 21:23 Whoso keepeth his mouth and his tongue keepeth his soul from troubles.

> *(Beck)* Guard your mouth and your tongue, and you'll keep out of trouble.
>
> *(Jer.)* He who keeps watch over his mouth and his tongue preserves himself from disaster.
>
> *(GNB)* If you want to stay out of trouble, be careful what you say.
>
> *(Mof.)* He who is careful of his lips and tongue will manage to keep clear of trouble.

PROVERBS 22:17 Bow down thine ear, and hear the words of the wise, and apply thine heart unto my knowledge.

> *(Jer.)* Give ear to my words and apply your heart to knowing them...

PROVERBS 22:18 For it is a pleasant thing if thou keep them within thee; they shall withal be fitted in thy lips.

> *(Jer.)* ...for it will be a delight to keep them deep within you to have them all ready on your lips.
>
> *(Douay)* ...in thy bowels and it shall flow in thy lips.
>
> *(Gspd.)* ...fix them firmly upon your lips.
>
> *(AMP)* ...your lips will be accustomed to [confessing] them.

PROVERBS 22:19 That thy trust may be in the Lord, I have made known to thee this day, even to thee.

(Jer.) So that your trust may be in Yahweh, today I propose to make your way known to you.

(Basic) So that your faith may be in the Lord, I have made them clear to you this day, even to you.

ISAIAH 55:10 For as the rain cometh down, and the snow from heaven, and returneth not thither, but watereth the earth, and maketh it bring forth and bud, that it may give seed to the sower, and bread to the eater...

(Beck) ...and make it produce and grow...

(Knox) Once fallen from the sky, does rain or snow return to it? Nay, it refreshes earth, soaking into it and making it fruitful, to provide the sower with fresh seed, the hungry mouths with bread.

(Jer.) Yes, as the rain and the snow come down from the heavens and do not return without watering the earth, making it yield and giving growth to provide seed for the sower and bread for the eating...

ISAIAH 55:11 So shall my word be that goeth forth out of my mouth: it shall not return unto me void, but it shall accomplish that which I please, and it shall prosper in the thing whereto I sent it.

(Basic) ...it will not come back to me with nothing done, but it will give effect to my purpose, and do that which I have sent it.

(TLB) ...So also is my Word. I sent it out and it always produces fruit.

(Young) So is My Word that goeth out of My mouth. It turneth not back unto Me empty, But hath done that which I desired, And prosperously effected that for which I sent it.

(Knox) So it is with the word by these lips of mine once uttered; it will not come back, an empty echo, the way it went; all my will it carries out, speeds on its errand.

(NAB) ...achieving the end for which I sent it.

(Jer.) ...so the word that goes from my mouth does not return to me empty, without carrying out my will and succeeding in what it was sent to do.

(Leeser) ...it shall not return unto me without effect...

JEREMIAH 1:12 Then said the Lord unto me, Thou hast well seen: for I will hasten my word to perform it.

(Beck) ...I'm watching over My word to make it come true.

(Leeser) ...I am watching over my word to perform it.

JEREMIAH 1:12 (AMP) ...I am alert and active, watching over My word to perform it.

(Young) And Jehovah saith unto me, "Thou hast well seen: for I am watching over My word to do it."

(Smith, J.M.) I am watching over my word to put it into effect.

(Fenton) For I am watchful over My promises to perform them.

(Mof.) ...I am wakeful over my word, to carry it out.

(GNB) ...I am watching to see that my words come true.

MATTHEW 7:24 Therefore whosoever heareth these sayings of mine, and doeth them, I will liken him unto a wise man, which built his house upon a rock:...

(K. & L.) ...whoever hears these words of mine and acts accordingly is like a sensible man...

(Authentic) Whoever, therefore, hears these sayings of mine and carries them out...

(Crickmer) ...whosoever that-is listening-to these truths of Mine, and is-carrying-them into practice, I-will-liken him to-a sensible man...

(Johnson) With this presentation I have summarized my teaching about the Spirit dimension. If you can hear what I am saying to you and shape your life according to the principles which I have laid down, you will be like a wise person who built his house upon a firm foundation.

(20th C. 1) Every one, then, that listens to this teaching of mine and acts upon it may be compared to a prudent man...

(NIV, NAB, Berk.) ...and puts them into practice...

(Phil.) Everyone then who hears these words of mine and puts them into practice is like a sensible man...

(Rieu) Anyone then who listens to these sayings of mine and acts accordingly...

(Mof.) Now, everyone who listens to these words of mine and acts upon them will be like a sensible man...

(NEB) What then of the man who hears these words of mine and acts upon them? He is like a man who had the sense to build his house on rock.

MATTHEW 7:25 And the rain descended, and the floods came, and the winds blew, and beat upon that house; and it fell not: for it was founded upon a rock.

(Johnson) And all the elements in nature tried to destroy that house: it rained, it flooded, the winds blew, the trees fell, but the house stood firm because it had a solid foundation.

(Berk.) ...it never collapsed, for it was based on the rock.

(Basic) ...it was not moved; because it was based on the rock.

(NEB) ...it did not fall, because its foundations were on rock.

(20th C. 1) ...its foundations are upon rock.

MATTHEW 7:26 And every one that heareth these sayings of mine, and doeth them not, shall be likened unto a foolish man, which built his house upon the sand...

> *(K. & L.)* ...whoever hears these words of mine and does not act accordingly...
>
> *(Authentic)* Everyone, however, who hears these sayings of mine and fails to carry them out will be like a stupid man...
>
> *(Johnson)* And those of you who are hearing the sound of my words, but making no decision about your behavior, will be like a foolish person who erected his house on sand.
>
> *(Rieu)* And anyone who listens to these sayings of mine and does not act accordingly...
>
> *(Mof.)* And everyone who listens to these words of mine and does not act upon them will be like a stupid man...
>
> *(NEB)* But what of the man who hears these words of mine and does not act upon them?
>
> *(20th C. 1)* But every one that listens to this teaching of mine and does not act upon it...
>
> *(NIV, NAB)* ...and does not put them into practice...
>
> *(Berk.)* ...who hears these saying of Mine and fails to practice them shall be like a foolish man...

MATTHEW 7:27 And the rain descended, and the floods came, and the winds blew, and beat upon that house; and it fell: and great was the fall of it.

> *(Berk.)* ...it collapsed. And the wreck of it was complete.
>
> *(Johnson)* When the rain and wind and floods came, that house collapsed, and its destruction was a tragedy.

MATTHEW 8:13 And Jesus said unto the centurion, Go thy way; and as thou hast believed, so be it done unto thee. And his servant was healed in the selfsame hour.

> *(Wms.)* Then Jesus said to the captain, "Go, it must be done for you as you have believed."
>
> *(NEB)* ...because of your faith, so let it be.
>
> *(Crickmer)* ...in the same measure-as thou-didst-get-to-trust so-let-it-have-got-to-be to-thee.
>
> *(Barclay)* ...Because you have a faith like this, your prayer is granted.
>
> *(Knox)* ...let it be done to thee as thy faith foretold.

MATTHEW 9:28 And when he was come into the house, the blind men came to him: and Jesus saith unto them, Believe ye that I am able to do this? They said unto him, Yea, Lord.

> *(Barclay)* ..."Do you really believe that I can do this?"
>
> *(NEB)* "Do you believe that I have the power to do what you want?"

MATTHEW 9:29 Then touched he their eyes, saying, According to your faith be it unto you.

> *(Berk.)* ...to the measure of your faith it shall be to you.
>
> *(Johnson)* ...What you have believed in the depths of your being will be true in your body.
>
> *(Fenton)* As your faith, so shall the result be.
>
> *(Knox)* ...your faith shall not be disappointed.
>
> *(Barclay)* ...Let your prayer be answered in proportion to your faith...
>
> *(Wms.)* Then He touched their eyes, and said, "In accordance with your faith it must be done for you."
>
> *(Beck)* As you believed, so it must be done to you!
>
> *(Gspd.)* Have what your faith expects!
>
> *(Wade)* ...the result for you shall be proportionate to your faith.
>
> *(Crickmer)* ...According-to your trust let-it-have-got-to-be-to-you.

MATTHEW 14:30 But when he saw the wind boisterous, he was afraid; and beginning to sink, he cried, saying, Lord save me.

> *(Phil.)* But when he saw the fury of the wind he panicked and began to sink...
>
> *(20th C. 1)* ...but when he felt the wind, he was frightened...
>
> *(Jer.)* ..but as soon as he felt the force of the wind, he took fright and began to sink...
>
> *(Wade)* But feeling the force of the wind, he grew afraid...
>
> *(Weym.)* But when he felt the wind he grew frightened...

MATTHEW 14:31 And immediately Jesus stretched forth his hand, and caught him, and said unto him, O thou of little faith, wherefore didst thou doubt?

> *(Berk.)* ...You faint believer, why did you doubt?
>
> *(20th C. l)* "How little faith you have!" he said, "What made you hesitate?"
>
> *(20th C.R.)* "O man of little faith!" he said, "Why did you falter?"
>
> *(Knox)* ...Why didst thou hesitate, man of little faith?
>
> *(Wuest)* ...O you of little faith. Why did you waver?
>
> *(Pl. Eng.)* ...O little-faith, why were you in two minds?

MATTHEW 17:20 And Jesus said unto them, Because of your unbelief: for verily I say unto you, If ye have faith as a grain of mustard seed, ye shall say unto this mountain, Remove hence to yonder place; and it shall remove; and nothing shall be impossible unto you.

> *(AMP)* He said to them, Because of the littleness of your faith [that is, your lack of firmly relying trust]. For truly I say to you, if you have faith [that is living] like a grain of mustard seed, you can say to this mountain, Move from here to yonder place, and it will move; and nothing will be impossible to you.

MATTHEW 17:20 (TLB) Because of your little faith, Jesus told them. For if you had faith even as small as a tiny mustard seed you could say to this mountain, "Move!" and it would go far away. Nothing would be impossible.

(*Message*) "Because you're not taking God seriously," said Jesus. "The simple truth is that if you had a mere kernel of faith, a poppy seed, say, you would tell this mountain, 'Move!' and it would move. There is nothing you wouldn't be able to tackle."

MATTHEW 21: 21, 22 Jesus answered and said unto them, Verily I say unto you, If ye have faith, and doubt not, ye shall not only do this which is done to the fig tree, but also if ye shall say unto this mountain, Be thou removed, and be thou cast into the sea; it shall be done. And all things, whatsoever ye shall ask in prayer, believing, ye shall receive.

(*AMP*) And Jesus answered them, Truly I say to you, if you have faith (a firm relying trust) and do not doubt, you will not only do what has been done to the fig tree, but even if you say to this mountain, Be taken up and cast into the sea, it will be done. And whatever you ask for in prayer, having faith and [really] believing, you will receive.

(*TLB*) Then Jesus told them, Truly, if you have faith, and don't doubt, you can do things like this and much more. You can even say to this Mount of Olives, "Move over into the ocean," and it will. You can get anything—anything you ask for in prayer—if you believe.

(*Message*) But Jesus was matter-of-fact: Yes—and if you embrace this kingdom life and don't doubt God, you'll not only do minor feats like I did to the fig tree, but also triumph over huge obstacles. This mountain, for instance, you'll tell, "Go jump in the lake," and it will jump. Absolutely everything, ranging from small to large, as you make it a part of your believing prayer, gets included as you lay hold of God.

MATTHEW 24:35 Heaven and earth shall pass away, but my words shall not pass away.

(*Godbey*) Heaven and earth shall pass away, but my words can not pass away.

(*Weym.*) Earth and sky will pass away, but it is certain that my words will not pass away.

(*K. & L.*) Heaven and earth will fail; my words will never fail.

(*Johnson*) The earth and sky may disintegrate, but the promises and predictions which I have made will stand.

(*Knox*) Though heaven and earth should pass away, my words will stand.

MARK 5:25-34 And a certain woman, which had an issue of blood twelve years, And had suffered many things of many physicians, and had spent all that she had, and was nothing bettered, but rather grew worse, When she had heard of Jesus, came in the press behind, and touched His garment. For she said, "If I may touch but His clothes, I shall be whole." And straightway the fountain of her blood was dried up; and she felt in her body that she was healed of that plague. And Jesus, immediately knowing in Himself that virtue had gone out of Him, turned Him about in the press, and said, "Who touched my clothes" And His disciples said unto Him, "Thou seest the multitude thronging thee, and sayest thou, "Who touched me?" And He looked round about to see her that had done this thing. But the woman fearing and trembling, knowing what was done in her, came and fell down before Him, and told Him all the truth. And He said unto her, "Daughter, thy faith hath made thee whole; go in peace, and be whole of thy plague."

    (AMP) For she kept saying, If I only touch His garments, I shall be restored to health.

    (Wms.) ...for she kept saying, "If I can only touch His clothes, I shall get well."

    (Wuest) ...for she kept saying, "If I touch even His garments, I shall be made whole."

    (Phil.) ...she kept saying...

    (Authentic) Jesus also was immediately aware that power had been drawn from Him...

    (Wade) ...Jesus, becoming conscious that the healing power within Him had been in active operation...

    (Smith, J.M.) Jesus instantly perceived that healing Power had passed from him...

    (20th C. 1) Jesus instantly became conscious that there had been a demand upon his powers...

    (AMP) Still He kept looking to see her who had done it.

    (Johnson) Jesus studied the faces in the crowd to see who had made contact with him.

    (20th C. 1) "...your own faith has made you well..."

    (Barclay) ...Go and enjoy your new health, free from the trouble that was your scourge...

    (Phil.) ...it is your faith that has healed you.

    (AMP) ...your faith (your trust and confidence in Me, springing from faith in Me, springing from faith in God) has restored you to health. Go in (into) peace and be continually healed and freed from your (distressing bodily) disease.

    (NEB) ...Go in peace, free for ever from this trouble.

    See divine healing p. 277

MARK 6:5, 6 And he could there do no mighty work, save that he laid his hands upon a few sick folk, and healed them. And he marvelled because of their unbelief. And he went round about the villages, teaching.

    (Wms.) He could not do any mighty deeds there, except that He put His hands on a few ailing (suffering with minor diseases) people and cured them.

MARK 6:5, 6 (Godbey) And He was not able to do any miracle there, except laying hands on a few sick people, He healed them. And He was astonished on account of their unbelief.

 (20th C. 1) And he could not work any miracle there, except that he placed his hands upon a few invalids, and cured them;...

 (Berk., Weym.) And He wondered at their unbelief. So He went around the nearby villages teaching.

 (Knox) ...he was astonished at their unbelief. And so he went on round about the villages preaching.

MARK 9:23 Jesus said unto him, If thou canst believe, all things are possible to him that believeth.

 (Berk.) Jesus said to him, If you can do anything? Everything is possible for a believer!

 (Fenton) "That depends upon yourself," said Jesus to him; "if you only believe, all is possible to the believer."

 (Norlie) ...all things are possible to the believer.

MARK 10:46-52 And they came to Jericho: and as he went out of Jericho with his disciples and a great number of people, blind Bartimeus, the son of Timeus, sat by the highway side begging. And when he heard that it was Jesus of Nazareth, he began to cry out, and say, Jesus, thou son of David, have mercy on me. And many charged him that he should hold his peace: but he cried the more a great deal, Thou son of David, have mercy on me. And Jesus stood still, and commanded him to be called. And they call the blind man, saying unto him, Be of good comfort, rise; he calleth thee. And he, casting away his garment, rose, and came to Jesus. And Jesus answered and said unto him, What wilt thou that I should do unto thee? The blind man said unto him, Lord, that I might receive my sight. And Jesus said unto him, Go thy way; thy faith hath made thee whole. And immediately he received his sight, and followed Jesus in the way.

 (RSV) ...Go your way; your faith has made you well.

 (NEB) ...Go; your faith has cured you.

 (Berk.) ...Go! Your faith has restored you.

MARK 11:14 And Jesus answered and said unto it, No man eat fruit of thee hereafter for ever. And his disciples heard it.

 (Rieu) ...he dealt with the tree by saying to it...

 (Knox) And he said to it aloud, in the hearing of his disciples...

 (Crickmer) And Jesus went-and-challenged-it and said to-it...

MARK 11:22 And Jesus answering saith unto them, Have faith in God.

 (Cent.) Take hold on God's faithfulness...

 (Roth. 2, Young) ...Have faith of God.

MARK 11:22 (Worrell, Douay) ...Have the faith of God.

    (Godbey) ...Have God's faith.

    (Conc.) ...faith of God...

    (Mar.) ...Have [the] faith of God.

MARK 11:23 For verily I say unto you, That whosoever shall say unto this mountain, Be thou removed, and be thou cast into the sea; and shall not doubt in his heart, but shall believe that those things which he saith shall come to pass; he shall have whatsoever he saith.

    (NEB) ...if anyone says to this mountain, "Be lifted from your place and hurled into the sea," and has no inward doubts, but believes that what he says is happening, it will be done for him.

    (K. & L.) I tell you positively...

    (Rieu) ...if any man orders this mountain to be removed and cast into the sea, and does not waver in his heart, but believes that what he says is done, it will be done for him.

    (Pl. Eng.) ...but believes that what he says is being done...

    (Syriac) ...to him will be the thing he spoke.

    (Godbey) ...believe that what he says does take place; it shall be unto him.

    (Mar.) ...Be thou taken and be thou cast into the sea, and not doubts in the heart of him but believes that what he says happens, it will be to him (he will have it).

    (Young) ...but may believe that the things that he saith do come to pass, it shall be to him whatever he may say.

    (Norlie) ..."Move! Throw yourself into the sea..."

    (Knox) ...has no hesitation in his heart, but is sure that what he says is to come about...

    (N. Berk.) ...and entertains no inner doubt...

    (Weym.) In solemn truth I tell you that if any one shall say to this mountain, "Remove, and hurl thyself into the sea," and has no doubt about it in his heart, but stedfastly believes that what he says will happen, it shall be granted him.

    (Jer.) ..."Get up and throw yourself into the sea," with no hesitation in his heart...

    (Book) ...and shall not waver in his heart, but shall believe that what he says comes to pass...

    (Douay) ...and shall not stagger in his heart...

    (Berk.) ...and entertains no inner doubt...

    (Johnson) Truly, anyone who speaks to that mountain yonder saying, "Dump yourself in the lake," and does not become separated from the statement he makes—that person will actualize his statement. When anyone's expression in prayer is congruent with his inner being, his desire will be actualized.

MARK 11:24 Therefore I say unto you, What things soever ye desire, when ye pray, believe that ye receive them, and ye shall have them.

    (Book) ...believe that you have received them...

MARK 11:24 (Johnson) Because of this principle, when you discover your soul's deepest desires, state them in your prayers, and consider them to have occurred—they will!

(Knox) I tell you, then, when you ask for anything in prayer, you have only to believe that it is yours, and it will be granted you.

(Godbey) ...believe that you just now received them, and they shall be unto you.

(N. Berk.) ...believe that you have received it and it will be yours.

(NASB) ...believe that you will receive it, and you will have it.

(NEB, Condon, Phil., NEB) ...believe that you have received it, and it will be yours.

(GNB) ...believe that you have received it, and you will be given whatever you ask for.

(Jer.) ...believe that you have it already, and it will be yours.

(Wade) ...believe that you have as good as received, and you will get them.

(20th C. 1) Have faith that whatever you ask for in prayer is already granted you, and it will be yours.

(NAB) I give you my word...

(Wuest) ...be believing that you received them, and they shall be yours.

(Wms.) ...have faith that it has been granted you, and you will get it.

(Mof.) ...believe you have got it, and you shall have it.

(Roth.) ...All things whatsoever ye are praying for and asking believe that ye have received, and they shall be yours.

(AMP) ...believe (trust & be confident) that it is granted to you, and you will [get it].

(River.) ...believe that you have obtained them and you will have them.

See prayer p. 230

LUKE 1:37 For with God nothing shall be impossible.

(ASV) For no word from God shall be void of power.

(Weym.) For no promise from God will be impossible of fulfilment.

(Phil.) For no promise of God can fail to be fulfilled.

(Cent.) For no word of God shall be void of power.

(Roth.) Because no declaration from God shall be void of power.

(Syriac) Because nothing is difficult for God.

(20th C.R.) No promise from God shall fail to be fulfilled.

(River.) For no word that comes from God will fail.

(20th C. 1) For not one word from God will prove powerless!

LUKE 1:38 And Mary said, Behold the handmaid of the Lord; be it unto me according to thy word. And the angel departed from her.

(Barclay) Mary said: "I am the Lord's servant. Whatever you say, I accept."

(K. & L.) ...May all that you have said be fulfilled in me!...

LUKE 1:45 And blessed is she that believed: for there shall be a performance of those things which were told her from the Lord.

> *(Roth.)* And happy is she who hath believed that there shall be a perfecting of the things which have been spoken to her from the Lord!
>
> *(Berk.)* And blessed is she who believed that the things told her by the Lord shall be accomplished.
>
> *(TLB)* You believed that God would do what he said; that is why he has given you this wonderful blessing!

LUKE 5:5 And Simon answering said unto him, Master, we have toiled all the night, and have taken nothing: nevertheless at thy word I will let down the net.

> *(Rieu)* "Master," replied Peter, "we toiled away all night and caught nothing. However, I will take your word for it and lower the nets."
>
> *(AMP)* ...on the ground of Your word, I will lower the nets [again].
>
> *(Weekes)* ...yet on thy word I will let down the nets.

LUKE 5:15 But so much the more went there a fame abroad of him: and great multitudes came together to hear, and to be healed by him of their infirmities.

> *(Basic)* ...to give hearing to his words and to be made well from their diseases.
>
> *(Berk.)* ...to listen and to be healed of their diseases.

LUKE 5:16-20 And he withdrew himself into the wilderness, and prayed. And it came to pass on a certain day, as he was teaching, that there were Pharisees and doctors of the law sitting by, which were come out of every town of Galilee, and Judea, and Jerusalem: and the power of the Lord was present to heal them. And, behold, men brought in a bed a man which was taken with a palsy: and they sought means to bring him in, and to lay him before him. And when they could not find by what way they might bring him in because of the multitude, they went upon the housetop, and let him down through the tiling with his couch into the midst before Jesus. And when he saw their faith, he said unto him, Man, thy sins are forgiven thee.

> *(AMP)* And when He saw [their confidence in him, springing from] their faith,...
>
> *(Conc.)* ...And, perceiving their faith...

LUKE 17:5, 6 And the apostles said unto the Lord, Increase our faith. And the Lord said, If ye had faith as a grain of mustard seed, ye might say unto this sycamine tree, Be thou plucked up by the root, and be thou planted in the sea; and it should obey you.

(AMP) ...If you had faith (trust and confidence in God) even [so small] like a grain of mustard seed, you could say to this mulberry tree, Be pulled up by the roots, and be planted in the sea, and it would obey you.

(TLB) ...We need more faith; tell us how to get it. If your faith were only the size of a mustard seed, Jesus answered, it would be large enough to uproot that mulberry tree over there and send it hurtling into the sea! Your command would bring immediate results!

(Message) You don't need more faith. There is no 'more' or 'less' in faith. If you have a bare kernel of faith, say the size of a poppy seed, you could say to this sycamore tree, "Go jump in the lake," and it would do it.

LUKE 17:14 And when he saw them, he said unto them, Go show yourselves unto the priests. And it came to pass, that, as they went, they were cleansed.

(Berk.) ...and as they went they were being cleansed.

(Young) ...and it came to pass, in their going, they were cleansed.

LUKE 17:15 And one of them, when he saw that he was healed, turned back, and with a loud voice glorified God...

(Barclay) One of them (lepers), when he saw he was cured, turned back praising God at the top of his voice.

LUKE 18:8 I tell you that he will avenge them speedily. Nevertheless when the Son of man cometh, will he find faith on the earth?

(AMP) ...will He find [persistence in] faith on the earth?

(TLB) ...When I, the Messiah, return, how many will I find who have faith [and are praying]?

(Message) He will not drag his feet. But how much of that kind of persistent faith will the Son of Man find on the earth when he returns?

LUKE 22:31, 32 And the Lord said, Simon, Simon, behold, Satan hath desired to have you, that he may sift you as wheat: But I have prayed for thee, that thy faith fail not: and when thou art converted, strengthen thy brethren.

(AMP) ...Satan has asked excessively that [all of] you be given up to him [out of the power and keeping of God], and that he might sift [all of] you like grain, But I have prayed especially for you [Peter], that your [own] faith may not fail; and when you yourself have turned again, strengthen and establish your brethren.

LUKE 22:31, 32 (TLB) ...Satan has asked to have you, to sift you like wheat, but I have pleaded in prayer for you that your faith should not completely fail. So when you have repented and turned to me again, strengthen and build up the faith of your brothers.

> *(Message)* ...stay on your toes. Satan has tried his best to separate all of you from me, like chaff from wheat...I've prayed for you in particular that you not give in or give out. When you have come through the time of testing, turn to your companions and give them a fresh start.

JOHN 4:49, 50 The nobleman saith unto him, Sir, come down ere my child die. Jesus saith unto him, Go thy way; thy son liveth. And the man believed the word that Jesus had spoken unto him, and he went his way.

> *(Beck)* "Go," Jesus told him, "your boy is well."
>
> *(Rieu)* "You can go back," said Jesus. "Your son is living." And the man set out, convinced that he had heard the truth from Jesus.
>
> *(NIV)* ...the man took Jesus at his word and departed.
>
> *(Knox)* And the man began his journey home, putting his trust in the words Jesus had spoken to him.
>
> *(TLB)* ...the man believed Jesus and started home.
>
> *(AMP)* ...the man put his trust in what Jesus said...

JOHN 11:40 Jesus saith unto her, Said I not unto thee, that, if thou wouldest believe, thou shouldest see the glory of God?

> *(Knox)* ...thou wilt see God glorified?
>
> *(TLB)* "But didn't I tell you that you will see a wonderful miracle from God if you believe?"

JOHN 15:7 If ye abide in me, and my words abide in you, ye shall ask what ye will, and it shall be done unto you.

> *(NAB)* If you live in me, and my words stay part of you...
>
> *(Berk.)* If you remain in Me and My words remain in you, then you may ask what you want and it will take place for you.
>
> *(Wuest)* If you maintain a living communion with me and my words are at home in you, I command you to ask, at once, something for yourself, whatever your heart desires, and it will become yours.
>
> *(New Life)* If you get your life from Me and My Words live in you, ask whatever you want. It will be done for you.

JOHN 15:7 (Crickmer) Supposing ye-shall-have-got-to-stop in-organic oneness with Me, and-moreover the flowing sap of the utterances of Me working organically-in you shall-have-got-to-stopunimpeded in their circulation, whatever ye-like ye-shall-be-asking, and to-you actually realized-shall-it-be-Fruit making word.

> *(Gspd.)* If you remain united to me and my words remain in your hearts, ask for whatever you please and you shall have it.
>
> *(Wms.)* If you remain in union...
>
> *(K. & L.)* As long as you remain united wth me, and my teachings remain your rule of life, you may ask for anything you wish, and you shall have it.
>
> *(Mof.)* ...ask whatever you like and you shall have it.
>
> *(Roth.)* ...and my sayings in you abide, whatsoever ye may be desiring ask! And it shall be brought to pass for you.
>
> *(20th C. 1)* If you remain united to me, and my teaching remains in your hearts, ask whatever you wish and you shall have it.
>
> *(Roth.)* If perchance ye abide in me and my sayings in you abide, whatsoever ye desire, ask! and it shall be brought to pass for you.
>
> *(Cent.)* ...ask whatever your will is, and it shall be yours.
>
> *See prayer p. 231*

JOHN 20:27 Then saith he to Thomas, Reach hither thy finger, and behold my hands; and reach hither thy hand, and thrust it into my side: and be not faithless, but believing.

> *(Norlie)* ...Do not be a doubter, but a believer.
>
> *(NIV)* ...Stop doubting and believe.
>
> *(Wuest)* ...call a halt to your progressive state of unbelief, but become one who is believing.
>
> *(Knox)* ...Cease thy doubting, and believe.
>
> *(NAB)* ...Do not persist in your unbelief, but believe!

JOHN 20:29 Jesus saith unto him, Thomas, because thou hast seen me, thou hast believed: blessed are they that have not seen, and yet have believed.

> *(Knox)* ...Blessed are those who have not seen, and yet have learned to believe.

ACTS 27:25 Wherefore, sirs, be of good cheer: for I believe God, that it shall be even as it was told me.

> *(Mof.)* Cheer up, men!
>
> *(Roth.)* Wherefore be of good courage, Sirs...
>
> *(RSV)* So take heart, men...
>
> *(Rieu)* ...I have faith in God...
>
> *(Wms.)* ...for I have confidence in my God...

ACTS 27:25 (Knox) ...I trust in God...

(20th C.R.) ...that everything will happen exactly as I have been told.

(N. Berk.) ...for I have faith in God that it will happen in accord with what was told me.

(Berk.) ...in agreement...

ROMANS 1:16, 17 For I am not ashamed of the gospel of Christ: for it is the power of God unto salvation to every one that believeth; to the Jew first, and also to the Greek. For therein is the righteousness of God revealed from faith to faith: as it is written, The just shall live by faith.

(Johnson) I am confident that the good news will release God's dynamic energy which makes all persons whole.

(Richert) In the meantime, I am pleased to present in writing the substance of my message which will reveal the Master's dynamic method of rendering safe and sound all who subscribe to it.

(Way) In the Glad-tidings there is no feature of which I am ashamed. It is the means through which God exerts His power for the salvation of every one who puts faith in the Message... God's gift of righteousness is revealed in it, lifting men from one step of faith to another. This is the import of that passage of Scripture, which says, "It is from the soil of faith that the righteous shall grow up into real life."

(Pilcher) For I am not ashamed of this message, this Gospel. I have witnessed its divine power to free men from the bondage of sin, if only they will surrender themselves to Jesus Christ in loyal acceptance and trust...For in this Gospel the righteousness of God is revealed in a system connected from first to last with faith...

(GNB) I have complete confidence in the gospel; it is God's power to save all who believe...For the gospel reveals how God puts people right with himself: it is through faith from beginning to end...

(Phil.) I see in it God's plan for imparting righteousness to men...

(Noli) I am proud of the Gospel of Christ. It is a message of divine power. It brings salvation to every believer...It reveals that divine righteousness comes from faith and faith only.

(Hayman) ...it being God's own weapon of might...The means of becoming righteous before God is being revealed in it, springing out of, leading up to faith, as Scripture says, "Now the righteous who is so by faith shall have Life."

(Lovett) ...It is a power which emanates from God and saves all who believe in it... It reveals God's way of making men as righteous as Himself. It is a process which, from beginning to end, is entirely by faith. As the scripture says, "He who receives his life by faith is made right with God."

ROMANS 1:16, 17 (Stevens) The gospel, I say, can save men, for in it a way is revealed in which sinful men may be accepted before God and may stand in his presence approved and forgiven. Faith is the condition-the procuring cause, on the human side, of this acceptance-and also its result.

(20th C. 1) For in it there is a revelation of a righteousness which comes from God, the result of faith and leading to faith; as Scripture says—"Those who stand right with God will find Life as the result of faith."

(Deaf) The Good News shows how God makes people right with himself. God's way of making people right begins and ends with faith...

(Wms.) For in the good news God's Way of man's right standing with Him is uncovered, the Way of faith that leads to greater faith...

(Weym.) For in the Good News a righteousness which comes from God is being revealed, depending on faith and tending to produce faith...

(Wade) ...a right standing with God, granted by Him in consequence of rudimentary faith, and resulting in a more developed faith...

(Trans.) ...the beginning and the end of the process by which God puts men right with himself is faith...

(NIV) ...a righteousness that is by faith from first to last...

See righteousness p. 29

ROMANS 2:28, 29 For he is not a Jew, which is one outwardly; neither is that circumcision, which is outward in the flesh: But he is a Jew, which is one inwardly; and circumcision is that of the heart, in the spirit, and not in the letter; whose praise is not of men, but of God.

(Wms.) The real Jew is the man who is a Jew on the inside...

(Berk.) ...but a Jew is such deep in his heart, and so is circumcision not a literal but a spiritual heart affair...

(Authentic) The real Jew is he who is one internally, and the real circumcision is that of the heart, spiritual, not literal...

(Wuest) But he who is so in the sphere of the inner man is a Jew, and circumcision is of the heart, in the sphere of the spirit, not in the sphere of the letter, concerning whom the praise is not from men but from God.

(Barclay) The real Jew is the man who is a Jew in his inner being, and the real circumcision is a thing of the heart. It is a spiritual thing, not conformity to any set of rules and regulations.

ROMANS 3:4 God forbid: yea, let God be true, but every man a liar; as it is written, That thou mightest be justified in thy sayings, and mightest overcome when thou art judged.

(Way) Let us be very sure that God is ever true to His word, though we should have to admit that no man can be relied on to keep faith.

ROMANS 3:4(K. & L.) ...even if all men are fickle...

    (Pl. Eng.) Let God be true to his word, though every man be a liar; as it is written: That thou mightest be proved just in thy words, and win the victory, when thou art judged.

    (TLB) ...God's words will always prove true and right, no matter who questions them.

    (Knox) ...God must prove true to his word, though all men should play him false...

ROMANS 4:16 Therefore it is of faith, that it might be by grace; to the end the promise might be sure to all the seed; not to that only which is of the law, but to that also which is of the faith of Abraham; who is the father of us all...

    (Berk.) For this reason it is a matter of faith, so that the promise may be made sure as a matter of grace...

    (Knox) ...the promise is made good to all Abraham's posterity, not only that posterity of his which keeps the law, but that which imitates his faith.

    (Norlie) ...not only to those who hold to the law, but also to those who have a faith like Abraham's. He is the Father of us all.

    (20th C. 1) That is why all is made to depend upon faith, that all may be God's gift, and in order that the fulfillment of the promise may be certain for all Abraham's descendants— not only for those who take their stand on the law, but also those who take their stand on the faith of Abraham.

    (Weym.) All depends on faith, and for this reason—that acceptance with God might be an act of pure grace...

ROMANS 4:17 (As it is written, I have made thee a father of many nations), before him whom he believed, even God, who quickeneth the dead, and calleth those things which be not as though they were.

    (Tomanek) ...calling the things not being, as being.

    (Berk.) ...and calls into existence what has no being.

    (Authentic) ...he relied on God the "Giver of life to the dead," and the Namer of things as existing which as yet are non-existent.

    (20th C. 1) ...who gives life to the dead, and speaks of what does not yet exist as if it did...

    (Godbey) ...calls things which are not as really existing.

    (Mof.) ...a God...who calls into being what does not exist.

      See eternal life p. 373

ROMANS 4:18 Who against hope believed in hope, that he might become the father of many nations, according to that which was spoken, So shall thy seed be.

    (20th C. 1) Though things looked hopeless, Abraham, sustained by hope, put faith in God...

ROMANS 4:19 And being not weak in faith, he considered not his own body now dead, when he was about an hundred years old, neither yet the deadness of Sarah's womb...

(Knox) There was no wavering in his faith; he gave no thought to the want of life in his own body...nor to the deadness of Sara's womb.

(Young) ...he did not consider his own body...and the deadness of Sarah's womb.

(Syriac) And he was not sickly in his faith...

(20th C. 1) ...yet his faith did not fail him...

(TLB) And because his faith was strong, he didn't worry...

(Message) Abraham didn't focus on his own impotence and say, "It's hopeless..."

ROMANS 4:20 He staggered not at the promise of God through unbelief; but was strong in faith, giving glory to God.

(Black.) Indeed, because of the promise of God, he did not waver between certainty and uncertainty, but was empowered by faith.

(Hudson) He was not led by lack of faith to doubt God's promise. On the contrary, by confessing God's power [literally: by giving God glory]...

(Knox) ...he shewed no hesitation or doubt at God's promise, but drew strength from his faith, confessing God's power...

(Godbey) ...but was filled up with dynamite through faith, having given glory to God.

(Roth.) In respect however of the promise of God he was not led to hesitate by unbelief, but received power by his faith, giving glory unto God.

(TLB) ...he praised God for this blessing even before it happened.

(Pl. Eng.) ...he became stronger in faith, as he gave glory to God.

(Jordan) Still he never concluded that the contract with God had been canceled, but stoutly maintained his faithfulness...

(Berk.) He did not in unbelief hesitate about God's promise, but, empowered by faith...

(Way) But, when he turned his eyes towards the promise of God, there came no distrust to make him waver. Nay, rather it was by that faith that he was filled with virile vigour, when once he had, by this trusting in God, rendered glory to Him...

(Authentic) ...fortified by faith he gave God credit...

ROMANS 4:21 And being fully persuaded that, what he had promised, he was also able to perform.

(Hudson) 21...and by being convinced that [God] could do as well as promise what he had promised, 22it was by faith he was endowed with vital force.

(Jordan) ...giving God credit for being able to carry out his end of the bargain.

(Berk.) 20...he rendered praise to God 21in the complete conviction that He was able to make good His promise.

ROMANS 4:21 (Authentic) ...and was fully assured that what he had promised was practicable, and that he would carry it out.

(Way) ...and was possessed by the conviction that God can perform whatever He has promised.

(Knox) ...fully convinced that God was able to perform what he had promised.

(Barclay) ...he praised God in the unshakable conviction that God is able, not only to make promises, but also to make his promises come true.

(20th C. 1) ...he praised God, in the firm conviction that what God has promised he is able also to carry out.

(Weym.) ...and being absolutely certain that whatever promise He is bound by He is able also to make good.

(NIV) ...that God had power to do what he had promised.

(Message) He plunged into the promise and came up strong...

ROMANS 10:8 But what saith it? The word is nigh thee, even in thy mouth, and in thy heart: that is the word of faith, which we preach;...

(AMP) ...The Word (God's message in Christ) is near you, on your lips and in your heart; that is, the Word—the message, the basis, and object—of faith which we preach.

ROMANS 10:9 That if thou shalt confess with thy mouth the Lord Jesus, and shalt believe in thine heart that God hath raised him from the dead, thou shalt be saved.

(NEB) If on your lips is the confession, "Jesus is Lord," and in your heart the faith that God raised him from the dead, then you will find salvation.

(Syriac) ...thou shalt live (or, be saved).

See righteousness p. 38

ROMANS 10:10 For with the heart man believeth unto righteousness; and with the mouth confession is made unto salvation.

(NEB) For the faith that leads to righteousness is in the heart, and the confession that leads to salvation is upon the lips.

(Syriac) For the heart that believeth in him, is justified; and the mouth that confesseth him is restored to life (or, is saved).

(Black.) For with the heart a person exercises faith that brings righteousness, and with the mouth he makes the acknowledgment that brings salvation.

(Way) For with the inmost heart must we believe, as the first step towards attaining righteousness; but secret belief will not suffice—with the lips must the profession of that belief be made, as the indispensable condition for salvation.

ROMANS 10:10 (Jer.) By believing from the heart you are made righteous; by confessing with your lips you are saved.

> *(Cony.)* For faith unto righteousness is in the heart, and confession unto salvation is from the mouth.
>
> *(20th C. 1)* For with their hearts men believe and so attain to righteousness, and with their lips they make open acknowledgment and so find Salvation.
>
> *(Wms.)* For in their hearts people exercise the faith that leads to right standing, and with their lips they make the acknowledgment which means salvation.
>
> *(Phil.)* For it is believing in the heart that makes a man righteous before God, and it is stating his belief by his own mouth that confirms his salvation.
>
> *(Beck)* With your heart you believe and become righteous.
>
> *See righteousness p. 38*

ROMANS 10:17 So then faith cometh by hearing, and hearing by the word of God.

> *(Berk.)* Faith, then, results from hearing...
>
> *(20th C. 1)* ...faith results from hearing a message, and the message comes through the teaching of Christ.
>
> *(NEB)* We conclude that faith is awakened by the message, and the message that awakens it comes through the word of Christ.
>
> *(Weekes)* So belief cometh from teaching, and the teaching through the word of Christ.
>
> *(Young)* ...so then the faith is by a report, and the report through a saying of God.
>
> *(Cony.)* So, then, faith comes by teaching; and our teaching comes by the Word of God.

ROMANS 12:3 For I say, through the grace given unto me, to every man that is among you, not to think of himself more highly than he ought to think; but to think soberly, according as God hath dealt to every man the measure of faith.

> *(Godbey)* ...God has imparted to each one the measure of faith.

II CORINTHIANS 4:13 We having the same spirit of faith, according as it is written, I believed, and therefore have I spoken; we also believe, and therefore speak;...

> *(NEB)* But Scripture says, "I believed, and therefore I spoke out," and we too, in the same spirit of faith, believe and therefore speak out...
>
> *(AMP)* ...we have the same spirit of faith...
>
> *(TLB)* We boldly say what we believe...

II CORINTHIANS 4:18 While we look not at the things which are seen, but at the things which are not seen: for the things which are seen are temporal; but the things which are not seen are eternal.

> *(Knox)* ...if only we will fix our eyes on what is unseen, not on what we can see. What we can see, lasts but for a moment; what is unseen is eternal.

II CORINTHIANS 4:18 (NIV) So we fix our eyes not on what is seen, but on what is unseen...

(Berk.) ...we do not fasten our eyes on the visible but on the unseen.

(NAB) We do not fix our gaze on what is seen but on what is unseen...

(GNB) For we fix our attention, not on things that are seen, but on things that are unseen.

(Mof.) ...for those of us whose eyes are on the unseen, not on the seen...

(Jordan) We just don't put any stock in outward things but in inner things. For outward things are perishable, while inner things are eternal.

II CORINTHIANS 5:7 For we walk by faith, not by sight:

(NIV) We live by faith, not by sight.

(Weym.) ...for we are living a life of faith, and not one of sight.

(20th C. 1) For we guide our lives by faith, and not by what we see.

(Wms.) ...(for here I live by what I believe and not by what I see).

(Basic) (...for we are walking by faith, not by seeing.)

(AMP) For we walk by faith...not by sight or appearance.

EPHESIANS 6:16 Above all, taking the shield of faith, wherewith ye shall be able to quench all the fiery darts of the wicked.

(Wms.) ...take on the shield which faith provides, for with it you will be able to put out all the fire-tipped arrows shot by the evil one.

(Basic) ...And most of all, using faith as a cover to keep off all the flaming arrows of the Evil One.

(NAB) In all circumstances hold faith up before you as your shield.

(New Life) Most important of all, you need a covering of faith in front of you.

(Barclay) Through thick and thin take faith as your shield.

(Roth.) With all having taken up the shield of faith wherewith ye shall have power all the ignited darts of the wicked one to quench.

(Jordan) Above all, take the bulletproof vest of faith, with which you'll be able to stop the tracer bullets of the evil one.

(Gspd.) ...the flaming missiles of the evil one.

See authority of the believer p. 219

II THESSALONIANS 1:3 We are bound to thank God always for you, brethren, as it is meet, because that your faith groweth exceedingly, and the charity of every one of you all toward each other aboundeth.

(Knox) We owe a constant debt of thanksgiving to God, brethren, on your behalf; we have good reason for it, when your faith thrives so well, and your love for one another exceeds all measure.

II THESSALONIANS 1:3 (Message) ...thanking God over and over for you is not only a pleasure; it's a must. We have to do it. Your faith is growing phenomenally; your love for each other is developing wonderfully.

(Mof.) ...your faith grows apace and your mutual love one and all is increasing.

(TLB) ...because of the really wonderful way your faith has grown, and because of your growing love for each other.

(Basic) ...because of the great increase of your faith, and the wealth of your love for one another.

(NASB) ...because your faith is greatly enlarged.

(20th C. 1) ...and because, without exception, your love for one another is continually increasing.

I TIMOTHY 6:12 Fight the good fight of faith, lay hold on eternal life, whereunto thou art also called, and hast professed a good profession before many witnesses.

(Cent.) Keep contending in the noble contest of the faith...

(Gspd.) Take part in the great contest of faith!

(20th C. 1) Run the great race of the Faith.

See eternal life p. 389

II TIMOTHY 3:16 All scripture is given by inspiration of God, and is profitable for doctrine, for reproof, for correction, for instruction in righteousness.

(Godbey, NIV, Black.) All Scripture is God-breathed...

(Young) ...every Writing is God-breathed, and profitable for teaching, for conviction, for setting aright, for instruction that is in righteousness...

(Roth.) Every scripture is God-breathed and profitable.

(AMP) Every Scripture is God-breathed.

II TIMOTHY 3:17 That the man of God may be perfect, thoroughly furnished unto all good works.

(Berk.) ...so that the man of God may be well-fitted & adequately equipped for all good work.

(Black.) ...so that the man of God may be competent, fully equipped for every excellent work.

(Roth.) ...that the man of God may be ready, unto every good work having been put in readiness.

(Young) ...that the man of God may be fitted-for every good work having been completed.

HEBREWS 3:1 Wherefore, holy brethren, partakers of the heavenly calling, consider the Apostle and High Priest of our profession, Christ Jesus.

(Roth.) ...attentively consider the Apostle and High-priest of our confession—Jesus.

HEBREWS 3:1 (AMP) So then, brethren, consecrated and set apart for God, who share in the heavenly calling, [thoughtfully and attentively] consider Jesus, the Apostle and High Priest Whom we confessed [as ours when we embraced the Christian faith].

HEBREWS 4:3 For we which have believed do enter into rest, as he said, As I have sworn in my wrath, if thy shall enter into my rest: although the works were finished from the foundation of the world.

> *(Knox)* ...and this rest is only to be attained by those who, like ourselves, have learned to believe...

HEBREWS 4:14 Seeing then that we have a great high priest, that is passed into the heavens, Jesus the Son of God, let us hold fast our profession.

> *(Cent.)* ...let us hold fast to the Faith which we have professed.
> *(Pl. Eng.)* ...let us hold fast to the declaration of our faith.
> *(N. Berk)* ...let us hold firmly to our confession.
> *(Barclay)* ...we must never lose our grip of the faith we have publicly professed.
> *(Cony., Conf.)* ...let us hold fast our confession.
> *(Mof.)* ...let us hold fast to our confession.
> *(AMP)* ...let us hold fast our confession [of faith in Him].
> *(Phil.)* ...let us hold firmly to our faith.
> *(Bart. & Pet.)* ...let us cling to our confession.
> *See redemption p. 128*

HEBREWS 6:17 Wherein God, willing more abundantly to show unto the heirs of promise the immutability of his counsel, confirmed it by an oath:

> *(Knox)* ...and God, in the same way, eager to convince the heirs of the promise that his design was irrevocable, pledged himself by an oath.
> *(NEB)* ...and so God...guaranteed it by oath.
> *(Berk.)* In this way God, in His extreme desire to show the heirs of the promise the unchangeableness of His purpose, gave surety with an oath...
> *(NAB)* God, wishing to give the heirs of his promise even clearer evidence that his purpose would not change, guaranteed it by oath.
> *(N. Berk.)* In this way God, in His desire to show the heirs of the promise the unchangeableness of His purpose, guaranteed it with an oath.
> *(Gspd.)* Therefore, God in his desire to make it perfectly clear to those to whom he made his promise, that his purpose was unalterable, bound himself with an oath...
> *(Syriac)* Therefore, God, being abundantly willing to show to the heirs of the promise, that his promising was irreversible, bound it up in an oath.

HEBREWS 6:17 (20th C. 1) And therefore God, in his desire to show, with unmistakeable plainness, to those who were to enter on the enjoyment of what he had promised, the unchangeableness of his purpose, bound himself with an oath.

HEBREWS 6:18 That by two immutable things, in which it was impossible for God to lie, we might have a strong consolation, who have fled for refuge to lay hold upon the hope set before us...

> *(Knox)* Two irrevocable assurances, over which there could be no question of God deceiving us, were to bring firm confidence to us...
>
> *(Berk.)* ...so that by two unalterable facts in which it is impossible for God to play false, we, who have fled the world to get hold of the hope that lies ahead of us, might enjoy mighty encouragement.
>
> *(Hudson)* ...God, by his very nature, cannot prove false...
>
> *(NEB)* Here, then, are two irrevocable acts in which God could not possibly play us false, to give powerful encouragement to us, who have claimed his protection by grasping the hope set before us.
>
> *(Gspd.)* ...so that by these two unalterable things, which make it impossible for God to break his promise, we who have taken refuge with him may be greatly encouraged to seize upon the hope that is offered to us.
>
> *(Weym.)* ...we may possess mighty encouragement.
>
> *(20th C. l)* For he meant that we should find great encouragement in these two unchangeable things, which make it impossible for God to prove false—we, I mean, who have fled for safety where we might lay hold on the hope set before us.

HEBREWS 7:22 By so much more was Jesus made a surety of a better testament.

> *(Mof.)* And this makes Jesus surety for a superior covenant.
>
> *(NIV, GNB, NASB)* ...the guarantee...
>
> *(Noli)* ...Jesus became the eternal guarantee...
>
> *(Weym.)* ...so much the more also is the Covenant of which Jesus has become the guarantor, a better covenant.
>
> *(Gspd.)* ...the agreement which he guarantees is better than the old one.
>
> *(Cent.)* And by so much Jesus becomes the guarantor of a better covenant.
>
> *(Phil.)* And he is, by virtue of this fact, himself the living guarantee of a 'better' agreement.
>
> *(GNB)* This difference, then, also makes Jesus the guarantee of a better covenant.
>
> *(Wms.)* ...so much the more Jesus has become the guarantee of a better covenant.
>
> *(Norlie)* This makes Jesus a guarantee of a much better covenant.
>
> *(AMP)* In keeping with [the oath's greater strength and force], Jesus has become the Guarantee of a (stronger) agreement [a more excellent and more advantageous covenant].

HEBREWS 7:22 (Pl. Eng.) Therefore the bond which Jesus makes sure is a better bond.

> *(Lovett)* ...the living guarantee...

> *See redemption p. 128*

HEBREWS 11:1 Now faith is the substance of things hoped for, the evidence of things not seen.

> *(Berk.)* But faith forms a solid ground for what is hoped for, a conviction of unseen realities.
> *(Authentic)* Now faith forms a solid ground for our expectations, the proof of unseen actualities.
> *(Knox)* What is faith? It is that which gives substance to our hopes, which convinces us of things we cannot see.
> *(Mof.)* Now faith means that we are confident of what we hope for, convinced of what we do not see.
> *(Roth.)* But faith is of things hoped for a confidence of facts, a conviction when they are not seen...
> *(Gspd.)* Faith means the assurance of what we hope for; it is our conviction about things that we cannot see.
> *(NEB)* And what is faith? Faith gives substance to our hopes, and makes us certain of realities we do not see.
> *(Fenton)* ...the conviction of unseen facts.
> *(Weym.)* Now faith is a well-grounded assurance of that for which we hope, and a conviction of the reality of things which we do not see.
> *(Barclay)* Faith is the confidence that the things which as yet we only hope for really do exist. It is the conviction of the reality of the things which as yet are out of sight.
> *(GNB)* To have faith is to be sure of the things we hope for, to be certain of the things we cannot see.
> *(Wand)* Now faith is a conviction of the fulfillment of our hopes, and a continual reliance upon the unseen world.
> *(Wms.)* Now faith is the assurance of the things we hope for, the proof of the reality of the things we cannot see.
> *(Jordan)* Now faith is the turning of dreams into deeds; it is betting your life on the unseen realities.
> *(Cent., Wuest)* Now faith is the title-deed of things hoped for...
> *(Beck.)* Faith is being sure of the things we hope for, being convinced of the things we can't see.
> *(Syriac)* Now faith is the persuasion of the things that are in hope, as if they were in act; and [it is] the manifestness of the things not seen.

HEBREWS 11:1 (AMP) Now faith is the assurance (the confirmation, the title deed) of the things [we] hope for, being the proof of things [we] do not see and the conviction of their reality [faith perceiving as real fact what is not revealed to the senses].

HEBREWS 11:3 Through faith we understand that the worlds were framed by the word of God, so that things which are seen were not made of things which do appear.

> *(Barclay)* It is by faith that we understand that the universe was constructed by the word of God, for the seen had to take its origin from the unseen.
>
> *(Wand)* It is faith that reveals how the worlds were created by the Word of God, so that what is seen owes its origin to what is not seen.
>
> *(Weym.)* Through faith we understand that the worlds came into being, and still exist, at the command of God, so that what is seen does not owe its existence to that which is visible.
>
> *(Jer.)* It is by faith that we understand that the world was created by one word from God, so that no apparent cause can account for the things we can see.
>
> *(Mof.)* It is by faith we understand that the world was fashioned by the word of God, and thus the visible was made out of the invisible.
>
> *(Berk.)* By faith we understand that the worlds were put in order at God's command so that what we now see did not come from visible things.
>
> *(Wade)* ...what we see has had its origin from things invisible to the senses.
>
> *(NEB)* ...the visible came forth from the invisible.
>
> *(NIV)* ...the universe was formed at God's command...
>
> *(Phil.)* ...the whole scheme of time and space was created by God's command...
>
> *(GNB)* ...the universe was created by God's word...
>
> *(Norlie)* ...the things we see did not evolve out of existing matter...
>
> *(Jordan)* ...the seen event is a projection of the Unseen Intent.

HEBREWS 11:6 But without faith it is impossible to please him; for he that cometh to God must believe that he is, and that he is a rewarder of them that diligently seek him.

> *(Jordan)* Without living by the Unseen, it's impossible to get such approval. For anyone who is serious about the God-life, must stake everything on the fact that God is, and that he amply rewards those who make him their quest.
>
> *(Gspd.)* ...for whoever would approach God must have faith in this existence and in his willingness to reward those who try to find him.
>
> *(Mof.)* ...apart from faith it is impossible to satisfy him,...
>
> *(Cent.)* ...and that he ever rewards those who are seeking.
>
> *(Berk.)* But without faith it is impossible to give Him pleasure; for he who comes to God must believe that He exists and that He becomes the Rewarder of those who search for Him.

HEBREWS 11:11 Through faith also Sarah herself received strength to conceive seed, and was delivered of a child when she was past age, because she judged him faithful who had promised.

(AMP) ...she considered [God] Who had given her the promise to be reliable and trustworthy and true to His word.

(Phil.) ...she believed that the one who had given the promise was utterly trustworthy.

(Jordan) Living by the Unseen, Sarah herself had a full-term pregnancy, even though she had passed her menopause. She was sure all along that God would carry through on what he had promised.

(Mof.) ...she considered that she could rely on Him who gave the promise.

(Berk.) Also by faith Sarah personally received potency for conception and that when past the normal age, because she regarded the Promiser trustworthy.

(Norlie) Faith also gave Sarah power to conceive after she was far beyond the years of child bearing, and the reason for this was that she believed that He who had given His promise was trustworthy.

(20th C. 1) Again, it was faith that enabled Sarah to conceive (though she was past the age for child-bearing), because she felt sure that he who had given her the promise might be trusted.

(Knox) ...she believed that God would be faithful to his word.

HEBREWS 11:30 By faith the walls of Jericho fell down, after they were compassed about seven days.

(AMP) Because of faith, the walls of Jericho fell down...

(Wand) It was faith that caused the walls of Jericho to fall down...

(GNB) It was faith that made the walls of Jericho fall down...

(20th C. 1) Faith caused the walls of Jericho to fall...

(NAB) Because of Israel's faith, the walls of Jericho fell...

(Gspd.) Faith made the walls of Jericho fall...

(TLB) It was faith that brought the walls of Jericho tumbling down...

(Knox) Faith pulled down the walls of Jericho...

HEBREWS 12:1, 2 Wherefore seeing we also are compassed about with so great a cloud of witnesses, let us lay aside every weight, and the sin which doth so easily beset us, and let us run with patience the race that is set before us, Looking unto Jesus the author and finisher of our faith; who for the joy that was set before him endured the cross, despising the shame, and is set down at the right hand of the throne of God.

HEBREWS 12:1, 2 (AMP) Therefore then, since we are surrounded by so great a cloud of witnesses [who have borne testimony to the Truth], let us strip off and throw aside every encumbrance [unnecessary weight] and that sin which so readily (deftly and cleverly) clings to and entangles us, and let us run with patient endurance and steady and active persistence the appointed course of the race that is set before us, Looking away [from all that will distract] to Jesus, Who is the Leader and the Source of our faith [giving the first incentive for our belief] and is also its Finisher [bringing it to maturity and perfection]. He, for the joy [of obtaining the prize] that was set before Him, endured the cross, despising and ignoring the shame, and is now seated at the right hand of the throne of God.

HEBREWS 13:5 Let your conversation be without covetousness; and be content with such things as ye have: for he hath said, I will never leave thee, not forsake thee.

> *(Berk.)* ...for He has said, "I will neither give you up nor ever at all desert you..."
> *(Roth.)* Without fondness of money be your way of life...
> *(Barclay)* Never let the love of money dominate your life. Be content with what you have. God himself has said: "I will never let go my grip of you; I will never abandon you."
> *(Wand)* Let your way of life be free from all love of money, and be satisfied with such possessions as you have. For has not God Himself said, "I will not leave you or forsake you?"
> *(Syriac)* Let not your mind love money; but let what ye have, satisfy you. For the Lord himself hath said, I will never leave thee, nor slacken the hand towards thee.
> *(Wade)* Have no leaning towards the love of money, and be content with what you have got, for God Himself has declared, "I will never let thee go, and will never forsake thee;..."
> *(Jordan)* Don't let the desire for money dominate your life. Make do with what's on hand, for he himself has said, "Never will I abandon you or run off and leave you."
> *(AMP)* ...[I will] not, [I will] not, [I will] not in any degree leave you helpless, nor forsake nor let [you] down.
> *(Wuest)* ...For He Himself has said, and the statement is on record, I will not, I will not cease to sustain and uphold you. I will not, I will not, I will not let you down.

HEBREWS 13:6 So that we may boldly say, The Lord is my helper, I will not fear what man shall do unto me.

> *(Berk.)* ...so that we are to say boldly, "The Lord is my Helper, I will not fear! What can man do to me?"
> *(Barclay)* If that is so, we can meet life fearlessly, for we can say: "The Lord is my helper. I shall not be afraid. What can any man do to me?"
> *(Wand)* And that encourages us to reply, "Since the Lord is my helper, I will not be afraid: what power has any human being to do us harm?"
> *(Syriac)* And it belongeth to us, to say confidently, My Lord is my aider, I will not fear. What can man do to me?

HEBREWS 13:6 (Wade) ...so that we may with good courage say, "The Lord is my Helper, I will dismiss all fear: what harm can man do unto me?"

(Jordan) That's why we can say with calm assurance: "The Lord is my provider; I shall never be ruled by fear. How shall a human do me in?"

JAMES 1:5 If any of you lack wisdom, let him ask of God, that giveth to all men liberally, and upbraideth not; and it shall be given him.

(AMP) If any of you is deficient in wisdom, let him ask of the giving God (Who gives) to everyone liberally and ungrudgingly, without reproaching or faultfinding, and it will be given him.

(Weym.) ...who gives with open hand...

See prayer p. 260

JAMES 1:6 But let him ask in faith, nothing wavering. For he that wavereth is like a wave of the sea driven with the wind and tossed.

(AMP) Only it must be in faith that he asks with no wavering (no hesitating, no doubting). For the one who wavers (hesitates, doubts) is like the billowing surge out at sea that is blown hither and thither and tossed by the wind.

(20th C.R.) ...with confidence, never doubting.

See prayer p. 260

JAMES 1:7 For let not that man think that he shall receive anything of the Lord.

(Gspd.) Such a man must not expect to get anything from the Lord.

(AMP) For truly, let not such a person imagine that he will receive anything (he asks for) from the Lord.

See prayer p. 260

JAMES 1:21 Wherefore lay apart all filthiness and superfluity of naughtiness, and receive with meekness the engrafted word, which is able to save your souls.

(Weekes) ...receive with meekness the implanted word, which hath power to save your souls.

JAMES 1:22 But be ye doers of the word, and not hearers only, deceiving your own selves.

(Mof.) Act on the Word, instead of merely listening to it and deluding yourselves.

(NAB) Act on this word. If all you do is listen to it, you are deceiving yourselves.

(K. & L.) Carry it into action...

JAMES 1:23 For if any be a hearer of the word, and not a doer, he is like unto a man beholding his natural face in a glass:...

(Mof.) For whoever listens and does nothing, is like a man who glances at his natural face in a mirror...

(GNB) Whoever listens to the word but does not put it into practice...

(20th C. 1) For, if any one listens to it and does not practice it...

(Barclay) To listen to the word and not to act on it...

(Wand) He who listens to the word and does not act upon it...

(Beck) If anyone listens to the Word but doesn't do what it says...

(Knox) One who listens to the word without living by it...

JAMES 1:24 For he beholdeth himself, and goeth his way, and straightway forgetteth what manner of man he was.

(Mof.) ...he glances at himself, goes off, and at once forgets what he was like.

(Roth.) ...straightway it hath escaped him—what manner of man he was!

JAMES 1:25 But whoso looketh into the perfect law of liberty, and continueth therein, he being not a forgetful hearer, but a doer of the work, this man shall be blessed in his deed.

(Berk.) But whoever looks seriously into the perfect law of liberty and is faithful to it...

(NAB) There is, on the other hand, the man who peers into freedom's ideal law and abides by it...

(Mof.) Whereas he who gazes into the faultless law of freedom and remains in that position, proving himself to be no forgetful listener but an active agent, he will be blessed in his activity.

(GNB) But whoever looks closely into the perfect law that sets people free, who keeps on paying attention to it and does not simply listen and then forget it, but puts it into practice—that person will be blessed by God in what he does.

(20th C. 1) But those who look carefully into the perfect Law, the Law of Freedom, and continue to do so, not listening to it and forgetting it, but putting it into practice—those people will be happy in what they do.

(New Life) ...God's Word makes men free.

(Barclay) It is the man who looks into the perfect law, which is the source of liberty, and who takes his stand on it, the man who is not simply a forgetful listener, but who is an active doer, who will be blessed by God, because he is a man of action.

(NEB) But the man who looks closely into the perfect law, the law that makes us free, and who lives in its company, does not forget what he hears, but acts upon it; and that is the man who by acting will find happiness.

JAMES 1:25 (Jordan) But when one takes a good look at the mature idea of freedom, and hangs on through thick and thin, not being a wishy-washy hearer but a man of action, such a person will be really happy in his work.

> *(Wand)* But the man who has gazed upon the perfect law of liberty and keeps the vision of it constantly before him...

> *(Beck)* But if you look into God's perfect Word, which makes us free, and are loyal to it, if you don't merely listen and forget but do what it says, you'll be happy as you do it.

> *(Roth.)* But he that hath obtained a nearer view into the perfect law of liberty and hath taken up his abode by it, becoming not a forgetful hearer but a work doer, the same happy in his doing shall be.

> *(Phil.)* ...He puts that law into practice and he wins true happiness.

> *(Wuest)* But he who with eagerness and concentration has pored over the perfect law, the law of liberty, and has continued in it...

> *(Pl. Eng.)* But anyone that looks at the perfect law that makes men free, and stands by it, being not a hearer that forgets, but a doer that acts, that man shall be happy in his work.

JAMES 2:14 What doth it profit, my brethren, though a man say he hath faith, and have not works? can faith save him?

> *(Phil.)* Now what use is it, my brothers, for a man to say he "has faith" if his actions do not correspond with it? Could that sort of faith save anyone's soul?

> *(Wand)* What good is it, brethren, if a man asserts that he possesses faith but does not reveal it in his actions?

> *(GNB)* My brothers, what good is it for someone to say that he has faith if his actions do not prove it? Can that faith save him?

> *(Weym.)* What good is it, my brethren, if a man professes to have faith, and yet his actions do not correspond? Can such faith save him?

> *(Berk.)* What is the use, my brothers, for anyone to say he has faith, if he fails to act on it? His faith cannot save him, can it?

JAMES 2:17 Even so faith, if it hath not works, is dead, being alone.

> *(NEB)* So with faith; if it does not lead to action, it is in itself a lifeless thing.

> *(20th C. 1)* ...faith, if not followed by actions, is, by itself, a lifeless thing.

> *(Barclay)* Faith is like that. If faith does not issue in action, if it is all alone by itself, it is dead.

> *(Wand)* So faith, if it does not issue in act, expires with itself.

JAMES 2:20-22 But wilt thou know, O vain man, that faith without works is dead? Was not Abraham our father justified by works, when he had offered Isaac his son upon the altar? Seest thou how faith wrought with his works, and by works was faith made perfect?

> *(Wand)* Don't you realize, my poor fellow, that faith without action is an empty husk? Was it not by action that our father Abraham was justified when he offered his son Isaac upon the altar? Faith, you see, expresses itself in deeds and was rounded off with action.

I PETER 1:25 But the word of the Lord endureth for ever. And this is the word which by the gospel is preached unto you.

> *(Pl. Eng.)* But the word of the Lord stands fast for ever. That word is the good news of God that has been brought to you.
>
> *(Wms.)* But the word of the Lord lives on forever; that is, the message of the good news which has been brought to you.
>
> *(Wuest)* ...but the word of the Lord abides forever.
>
> *(Roth.)* But this is the declaration which was delivered as a joyful message unto you.

I PETER 3:4 But let it be the hidden man of the heart, in that which is not corruptible, even the ornament of a meek and quiet spirit, which is in the sight of God of great price.

> *(Roth.)* But the hidden character ("man"—Greek anthropos; Lat. homo "human being")
>
> *(Pl. Eng.)* ...but rather the hidden inward self, with the undying beauty of a quiet and gentle spirit, which is precious in the sight of God.
>
> *(NEB)* ...but in the inmost centre of your being, with its imperishable ornament, a gentle, quiet spirit, which is of high value in the sight of God.
>
> *(Jordan)* Don't let your good looks depend on external things, like fancy hairdos, expensive jewelry and fashionable clothes, but on the inner radiance of a gentle and sweet spirit which does not fade with age.
>
> *(GNB)* Instead, your beauty should consist of your true inner self, the ageless beauty of a gentle and quiet spirit.
>
> *(AMP)* But let it be the inward adorning and beauty of the hidden person of the heart...
>
> *(Barclay)* ...a beauty which the years cannot wither...
>
> *(Basic)* ...the unseen man of the heart...
>
> *(K. & L.)* ...the inner self...

I PETER 3:10 For he that will love life, and see good days, let him refrain his tongue from evil, and his lips that they speak no guile:...

> *(Wuest)* For he who desires to be loving life and to see good days, let him stop the natural tendency of his tongue from evil.

I PETER 3:10 (Norlie) If a man would enjoy life and see happier days, then he should keep his tongue from speaking evil and his lips from uttering deceit.

(Jordan) He should put the brakes on badness, and give the throttle to goodness.

I JOHN 5:4 For whatsoever is born of God overcometh the world: and this is the victory that overcometh the world, even our faith.

(Deaf) ...every person that is a child of God has the power to win against the world.

(Adams) ...since whoever has been born of God defeats the world. And this is what defeats the world: our faith.

(20th C. R.) ...because all that has received the new Life from God conquers the world. And this is the power that has conquered the world—our faith!

(20th C. 1) ...all that has derived its Life from God masters the world. This is the power that has mastered the world-our faith!

(Wand) ...all God's children conquer the world. The means by which we conquer the world is our faith.

(GNB) ...because every child of God is able to defeat the world. And we win the victory over the world by means of our faith.

(Gspd.) ...every child of God is victorious over the world. The victory that has triumphed over the world is our faith.

(Barclay) ...to be a child of God is to be victorious over the world, and the victory which conquers the world is our faith.

(Phil.) ...for God's "heredity" within us will always conquer the world outside us. In fact, this faith of ours is the only way in which the world has been conquered.

(Wuest) ...is constantly coming off victorious over the world. And this is the victory that has come off victorious over the world, our faith.

(Godbey) ...everything which has been born of God conquers the world: and this is \ the victory which has conquered the world, our faith.

(Mof.) Our faith, that is the conquest which conquers the world. Who is the world's conqueror but he who believes that Jesus is the Son of God?

(N. Berk.) ...this is the victory that triumphs over the world, the faith that we have. Who is the world's victor...?

(Weym.) ...the victorious principle which has overcome the world is our faith.

See redemption p. 99; eternal life p. 399

REVELATION 12:11 And they overcame him by the blood of the Lamb, and by the word of their testimony; and they loved not their lives unto death.

(K. & L.) But they conquered him by means of the blood of the Lamb and the word of their testimony...

REVELATION 12:11 (Barclay) The blood of the Lamb, and their fearless declaration of their faith, have won for them the victory over him...

(NEB) By the sacrifice of the Lamb, they have conquered him, and by the testimony which they uttered...

(Young) ...and they did overcome him because of the blood of the Lamb, and because of the word of their testimony...

(Knox) ...but because of the Lamb's blood and because of the truth to which they borewitness, they triumphed over him, holding their lives cheap till death overtook them.

(Weekes) And they prevailed over him by means of the blood of the Lamb, and by means of the Word of their testimony...

(Weym.) But they have gained the victory over him because of the blood of the Lamb and of the testimony which they have borne...

(20th C. 1) Their victory was due to the sacrifice of the Lamb, and to the Message to which they bore their testimony...

(Phil.) Now they have conquered him through the blood of the Lamb, and through the Word to which they bore witness. They did not cherish life even in the face of death!

(Wms.) But they have conquered him because of the blood of the Lamb and because of the message to which they bore testimony...

(Mof.) But they have conquered him...

(Pl. Eng.) And they themselves have conquered him through the blood of the Lamb, and through the word of their confession,...

(TLB) They defeated him by the blood of the Lamb, and by their testimony...

(NAB) They defeated him...

Notes on Faith

God's

HEAD-BYPASS OPERATION:

Speaking...in the Holy Ghost.

Mark Hankins
11:23: THE LANGUAGE OF FAITH

ISAIAH
28:11 179
LUKE
4:18 179
4:19 179
JOHN
7:38 179
14:15 180
14:16 180
14:17 180
16:13 180
16:14 181
16:15 181
ACTS
1:8 181
2:4 181
2:13 182
2:15 182
2:16 182
2:17, 18 182
4:31 183
7:55, 56 183
8:15-17 184
9:17 184
10:44-47 184
11:14, 15 185
13:2-4 185
13:52 185
15:28 185
19:6 186
ROMANS
8:11 186
8:14 187
8:16 187
8:26 187
8:27 188
11:29 188
I CORINTHIANS
2:9 188
2:10 189
2:11 189
2:12 189
2:13 189
2:14 189
3:16 190
6:19 190
12:7 191
12:9 191
12:10 191
12:11 191
II CORINTHIANS
3:17 191
3:18 191
6:16 192
EPHESIANS
3:16 192
5:18 192
5:19 193
PHILIPPIANS
1:6 193
2:13 193
I THESSALONIANS
5:23 194
II TIMOTHY
1:14 194
I PETER
1:5 194
I JOHN
4:4 195

The Spirit of God doesn't land everywhere. **FAITH** is the landing strip that the **HOLY SPIRIT** lands on.

Mark Hankins
11:23: THE LANGUAGE OF FAITH

ISAIAH 28:11 For with stammering lips and another tongue will he speak to this people.

(AMP) No, but (the Lord will teach the rebels in a more humiliating way) by men with stammering lip and another tongue will speak to this people (says Isaiah, and teach them His lessons).

(Roth.) For with a jabbering lip, and with an alien tongue must he speak unto this people!

See prayer p. 227

LUKE 4:18 The Spirit of the Lord is upon me, because he hath anointed me to preach the gospel to the poor; he hath sent me to heal the broken-hearted, to preach deliverance to the captives, and recovering of sight to the blind, to set at liberty them that are bruised...

(Weym.) ...to proclaim Good News to the poor...to announce release to the prisoners of war...to send away free those whom tyranny has crushed...

(Wade) ...He hath consecrated me to impart Good News to needy men; He hath sent me to proclaim to captives Release and to blind men Recovery of Sight; to send away in Freedom men crushed by oppression...

(Jordan) ...to help those who have been grievously insulted to find dignity...

(Roth. 2) ...he anointed me to deliver a joyful message to [the] destitute...

(Barclay) ...to send away in freedom those who have been broken by life...

(Wuest) ...to send away in release those who are broken by calamity...

(Mof.) ...to set free the oppressed...

(Beck) ...He sent Me to announce to prisoners, You are free...

(Worrell) ...to send away the crushed in freedom...

LUKE 4:19 To preach the acceptable year of the Lord.

(Weym.) ...the year of acceptance with the Lord.

(Jordan) ...to proclaim the Lord's new era.

(AMP) To proclaim the acceptable year of the Lord (the day when salvation and the free favors of God profusely abound).

(Wade) ...to proclaim the year which the Lord has fixed for accepting His people.

(Barclay) ...to announce that the year when the favour of God will be shown has come.

(Beck) ...to announce a season when the Lord welcomes people.

JOHN 7:38 He that believeth on me, as the scripture hath said, out of his belly shall flow rivers of living water.

(Norlie) Out of the heart...

(AMP) Out from his innermost being...shall flow (continuously)...

(Jordan) From the heart of the man who lives, my life will flow, as the Bible says, floods of life giving water.

JOHN 7:38 (Authentic) ...from his interior streams of living water will flow...

> *(Wade)* ...From His breast there will flow streams of Life-imparting water.
>
> *(Conc.)* ...shall gush rivers of living water.
>
> *(Knox)* ...Fountains of living water shall flow...
>
> *(GNB)* ...streams of life-giving water will pour out from his heart.
>
> *(Crickmer)* ...rivers out-from his inward-parts shall-be-flowing of-Water,—all-Alive-as it is.
>
> *(NEB)* Streams of living water shall flow out from within him.
>
> *See eternal life p. 367*

JOHN 14:15 If ye love me, keep my commandments.

> *(New Life)* If you love Me, you will do what I say.
>
> *(Authentic)* If you care for me, carry out my instructions...

JOHN 14:16 And I will pray the Father, and he shall give you another Comforter, that he may abide with you for ever.

> *(Wms., Barclay)* ...another Helper...
>
> *(River.)* ...another Counselor...
>
> *(Pl. Eng.)* ...another Friend...
>
> *(Knox)* ...another to befriend you...
>
> *(AMP)* ...another Comforter (Counselor, Helper, Intercessor, Advocate, Strengthener and Standby)...

JOHN 14:17 Even the Spirit of truth; whom the world cannot receive, because it seeth him not, neither knoweth him: but ye know him; for he dwelleth with you, and shall be in you.

> *(Wade)* ...whom the world cannot receive because it does not behold Him with physical vision, and so does not recognize Him...
>
> *(Basic)* ...Even the Spirit of true knowledge. That Spirit the world is not able to take to its heart because it sees him not and has no knowledge of him.
>
> *(Knox)* It is the truth-giving Spirit, for whom the world can find no room, because it cannot see him, cannot recognize him. But you are to recognize him; he will be continually at your side, nay, he will be in you.

JOHN 16:13 Howbeit when he, the Spirit of truth, is come, he will guide you into all truth; for he shall not speak of himself; but whatsoever he shall hear, that shall he speak: and he will show you things to come.

> *(Barclay)* ...he will tell you all about the things which are going to happen.
>
> *(Weym.)* ...He will make known the future to you.

JOHN 16:13 (Basic) ...the Spirit of true knowledge, has come, he will be your guide into all true knowledge...and he will make clear to you the things to come.

(Crickmer) ...and what is-coming will-be-accurately-informing you...

JOHN 16:14 He shall glorify me: for he shall receive of mine, and shall shew it unto you.

(Basic.) ...and make it clear to you.

(Gspd.) ...he will take what is mine and communicate it to you.

(Mof.) ...he will draw upon what is mine and disclose it to you.

(Crickmer) ...from-out-of My-own shall-He-be-receiving, and-then accurately-informing you.

JOHN 16:15 All things that the Father hath are mine: therefore said I, that he shall take of mine, and shall shew it unto you.

(AMP) Everything that the Father has is Mine. That is what I meant when I said that He (the Spirit) will take the things that are Mine and will reveal (declare, disclose, transmit) them to you.

(NASB) ...and shall disclose it to you.

(Wms.) ...and tell them to you.

ACTS 1:8 But ye shall receive power, after that the Holy Ghost is come upon you: and ye shall be witnesses unto me both in Jerusalem, and in all Judea, and in Samaria, and unto the uttermost part of the earth.

(Wuest) But you shall receive power of the kind which God has and exerts after the Holy Spirit has come upon you.

(GNB) But when the Holy Spirit comes upon you, you will be filled with power, and you will be witnesses for me...

(Jordan) ...you will get power and will be my agents...

(Syriac) ...ye will receive energy...

ACTS 2:4 And they were all filled with the Holy Ghost, and began to speak with other tongues, as the Spirit gave them utterance.

(AMP) And they were all filled (diffused throughout their souls) with the Holy Spirit and began to speak in other (different, foreign) languages (tongues), as the Spirit kept giving them clear and loud expression [in each tongue in appropriate words].

(Phil.) They were all filled with the Holy Spirit and began to speak in different languages as the Spirit gave them power to proclaim his message.

(Jordan) Everybody was bursting with Holy Spirit and started talking in whatever different languages the spirit directed.

ACTS 2:4 (Wuest) ...not in words of everyday speech but in words belonging to dignified and elevated discourse.

> *(Mof.)* ...they began to speak in foreign tongues, as the Spirit enabled them to express themselves.
>
> *(TLB)* ...for the Holy Spirit gave them this ability.
>
> *(NIV)* ...as the Spirit enabled them.

ACTS 2:13 Others mocking said, These men are full of new wine.

> *(Jordan)* Everybody was dumbfounded and puzzled, saying to one another, "What's the meaning of this?" But others sneered, "They're tanked up on white lightning."
>
> *(AMP)* But others made a joke of it and derisively said, They are simply drunk and full of sweet [intoxicating] wine.
>
> *(Mof.)* Some others sneered, "They are brim-full of new wine!"
>
> *(Basic)* But others, making sport of them...
>
> *(NASB)* ...They are full of sweet wine.
>
> *(NEB)* ...They have been drinking.

ACTS 2:15 For these are not drunken, as ye suppose, seeing it is but the third hour of the day.

> *(Wuest)* ...these are not intoxicated as you suppose...
>
> *(Basic)* For these men are not overcome with wine...
>
> *(AMP)* ...as you imagine...

ACTS 2:16 But this is that which was spoken by the prophet Joel...

> *(AMP)* But [instead,] this is [the beginning of what was spoken through the prophet Joel...
>
> *(Wuest)* ...has been spoken...of the prophet Joel and is on record.
>
> *(Basic)* But this is the thing...
>
> *(Weym.)* But that which was predicted through the Prophet Joel has happened...
>
> *(TLB)* ...was predicted centuries ago by the prophet Joel.
>
> *(Jordan)* ...this is the happening described in the book of Joel...

ACTS 2:17,18 And it shall come to pass in the last days, saith God, I will pour out my Spirit upon all flesh: and your sons and your daughters shall prophesy, and your young men shall see visions, and your old men shall dream dreams: And on my servants and on my handmaidens I will pour out in those days of my Spirit; and they shall prophesy...

> *(Wuest)* ...I will abundantly bestow my Spirit upon all flesh.

ACTS 2:17,18 (AMP) ...your sons and daughters shall prophesy [telling forth the divine counsels] and your young men shall see visions (that is, divinely granted appearances), and your old men shall dream [divinely suggested] dreams. Yes, and on My menservants also and on My maidservants in those days I will pour out of My Spirit, and they shall prophesy - telling forth the divine counsels and predicting future events pertaining especially to God's kingdom.

(Jordan) When the time is ripe, says God, I will share my spirit with all mankind, and your sons and your daughters will speak the truth. Your young people will catch visions and your old people will dream new dreams. Yes indeed, when the time is ripe I'll s hare my spirit with my boys and my girls and they will speak the truth.

(Basic) And on my men-servants and my women-servants I will send my Spirit, and they will be prophets.

(TLB) Yes, the Holy Spirit shall come upon all my servants, men and women alike, and they shall prophesy.

(Beck) ...will speak God's Word.

ACTS 4:31 And when they had prayed, the place was shaken where they were assembled together; and they were all filled with the Holy Ghost, and they spake the word of God with boldness.

(AMP) And when they had prayed, the place in which they were assembled was shaken; and they were all filled with the Holy Spirit, and they continued to speak the Word of God with freedom and boldness and courage.

(Phil.) When they had prayed their meeting-place was shaken; they were all filled with the Holy Spirit and spoke the Word of God fearlessly.

(Basic) ...the place where they were was violently moved, and they all became full of the Holy Spirit, preaching the word of God without fear.

(Roth) ...and they were filled one and all...

(Wuest) ...speaking the word of God with fearless confidence and freedom of speech.

(NASB) ...began to speak the word of God with boldness.

(Weym.) ...they were, one and all, filled with the Holy Spirit, and proceeded to tell God's Message with boldness.

(Jordan) ...were telling God's word like it is.

See prayer p. 234

ACTS 7:55, 56 But he, being full of the Holy Ghost, looked up stedfastly into heaven, and saw the glory of God, and Jesus standing on the right hand of God, And said, Behold, I see the heavens opened, and the Son of man standing on the right hand of God.

(AMP) But he, full of the Holy Spirit and controlled by Him, gazed into heaven and saw the glory (the splendor and majesty) of God, and Jesus standing at God's right hand; And he said, Look! I see the heavens opened, and the Son of man standing at God's right hand!

ACTS 7:55, 56 (Wuest) ...having fixed his gaze into heaven, saw God's glory...
>   *(Weym.)* But, full of the Holy Spirit and looking up to Heaven...
>   *(Jordan)* ...vibrant with the Holy Spirit...

ACTS 8:15-17 Who, when they were come down, prayed for them, that they might receive the Holy Ghost: (For as yet he was fallen upon none of them: only they were baptized in the name of the Lord Jesus.) Then laid they their hands on them, and they received the Holy Ghost.
>   *(NASB)* ...For He had not yet fallen upon any of them...Then they began laying their hands on them, and they were receiving the Holy Spirit.
>   *(Basic)* Who, when they came there, made prayer for them...Then they put their hands on them, and the Holy Spirit came on them.
>   *(Weym.)* Then the Apostles placed their hands upon them, and they received the Holy Spirit.

ACTS 9:17 And Ananias went his way, and entered into the house; and putting his hands on him said, Brother Saul, the Lord, even Jesus, that appeared unto thee in the way as thou camest, hath sent me, that thou mightest receive thy sight, and be filled with the Holy Ghost.
>   *(Basic)* ...the Lord Jesus, whom you saw when you were on your journey, has sent me, so that you may be able to see, and be full of the Holy Spirit.
>   *(TLB)* ...so that you may be filled with the Holy Spirit...

ACTS 10:44-47 While Peter yet spake these words, the Holy Ghost fell on all them which heard the word. And they of the circumcision which believed were astonished, as many as came with Peter, because that on the Gentiles also was poured out the gift of the Holy Ghost. For they heard them speak with tongues, and magnify God. Then answered Peter, Can any man forbid water, that these should not be baptized, which have received the Holy Ghost as well as we?
>   *(20th C.R.)* Before Peter had finished saying these words...
>   *(Basic)* ...the Holy Spirit came on all those who were hearing the word. And the Jews of faith ...were full of wonder, because the Holy Spirit was given to the Gentiles, And they were talking in tongues, and giving glory to God...
>   *(Mof.)* ...were amazed that the gift of the Holy Spirit had actually been poured out on the Gentiles...
>   *(AMP)* ...the free gift of the Holy Spirit had been bestowed and poured out largely even on the Gentiles. For they heard them talking in [unknown] languages and extolling and magnifying God...
>   *(Weym.)* For they heard them speaking in tongues and extolling the majesty of God...

ACTS 10:44-47 (Gspd.) ...speaking in foreign languages and declaring the greatness of God...

ACTS 11:14, 15 Who shall tell thee words, whereby thou and all thy house shall be saved. And as I began to speak, the Holy Ghost fell on them as on us at the beginning.

(AMP) He will give and explain to you a message by means of which you and all your household [as well] will be saved [from eternal death]. When I began to speak, the Holy Spirit fell on them just as on us at the beginning.

(Basic) Who will say words to you through which you and all your family may get salvation. And, while I was talking to them, the Holy Spirit came on them, as on us at first.

(Weym.) And, said Peter, no sooner had I begun to speak than the Holy Spirit fell upon them...

ACTS 13:2-4 As they ministered to the Lord, and fasted, the Holy Ghost said, Separate me Barnabas and Saul for the work whereunto I have called them. And when they had fasted and prayed, and laid their hands on them, they sent them away. So they, being sent forth by the Holy Ghost, departed unto Seleucia; and from thence they sailed to Cyprus.

(Mof.) As they were worshipping the Lord and fasting, the Holy Spirit said...

(Basic) ...the Holy Spirit said, Let Barnabas and Saul be given to me for the special work for which they have been marked out by me.

(AMP) Separate now for Me...

(TLB) Dedicate Barnabas and Saul for a special job I have for them.

(Gspd.) So after fasting and prayer...

(NASB) So, being sent out by the Holy Spirit,...

ACTS 13:52 And the disciples were filled with joy, and with the Holy Ghost.

(Phil.) And the disciples continued to be full of joy and the Holy Spirit.

(Jordan) And the Lord's learners were just bubbling over with joy and Holy Spirit.

(Wuest) ...continually filled with joy...

(Basic) And the disciples were full of joy and of the Holy Spirit.

(Weym.) ...more and more filled with joy and with the Holy Spirit.

See joy p. 341

ACTS 15:28 For it seemed good to the Holy Ghost, and to us, to lay upon you no greater burden than these necessary things...

(Weym.) For it has seemed good to the Holy Spirit and to us to lay upon you no burden heavier than these necessary requirements.

(Knox) It is the Holy Spirit's pleasure and ours...

(Mof.) ...not to impose any extra burden on you...

ACTS 19:6 And when Paul had laid his hands upon them, the Holy Ghost came on them; and they spake with tongues, and prophesied.

> *(Basic)* And when Paul had put his hands on them, the Holy Spirit came on them...

> *(Jordan)* And when Paul put his hands on them, the Holy Spirit came over them and they began tongue-talking and preaching.

> *(NASB)* ...the Holy Spirit came on them, and they began speaking with tongues and prophesying.

> *(Beck)* ...and they started to talk in other languages and to speak God's Word.

ROMANS 8:11 But if the Spirit of him that raised up Jesus from the dead dwell in you, he that raised up Christ from the dead shall also quicken your mortal bodies by his Spirit that dwelleth in you.

> *(Way)* If the Spirit of God, of Him who raised Jesus from the dead, has its home in you, then He who raised the Messiah Jesus from the dead will thrill with a new life your very bodies - those mortal bodies of yours - by the agency of His own Spirit, which now has its home in you.

> *(Barclay)* If the Spirit of God, who raised Jesus from the dead, has his home in you, God, who raised Christ from the dead, will give life even to your bodies, subject to death though they are, through the power of his Spirit, who comes and makes his home within you.

> *(NEB)* ...the God who raised Christ Jesus from the dead will also give new life to your mortal bodies through his indwelling Spirit.

> *(Phil.)* ...he will, by the same Spirit, bring to your whole being new strength and vitality.

> *(NIV, Weym.)* ...will also give life to...

> *(Cony.)* ...shall endow with life also your dying bodies...

> *(Wade)* ...Who raised Christ Jesus to Life from among the dead dwells in you, He Who raised Christ Jesus to Life from among the dead will endue with Life your own mortal bodies also, through His Spirit that resides in you.

> *(Godbey)* ...will also create life in your mortal bodies...

> *(Roth.)* ...your death-doomed bodies...

> *(Gspd.)* If the Spirit of him who raised Jesus from the dead has taken possession of you, he who raised Christ Jesus from the dead will also give your mortal bodies life through his Spirit that has taken possession of you.

> *(Wuest)* ...the Spirit of the One who raised up Jesus out from among the dead is in residence in you...the Spirit who is resident in you.

See divine healing p. 284; eternal life p. 381

ROMANS 8:14 For as many as are led by the Spirit of God, they are the sons of God.

> *(AMP)* For all who are led by the Spirit of God are sons of God.
>
> *(Phil.)* All who follow the leading of God's Spirit are God's own sons.
>
> *(Jordan)* For God's sons are they who are led by God's Spirit.
>
> *(Letters)* ...all people who let God's Spirit lead them are His children.
>
> *(Pilcher)* ...it is those who are under the sway of the Divine Spirit who are the sons of God.
>
> *(Gspd.)* For all who are guided by God's Spirit are God's sons.

ROMANS 8:16 The Spirit itself beareth witness with our spirit, that we are the children of God.

> *(AMP)* The Spirit Himself thus testifies together with our own spirit, assuring us that we are children of God.
>
> *(20th C.R.)* The Spirit himself unites with our spirit in bearing witness to our being God's children...
>
> *(Johnson)* By uniting with our own spirit, this Spirit confirms that we are God's children.
>
> *(Letters)* The Spirit Himself whispers deep inside us that we really are kids in the Father's family.
>
> *(Phil.)* The Spirit himself endorses our inward conviction...
>
> *(NEB)* In that cry the Spirit of God joins with our spirit in testifying...
>
> *(TLB)* For his Holy Spirit speaks to us deep in our hearts, and tells us...
>
> *(Knox)* The Spirit himself thus assures our spirit...
>
> *See redemption p. 124*

ROMANS 8:26 Likewise the Spirit also helpeth our infirmities: for we know not what we should pray for as we ought: but the Spirit itself maketh intercession for us with groanings which cannot be uttered.

> *(Wuest)* ...the Spirit lends us a helping hand with reference to our weakness, for the particular thing that we should pray for according to what is necessary in the nature of the case, we do not know with an absolute knowledge;...
>
> *(New Life)* ...the Holy Spirit prays to God for us with sounds that cannot be put into words.
>
> *(Phil.)* ...helps us in our present limitations...
>
> *(Basic)* ...the Spirit puts our desires into words which are not in our power to say...
>
> *(Pl. Eng.)* ...the Spirit prays on our behalf with inward cries beyond ordinary speech.
>
> *(NASB)* ...with groanings too deep for words.
>
> *(Gspd.)* ...with inexpressible yearnings...
>
> *(Trans.)* ...with our inarticulate cries.
>
> *(NEB)* ...We do not even know how we ought to pray, (or, what it is right to pray for) but through our inarticulate groans the Spirit himself is pleading for us...

ROMANS 8:26 (Black.) ...the Spirit gives assistance in our weakness—he takes hold [of our problems] on the other side...

(Barclay) ...the Spirit himself intercedes for us, when the only prayers that we can offer are inarticulate cries.

(Jer.) ...For when we cannot choose words in order to pray properly, the Spirit himself expresses our plea in a way that could never be put into words....

(Wand) ...We do not even know precisely what we ought to pray for. But the Spirit Himself comes to our assistance with inarticulate groanings.

(Johnson) ...we also have the Spirit, who compensates for our inadequacies...

(Authentic) Likewise the Spirit comes to the assistance of our limitations; for we do not know how to express ourselves adequately in prayer. But the Spirit itself makes intercession with speechless moans...

See prayer p. 235

ROMANS 8:27 And he that searcheth the hearts knoweth what is the mind of the Spirit, because he maketh intercession for the saints according to the will of God.

(Wuest) ...but the Spirit himself comes to our rescue by interceding with unutterable groanings.

(Jordan) ...he who X-rays our hearts...

(Weym.) ...His intercessions for God's people are in harmony with God's will.

(Authentic) ...and God who searches hearts knows what is the sense of the Spirit's utterances...

(Syriac) ...and the explorer of hearts, he knoweth what is the mind of the Spirit; because he prayeth for the saints, agreeably to the good pleasure of God.

See prayer p. 235

ROMANS 11:29 For the gifts and calling of God are without repentance.

(Wade) For God's Boons are incapable of being withdrawn, and His Call is incapable of being revoked.

(Way) God, in fact, does not repent of bounty once bestowed, nor withdraw an invitation once given.

(Beck) God never changes His mind when He gives anything or calls anyone.

(GNB) For God does not change his mind about whom he chooses and blesses.

(NASB) ...are irrevocable.

I CORINTHIANS 2:9 But as it is written, Eye hath not seen, nor ear heard, neither have entered into the heart of man, the things which God hath prepared for them that love him.

(Wade) ...Realities (in the words of Scripture) "Which eye hath not seen nor ear heard..."

(20th C. R.) ...for the Spirit fathoms all things, even the inmost depths of God's being.

I CORINTHIANS 2:10 But God hath revealed them unto us by his Spirit: for the Spirit searcheth all things, yea, the deep things of God.

 (Basic) But God has given us the revelation of these things through his Spirit...

 (Syriac) ...the Spirit exploreth all things, even the profound things of God.

 (Barclay) It is through the Spirit that God has given us the revelation of his truth...

 (Wand) This revelation God has given us through His Spirit...

I CORINTHIANS 2:11 For what man knoweth the things of a man, save the spirit of man which is in him? even so the things of God knoweth no man, but the Spirit of God.

 (20th C. R.) For what man is there who knows what a man is, except the man's own spirit within him? So, also, no one comprehends what God is, except the Spirit of God.

I CORINTHIANS 2:12 Now we have received, not the spirit of the world, but the Spirit which is of God; that we might know the things that are freely given to us of God.

 (Wade) But we have received, not the spirit of the world, but the Spirit which proceeds from God, that we may understand the Favours lavished by God upon us...

 (Wms.) ...that we may get an insight into the blessings God has graciously given us.

 (20th C. R.) ...that we may realize the blessings given to us by him.

I CORINTHIANS 2:13 Which things also we speak, not in the words which man's wisdom teacheth, but which the Holy Ghost teacheth; comparing spiritual things with spiritual.

 (Wuest) ...fitly joining together Spirit-revealed truths with Spirit-taught words.

 (Wade) Favours of which we also speak, not in discourses taught by human philosophy, but in discourses taught by the Spirit, explaining spiritual truths in spiritual language.

 (20th C. R.) And we speak of these gifts, not in language taught by human philosophy, but in language taught by the Spirit, explaining spiritual things in spiritual words.

 (Wand) Those are the subjects of which we treat in our addresses...

 (Way) Yes, it is of these high themes that I then discourse, not in the rhetoric of the schools, in terms of human philosophy; but in terms learnt in the Spirit's school do I embody spiritual conceptions in spiritual language.

 (Roth. 2) ...to spiritual [men] spiritual things explaining.

I CORINTHIANS 2:14 But the natural man receiveth not the things of the Spirit of God: for they are foolishness unto him: neither can he know them, because they are spiritually discerned.

 (Wuest) But the unregenerate man of highest intellectual attainments does not grant access to the things of the Spirit of God, for to him they are folly, and he is not able to come to know them because they are investigated in a spiritual realm.

I CORINTHIANS 2:14 (Roth.) But a man of the soul doth not welcome the things of the Spirit of God, for they are foolishness unto him and he cannot get to know them because spiritually are they examined...

>*(Wade)* But the man who judges things only by the senses rejects the truths communicated by God's Spirit: to him they are sheer foolishness, and he cannot understand them, because it is only through spiritual insight that it is possible to penetrate to their meaning.

>*(20th C. R.)* The merely intellectual man rejects the teaching of the Spirit of God; for to him it is mere folly; he cannot grasp it, because it is to be understood only by spiritual insight. But the man with spiritual insight is able to understand everything, although he himself is understood by no one.

>*(Bruce)* The unspiritual man cannot take in the things which the Spirit of God imparts; they are folly to his way of thinking, and he is unable to apprehend them because they are assessed by the spiritual faculty.

>*(Roth. 2)* But a soulical man welcomes not the things of the Spirit of God; for they are foolishness to him, and he cannot ascertain [them], because spiritually are they searched out.

>*(Mof.)* ...they must be read with the spiritual eye.

>*(Godbey)* But the intellectual man receives not the things of the Spirit of God; for they are foolishness unto him; and he is not able to know them, because they are spiritually discerned (They are discerned by the human spirit, and not by the intellect.)

I CORINTHIANS 3:16 Know ye not that ye are the temple of God, and that the Spirit of God dwelleth in you?

>*(Basic)* ...you are God's holy house...

>*(Barclay)* Are you not aware that you are God's temple, and that the Holy Spirit has his home in you?

>*(Wms.)* Are you not conscious...?

>*(Wand)* Don't you realize that you are a temple of God, in which the Spirit of God resides?

I CORINTHIANS 6:19 What! know ye not that your body is the temple of the Holy Ghost which is in you, which ye have of God, and ye are not your own?

>*(Wms.)* Or, are you not conscious...?

>*(Barclay)* Are you not aware...?

>*(Basic)* Or are you not conscious that your body is a house for the Holy Spirit which is in you...?

I CORINTHIANS 12:7 But the manifestation of the Spirit is given to every man to profit withal.

(Way) Now, mark, it is for the benefit of the church that the manifestation of the Spirit is bestowed on this or that person.

(Basic) But to every man some form of the Spirit's working is given for the common good.

I CORINTHIANS 12:9 To another faith by the same Spirit; to another the gifts of healing by the same Spirit...

(Way) ...to another, borne on the breathings of the same Spirit, comes faith...

(Weym.) ...special faith...

I CORINTHIANS 12:10 To another the working of miracles; to another prophecy; to another discerning of spirits; to another divers kinds of tongues; to another the interpretation of tongues...

(Basic) ...to another the power of making clear the sense of the tongues...

(Roth. 2) ...inward workings of deeds of power...

(Godbey) ...and to another the workings of dynamites...

I CORINTHIANS 12:11 But all these worketh that one and the selfsame Spirit, dividing to every man severally as he will.

(Way) ...but, in all these, it is one and the same Spirit that is the energizing source.

(Roth. 2) But, all these, inwardly works the one and the same Spirit...

II CORINTHIANS 3:17 Now the Lord is that Spirit: and where the Spirit of the Lord is, there is liberty.

(Cony.) Now the Lord is the Spirit; and where the Spirit of the Lord abides, there bondage gives place to freedom.

(Jordan) ...where the Lord's Spirit rules, so does freedom.

(Weym.) ...where the Spirit of the Lord is, freedom is enjoyed.

(Mof.) ...there is open freedom.

II CORINTHIANS 3:18 But we all, with open face beholding as in a glass the glory of the Lord, are changed into the same image from glory to glory, even as the Spirit of the Lord.

(AMP) And all of us, as with unveiled face, [because we] continued to behold [in the Word of God] as in a mirror the glory of the Lord, are constantly being transfigured into His very own image in ever increasing splendor and from one degree of glory to another; [for this comes] from the Lord [Who is] the Spirit.

(TLB) ...we can be mirrors that brightly reflect the glory of the Lord. And as the Spirit of the Lord works within us, we become more and more like him.

II CORINTHIANS 3:18 (Message) ...our lives gradually becoming brighter and more beautiful as God enters our lives and we become like him.

II CORINTHIANS 6:16 And what agreement hath the temple of God with idols? for ye are the temple of the living God; as God hath said, I will dwell in them, and walk in them; and I will be their God, and they shall be my people.

    (TLB) For you are God's temple, the home of the living God...

    (Basic) ...we are a house of the living God...

    (Wuest) ...we are an inner sanctuary of the living God, even as God said, I will dwell in them in fellowship with them as in a home and I will live my life in and through them.

    (Jer.) ...that is what we are - the temple of the living God. We have God's word for it: I will make my home among them and live with them...

EPHESIANS 3:16 That he would grant you, according to the riches of his glory, to be strengthened with might by his Spirit in the inner man...

    (Jordan) ...I beg him to give you, out of his glorious abundance, the power to win by his Spirit ruling your inner life.

    (Wand) I pray then that out of the wealth of His glory He will grant you to be mightily strengthened by His Spirit in the very core of your being...

    (Way) I pray that He may, with a fullness measured only by the wealth of His own glory, vouch safe to you to be made strong with power infused by His Spirit into your inmost nature.

    (Jer.) Out of his infinite glory, may he give you the power through his Spirit for your hidden self to grow strong...

    (Wms.) ...mightily strengthened by His Spirit in your inmost being...

    (Weym.) ...strengthened by His Spirit with power penetrating to your inmost being.

    (Barclay) ...strengthened in power through his Spirit in your inner being...

    (Berk) ...empowered with strength in the inner self...

    (Tomanek) ...in the man within...

        See authority of the believer p. 211; prayer p. 245

EPHESIANS 5:18 And be not drunk with wine, wherein is excess; but be filled* with the Spirit... (* Greek - be being filled - continuously)

    (AMP) And do not get drunk on wine...but be ever filled and stimulated with the *(Holy)* Spirit.

    (Jordan) Don't get drunk on wine and carry on a lot of foolishness; tank up on the Spirit...

    (Basic) And do not take overmuch wine by which one may be overcome, but be full of the Spirit...

EPHESIANS 5:18 (Weym.) Do not over-indulge in wine-a thing in which excess is so easy-but drink deeply of God's Spirit.

(Black.) ...But keep filled with the Spirit.

(TLB) ...be filled instead with the Holy Spirit...

(Message) Drink the Spirit of God, huge draughts of him.

EPHESIANS 5:19 Speaking to yourselves in psalms and hymns and spiritual songs, singing and making melody in your heart to the Lord.

(Jordan) ...do your talking to each other with hymns and songs and spirituals, singing and strumming in your hearts to the Lord.

(AMP) ...offering praise with voices [and instruments], and making melody with all your heart...

(Basic) Joining with one another in holy songs of praise and of the Spirit...

(Weym.) ...Sing and offer praise in your hearts to the Lord.

(Knox) ...your tongues unloosed in psalms and hymns and spiritual music...

(Phil.) Express your joy in singing...

(TLB) Talk with each other much about the Lord...making music in your hearts...

(Message) Sing praises over everything, any excuse for a song to God...

PHILIPPIANS 1:6 Being confident of this very thing, that he which hath begun a good work in you will perform it until the day of Jesus Christ.

(Cent.) Of this I am fully persuaded, that He who has begun a good work in you will go on completing it until the day of Jesus Christ.

(Pl. Eng.) ...for I am sure that he that began a good work in you will go on making it better and better until the day of Jesus Christ.

PHILIPPIANS 2:13 For it is God which worketh in you both to will and to do of his good pleasure.

(GNB) ...God is always at work in you to make you willing and able to obey his own purpose.

(Wuest) ...God is the One who is constantly putting forth His energy in you, both in the form of your being desirous of and of your doing His good pleasures.

(Berk.) ...for God is the Energizer within you, so as to will and to work for His delight.

(Weym.) It is God Himself whose power creates within you the desire to do His gracious will and also brings about the accomplishment of the desire.

(Way) ...it is God who is all the while supplying the impulse, giving you the power to resolve, the strength to perform, the execution of His good pleasure.

PHILIPPIANS 2:13 (Barclay) For it is God who is at work in you, to put into you the will to desire and the power to achieve what his purpose has planned for you.

(Norlie) It is really God who works in you, so that you are not only willing but also able to carry out His loving purposes.

See divine healing p. 285

I THESSALONIANS 5:23 And the very God of peace sanctify you wholly, and I pray God your whole spirit and soul and body be preserved blameless unto the coming of our Lord Jesus Christ.

(Mof.) May the God of peace consecrate you through and through!

(N. Berk.) ...May your whole being...

(GNB) May the God who gives us peace make you holy in every way and keep your whole being - spirit, soul, and body - free from every fault at the coming of our Lord Jesus Christ.

(Gspd.) ...Spirit, soul, and body, may be kept sound...

(Cent.) ...be kept altogether faultless until the coming of our Lord Jesus Christ.

(Berk) And may the God of peace Himself make you holy through and through. May your spirit be without a flaw and your soul* and body maintained blameless... (*With Paul the human spirit is the unseen self related to God, while the soul is thought of as related to the visible world. Soul may mean spirit, but not in its highest functions. At times the soul is so involved with the passions, that antagonism against the spirit is felt.)

II TIMOTHY 1:14 That good thing which was committed unto thee keep by the Holy Ghost which dwelleth in us.

(TLB) Guard well the splendid, God-given ability you received as a gift from the Holy Spirit who lives within you.

(Cent.) Guard the glorious trust which has been committed to you by the aid of the Holy Spirit who makes his home in us.

(Weym.) That precious treasure which is in your charge, guard through the Holy Spirit who has His home in our hearts.

(Wms.) Guard this fine deposit of truth by the aid of the Holy Spirit who has His home in our hearts.

I PETER 1:5 Who are kept by the power of God through faith unto salvation ready to be revealed in the last time.

(Beck) And you by believing are protected by God's power...

(Barclay) Your faith has made the power of God the guardian of your lives...

(Cent.) ...you who, through faith, are continuously guarded by the power of God...

(Phil.) ...you are guarded by the power of God operating through your faith...

I PETER 1:5 (Jordan) ...who are sheltered by God's power. This power is yours because of your faith in the solution that's ready to be made crystal clear at the last roundup.

I JOHN 4:4 Ye are of God, little children, and have overcome them: because greater is he that is in you, than he that is in the world.

(Norlie) ...He who is in you is mightier than he who is in the world.

(Barclay) But, my dear children, your life has its source in God, and yours is the victory over them, because the Spirit who is in you is greater than the spirit who is in the world.

(Gspd.) ...he who is in our hearts...

(Jer.) ...you are from God and you have in you one who is greater than anyone in this world...

Every breakthrough **IN FAITH** comes from a breakthrough **IN REVELATION KNOWLEDGE,** not necessarily new information.

Mark Hankins
REVOLUTIONARY REVELATION

PSALM
110:2 199
MATTHEW
18:18 199
MARK
16:17 199
16:18 200
LUKE
10:19 200
JOHN
14:12 200
ROMANS
5:17 201
II CORINTHIANS
10:4 201
10:5 202
EPHESIANS
1:16, 17 202
1:18 203
1:19, 20 205
1:21 207
1:22 208
1:23 209
2:4, 5 210
2:6 210
3:14 211
3:15 211
3:16 211
3:17 213
3:18 213
3:19 214
3:20 215
3:21 216
4:27 216
6:10 216
6:11 217
6:12 217
6:13 218
6:14 219
6:15 219
6:16 219
PHILIPPIANS
2:9 219
2:10 220

COLOSSIANS
2:15 220
HEBREWS
2:14, 15 221
JAMES
4:7 222
I PETER
5:8 223
5:9 223

YOU are the believer and **GOD** is the performer.

Mark Hankins
11:23: THE LANGUAGE OF FAITH

PSALM 110:2 The Lord shall send the rod of thy strength out of Zion: rule thou in the midst of thine enemies.

> *(Mof.)* Yes, the Eternal shall send you from Sion the sceptre of your sway, that you may reign amid your foes, arrayed in sacred vestments.
>
> *(NEB)* When the Lord from Zion hands you the sceptre, the symbol of your power, march forth through the ranks of your enemies.
>
> *(Basic)* ...be king over your haters.

MATTHEW 18:18 Verily I say unto you, Whatsoever ye shall bind on earth shall be bound in heaven; and whatsoever ye shall loose on earth shall be loosed in heaven.

> *(Condon, Trans., NEB, Cunn.)* ...forbid...forbidden...allow...allowed...
>
> *(Basic)* Whatever things are fixed by you on earth will be fixed in heaven: and whatever you make free on earth will be made free in heaven.
>
> *(Pl. Eng., Cent.)* ...forbid...forbidden...permit...permitted.
>
> *(Rieu)* ...whatever you forbid on earth shall be forbidden by Heaven, and whatever you allow on earth shall be allowed by Heaven.
>
> *(Mof.)* ...prohibit...prohibited...permit...permitted...
>
> *(Barclay)* I tell you truly, all that you forbid on earth will be forbidden in heaven, and all that you allow on earth will be allowed in heaven.
>
> *(GNB)* And so I tell all of you:...prohibit...prohibited...permit...permitted...
>
> *See prayer p. 229*

MARK 16:17 And these signs shall follow them that believe; In my name shall they cast out devils; they shall speak with new tongues;...

> *(New Life)* These special powerful works will be done by those who have put their trust in Me. In My name they will put out demons.
>
> *(NEB)* Faith will bring with it these miracles: believers will cast out devils in my name...
>
> *(Wms.)* ...By using my name they will drive out demons...
>
> *(Knox)* Where believers go, these signs shall go with them;...
>
> *(Phil.)* ...they will drive out evil spirits in my name;...
>
> *(Gspd.)* ...with my name they will drive out demons.
>
> *(Weym.)* ...making use of my name they shall expel demons.
>
> *(Trans.)* Wherever men believe, these signs will be found...
>
> *(Wade)* ...By the use of my Name they will expel demons; they will speak rapturously in strange languages...
>
> *(Wuest)* ...And these attesting miracles will accompany those who believe...
>
> *See divine healing p. 278; signs and wonders p. 409*

MARK 16:18 They shall take up serpents; and if they drink any deadly thing, it shall not hurt them; they shall lay hands on the sick, and they shall recover.

> *(Knox)* ...they will lay their hands upon the sick and make them recover.
> *(Fenton)* ...they shall lay their hands upon the sick, and fully restore them to strength.
> *(Norlie)* ...they will lay their hands on the sick and make them well again.
> *(Wade)* ...they will place their hands upon invalids, and they will be restored to health.
> *See divine healing p.279; signs and wonders p. 409*

LUKE 10:19 Behold, I give unto you power to tread on serpents and scorpions, and over all the power of the enemy; and nothing shall by any means hurt you.

> *(Norlie)* I have given you authority to trample on serpents and scorpions and all the might of the satanic foe, and nothing will harm you in any way.
> *(Wms.)* Listen! I have given you power to tread on snakes and scorpions, and to trample on all the power of the enemy, and nothing at all will ever harm you.
> *(Fenton)* ...upon all the might of the enemy; and none can resist you.
> *(Jordan)* ...nothing will be able to stop you.
> *(Authentic)* I have indeed invested you with power to stamp on snakes and scorpions...
> *(Mof.)* ...trampling down all the power of the Enemy; nothing shall injure you.
> *(Knox)* ...I have given you the right to...
> *(AMP)* Behold! I have given you authority and power to trample upon serpents and scorpions, and (physical and mental strength and ability) over all the power that the enemy (possesses); and nothing shall in any way harm you.
> *(New Life)* ...I have given you power over all the power of the one who works against you.
> *(Conc.)* Lo! I have given you authority to be treading upon serpents and scorpions and over the entire power of the enemy, and nothing shall be injuring you under any circumstances.
> *(Trans.)* ...he shall not do you any injury.
> *(Weym.)* I have given you power to tread serpents and scorpions underfoot, and to trample on all the power of the Enemy; and in no case shall anything do you harm.
> *(Condon)* Yes, I have given you power to trample every evil under foot, to counter all the might of the enemy; nothing whatever shall harm you.
> *See divine healing p. 280*

JOHN 14:12 Verily, Verily, I say unto you, He that believeth on me, the works that I do shall he do also; and greater works than these shall he do; because I go unto my Father.

> *(Authentic)* I tell you for a positive fact...
> *(Tomanek)* ...and more of these he shall do...
> *See divine healing p. 282; signs and wonders p. 409*

ROMANS 5:17 For if by one man's offense death reigned by one; much more they which receive abundance of grace and of the gift of righteousness shall reign in life by one, Jesus Christ.

(Weym.) For if, through the transgression of the one individual, Death made use of the one individual to seize the sovereignty, all the more shall those who receive God's overflowing grace and gift of righteousness reign as kings in Life through the one individual, Jesus Christ.

(Way) If, in consequence of that single first transgression, death became king of men's lives, through the one man's demerit, all this will be far more compensated when those who receive the measureless wealth of God's grace and God's gift of righteousness shall be kings in the New Life, through the merit of the One, Jesus the Messiah.

(Beck) If one man by his sin made death a king, we, on whom God has poured His love and His gift of righteousness, are all the more certain the one Jesus Christ makes us live and be kings.

(Wand) If then by one man's transgression all became the subjects of death, much more shall those who receive the bounty of God and the gift of righteousness through the Unique Person Jesus Christ become the lords of life.

(Lau.) That one man, Adam, when he sinned, put all men under the rule of death. But that other Man, Jesus Christ, makes men right with God so that they shall live and rule like kings. This He does for all who accept God's rich forgiving love and His free gift.

(AMP) ...those who receive (God's) overflowing grace (unmerited favor) and the free gift of righteousness (putting them into right standing with Himself) reign as kings in life...

See redemption p. 102; righteousness p. 34; eternal life p. 375

II CORINTHIANS 10:4 (For the weapons of our warfare are not carnal, but mighty through God to the pulling down of strongholds;)

(Tomanek) For our arms of warfare are not fleshly, but powerful in God for casting down of fortresses.

(Lau.) ...Our weapons have the power of God to destroy the defenses of evil...

(Trans.) The weapons that we fight with are not just ordinary weapons; under God they are powerful enough to destroy fortresses. We demolish false arguments...

(New Life) We do not use those things to fight with that the world uses. We use the things God gives to fight with and they have power. Those things God gives to fight with destroy the strong places of the devil.

(Pl. Eng.) ...for the weapons of our warfare are not weapons of the flesh, they are full of power for God...

(TLB) I use God's mighty weapons. not those made by men, to knock down the devil's strongholds.

(Barclay) The weapons we use in our campaign are not the weapons the world uses. They are filled with divine power to demolish strongholds. We demolish false arguments...

II CORINTHIANS 10:4 (Way) ...but, in the strength of God, they are mighty enough to raze all strongholds of our foes.

(Jordan) For even though we live in the world, we do not fight on its level. Our implements of war are not manufactured by the world but loaded by God for smashing fortresses. With them we explode learned discourses and every highfalutin wisecrack against the true knowledge of God.

(Fenton) For the weapons of our campaign are not corporeal: but powers from God, for the purpose of destroying fortresses; defeating opponents, and every pride exalting itself against the knowledge of God...

(Berk.) ...are not physical...

II CORINTHIANS 10:5 Casting down imaginations, and every high thing that exalteth itself against the knowledge of God, and bringing into captivity every thought to the obedience of Christ...

(Trans.) ...and pull down every towering obstacle reared up against the knowledge of God; we take every thought prisoner and make it obey Christ...

(New Life) We break down every thought and proud thing that puts itself up against the wisdom of God. We take hold of every thought and make it obey Christ.

(Barclay) ...and every towering obstacle, erected to prevent men from knowing God.

(Wade) We demolish opposing Reasonings and all presumptuous Unbelief that, like a towering fortress, rears itself against the knowledge of God; and we take captive and render submissive to the Christ every defiant thought.

(Worrell) ...casting down reasonings...

(NASB) ...speculations...

(TLB) These weapons can break down every proud argument against God and every wall that can be built to keep men from finding him. With these weapons I can capture rebels and bring them back to God, and change them into men whose hearts' desire is obedience to Christ.

EPHESIANS 1:16, 17 Cease not to give thanks for you, making mention of you in my prayers. That the God of our Lord Jesus Christ, the Father of glory, may give unto you the spirit of wisdom and revelation in the knowledge of him.

(TLB) ...I pray for you constantly, asking God, the glorious Father of our Lord Jesus Christ, to give you wisdom to see clearly and really understand who Christ is and all that he has done for you.

(Jer.) May the God of our Lord Jesus Christ, the Father of glory, give you a spirit of wisdom and perception of what is revealed, to bring you to full knowledge of him.

EPHESIANS 1:16, 17 (Barclay) For it is my prayer that the God of our Lord Jesus Christ, the glorious Father, may give you the Spirit to make you wise in heavenly things, and to reveal to you full knowledge of himself.

(NEB) I pray that the God of our Lord Jesus Christ, the all-glorious Father, may give you the spiritual powers of wisdom and vision, by which there comes the knowledge of him.

(Hudson) May the God of our Lord Jesus Christ, the Father all glorious, give you a spirit that grasps principles [and receives] God's revelation in the sphere of [or, as regards] full knowledge of himself...

(Way) that the God of our Lord Jesus the Messiah, the Father glory-clad, may, in bestowing the full knowledge of Himself, bestow on you the Spirit which is manifested in divine illumination and insight into the mysteries of God...

(Carpenter) ...May the eternal wisdom make you wise. May all the veils be torn away, so far as that may be in this life, and the full glory of the Revelation come flooding in upon you, so that your knowledge may be directed to the true end.

(Cornish) ...this prayer is one for further light and increased understanding on your part, that the God of our Lord Jesus Christ, Father of all glory, may give you the spiritual wisdom & revelation, which are found in the clear full knowledge of Him...

(AMP) ...that He may grant you a spirit of wisdom and revelation—of insight into mysteries and secrets—in the [deep and intimate] knowledge of Him.

(Conc.) ...a spirit of wisdom and revelation in the realization of Him...

(Wms.) ...wisdom and revelation which come through a growing knowledge of Him...

(Dist.) I pray that you new Christians will understand the mighty position with Christ which your congregations occupy.

(Fenton) ...a spirit of wisdom, and comprehension of what is contained in a full knowledge of Him...

(Roth. 2) ...a spirit of wisdom and revelation in gaining a full knowledge of him...

(Conf.) ...the spirit of wisdom and revelation in deep knowledge of him...

(Black.) ...in the deeper knowledge of himself...

(NIV) I keep asking...

(ABV, Tomanek, Estes) ...full knowledge...

(Noli) ...a spirit of wisdom, revelation, and divine knowledge.

(Cony.) ...a spirit of wisdom and of insight...

See prayer p. 238

EPHESIANS 1:18 The eyes of your understanding being enlightened; that ye may know what is the hope of his calling, and what the riches of the glory of his inheritance in the saints...

(NEB) I pray that your inward eyes may be illumined, so that you may know what is the hope to which he calls you, what the wealth and glory of the share he offers you among his people in their heritage...

EPHESIANS 1:18 (Phil.) ...that you may receive that inner illumination of the spirit which will make you realize how great is the hope to which he is calling you - the magnificence and splendor of the inheritance promised to Christians.

(Way) ...and may flood with light the eyes of your understanding. So shall you know what it really is, that hope which springs up in those who hearken His invitation: so shall you know what riches are comprised in the magnificence of the inheritance which He gives you among His consecrated ones...

(Cornish) ...and illuminate your inner vision, the eyes of your heart, thereby explaining and opening to you the full nature of his calling and its aim and expectation, revealing too what an abundance of glory is implied in this inheritance of the saints...

(Dodd.) ...the eyes of your understanding enlightened still more and more; that, being thus illuminated, ye may know, in a more comprehensive manner than you now do...

(Jordan) ...May you know the hope which his call inspires and the wonderful resources available to Christians because of their membership in his family.

(Lovett) Specifically I pray that the eyes of your heart may be enlightened, so that you may behold the intimate details of his plan...

(Letters) ...what is actually ours now and in the future because of what Jesus has done for you.

(Conc.) ...for you to perceive what is the expectation of His calling, and what the riches of the glory of the enjoyment of His allotment among the saints...

(Fenton) ...who enlightens the eyes of your hearts: to show you what is the hope of His calling...

(Basic) ...And that having the eyes of your heart full of light, you may have knowledge of...

(Pl. Eng.) ...that your inward eyes may be filled with his light...and what a wealth of glory is laid up for our possession among the people of God...

(Barclay) I pray that your inner vision may be flooded with light, to enable you to see...

(Cress.) I ask him that you may see these things in your hearts.

(Berk.) ...granting you illumined eyes of the heart...

(Wuest) ...the eyes of your heart being in an enlightened state...

(Bruce) I pray for the enlightenment of your spiritual vision...

(GNB) ...how rich are the wonderful blessings he promises his people...

(Knox) May your inward eye be enlightened...

(Jer.) ...so that you can see what hope his call holds for you...

(Roth.) ...the eyes of your heart having been enlightened...

(Tomanek) ...of his inheritance in the Holy one...

(Black.) ...that the perception of your heart may be illumined...

(Cent.) ...that the eyes of your heart may be flooded with light...

(AMP) By having the eyes of your heart flooded with light...

EPHESIANS 1:18 (New Life) I pray that your hearts will be able to understand...

(*TLB*) I pray that your hearts will be flooded with light...

See prayer p. 239

EPHESIANS 1:19, 20 And what is the exceeding greatness of his power to usward who believe, according to the working of his mighty power. Which he wrought in Christ, when he raised him from the dead, and set him at his own right hand in the heavenly places.

(*GNB*) ...and how very great is his power at work in us who believe. This power working in us is the same as the mighty strength which he used when he raised Christ from death and seated him at his right side in the heavenly world.

(*Trans.*) ...and the limitless scope of his power at work in us once we believe in him. This is that same stupendous power which he exerted when he raised Christ from death and enthroned him at his right hand in the supernatural world.

(*Johnson*) ...and that you will be aware of the incredibly immense strength which is available to us. You see, we have access to resurrection - to the strength and power God demonstrated in Christ when he raised him from death and gave him supreme authority.

(*Lau.*) I pray that you may realize that His power in us who believe, is great beyond measure. It is the same mighty power that worked in Christ. By that power God raised Him from the dead and had Him sit at His right hand in heaven.

(*Weym.*) ...and what the transcendent greatness of His power in us believers as seen in the working of His infinite might when He displayed it in Christ by raising Him from the dead and seating Him at His own right hand in the heavenly realms...

(*Cornish*) ...and unfolding to your apprehension the extraordinary power which reacts from him upon all who believe. It is the enormous overmastering supremacy which the Christ showed forth, which operated in him, raising him from the dead.

(*Bruce*) ...and what the surpassing greatness of His power displayed in us who believe. That power is the effective operation of His mighty strength which He exerted in the case of Christ, when He raised Him from the dead and made Him sit at His right hand in the heavenly realm.

(*Cent.*) ...the surpassing greatness of his might in us who believe, as seen in the energy of that resistless might which he exercised in raising Christ from the dead, and in seating him at his right hand in the heavenly heights...

(*Jordan*) May you experience the incredible outburst of his power in us who rely on his might and his abundant energy. This same energy working in Christ raised him from the dead and gave him spiritual victory and authority over every ruler...

EPHESIANS 1:19, 20 (Carpenter) Calculate, if you can, the gigantic power behind all this. Sons, quickened into life and consciousness. We say that we believe. Yes, but what a miracle that is! It means that there is a bridge which joins time with eternity, a road which leads from earth to heaven, and the feet of believers have been set on it...Christ is in countless ways the reversal of human expectations, and in no way more startlingly than by the Resurrection. If there was one thing that all men had, willy-nilly, to acknowledge, it was the fact that at the end of life comes death. Christ lived and died. Death had his usual triumph. But it was a short-lived mastery. "Death's pale-flag" was hoisted for a day and for a second day, and on the third day it was hauled down. And the Lamb of God, flying His own flag, was raised from the dead and entered into His glory. It was the beginning of the resumption of the original glory, which He had with the Father before the world was, but that glory was touched now with an added quality. The victory had been won within the terms of human life. The Risen Christ is victorious Mankind. In what we call the Ascension, which follows hard upon the triumph over death, the Son of God finally resumes the attributes of Godhead, but He is still Son of Man, Ambassador of Humanity, High Priest of Earth. He has taken our nature, not for one human generation only, but so as never more to lay it off, and thus it is that in Him man is now lifted to the divine level, where God is.

(Wade) ...and how transcendently great is His power manifested in us who have faith. That power in us is due to the same exercise of His Mighty Sovereignty as was displayed in the instance of the Christ...

(Beck) ...the vast resources of His power working in us who believe. It is the same mighty power with which He worked in Christ, raised Him from the dead...

(Lamsa) And what is the exceeding greatness of his power in us as the result of the things we believe, according to the skill of his mighty power.

(N. Berk.) ...how overwhelmingly great is His power...

(NEB) ...and how vast the resources of his power open to us who trust in him.

(Basic) ...And how unlimited is his power to us who have faith...

(Noli) ...and how immeasurable is his power in us who believe in him...

(Fenton) ...the exceeding greatness of His power in us believers, through His mighty energy, which energized in Christ...

(Wuest) ...the super abounding greatness of His inherent power to us who are believing ones as measured by the operative energy, of the manifested strength of His might...

(Swann) ...like the energy of the mighty powers which he exercised in the Christ...

(Pl. Eng.) ...this power works with the force of the might which he exercised in Christ, when he raised him from the dead, and seated him at his right hand in the heavenly world...

(AMP) ...His power in and for us who believe...

(Roth.) ...according to the working of the strength of His might, which he wrought in Christ, when He raised Him from the dead...

EPHESIANS 1:19, 20 (Kling.) ...the erupting greatness of his power...

(Syriac) ...what is the excellence of the majesty of his power in us who believe...

(NIV) ...incomparably great power...

(NAB) ...the immeasurable scope of his power in us who believe...

(RSV) ...in us who believe...

(Conc.) ...from among the dead...

(Stevens) ...whereby he has placed him in the supreme seat of authority in heaven.

(ABV) ...in the heavenly places...

(Phil.) That power is the same divine energy which was demonstrated in Christ when he raised him from the dead and gave him the place of supreme honor in Heaven...

(Authentic) ...indicated by the operation of the mighty force God employed in the case of Christ in raising him from the dead...

(Barclay) ...that power demonstrated in the action of the mighty strength which was operative in the case of Christ...

See redemption p. 72; prayer p. 240

EPHESIANS 1:21 Far above all principality and power, and might, and dominion and every name that is named, not only in this world, but also in that which is to come.

(GNB) Christ rules there above all heavenly rulers, authorities, powers, and lords; he has a title superior to all titles of authority in this world and in the next.

(Lau.) There Jesus sits above all rulers, above all authority, above all power, above all lords...

(Weym.) ...high above all other government and authority and power and dominion, and every title of sovereignty used either in this age or in the age to come.

(Carpenter) ...Above every kind of being that imagination can conceive, present or future, good or evil, Christ is supreme.

(Cornish) ...supreme in every way, untouched, unimpeded by the innumerable authorities, influences, powers, potentates of the world, having power over all other names to which authority is lent not only in this age, but in the next.

(Bruce) There now He sits enthroned, high above all principality and power, might and dominion, and every name of renown whether belonging to this present age or to the age to come.

(Phil.) ...a place that is infinitely superior to any conceivable command, authority, power or control, and which carries with it a name far beyond any name that could ever be used in this world or the world to come.

(Wms.) ...far above every other government, authority, power, and dominion, yea, far above every other title that can be conferred,...

(Barclay) There he gave him a place far above all spiritual powers, above every ruler and authority, and power and lord, above every possible title of honour...

See redemption p. 72; prayer p. 242

EPHESIANS 1:22 And hath put all things under his feet, and gave him to be the head over all things to the church.

(Johnson) In addition to all of creation, Christ also has full authority over the Church, the fellowship of Christpersons, to give it direction.

(K. & L.) He has subjected every single thing to his authority and has appointed him sovereign head of the Church...

(Wand) He hath put the universe under His feet. In so exalting Christ He has made Him Head of a Body, the Church.

(Gspd.) He has put everything under his feet and made him the indisputable head of the church...

(Barclay) He subjected everything to him, and he gave him as the supreme head to the church.

(Wade) He has reduced all things to subjection beneath His feet, and has given Him to the Church to be the Head over all...

(Noli) He has put all the universe under his rule, and made him the head of the Church.

(NEB) He put everything in subjection beneath his feet, and appointed him as supreme head to the church...

(Letters) God has put everything under Jesus and made Him the head of God's family of believers.

(Berk., N. Berk.) God has placed everything under His feet and has given Him as head over everything for the church...

(Knox) He has put everything under his dominion, and made him the head to which the whole Church is joined.

(GNB) God put all things under Christ's feet and gave him to the church as supreme Lord over all things.

(Weym.) God has put all things under His feet, and has appointed Him universal and supreme Head of the Church.

(Carpenter) But perhaps someone will say, "What is this to us? We do not doubt that your picture is true enough, and that the Lord Jesus is above all. But heaven is far away." My brother, heaven is here.

(Cornish) God has "put all things under his feet," made him the head of all things for the Church...

(Stevens) ...and has subordinated to him all existing powers and made him Sovereign over his church...

(Phil.) God has placed everything under the power of Christ and has set him up as head of everything for the Church.

(Mof.) ...and set him as head over everything for the church...

(Hudson) ...and appointed him supreme head of the church, his body...

EPHESIANS 1:22 (Pl. Eng.) ...and made him the head over all things for the church...

(*RSV*) ...for the church...

See prayer p. 243

EPHESIANS 1:23 Which is his body, the fulness of him that filleth all in all.

(*20th C.R.*) For the Church is Christ's Body, and is filled by him who fills all things everywhere with his presence.

(*Cress.*) The church is his body. The church has everything Christ has. And he has everything everywhere.

(*K. & L.*) ...which is truly his body, the complement of him who fills all the members with all graces.

(*Wand*) That Body provides a universal means of expression for one who is Himself a universal Personality.

(*Gspd.*) ...which is his body, filled by him who fills everything everywhere.

(*Barclay*) ...and the church is his body, the complement of him who completes all things everywhere.

(*NEB*) ...which is his body and as such holds within it the fullness of him who himself receives the entire fullness of God. (or, as supreme head to the church which is his body, and to be all that he himself is who fills the universe in all its parts.)

(*Letters*) ...which is filled with Jesus Himself, the one who makes us complete.

(*Knox*) ...so that the Church is his body, the completion of him who everywhere and in all things is complete.

(*GNB*) The church is Christ's body, the completion of him who himself completes all things everywhere.

(*Carpenter*) This same Jesus, Who is exalted at the right hand of God the Father, is the Head of the Church...The body is the instrument which every person has wherewith to accomplish the purposes of his will. In the Church the purpose and the will are those of Christ. We are the instrument...

(*Stevens*) ...his mystical body, which is filled and penetrated by his life.

(*Phil.*) For the Church is his body, and in that body lives fully the one who fills the whole wide universe.

(*Mof.*) ...the church which is his Body, filled by him who fills the universe entirely.

(*AMP*) ...for in that body lives the full measure of Him who makes everything complete, and who fills everything everywhere (with Himself).

(*Jordan*) ...his body, the full expression of him...

(*Black.*) ...the means of expression for him whose plentitude pervades all creation.

(*Bruce*) ...the body or complement, that is to say, of the One who fills the whole universe with His presence.

EPHESIANS 1:23 (Lau.) The church is His body and it is filled with Him...
See prayer p. 244

EPHESIANS 2:4, 5 But God, who is rich in mercy, for his great love wherewith he loved us, Even when we were dead in sins, hath quickened us together with Christ, (by grace ye are saved.)

(20th C. R.) Yet God, in his abundant compassion, and because of the great love with which he loved us, even though we were dead because of our offenses, gave life to us in giving Life to the Christ...

(GNB) But God's mercy is so abundant, and his love for us is so great, that while we were spiritually dead in our disobedience he brought us to life with Christ...

(K. & L.) ...was moved by the intense love with which he loved us...he made us live with the life of Christ...

(Jordan) ...God in his overflowing sympathy and great love breathed the same new life into us as into Christ.

(Noli) ...out of his excessive love for us.

(AMP) ...Because of and in order to satisfy the great and wonderful and intense love with which He loved us...He gave us the very life of Christ Himself, the same new life which He quickened Him.

(Way) Even when in trespasses we lay dead, Thrilled us with the same new life wherewith He quickened our Messiah - By free grace alone have ye obtained salvation!

(Knox) Our sins had made dead men of us, and he, in giving life to Christ, gave life to us too...

(Cony.) ...called us to share the life in Christ...

(Godbey) ...created life in us in Christ...

(Weekes, Basic, Phil.) ...gave us life together with Christ...

(Wade) ...spiritually dead...spiritually alive...

(Mar., Young) ...(by grace ye are having been saved)

(Lau., Wand, New Life) ...we have been saved.

(Cunn., Weym., NASB, NIV, Conf., Wade, 20th C. R., Godbey, Wms., Norlie, Pl. Eng., N. Berk., Trans., Mof., GNB, Jer., Gspd., RSV) ...you have been saved.

(ASV) ...have ye been saved.
See redemption p. 82; eternal life p. 386

EPHESIANS 2:6 And hath raised us up together, and made us sit together in heavenly places in Christ Jesus.

(AMP) And He raised us up together with Him and made us sit down together [giving us joint seating with Him] in the heavenly sphere [by virtue of our being] in Christ Jesus (the Messiah, the Anointed One).

EPHESIANS 2:6 (20th C. R.) And, through our union with Christ Jesus, God raised us with him, and caused us to sit with him on high.

>*(GNB)* In our union with Christ Jesus, he raised us up with him to rule with him in the heavenly world.
>
>*(K. & L.)* Together with Christ Jesus and in him, he raised us up and enthroned us in the heavenly realm...
>
>*(Way)* And with Him He raised us from the death sleep, and with Him throned us in the high Heavens, by virtue of our union with Messiah Jesus.
>
>*(Knox)* ...raised us up too, enthroned us too above the heavens, in Christ Jesus.
>
>*(Wms.)* And He raised us with Him and through union with Christ Jesus He made us sit down with Him in the heavenly realm...
>
>*(Barclay)* Because of our union with Christ Jesus he raised us from spiritual death, and gave us a seat with him in the heavenly places.
>
>*See redemption p. 83*

EPHESIANS 3:14 For this cause I bow my knees unto the Father of our Lord Jesus Christ.

>*(TLB)* When I think of the wisdom and scope of his plan I fall down on my knees and pray to the Father...
>
>*(Dist.)* I am overwhelmed with the immense significance of all this.
>
>*(Knox)* With this in mind, then, I fall on my knees...
>
>*See prayer p. 245*

EPHESIANS 3:15 Of whom the whole family in heaven and earth is named.

>*(Barclay)* ...that Father who is the origin and ideal of all fatherhood in heaven and on earth...
>
>*(20th C.R.)* ...from whom all 'fatherhood' in Heaven and on earth derives its name.
>
>*(ASV)* ...from whom every family...
>
>*(Knox)* ...takes its title.
>
>*See prayer p. 245*

EPHESIANS 3:16 That he would grant you, according to the riches of his glory, to be strengthened with might by his Spirit in the inner man.

>*(Wade)* ...that He may enable you, in virtue of the inexhaustible resources of His glorious Perfection, to become strengthened powerfully in your inmost selves through His Spirit...
>
>*(Johnson)* May he give you an infusion of strength in the depths of your being by the Spirit.
>
>*(Way)* I pray that He may, with a fulness measured only by the wealth of His own glory, vouch-safe to you to be made strong with power infused by His Spirit into your inmost nature.

EPHESIANS 3:16 (Wand) I pray then that out of the wealth of His glory He will grant you to be mightily strengthened by His Spirit in the very core of your being...

(Jer.) Out of his infinite glory, may he give you the power through his Spirit, for your hidden self to grow strong...

(Phil.) ...and I pray that out of the glorious richness of his resources he will enable you to know the strength of the Spirit's inner reinforcement...

(Letters) We ask to use His unlimited resources to make your spirit strong by His Spirit.

(Knox) May he, out of the rich treasury of his glory, strengthen you through his Spirit with a power that reaches your innermost being.

(Jordan) ...I beg him to give you, out of his glorious abundance, the power to win by his Spirit ruling your inner life.

(Carpenter) ...I am thinking of your inner selves, the deep well of character, whence actions and habits are thrown up. As a rich man keeps his chief treasures in an inner strong-room of his house, I want the deep centre of your life to be a stronghold where the Holy Spirit reigns, the Strengthener, the Comforter, where He and you together, He, the giver of Life, and you with your glad obedience, make up a mansion where our Lord can come and dwell.

(Dodd.) ...out of those redundant stores of goodness in his gracious heart which can never be exhausted, to be mightily strengthened by the effectual operation of his Spirit, invigorating and increasing every grace, and carrying on his work with abundant success, in the inner man...

(Smith, J. M.) ...strengthened with power by his Spirit in the interior man...For Christ to dwell by faith in your hearts; in love being rendered firm, and the foundation laid... endowed with power through His Spirit to the inmost core of your being.

(Berk., N. Berk.) ...empowered with strength in the inner self by His Spirit...

(Weym.) ...to be strengthened by His Spirit with power penetrating to your inmost being.

(Cent.) ...strengthened with might by his Spirit in your inmost being...

(K. & L.) ...strengthened with power through the Spirit for the development of your inner selves...

(Cornish) ...for the strengthening of that man who is invisible within, for infinite power to be given you according to the wealth of His glory spiritually...

(Conc.) ...to be made staunch with power, through His Spirit, in the man within...

(MacK.) ...endowing you with the knowledge of your privileges as believers, and with courage to maintain them.

(Conf.) ...strengthened with power through his Spirit unto the progress of the inner man...

(Adams) ...strengthened with power in the inner person...

(Trans.) ...strength and power through his Spirit in your inmost being...

(GNB) ...power to be strong in your inner selves...

EPHESIANS 3:16 (Authentic) ...powerfully strengthened in the inner self.

(Tomanek) ...in the man within...

(NIV, NEB) ...in your inner being...

(Wms.) ...in your inmost being...

See Holy Spirit p. 192; prayer p. 245

EPHESIANS 3:17 That Christ may dwell in your hearts by faith; that ye, being rooted and grounded in love.

(Wand) ...and that in response to your faith Christ will take up his abode in your hearts. Then you will be deeply rooted and securely grounded in love...

(Jordan) God grant that Christ, through your faith, might establish residence in your hearts. May love be your tap root and foundation.

(Weym.) I pray that Christ may make His home in your hearts through your faith; so that having your roots deep and your foundations strong in love...

(Wuest) ...that the Christ might finally settle down and feel completely at home in your hearts through your faith...

(Syriac) ...the Messiah may dwell by faith, and in your hearts by love, while your root and your foundation waxeth strong...

(Lamsa) That Christ may dwell in your inner man by faith, and in your hearts by love, strengthening your understanding and your foundation.

(Barclay) ...that love may be that in which your life is rooted and on which it is founded.

(TLB) ...May your roots go down deep into the soil of God's marvelous love...

(Lau.) ...I pray that the roots of your faith may grow deep in the ground of His love.

(Jer.) ...planted in love and built on love.

(Dodd.) ...by the continual exercise of a lively faith, by means of which a constant intercourse with him will be maintained...

(Cornish) ...I pray for those spiritual roots and foundations to be in you...

(NIV) ...rooted and established in love...

(Godbey) ...being rooted and grounded in divine love...

See prayer p. 247

EPHESIANS 3:18 May be able to comprehend with all saints what is the breadth, and length, and depth, and height...

(Wand) ...and you will be strong enough with the rest of the Brethren to grasp in all its breadth and length and height and depth.

(Johnson) I hope that you will be able to grasp with all God-persons the multidimensional love of God - a love broad enough to include everybody, long enough to reach to the ends of the earth, deep enough to unify our human fragmentation, and high enough to reach the very heart of God.

EPHESIANS 3:18 (Carver) ...yea even to know in all its dimensions the love of the Christ, his love for the world and God's love of which he is the embodiment and the perfect expression. We must do our utmost to know that love which in its full reaches is beyond knowing...

(K. & L.) Thus will you have the power to grasp fully together with all the saints, what is the breadth and length and height and depth (of this mystery)...

(Adams) ...may you, together with all of the saints, have the capacity to get a grasp of how broad, how long, how high and how deep Christ's love is...

(Dist.) I pray you will all grasp more & more of the profound scope of your spiritual position.

(Syriac) ...and that ye may be able to explore, with all the saints, what is the height and depth, and length and breadth...

(RSV) ...may have power to comprehend...

(Tomanek) ...so that you may be able to fully understand...

(Kling.) ...that you may be entirely able to lay hold with all saints...

(Roth. 2) ...that ye may be full mighty to grasp firmly...

(Johnson) Experiencing love like this, may you be overwhelmed with the awareness of the presence of God.

See prayer p. 247

EPHESIANS 3:19 And to know the love of Christ, which passeth knowledge, that ye might be filled with all the fulness of God.

(Wand) ...the conception of the love of Christ. That is a subject of knowledge which surpasses knowledge. Nevertheless through it you will attain to the complete measure of the Wholeness which is God.

(Carpenter) God is the Plenitude of power and glory. May He fill you to the utmost limits of your being with all that you can receive of what He has to give, and bring you in the end, just men made perfect, to the full and open vision of Himself...

(AMP) ...that you may be filled (through all your being) unto all the fulness of God— [that is] may have the richest measure of the divine Presence, and become a body wholly filled and flooded with God Himself!

(Wade) ...to the end that you may be made complete, up to the full measure of all God's completeness.

(Bruce) ...so may you be filled up to the measure of God's own fulness!

(Weym.) ...so that you may be made complete in accordance with God's own standard of completeness.

(Dodd.) ...that your expanded hearts, being dialated more and more, may be rendered capable of admitting larger degrees than ever of Divine love, and more ample indwellings of Divine consolation...

(NEB) So may you attain to fullness of being, the fullness of God himself.

EPHESIANS 3:19 (GNB) ...and so be completely filled with the very nature of God.

(*Knox*) ...May you be filled with all the completion God has to give.

(*Phil.*) ...May you be filled through all your being with God himself!

(*20th C. 1*) ...filled to the full with God himself.

(*Cony.*) ...that you may be filled therewith, even to the measure of the fulness of God.

(*Hudson*) ...filled with the full content of the divine nature.

(*Beck*) ...so you will be filled with all that is in God.

(*Basic*) ...so that you may be made complete as God himself is complete.

(*Fenton*) ...and to gain an idea how far the love of Christ exceeds our research...

(*Kling.*) ...that you might know the erupting knowledge of the love of Christ...

(*Cornish*) ...and to understand the love of the Christ which goes far beyond all material comprehension...

(*Godbey*) ...and to know the divine love of Christ...

(*Authentic*) ...filled with the immensity of God.

See prayer p. 248

EPHESIANS 3:20 Now unto him that is able to do exceeding abundantly above all that we ask or think, according to the power that worketh in us...

(*Wade*) To Him Who is able to transcend all limits - to do far in excess of all that we request or imagine, in virtue of His Power which is active in us...

(*Weym.*) Now to Him who, in the exercise of His power that is at work within us, is able to do infinitely beyond all our highest prayers or thoughts...

(*Knox*) He whose power is at work in us is powerful enough, and more than powerful enough, to carry out his purpose beyond all our hopes and dreams...

(*Authentic*) Now to him who is supremely powerful to do infinitely more than we can ask or think, in accordance with the power that operates in us.

(*Norlie*) He who exerts His power within us is able to do in full measure far more than all that we ask for or can think of.

(*Mof.*) Now to him who by the action of his power within us is able to do all things, aye far more than we can ever ask or imagine...

(*Conc.*) Now to Him Who is able to do superexcessively above all that we are requesting or apprehending, according to the power that is operating in us...

(*Barclay*) Now unto him who can do for us far more than our lips can ask or our minds conceive through that power of his which is at work in us...

(*Dist.*) Results beyond our thoughts will arise from these beginnings in which we now participate.

(*NEB*) Now to him who is able to do immeasurably more than all we can ask or conceive...

EPHESIANS 3:20 (Way) ...To an extent whose measure is that mighty impulse which thrills us through...

> *(Conf.)* Now, to him who is able to accomplish all things in a measure far beyond what we ask or conceive...
>
> *(Jordan)* Now to him who is able, by the power energizing us...
>
> *(TLB)* ...infinitely beyond our highest prayers, desires, thoughts, or hopes.
>
> *(Syriac)* ...by his almighty power...
>
> *(Roth.)* ...according to the power which doth energize itself within us...
>
> *(Roth. 2)* ...according to the power that is inwardly working itself in us...
>
> *(Fenton)* ...by means of His power energizing in us...
>
> *(Johnson)* Now to God, who can do by the power that exists in us greater things than we are able even to imagine or request...
>
> *See prayer p. 249*

EPHESIANS 3:21 Unto him be glory in the church by Christ Jesus throughout all ages, world without end. Amen.

> *(New Life)* May we see His shining greatness in the church...
>
> *See prayer p. 250*

EPHESIANS 4:27 Neither give place to the devil.

> *(AMP)* Leave no (such) room or foothold for the devil - give no opportunity to him.
>
> *(NEB)* ...leave no loop-hole for the devil.
>
> *(Wms.)* ...stop giving the devil a chance.
>
> *(Knox)* Do not give the devil his opportunity.
>
> *(Barclay)* Give the Devil no place or opportunity in your life.
>
> *(Mof.)* ...give the devil no chance.
>
> *(Jordan)* ...don't give in one inch to the Devil.
>
> *(Pl. Eng.)* ...do not make room for the devil...
>
> *(Trans.)* ...and do not give the devil a chance.
>
> *(Weym.)* ...do not leave room for the Devil.
>
> *(Berk.)* Do not give the devil an opportunity.
>
> *(Jer.)* ... never let the sun set on your anger or else you will give the devil a foothold.
>
> *(Wand)* It is when we are in a sulky frame of mind that the devil has his greatest opportunity.
>
> *(Beck)* Don't give the devil a chance to work.
>
> *See divine healing p. 285*

EPHESIANS 6:10 Finally, my brethren, be strong in the Lord, and in the power of his might.

> *(Cony.)* ...let your hearts be strengthened in the Lord and in the conquering power of His might.

EPHESIANS 6:10 (GNB) Finally, build up your strength in union with the Lord and by means of his mighty power.

> *(Barclay)* Finally, your union with the Lord and with his mighty power must give you a dynamic strength.
>
> *(Knox)* ...draw your strength from the Lord, from that mastery which his power supplies.
>
> *(TLB)* ...your strength must come from the Lord's mighty power within you.
>
> *(Phil.)* In conclusion, be strong - not in yourselves but in the Lord, in the power of his boundless resource.
>
> *(AMP)* ...be empowered through your union with Him; draw your strength from Him - that strength which His (boundless) might provides.
>
> *(Trans.)* Finally, draw upon the Lord's power and let him supply you with his mighty strength.
>
> *(Weym.)* In conclusion, strengthen yourselves in the Lord and in the power which His supreme might imparts.
>
> *(Wand)* For the rest let all alike realize the strength they possess in the Lord and in the power of His might.

EPHESIANS 6:11 Put on the whole armour of God, that ye may be able to stand against the wiles of the devil.

> *(Jordan)* Put on God's uniform so as to be able to withstand all the Devil's tricks.
>
> *(Authentic)* Array yourselves in the full armour of God, so that you may stand up to the cunning of the Adversary.
>
> *(Knox)* You must wear all the weapons in God's armoury, if you would find strength to resist the cunning of the devil.
>
> *(TLB)* ...so that you will be able to stand safe against all strategies and tricks of Satan.
>
> *(Phil.)* Put on God's complete armor so that you can successfully resist all the devil's methods of attack.
>
> *(AMP)* ...that you may be able successfully to stand up against (all) the strategies and the deceits of the devil.
>
> *(Basic)* Take up God's instruments of war...
>
> *(Wand)* Arm yourselves with the full equipment that God has provided to enable His soldiers to hold their own against the tactics of the Devil.

EPHESIANS 6:12 For we wrestle not against flesh and blood, but against principalities, against powers, against the rulers of the darkness of this world, against spiritual wickedness in high places.

> *(Jer.)* For it is not against human enemies that we have to struggle, but against the Sovereignties and the Powers who originate the darkness in this world, the spiritual army of evil in the heavens.

EPHESIANS 6:12 (Way) ...with Principalities, with Powers, with the Lords of Darkness whose present sway is world wide, with the spirit-host of Wicked Beings that haunt the upper air.

(Barclay) For our struggle is not against any human foe...

(Roth. 2) ...against the world-holders of this darkness...

(TLB) For we are not fighting against people made of flesh and blood, but against persons without bodies - the evil rulers of the unseen world, those mighty satanic beings and great evil princes of darkness who rule this world; and against huge numbers of wicked spirits in the spirit world.

(Phil.) For our fight is not against any physical enemy: it is against organizations and powers that are spiritual. We are up against the unseen power that controls this dark world, and spiritual agents, from the very headquarters of evil.

(New Life) Our fight is not with people...

(Trans.) We are not fighting against human enemies, but against the rulers and the authorities, against the world-rulers of this dark age, against the spirit-forces of evil in the supernatural world.

(Weym.) For ours is not a conflict with mere flesh and blood, but with the despotisms, the empires, the forces that control and govern this dark world - the spiritual hosts of evil arrayed against us in the heavenly warfare.

(Wand) We need it all, for our contest is not against flesh and blood but against demonic rulers, potentates, dictators of this dark age, forces of evil in the spiritual sphere.

EPHESIANS 6:13 Wherefore take unto you the whole armor of God, that ye may be able to withstand in the evil day, and having done all, to stand.

(Cony.) ...and having overthrown them all, to stand unshaken.

(Norlie) ...In that way you may be able to make a stand when the evil day comes and, when it is all over, you will still be holding your own.

(Authentic) ...and having overcome completely to go on standing.

(Way) ...to stand unstaggered still.

(Mof.) ...that you may be able to make a stand upon the evil day and hold your ground by overcoming all the foe.

(TLB) So use every piece of God's armor to resist the enemy whenever he attacks, and when it is all over, you will still be standing up.

(Weym.) Therefore put on the complete armour of God, so that you may be able to stand your ground on the day of battle, and, having fought to the end, to remain victors on the field.

(Wand) Therefore take the whole divine equipment, which will enable you to maintain your stand in the evil day and to remain victorious on the field of battle.

(Beck) ...then you can resist when things are at their worst and having done everything, you can hold your ground.

EPHESIANS 6:14 Stand therefore, having your loins girt about with truth, and having on the breastplate of righteousness...

(Wms.) Hold your position, then...

(Mof.) Hold your ground...

(Barclay) So then take your stand.

EPHESIANS 6:15 And your feet shod with the preparation of the gospel of peace...

(Way) Your feet shod with that preparedness to face the foe which is a fruit of the Gladtidings of peace.

EPHESIANS 6:16 Above all, taking the shield of faith, wherewith ye shall be able to put out all the fire-tipped arrows shot by the evil one...

(Wms.) ...take on the shield which faith provides, for with it you will be able to quench all the fiery darts of the wicked.

(Basic) ...And most of all, using faith as a cover to keep off all the flaming arrows of the evil one.

(NAB) In all circumstances hold faith up before you as your shield...

(New Life) Most important of all, you need a covering of faith in front of you...

(Barclay) Through thick and thin take faith as your shield.

(Roth.) With all having taken up the shield of faith wherewith ye shall have power over all the ignited darts of the wicked one to quench...

(Jordan) Above all, take the bulletproof vest of faith, with which you'll be able to stop the tracer bullets of the evil one.

(Gspd.) ...the flaming missiles of the evil one...

See faith p. 161

PHILIPPIANS 2:9 Wherefore God also hath highly exalted him, and given him a name which is above every name:...

(Weym.) ...[God] has conferred on Him the Name which is supreme above every other...

(Fenton) ...the Name surpassing every name;...

(Worrell) ...bestowed upon Him the name...

(Wand) ...God has ennobled Him and given Him a title above all others...

(20th C. 1) ...God raised him to the very highest place, and gave him the Name which ranks above all others...

(Barclay) That is why God has given him the highest place, and has conferred on him the name that is greater than any name...

(Trans.) ...God raised him to the highest place and conferred on him the name that is above all others...

PHILIPPIANS 2:9 (Tomanek) ...God supremely exalted Him...

PHILIPPIANS 2:10 That at the name of Jesus every knee should bow, of things in heaven, and things in earth, and things under the earth...

>*(Weym.)* ...in order that in the Name of Jesus every knee should bow, of beings in Heaven, of those on the earth, and of those in the underworld...

>*(Fenton)* ...so that in presence of the name of Jesus every knee should bend...

>*(Jer.)* ...so that all beings in the heavens, on earth and in the underworld...

>*(Barclay)* ...so that at the name of Jesus every creature in heaven, and on earth, and beneath the earth should kneel in reverence and submission...

>*(Roth. 2)* ...of beings in heaven, and on earth and underground...

>*(Wand)* ...so that at the mere mention of it every living being in the whole universe, whether in Heaven, on earth, or in hell, must do humble reverence...

>*(Way)* ...dwellers in heaven, on earth, in the underworld, And every tongue shall utter this confession, "Jesus the Messiah is Lord!" So rendering glory to God the Father.

COLOSSIANS 2:15 And having spoiled principalities and powers, he made a show of them openly, triumphing over them in it.

>*(20th C.R.)* He rid himself of all the Powers of Evil, and held them up to open contempt, when he celebrated his triumph over them on the cross!

>*(Barclay)* On the cross he stripped the demonic powers and authorities of their power, and made a public spectacle of them, as if they had been captives in a victor's triumphal procession.

>*(Way)* He stripped away from Himself all trammels of "Principalities and Powers:" He paraded them unsparingly, as He haled them in the Triumph of the Cross.

>*(Cony.)* And He disarmed the Principalities and the Powers [which fought against Him], and put them to open shame, leading them captive in the triumph of Christ.

>*(Phil.)* And then, having drawn the sting of all the powers ranged against us, he exposed them, shattered, empty and defeated, in his final glorious triumphant act!

>*(Weym.)* And the hostile princes and rulers He shook off from Himself, and boldly displayed them as His conquests, when by the Cross He triumphed over them.

>*(Trans.)* There *Christ stripped** the demonic rulers and authorities of their power over him, and in his own triumph made a public show of them. (* "en auto" – may mean "in him" or "in it"– the cross. ** The verb here translated "stripped," used for the stripping off of clothes may denote an action done by oneself or by someone else.)

>*(Wand)* ...he stripped away like a cast-off garment every demonic Rule and Authority and made a public exhibition of them...

COLOSSIANS 2:15 (Noli) He despoiled the infernal dominions and realms. He dragged their rulers as captives in procession, and through his Cross he led us all to triumph.

(Lau.) And He tore the swords from the hands of all the spirit rulers and the powers in the spirit.

(Alf.) ...in him.

(Douay) ...in himself.

See redemption p. 68

HEBREWS 2:14, 15 Forasmuch then as the children are partakers of flesh and blood, he also himself likewise took part of the same; that through death he might destroy him that had the power of death, that is, the devil; And deliver them, who through fear of death were all their lifetime subject to bondage.

(Jer.) ...so that by his death were all their lifetime subject to bondage.

(Jordan) ...he might break the grip of the one who controls death...

(Wuest) ...He might render inoperative the one having the dominion of death, that is, the devil, and effect the release of those...

(Weekes) ...he might put an end to him who possesseth the lordship of death...

(Norlie) ...who has the power of death...

(Alf.) ...hath...

(Cent.) ...he might render powerless him...

(River.) ...he might defeat him...

(Wand) ...He might frustrate...

(Godbey) ...he might set at naught him who has the power of death...

(Cony.) ...He might destroy the lord of death, that is, the Devil.

(Phil.) ...so that by going through death as a man...

(Roth.) ...He might paralyze hirn...

(Wms.) ...He by His death might put a stop to the power of him who has the power of death; that is, the devil.

(Authentic) ...he might put out of commission him who wields the power of death, namely the Devil...

(Wade) ...He might reduce to impotence him who has in Death the instrument of his sway, that is, the Devil...

(Noli) ...to overthrow the devil who has the power of death.

(Way) He did this, that he might be able to die, and by His death might annihilate the power of him who sways the sceptre of death's terrors - that is, the devil - and so might transfer into a new existence those who through the haunting dread of death were all their lifetime bowed beneath a yoke of veritable slavery.

HEBREWS 2:14, 15 (Pl. Eng.) ...by death he might bring to nothing the lord of death, that is the devil, and might set free from slavery all those that all their lives had lived in fear of death.

(Knox) ...he would depose the prince of death...he would deliver those multitudes who lived all their while as slaves, made over to the fear of death.

(Gspd.) ...he might dethrone the lord of death, the devil, and free from their slavery men who had always lived in fear of death.

(NASB) ...He might render powerless...

(Weym.) ...He might render powerless him who had authority over death, that is, the Devil, and might set at liberty all those...

(AMP) ...that by (going through) death He might bring to naught and make of no effect him who had the power of death...And also that He might deliver and completely set free all those who through the (haunting) fear of death were held in bondage through the whole course of their lives.

(Basic) ...he took a body himself and became like them; so that by his death he might put an end to him who had the power of death, that is to say, the Evil One; And let those who all their lives were in chains because of their fear of death, go free.

(Lau.) ...He died as we die, so that He might destroy the devil, who is the king of death. He set us free from death. We need no longer be slaves to the fear of death.

(Mof.) ...he might crush him who wields the power of death (that is to say, the devil) and release from thraldom those who lay under a life-long fear of death.

(TLB) ...for only as a human being could he die and in dying break the power of the devil who had the power of death. Only in that way could he deliver those...

(20th C. R.) ...that by death he might render powerless him whose power lies in death - that is, the Devil - and so might deliver all those who, from fear of death, had all their lives been living in slavery.

See redemption p. 70

JAMES 4:7 Submit yourselves therefore to God. Resist the devil, and he will flee from you.

(Roth. 2) Range yourselves, therefore, under God; but withstand the adversary, and he will flee from you.

(Jordan) ...Put up a fight against the devil, and he'll run from you.

(NEB) ...Stand up to the devil and he will turn and run.

(Wuest) ...Stand immovable against the onset of the devil and he will flee from you.

(Fenton) ...repel the Devil...

(Barclay) So then, accept the authority of God. Take a stand against the devil, and he will run away from you.

(Basic) ...be ruled by God; but make war on the Evil One and he will be put to flight before you.

See divine healing p. 286

I PETER 5:8 Be sober, be vigilant; because your adversary the devil, as a roaring lion, walketh about, seeking whom he may devour...

> *(Wand)* Don't get excited but be continually on the watch, for the Devil like a roaring lion is continually on the prowl to see of whom he can make a meal.
>
> *(Beck)* Keep a clear head and watch!
>
> *(Berk.)* Be composed! Be on your guard. Your accuser...
>
> *(20th C. 1)* ...prowling about eager to devour you.
>
> *(Wms.)* Be calm and alert. Your opponent the devil...
>
> *(Jordan)* Sober up now, and get with it. That old roaring lion - your adversary, the Devil - is stalking around looking for someone to gobble up.
>
> *See divine healing p. 287*

I PETER 5:9 Whom resist stedfast in the faith, knowing that the same afflictions are accomplished in your brethren that are in the world.

> *(Jordan)* Put steel in your faith and stand up to him...
>
> *(Barclay)* You must resist him with a rock-like faith...
>
> *(Knox)* ...but you, grounded in the faith, must face him boldly...
>
> *(Wuest)* Stand immovable against his onset, solid as a rock in your faith...
>
> *(NEB)* Stand up to him...
>
> *(AMP)* ...be firm in faith [against his onset], - rooted, established, strong, immovable and determined...
>
> *See divine healing p. 287*

Our **ONLY** safeguard from dropping back into our natural mind with which we can receive nothing from God is by **BEING FILLED** and filled again with the Holy Spirit.

Smith Wigglesworth

PSALM

37:4 227

55:22 227

100:2 227

100:4 227

ISAIAH

28:11 227

28:12 227

43:26 228

JEREMIAH

33:3 228

MATTHEW

7:7 228

7:8 228

7:11 229

18:18 229

18:19 230

MARK

11:24 230

11:25 231

JOHN

15:7 231

16:23 232

16:24 232

ACTS

4:24 232

4:29 233

4:30 233

4:31 234

4:32 234

16:25 234

ROMANS

8:26 235

8:27 235

8:28 236

I CORINTHIANS

14:2 236

14:4 236

14:14 237

14:15 237

EPHESIANS

1:16, 17 238

1:18 239

1:19, 20 240

1:21 242

1:22 243

1:23 244

3:14 245

3:15 245

3:16 245

3:17 247

3:18 247

3:19 248

3:20 249

3:21 250

6:18 250

PHILIPPIANS

4:6 251

4:7 252

COLOSSIANS

1:9 252

1:10 253

1:11 254

1:12 255

1:13 256

1:14 257

3:16 257

I TIMOTHY

2:1 258

2:2 258

2:3 258

2:4 259

2:8 259

HEBREWS

13:15 259

JAMES

1:5-7 260

5:13-18 260

I PETER

3:12 262

5:7 262

I JOHN

5:14 263

5:15 263

JUDE

20 264

You can never take a vacation from your **PRAYER** life.

Mark Hankins

PSALM 37:4 Delight thyself also in the Lord; and he shall give thee the desires of thine heart.
   (Knox) ...all thy longing fixed in the Lord; so he will give thee what thy heart desires.
   (NEB) Depend upon the Lord, and he will grant you your heart's desire.
   (Jer.) ...make Yahweh your only joy and he will give you what your heart desires.
   (Young) ...the petitions of thy heart.

PSALM 55:22 Cast thy burden upon the Lord, and he shall sustain thee: he shall never suffer the righteous to be moved.
   (AMP) Cast your burden on the Lord [releasing the weight of it] and He will sustain you; He will never allow the [consistently] righteous to be moved—made to slip, fall or fail.
   (Har.) Commit your problems to the Lord and He will uphold you...
   (TLB) Give your burdens to the Lord. He will carry them....
   (NIV) ...he will never let the righteous fall.
   (NAB) ...never will he permit the just man to be disturbed.

PSALM 100:2 Serve the Lord with gladness: come before his presence with singing.
   (Beck) ...come before Him shouting happily.
   (Basic) Give worship to the Lord with joy...
   (Roth.) Serve Yahweh with rejoicing, enter before him, with shouts of triumph.
   (Douay) ...Come in before his presence with exceeding great joy.
   (Jer.) ...serve Yahweh gladly, come into his presence with songs of joy!

PSALM 100:4 Enter into his gates with thanksgiving, and into his courts with praise: be thankful unto him, and bless his name.
   (Jer.) Walk through his porticoes giving thanks, enter his courts praising him, give thanks to him, bless his name!

ISAIAH 28:11 For with stammering lips and another tongue will he speak to this people.
   (Roth.) For with a jabbering lip, and with an alien tongue must he speak unto this people!
   See holy spirit p. 179

ISAIAH 28:12 To whom he said, This is the rest wherewith ye may cause the weary to rest; and this is the refreshing: yet they would not hear.
   (Basic) ...and by this you may get new strength...
   (TLB) They could have rest in their own land if they would obey him, if they were kind and good...
   (AMP) This is the true rest [the way to true comfort and happiness]...
   See peace p. 349

ISAIAH 43:26 Put me in remembrance; let us plead together: declare thou, that thou mayest be justified.

> *(ASV)* ...set thou forth thy cause...
>
> *(Jer.)* ...state your own case...
>
> *(Knox)* ...tell me what plea thou hast to bring forward.

JEREMIAH 33:3 Call unto me, and I will answer thee, and shew thee great and mighty things, which thou knowest not.

> *(TLB)* Ask me and I will tell you some remarkable secrets about what is going to happen here.
>
> *(AMP)* Call to Me and I will answer you and show you great and mighty things, fenced in and hidden, which you do not know (do not distinguish and recognize, have knowledge of and understand).
>
> *(Basic)* Let your cry come to me, and I will give you an answer...
>
> *(NIV)* ...and tell you great and unsearchable things you do not know.

MATTHEW 7:7 Ask, and it shall be given you; seek, and ye shall find; knock, and it shall be opened unto you...

> *(Johnson)* Here are three simple directives for living in the Spirit dimension...
>
> *(Knox)* Ask, and the gift will come...
>
> *(Wade)* Ask, and what you ask for will be given to you; seek, and what you seek you will find; knock, and the door at which you knock will be opened to you.
>
> *(Basic)* Make a request, and it will be answered; what you are searching for you will get; give the sign, and the door will be open to you...
>
> *(New Life)* Ask, and what you are asking for will be given to you. Look, and what you are looking for you will find. Knock, and the door you are knocking on will be opened to you.
>
> *(K. & L.)* ...knock, and you will gain admission.
>
> *(TLB)* Ask, and you will be given what you ask for...
>
> *(Mof.)* Ask and the gift will be yours...

MATTHEW 7:8 For every one that asketh receiveth; and he that seeketh findeth; and to him that knocketh it shall be opened.

> *(Basic)* Because to everyone who makes a request, it will be given; and he who is searching will get his desires, and to him who gives the sign, the door will be open.
>
> *(Jer.)* ...the one who knocks will always have the door opened to him.
>
> *(Phil.)* The one who asks will always receive; the one who is searching will always find...

MATTHEW 7:8 (New Life) Everyone who asks receives what he asks for. Everyone who looks finds what he is looking for...

(K. & L.) In fact, only he who asks receives; only he who seeks finds; only he who knocks will gain admission.

(Mof.) ...for everyone who asks receives, the seeker finds, the door is opened to anyone who knocks.

MATTHEW 7:11 If ye then, being evil, know how to give good gifts unto your children, how much more shall your Father which is in heaven give good things to them that ask him?

(Phil.) If you, then, for all your evil, quite naturally give good things to your children, how much more likely is it that your Heavenly Father will give good things to those who ask him?

(Wade) ...how much more readily will your Father that is in the Heavens give what is good to those who ask Him?

(Barclay) ...how much more can you depend on your Father in heaven to give good things...

(N. Berk.) ...how much more surely...

(TLB) And if you hardhearted, sinful men know how to give good gifts to your children, won't your Father in heaven even more certainly give good gifts to those who ask him for them?

(Knox) Why then, if you, evil as you are, know well enough how to give your children what is good for them, is not your Father in heaven much more ready to give wholesome gifts to those who ask him?

(Johnson) If you, then, being human respond to the legitimate desires and needs of your children, do you not know that to a greater extent, your Father, the source of all being, will give you the true needs and desires of your life?

(Gspd.) So if you, bad as you are, know enough to give your children what is good, how much more surely will your Father in heaven give what is good to those who ask him for it!

See finances p. 303

MATTHEW 18:18 Verily I say unto you, Whatsoever ye shall bind on earth shall be bound in heaven; and whatsoever ye shall loose on earth shall be loosed in heaven.

(Condon, Trans., NEB, Cunn.) ...forbid...forbidden...allow...allowed...

(Basic) Whatever things are fixed by you on earth will be fixed in heaven: and whatever you make free on earth will be made free in heaven.

(Pl. Eng., Cent.) ...forbid...forbidden...permit...permitted.

(Rieu) ...whatever you forbid on earth shall be forbidden by Heaven, and whatever you allow on earth shall be allowed by Heaven.

MATTHEW 18:18 (Mof.) ...prohibit...prohibited...permit...permitted...

(*Barclay*) I tell you truly, all that you forbid on earth will be forbidden in heaven, and all that you allow on earth will be allowed in heaven.

(*GNB*) And so I tell all of you:...prohibit...prohibited...permit...permitted...

See authority of the believer p. 199

MATTHEW 18:19 Again I say unto you, That if two of you shall agree on earth as touching anything that they shall ask, it shall be done for them of my Father which is in heaven.

(*Cent.*) ...if two of you on earth symphonize your praying...

(*K. & L.*) But I tell you with the same assurance...

(*Knox*) ...if two of you agree over any request that you make on earth, it will be granted them by my Father who is in heaven.

(*Beck*) ...My Father in heaven will certainly do it for you.

(*Authentic*) ...my heavenly Father will undertake it for you.

(*Jordan*) ...if two of you in the physical realm covenant together about any matter of concern, it will be acted on for them by my spiritual Father.

(*Condon*) ...whenever two of you on earth pray together with one voice for something they need...

(*AMP*) ...agree (harmonize together, make a symphony together) about whatever [anything and everything] they may ask...

(*Norlie*) ...if two of you agree on earth about any request, you will certainly obtain it from my Father in heaven.

(*Johnson*) ...If two of you can be in harmony...

(*River.*) ...if two of you agree on earth regarding any matter, whatever they pray for will come to them from my Father in heaven.

(*Jer.*) ...anything at all...

MARK 11:24 Therefore I say unto you, What things soever ye desire, when ye pray, believe that ye receive them, and ye shall have them.

(*Book*) ...believe that you have received them...

(*Johnson*) Because of this principle, when you discover your soul's deepest desires, state them in your prayers, and consider them to have occurred - they will!

(*Knox*) I tell you, then, when you ask for anything in prayer, you have only to believe that it is yours, and it will be granted you.

(*Godbey*) ...believe that you just now received them, and they shall be unto you.

(*N. Berk.*) ...believe that you have received it and it will be yours.

(*NASB, NEB, Condon, Phil., GNB, Cent.*) ...believe that you have received them, and they shall be granted you.

MARK 11:24 *(Jer.)* ...believe that you have it already, and it will be yours.

(Wade) ...believe that you have as good as received, and you will get them.

(20th C. 1) ...Have faith that whatever you ask for in prayer is already granted you, and it will be yours.

(NAB) I give you my word...

(Wuest) ...be believing that you received them, and they shall be yours.

(Wms.) ...have faith that it has been granted you, and you will get it.

(Mof.) ...believe you have got it, and you shall have it.

(Roth.) ...All things whatsoever ye are praying for and asking believe that ye have received, and they shall be yours.

(AMP) ...believe (trust and be confident) that it is granted to you, and you will [get it].

(River.) ...believe that you have obtained them and you will have them.

> *See faith p. 149*

MARK 11:25 And when ye stand praying, forgive, if you have ought against any; that your Father also which is in heaven may forgive you your trespasses.

(Gspd.) ...if you have a grievance against anyone, forgive him...

(NIV) ...if you hold anything against anyone...

(AMP) ...if you have anything against any one, forgive him and let it drop (leave it, let it go) in order that your Father who is in heaven may also forgive you your [own] failings and shortcomings and let them drop.

(Noli) ...forgive any grievance you have against anyone...

(Phil.) ...you must forgive anything that you are holding against anyone else...

JOHN 15:7 If ye abide in me, and my words abide in you, ye shall ask what ye will, and it shall be done unto you.

(NAB) If you live in me, and my words stay part of you...

(Wms.) If you remain in union...

(Berk.) If you remain in Me and My words remain in you, then you may ask what you want and it will take place for you.

(Wuest) If you maintain a living communion with me and my words are at home in you, I command you to ask, at once, something for yourself, whatever your heart desires, and it will become yours.

(New Life) If you get your life from Me and My Words live in you, ask whatever you want. It will be done for you.

(Crickmer) Supposing ye-shall-have-got-to-stop in-organic oneness with Me, and-moreover the flowing sap of the utterances of Me working organically-in you shall-have-got-to-stop unimpeded in their circulation, whatever ye-like ye-shall-be-asking, and to-you actually realized-shall-it-be-Fruit making word.

JOHN 15:7 (Gspd.) If you remain united to me and my words remain in your hearts, ask for whatever you please and you shall have it.

> *(K. & L.)* As long as you remain united with me, and my teachings remain your rule of life, you may ask for anything you wish, and you shall have it.
> *(Mof.)* ...ask whatever you like and you shall have it.
> *(Roth.)* ...and my sayings in you abide whatsoever ye may be desiring ask! And it shall be brought to pass for you.
> *(20th C. 1)* If you remain united to me, and my teaching remains in your hearts, ask whatever you wish, and you shall have it.
> *(Roth. 2)* If perchance ye abide in me, and my sayings in you abide, whatsoever ye desire, ask! And it shall be brought to pass for you.
> *(Cent.)* ...ask whatever your will is, and it shall be yours.
> *See faith p. 153*

JOHN 16:23 And in that day ye shall ask me nothing. Verily, verily, I say unto you, Whatsoever ye shall ask the Father in my name, he will give it you.

> *(Tomanek)* ...you will not ask Me for anything.
> *(TLB)* At that time you won't need to ask me for anything, for you can go directly to the Father and ask him, and he will give you what you ask for because you use my name.
> *(Knox)* ...Believe me, you have only to make any request of the Father in my name, and he will grant it to you.
> *(Wms.)* ...the Father will give you, as bearers of my name, whatever you ask Him for.
> *(New Life)* ...For sure, I tell you...

JOHN 16:24 Hitherto have ye asked nothing in my name: ask, and ye shall receive, that your joy may be full.

> *(TLB)* You haven't tried this before, [but begin now]. Ask, using my name, and you will receive, and your cup of joy will overflow.
> *(Knox)* Until now, you have not been making any requests in my name; make them, and they will be granted, to bring you gladness in full measure.
> *(Wms.)* Up to this time you have not asked for anything as bearers of my name, but now you must keep on asking, and you will receive, that your cup of joy may be full to the brim.
> *See joy p. 341*

ACTS 4:24 And when they heard that, they lifted up their voice to God with one accord, and said, Lord, thou art God, which hast made heaven, and earth, and the sea, and all that in them is...

> *(Godbey)* ...they unanimously lifted up their voice to God...

ACTS 4:24 (RSV) ...they lifted their voices together to God...

    (N. Berk.) ...unitedly raised their voices to God...

    (Rieu) ...they raised their voices to God in unity of spirit...

    (Jer.) ...they lifted up their voice to God all together...

    (Wade) ...raised in concert their voices to God...

    (Wms.) ...with one united prayer to God...

    (Barclay) ...they joined in united prayer to God...

    (NEB) ...they raised their voices as one man and called upon God...

    (20th C. R.) ...moved by a common impulse, raised their voices to God in prayer...

    (Trans.) ...they all prayed out loud to God together...

    (Authentic) ...they cried aloud to God with one accord...

    (Phil.) ...they raised their voices to God in united prayer...

    (Jordan) ...all of them lifted up a united voice to God...

ACTS 4:29 And now, Lord, behold their threatenings: and grant unto thy servants, that with all boldness they may speak thy word,...

    (Roth. 2) ...give to thy servants with all freedom of utterance to be speaking thy word...

    (Phil.) ...give thy servants courage to speak thy word fearlessly...

    (Barclay) ...grant to your servants fearlessly and freely to speak your word...

    (Wuest) ...grant at once to your bondslaves the ability to be speaking your word with all fearless confidence and freedom of speech...

    (AMP) ...grant to Your bond servants [full freedom] to declare Your message fearlessly...

    (Berk.) ...endow thy servants with fearlessness to speak Thy word...

    (Jordan) ...and give us, your slaves, the guts to tell your word like it is...

    (Noli) ...Grant to your servants the power to proclaim your message fearlessly.

    (NAB) ...Grant to your servants, even as they speak your words, complete assurance...

    (Mof.) ...grant that thy servants may be perfectly fearless in speaking thy word...

    (Deaf) ...Help us to speak the things you want us to say without fear.

    (K. & L.) ...grant to your servants courage to speak your message with complete and firm assurance...

      See signs and wonders p. 410

ACTS 4:30 By stretching forth thine hand to heal; and that signs and wonders may be done by the name of thy holy child Jesus.

    (Barclay) ...and act yourself to heal and to cause wonderful demonstrations of your power to happen through the name of your holy servant Jesus.

    (Wuest) ...while you stretch out your hand to heal, and grant that attesting miracles and miracles which arouse wonder may be done...

ACTS 4:30 (AMP) ...While You stretch out Your hand to cure and to perform signs and wonders through the authority and by the power of the name of Your Holy Child and Servant Jesus.

> *(Mof.)* ...when thy hand is stretched out to heal...
>
> *(Berk.)* ...as Thou reachest out Thy hand to heal and to work signs and wonders through the name of Thy holy Servant Jesus.
>
> *(Wade)* ...by exerting Thy Active Power to bring about Healing...
>
> *See signs and wonders p. 410*

ACTS 4:31 And when they had prayed, the place was shaken where they were assembled together; and they were all filled with the Holy Ghost, and they spake the word of God with boldness.

> *(Roth. 2)* ...speaking the word of God with freedom of utterance.
>
> *(Barclay)* ...and they freely and fearlessly spoke God's word.
>
> *(Wuest)* ...with fearless confidence and freedom of speech.
>
> *(AMP)* ...with freedom and boldness and courage.
>
> *(K. & L.)* ...and they continued to speak the message of God with firm assurance.
>
> *(Deaf)* ...they continued to speak God's message without fear.
>
> *(NAB)* ...and continued to speak God's word with confidence.
>
> *(Noli)* ...and fearlessly proclaimed the message of God.
>
> *(Phil.)* ...and spoke the Word of God fearlessly.
>
> *(NEB)* ...the building where they were assembled rocked...
>
> *(Knox)* ...the place in which they had gathered rocked to and fro...
>
> *See Holy Spirit p. 183*

ACTS 4:32 And the multitude of them that believed were of one heart and of one soul: neither said any of them that aught of the things which he possessed was his own; but they had all things common.

> *(Barclay)* The whole body of those who had placed their faith in Jesus was united in heart and soul.
>
> *(Jer.)* The whole group of believers was united, heart and soul; no one claimed for his own use anything that he had, as everything they owned was held in commom.
>
> *(Knox)* There was one heart and one soul in all the company of believers; none of them called any of his possessions his own, everything was shared in common.

ACTS 16:25 And at midnight Paul and Silas prayed, and sang praises unto God: and the prisoners heard them.

> *(Wuest)* ...while they were praying were also singing praises to God, mingling petitions with songs of praise...
>
> *(Worrell)* ...while engaged in prayer, were singing praise to God...

ROMANS 8:26 Likewise the Spirit also helpeth our infirmities: for we know not what we should pray for as we ought: but the Spirit itself maketh intercession for us with groanings which cannot be uttered.

(Wuest) ...the Spirit lends us a helping hand with reference to our weakness, for the particular thing we should pray for according to what is necessary in the nature of the case, we do not know with an absolute knowledge...

(New Life) ...the Holy Spirit prays to God for us with sounds that cannot be put into words.

(Phil.) ...helps us in our present limitations...

(Basic) ...the Spirit puts our desires into words which are not in our power to say.

(Pl. Eng.) ...the Spirit prays on our behalf with inward cries beyond ordinary speech.

(NASB) ...with groanings too deep for words.

(Gspd.) ...with inexpressible yearnings...

(Trans.) ...with our inarticulate cries.

(NEB) ...We do not even know how we ought to pray, (or, what it is right to pray for) but through our inarticulate groans the Spirit himself is pleading for us...

(Black.) ...the Spirit gives assistance in our weakness - he takes hold [of our problems] on the other side...

(Barclay) ...the Spirit himself intercedes for us, when the only prayers that we can offer are inarticulate cries.

(Jer.) For when we cannot choose words in order to pray properly, the Spirit himself expresses our plea in a way that could never be put into words.

(Wand) ...We do not even know precisely what we ought to pray for. But the Spirit Himself comes to our assistance with inarticulate groanings.

(Johnson) ...we also have the Spirit, who compensates for our inadequacies.

(Authentic) Likewise the Spirit comes to the assistance of our limitations; for we do not know how to express ourselves adequately in prayer. But the Spirit itself makes intercession with speechless moans...

See Holy Spirit p. 187

ROMANS 8:27 And he that searcheth the hearts knoweth what is the mind of the Spirit, because he maketh intercession for the saints according to the will of God.

(Wuest) ...but the Spirit himself comes to our rescue by interceding with unutterable groanings.

(Jordan) ...he who X-rays our hearts...

(Weym.) ...His intercessions for God's people are in harmony with God's will.

(Authentic) ...and God who searches hearts knows what is the sense of the Spirit's utterances...

(Syriac) ...and the explorer of hearts, he knoweth what is the mind of the Spirit; because he prayeth for the saints, agreeably to the good pleasure of God.

See Holy Spirit p. 188

ROMANS 8:28 For we know that all things work together for good to them that love God, to them who are the called according to his purpose.

    (New Life, N. Berk., NAB) ...God makes all things work together for the good...

    (Lau.) ...God works with those who love Him to bring good out of everything...

    (K. & L., 20th C.R.) ...God causes all things to work together for the good...

    (20th C. 1) ...God makes all things work in harmony for the good...

    (Trans.) ...the Spirit makes everything work harmoniously for good...

    (Authentic) ...God makes everything turn out for the best.

    (Jordan) ...God fully cooperates in a good cause...

    (Hudson) ...God co-operates in all things for [their] good.

    (Deaf) ...in everything God works for the good...

    (Mof.) ...those who love God, those who have been called in terms of his purpose, have his aid and interest in everything.

    (RSV) ...in everything God works for good with those who love him...

    (Gspd.) We know that in everything God works with those who love him, whom he has called in accordance with his purpose, to bring about what is good.

    (Jer.) We know that by turning everything to their good God co-operates with all those who love him...

    (Black.) ...God works all things together for good.

    (NEB) ...in everything, as we know, he co-operates for good...

    (Roth.) ...God causeth all things to work together for good...

    (GNB) ...in all things God works for good with those who love him...

I CORINTHIANS 14:2 For he that speaketh in an unknown tongue speaketh not unto men, but unto God: for no man understandeth him; howbeit in the spirit he speaketh mysteries.

    (Mof.) ...he is talking of divine secrets in the Spirit.

    (Hudson) ...by [his] spirit he is speaking [divine] secrets.

    (Cent.) ...in the Spirit he utters secret truths.

    (Authentic) ...He is speaking mysterious things in spirit language.

    (Wuest) ...he utters with his human spirit [as energized by the Holy Spirit] divine revelations not explained.

    (NIV) ...he utters mysteries with his spirit.

    (Pl. Eng.) ...he is speaking heavenly secrets in the spirit.

    (Weym.) ...in the Spirit he is speaking secret truths.

I CORINTHIANS 14:4 He that speaketh in an unknown tongue edifieth himself; but he that prophesieth edifieth the church.

    (AMP) ...edifies and improves himself...

I CORINTHIANS 14:4 (N. Berk.) He who speaks in a tongue improves himself...

    (NAB) ...builds up himself...

    (Roth.) ...buildeth up himself...

I CORINTHIANS 14:14 For if I pray in an unknown tongue, my spirit prayeth, but my understanding is unfruitful.

    (Basic) For if I make use of tongues in my prayers, my spirit makes the prayer, but not my mind.

    (GNB) ...my spirit prays indeed, but my mind has no part in it.

    (NEB) ...my intellect lies fallow.

    (NAB) ...my spirit is at prayer but my mind contributes nothing.

    (Jer.) ...my mind is left barren.

    (TLB) ...my spirit is praying but I don't know what I'm saying.

    (Cent.) ...my spirit prays, but my mind is barren.

    (N. Berk.) ...my spirit prays but my mind is unproductive.

    (Jordan) ...my mind is a blank.

    (Hoerber) ...my spirit doubtless prays, but my mind is a blank.

    (20th C. R.) ...my spirit indeed prays, but my mind is a blank.

    (Trans.) ...it is my spirit which prays, but my mind is unproductive.

    (Authentic) ...my spirit is engaged in prayer, but my intellect is not functioning.

    (Knox) ...my spirit is praying, but my mind reaps no advantage from it.

    (AMP) My spirit (by the Holy Spirit within me) prays, but my mind is unproductive...

    (NASB) ...my mind is unfruitful.

    (Wuest) ...my spirit [the human spirit as moved by the Holy Spirit] is praying...

    (Phil.) ...my spirit is praying but my mind is inactive.

    (Norlie) ...my spirit does the praying but my understanding is a blank.

    (Weym.) ...my spirit prays, but my understanding is barren.

    (Way) ...my spirit is engaged in prayer, but my intelligence is simply barren.

    (Wand) ...my spirit prays but my understanding derives no benefit.

    (Barclay) ...it is my spirit which prays. My mind is producing nothing at all.

I CORINTHIANS 14:15 What is it then? I will pray with the spirit, and I will pray with the understanding also: I will sing with the spirit, and I will sing with the understanding also.

    (AMP) ...I will pray with my spirit [by the Holy Spirit that is within me]...I will sing with my spirit [by the Holy Spirit that is within me]...

    (Wuest) I will pray by means of my spirit. But I will pray also with the aid of my intellect.

    (TLB) Well, then, what shall I do? I will do both. I will pray in unknown tongues and also in ordinary language that everyone understands. I will sing in unknown tongues & also in ordinary language, so that I can understand the praise I am giving.

EPHESIANS 1:16, 17 Cease not to give thanks for you, making mention of you in my prayers. That the God of our Lord Jesus Christ, the Father of glory, may give unto you the spirit of wisdom and revelation in the knowledge of him.

(TLB) ...I pray for you constantly, asking God, the glorious Father of our Lord Jesus Christ, to give you wisdom to see clearly and really understand who Christ is and all that he has done for you.

(Jer.) May the God of our Lord Jesus Christ, the Father of glory, give you a spirit of wisdom and perception of what is revealed, to bring you to full knowledge of him.

(Barclay) For it is my prayer that the God of our Lord Jesus Christ, the glorious Father, may give you the Spirit to make you wise in heavenly things, and to reveal to you full knowledge of himself.

(NEB) I pray that the God of our Lord Jesus Christ, the all-glorious Father, may give you the spiritual powers of wisdom and vision, by which there comes the knowledge of him.

(Hudson) May the God of our Lord Jesus Christ, the Father all glorious, give you a spirit that grasps principles [and receives] God's revelation in the sphere of [or, as regards] full knowledge of himself.

(AMP) ...that He may grant you a spirit of wisdom and revelation [of insight into mysteries and secrets] in the [deep and intimate] knowledge of Him.

(Way) That the God of our Lord Jesus the Messiah, the Father glory-clad, may, in bestowing the full knowledge of Himself, bestow on you the Spirit which is manifested in divine illumination and insight into the mysteries of God.

(Carpenter) ...May the eternal wisdom make you wise. May all the veils be torn away, so far as that may be in this life, and the full glory of the Revelation come flooding in upon you, so that your knowledge may be directed to the true end.

(Cornish) ...this prayer is one for further light and increased understanding on your part, that the God of our Lord Jesus Christ, Father of all glory, may give you the spiritual wisdom and revelation, which are found in the clear full knowledge of Him.

(Conc.) ...a spirit of wisdom and revelation in the realization of Him.

(Wms.) ...wisdom and revelation which come through a growing knowledge of Him.

(Dist.) I pray that you new Christians will understand the mighty position with Christ which your congregations occupy.

(Fenton) ...a spirit of wisdom, and comprehension of what is contained in a full knowledge of Him.

(Roth.) ...a spirit of wisdom and understanding in gaining a personal knowledge of him.

(Conf.) ...the spirit of wisdom and revelation in deep knowledge of him.

(Black.) ...in the deeper knowledge of himself.

(NIV) I keep asking...

(ABV, Tomanek, Estes) ...full knowledge...

EPHESIANS 1:16, 17 *(Noli)* ...a spirit of wisdom, revelation, and divine knowledge.

(Cony.) ...a spirit of wisdom and of insight...

See authority of the believer p. 202

EPHESIANS 1:18 The eyes of your understanding being enlightened; that ye may know what is the hope of his calling, and what the riches of the glory of his inheritance in the saints...

(NEB) I pray that your inward eyes may be illumined, so that you may know what is the hope to which he calls you, what the wealth and glory of the share he offers you among his people in their heritage...

(Phil.) ...that you may receive that inner illumination of the spirit which will make you realize how great is the hope to which he is calling you - the magnificence and splendor of the inheritance promised to Christians...

(Way) ...and may flood with light the eyes of your understanding. So shall you know what it really is, that hope which springs up in those who hearken His invitation: so shall you know what riches are comprised in the magnificence of the inheritance which He gives you among His consecrated ones...

(Cornish) ...and illuminate your inner vision, the eyes of your heart, thereby explaining and opening to you the full nature of his calling and its aim and expectation, revealing too what an abundance of glory is implied in this 'inheritance of the saints.'

(Carver) ...and so knowledge of the deeper meanings of truth and reality, a spirit which he will give by the eyes of your heart having been enlightened, since the source of issues and of living knowledge we found in the basal heart attitudes...that you may know in experience: first, what is God's optimistic aim in calling men into his redemption and fellowship, the hope of his calling...

(Dodd.) ...the eyes of your understanding enlightened still more & more; that being thus illuminated, ye may know, in a more comprehensive manner than you now do...

(Jordan) ...May you know the hope which his call inspires and the wonderful resources available to Christians because of their membership in his family.

(Lovett) Specifically I pray that the eyes of your heart may be enlightened, so that you may behold the intimate details of his plan...

(Letters) ...what is actually ours now and in the future because of what Jesus has done for you.

(Conc.) ...for you to perceive what is the expectation of His calling, and what the riches of the glory of the enjoyment of His allotment among the saints.

(Fenton) ...who enlightens the eyes of your hearts: to show you what is the hope of His calling...

(Basic) ...And that having the eyes of your heart full of light, you may have knowledge of...

(Pl. Eng.) ...that your inward eyes may be filled with his light...and what a wealth of glory is laid up for our possession among the people of God.

(Barclay) I pray that your inner vision may be flooded with light, to enable you to see...

EPHESIANS 1:18 (Cress.) I ask him that you may see these things in your hearts...

    (Berk.) ...granting you illumined eyes of the heart...

    (NAB) May he enlighten your innermost vision...

    (Wuest) ...the eyes of your heart being in an enlightened state...

    (Bruce) I pray for the enlightenment of your spiritual vision...

    (GNB) ...how rich are the wonderful blessings he promises his people.

    (Knox) May your inward eye be enlightened...

    (Jer.) ...so that you can see what hope his call holds for you...

    (Roth.) The eyes of your heart having been enlightened...

    (Tomanek) ...of his inheritance in the Holy one.

    (Black.) ...that the perception of your heart may be illumined...

    (Cent.) ...that the eyes of your heart may be flooded with light...

    (AMP) By having the eyes of your heart flooded with light...

    (New Life) I pray that your hearts will be able to understand...

    (TLB) I pray that your hearts will be flooded with light...

See authority of the believer p. 203

EPHESIANS 1:19, 20 And what is the exceeding greatness of his power to usward who believe, according to the working of his mighty power. Which he wrought in Christ, when he raised him from the dead, and set him at his own right hand in the heavenly places.

    (GNB) And how very great is his power at work in us who believe. This power working in us is the same as the mighty strength which he used when he raised Christ from death and seated him at his right side in the heavenly world.

    (Trans.) ...and the limitless scope of his power at work in us once we believe in him. This is that same stupendous power which he exerted when he raised Christ from death and enthroned him at his right hand in the supernatural world.

    (Johnson) And that you will be aware of the incredibly immense strength which is available to us. You see, we have access to resurrection - to the strength and power God demonstrated in Christ when he raised him from death and gave him supreme authority.

    (Lau.) I pray that you may realize that His power in us who believe, is great beyond all measure. It is the same mighty power that worked in Christ. By that power God raised Him from the dead and had Him sit at His right hand in heaven.

    (Weym.) ...and what the transcendent greatness of His power in us believers as seen in the working of His infinite might when He displayed it in Christ by raising Him from the dead and seating Him at His own right hand in the heavenly realms.

EPHESIANS 1:19, 20 (Carpenter) Calculate, if you can, the gigantic power behind all this. Sons, quickened into life and consciousness. We say that we believe. Yes, but what a miracle that is! It means that there is a bridge which joins time with eternity, a road which leads from earth to heaven, and the feet of believers have been set on it...Christ is in countless ways the reversal of human expectations, and in no way more startlingly than by the Resurrection. If there was one thing that all men had, willy-nilly, to acknowledge, it was the fact that at the end of life comes death. Christ lived and died. Death had his usual triumph. But it was a short-lived mastery. "Death's pale-flag" was hoisted for a day and for a second day, and on the third day it was hauled down. And the Lamb of God, flying His own flag, was raised from the dead and entered into His glory. It was the beginning of the resumption of the original glory, which He had with the Father before the world was, but that glory was touched now with an added quality. The victory had been won within the terms of human life. The Risen Christ is victorious Mankind. In what we call the Ascension, which follows hard upon the triumph over death, the Son of God finally resumes the attributes of Godhead, but He is still Son of Man, Ambassador of Humanity, High Priest of Earth. He has taken our nature, not for one human generation only, but so as never more to lay it off, and thus it is that in Him man is now lifted to the divine level, where God is.

(Cornish) ...and unfolding to your apprehension the extraordinary power which reacts from him upon all who believe. It is the enormous overmastering supremacy which the Christ showed forth, which operated in him, raising him from the dead...

(Bruce) ...and what the surpassing greatness of His power displayed in us who believe. That power is the effective operation of His mighty strength which He exerted in the case of Christ, when He raised Him from the dead and made Him sit at His right hand in the heavenly realm.

(Cent.) ...the surpassing greatness of his might in us who believe, as seen in the energy of that resistless might which he exercised in raising Christ from the dead, and in seating him at his right hand in the heavenly heights...

(Jordan) May you experience the incredible outburst of his power in us who rely on his might and his abundant energy. This same energy working in Christ raised him from the dead and gave him spiritual victory and authority over every ruler...

(Wade) ...and how transcendently great is His power manifested in us who have faith. That power in us is due to the same exercise of His Mighty Sovereignty as was displayed in the instance of the Christ...

(Beck) ...the vast resources of His power working in us who believe. It is the same mighty power with which He worked in Christ, raised Him from the dead...

(Lamsa) And what is the exceeding greatness of his power in us as the result of the things we believe, according to the skill of his mighty power.

(N. Berk.) ...how overwhelmingly great is His power...

EPHESIANS 1:19, 20 *(NEB)* ...and how vast the resources of his power open to us who trust in him.

(Basic) ...And how unlimited is his power to us who have faith...

(Noli) ...and how immeasurable is his power in us who believe in him...

(Fenton) ...the exceeding greatness of His power in us believers, through His mighty energy, which energized in Christ...

(Wuest) ...the superabounding greatness of His inherent power to us who are believing ones as measured by the operative energy of the manifested strength of His might...

(Swann) ...like the energy of the mighty powers which he exercised in the Christ...

(Pl. Eng.) ...this power works with the force of the might which he exercised in Christ, when he raised him from the dead, and seated him at his right hand in the heavenly world.

(AMP) ...His power in and for us who believe...

(Roth.) ...According to the energy of the grasp of his might which he energized in the Christ, when he raised him from among the dead...

(Kling.) ...the erupting greatness of his power...

(Syriac) ...what is the excellence of the majesty of his power in us who believe...

(NIV) ...incomparably great power...

(NAB) ...the immeasurable scope of his power in us who believe...

(RSV) ...in us who believe...

(Conc.) ...from among the dead...

(Stevens) ...whereby he has placed him in the supreme seat of authority in heaven.

(ABV) ...in the heavenly places...

(Phil.) That power is the same divine energy which was demonstrated in Christ when he raised him from the dead and gave him the place of supreme honor in Heaven.

(Authentic) ...indicated by the operation of the mighty force God employed in the case of Christ in raising him from the dead...

(Barclay) ...that power demonstrated in the action of the mighty strength which was operative in the case of Christ...

See redemption p. 72; authority of the believer p. 205

EPHESIANS 1:21 Far above all principality and power, and might, and dominion and every name that is named, not only in this world, but also in that which is to come.

(GNB) Christ rules there above all heavenly rulers, authorities, powers, and lords; he has a title superior to all titles of authority in this world and in the next.

(Lau.) There Jesus sits above all rulers, above all authority, above all power, above all lords.

(Weym.) ...high above all other government and authority and power and dominion, and every title of sovereignty used either in this Age or in the Age to come.

(Carpenter) ...Above every kind of being that imagination can conceive, present or future, good or evil, Christ is supreme.

EPHESIANS 1:21 (Cornish) ...supreme in every way, untouched, unimpeded by the innumerable authorities, influences, powers, potentates of the world, having power over all other names to which authority is lent not only in this age, but in the next.

> *(Bruce)* There now He sits enthroned, high above all principality and power, might and dominion, and every name of renown whether belonging to this present age or to the age to come.

> *(Phil.)* ...a place that is infinitely superior to any conceivable command, authority, power, or control, and which carries with it a name far beyond any name that could ever be used in this world or the world to come.

> *(Wms.)* ...far above every other government, authority, power, and dominion, yea, far above every other title that can be conferred,...

> *(Barclay)* There he gave him a place far above all spiritual powers, above every ruler and authority, and power and lord, above every possible title of honour...

> *See redemption p. 72; authority of the believer p. 207*

EPHESIANS 1:22 And hath put all things under his feet, and gave him to be the head over all things to the church.

> *(Johnson)* In addition to all of creation, Christ also has full authority over the Church, the fellowship of Christpersons, to give it direction.

> *(K. & L.)* He has subjected every single thing to his authority and has appointed him sovereign head of the Church...

> *(Wand)* "He hath put the universe under His feet." In so exalting Christ He has made Him Head of a Body, the Church.

> *(Gspd.)* He has put everything under his feet and made him the indisputable head of the church.

> *(Barclay)* He subjected everything to him, and gave him as the supreme head to the church.

> *(Wade)* He has reduced all things to subjection beneath His feet, and has given Him to the Church to be the Head over all.

> *(Noli)* He has put all the universe under his rule, and made him the head of the Church.

> *(NEB)* He put everything in subjection beneath his feet, and appointed him as supreme head to the church.

> *(Letters)* God has put everything under Jesus and made Him the head of God's family of believers.

> *(Berk., N. Berk.)* God has placed everything under His feet and has given Him as head over everything for the church.

> *(Knox)* He has put everything under his dominion, and made him the head to which the whole Church is joined.

> *(GNB)* God put all things under Christ's feet and gave him to the church as supreme Lord over all things.

EPHESIANS 1:22 (Weym.) God has put all things under His feet, and has appointed Him universal andsupreme Head of the Church.

(Carpenter) But perhaps someone will say "What is this to us? We do not doubt that your picture is true enough, and that the Lord Jesus is above all. But heaven is far away." My brothers, heaven is here.

(Cornish) God has put all things under his feet, made him the head of all things for the Church...

(Stevens) ...and has subordinated to him all existing powers, and made him Sovereign over his church.

(Phil.) God has placed everything under the power of Christ and has set him up as head of everything for the Church.

(Mof.) ...and set him as head over everything for the church...

(Hudson) ...and appointed him supreme head of the church, his body...

(Pl. Eng.) ...and made him the head over all things for the church...

(RSV) ...for the church...

(Carver) ...his Body, without which the Christ is incomplete as God's cosmic Authority. As the Body of the Christ functioning in human history, the Church is the full expression and historic content of the Christ...The Christ is the full expression of God, and the Church the full expression and fulfillment of the Christ.

See authority of the believer p. 208

EPHESIANS 1:23 Which is his body, the fulness of him that filleth all in all.

(20th C.R.) For the Church is Christ's Body, and is filled by him who fills all things everywhere with his presence.

(Cress.) The church is his body. The church has everything that Christ has. And he has everything everywhere.

(K. & L.) ...which is truly his body, the complement of him who fills all the members with all graces.

(Wand) That Body provides a universal means of expression for one who is Himself a universal Personality.

(Gspd.) ...which is his body, filled by him who fills everything everywhere.

(Barclay) ...and the church is his body, the complement of him who completes all things everywhere.

(NEB) ...which is his body and as such holds within it the fullness of him who himself receives the entire fullness of God. (or, as supreme head to the church which is his body, and to be all that he himself is who fills the universe in all its parts.)

(Letters) ...which is filled with Jesus Himself, the one who makes us complete.

(Knox) ...so that the Church is his body, the completion of him who everywhere and in all things is complete.

EPHESIANS 1:23 (GNB) The church is Christ's body, the completion of him who himself completes all things everywhere.

> *(Carpenter)* This same Jesus, Who is exalted at the right hand of God the Father, is the Head of the Church…The body is the instrument which every person has wherewith to accomplish the purposes of his will. In the Church the purpose and the will are those of Christ. We are the instrument…
>
> *(Stevens)* …his mystical body, which is filled and penetrated by his life.
>
> *(Phil.)* For the Church is his body, and in that body lives fully the one who fills the whole wide universe.
>
> *(Mof.)* …the church which is his Body, filled by him who fills the universe entirely.
>
> *(AMP)* …for in that body lives the full measure of Him who makes everything complete, and who fills everything everywhere (with Himself).
>
> *(Jordan)* …his body, the full expression of him…
>
> *(Black.)* …the means of expression for him whose plentitude pervades all creation.
>
> *(Bruce)* …the body or complement, that is to say, of the One who fills the whole universe with His presence
>
> *(Lau.)* The church is His body and it is filled with Him…
>
> *See authority of the believer p. 209*

EPHESIANS 3:14 For this cause I bow my knees unto the Father of our Lord Jesus Christ.

> *(TLB)* When I think of the wisdom and scope of his plan I fall down on my knees and pray to the Father.
>
> *(Dist.)* I am overwhelmed with the immense significance of all this.
>
> *See authority of the believer p. 211*

EPHESIANS 3:15 Of whom the whole family in heaven and earth is named.

> *(Barclay)* …that Father who is the origin and ideal of all fatherhood in heaven and on earth.
>
> *(20th C.R.)* …from whom all 'fatherhood' in Heaven and on earth derives its name.
>
> *(ASV)* …from whom every family…
>
> *(Knox)* …takes its title.
>
> *See authority of the believer p. 211*

EPHESIANS 3:16 That he would grant you, according to the riches of his glory, to be strengthened with might by his Spirit in the inner man.

> *(Wade)* …that He may enable you, in virtue of the inexhaustible resources of His glorious Perfection, to become strengthened powerfully in your inmost selves through His Spirit…
>
> *(Johnson)* May he give you an infusion of strength in the depths of your being by the Spirit.

EPHESIANS 3:16 (Way) I pray that He may, with a fulness measured only by the wealth of His own glory, vouch-safe to you to be made strong with power infused by His Spirit into your inmost nature.

(***Wand***) I pray then that out of the wealth of His glory He will grant you to be mightily strengthened by His Spirit in the very core of your being...

(***Jer.***) Out of his infinite glory, may he give you the power through his Spirit, for your hidden self to grow strong...

(***Phil.***) ...and I pray that out of the glorious richness of his resources he will enable you to know the strength of the Spirit's inner reinforcement...

(***Letters***) We ask to use His unlimited resources to make your spirit strong by His Spirit.

(***Knox***) May he, out of the rich treasury of his glory, strengthen you through his spirit with a power that reaches your innermost being.

(***Jordan***) ...I beg him to give you, out of his glorious abundance, the power to win by his Spirit ruling your inner life.

(***Carpenter***) ...I am thinking of your inner selves, the deep well of character, whence actions and habits are thrown up. As a rich man keeps his chief treasures in an inner strong-room of his house, I want the deep centre of your life to be a stronghold where the Holy Spirit reigns, the Strengthener, the Comforter, where He and you together, He, the Giver of Life, and you with your glad obedience, make up a mansion where our Lord can come and dwell.

(***Dodd.***) ...out of those redundant stores of goodness in his gracious heart which can never be exhausted, to be mightily strengthened by the effectual operation of his Spirit, invigorating and increasing every grace, and carrying on his work with abundant success, in the inner man...

(***Smith, J.M.***) ...strengthened with power by his Spirit in the interior man...For Christ to dwell by faith in your hearts; in love being rendered firm, and the foundation laid... endowed with power through His Spirit to the inmost core of your being.

(***Berk., N. Berk.***) ...empowered with strength in the inner self by His Spirit...

(***Weym.***) ...to be strengthened by His Spirit with power penetrating to your inmost being.

(***Cent.***) ...strengthened with might by his Spirit in your inmost being...

(***K. & L.***) ...strengthened with power through the Spirit for the development of your inner selves...

(***Cornish***) ...for the strengthening of that man who is invisible within, for infinite power to be given you according to the wealth of His glory spiritually...

(***Conc.***) ...to be made staunch with power, through His spirit, in the man within...

(***MacK.***) ...endowing you with the knowledge of your privileges as believers, and with courage to maintain them.

(***Conf.***) ...strengthened with power through his Spirit unto the progress of the inner man...

EPHESIANS 3:16 (Adams) ...strengthened with power in the inner person...

> *(Trans.)* ...strength and power through his Spirit in your inmost being...
>
> *(GNB)* ...power to be strong in your inner selves...
>
> *(Authentic)* ...powerfully strengthened in the inner self.
>
> *(Tomanek)* ...in the man within...
>
> *(NIV, NEB)* ...in your inner being.
>
> *(Wms.)* ...in your inmost being.
>
> *See Holy Spirit p. 192; authority of the believer p. 211*

EPHESIANS 3:17 That Christ may dwell in your hearts by faith; that ye, being rooted and grounded in love.

> *(Wand)* ...and that in response to your faith Christ will take up his abode in your hearts. Then you will be deeply rooted and securely grounded in love.
>
> *(Jordan)* God grant that Christ, through your faith, might establish residence in your hearts. May love be your tap root and foundation.
>
> *(Weym.)* I pray that Christ may make His home in your hearts through your faith; so that having your roots deep and your foundations strong in love...
>
> *(Wuest)* ...that the Christ might finally settle down and feel completely at home in your hearts through your faith...
>
> *(Syriac)* ...the Messiah may dwell by faith, and in your hearts by love, while your root and your foundation waxeth strong...
>
> *(Lamsa)* That Christ may dwell in your inner man by faith, and in your hearts by love, strengthening your understanding and your foundation...
>
> *(Barclay)* ...that love may be that in which your life is rooted and on which it is founded.
>
> *(TLB)* ...May your roots go down deep into the soil of God's marvelous love...
>
> *(Lau.)* ...I pray that the roots of your faith may grow deep in the ground of His love.
>
> *(Jer.)* ...planted in love and built on love...
>
> *(Dodd.)* ...by the continual exercise of a lively faith, by means of which a constant intercourse with him will be maintained...
>
> *(Cornish)* ...I pray for those spiritual roots and foundations to be in you...
>
> *(NIV)* ...rooted and established in love.
>
> *(Godbey)* ...being rooted and grounded in divine love...
>
> *See authority of the believer p. 213*

EPHESIANS 3:18 May be able to comprehend with all saints what is the breadth, and length, and depth, and height.

> *(Wand)* ...and you will be strong enough with the rest of the Brethren to grasp in all its breadth and length and height and depth...

EPHESIANS 3:18 (Johnson) I hope that you will be able to grasp with all God-persons the multidimensional love of God - a love broad enough to include everybody, long enough to reach to the ends of the earth, deep enough to unify our human fragmentation, and high enough to reach the very heart of God.

> *(Carver)* ...yea even to know in all its dimensions the love of the Christ, his love for the world and God's love of which he is the embodiment and the perfect expression. We must do our utmost to know that love which in its full reaches is beyond knowing...
>
> *(K. & L.)* Thus will you have the power to grasp fully, together with all the saints, what is the breadth and length and height and depth (of this mystery)...
>
> *(Adams)* ...may you, together with all of the saints, have the capacity to get a grasp of how broad, how long, how high and how deep Christ's love is...
>
> *(Dist.)* I pray you will all grasp more and more of the profound scope of your spiritual position.
>
> *(Syriac)* ...and that ye may be able to explore, with all the saints, what is the height and depth, and length and breadth...
>
> *(RSV)* ...may have power to comprehend...
>
> *(Tomanek)* ...so that you may be able to fully understand...
>
> *(Kling.)* ...that you may be entirely able to lay hold with all saints...
>
> *(Roth.)* ...that ye may be mighty enough to grasp firmly...
>
> *See authority of the believer p. 213*

EPHESIANS 3:19 And to know the love of Christ, which passeth knowledge, that ye might be filled with all the fulness of God.

> *(Wand)* ...the conception of the love of Christ. That is a subject of knowledge which surpasses knowledge. Nevertheless through it you will attain to the complete measure of the Wholeness which is God.
>
> *(Carpenter)* God is the Plenitude of power and glory. May He fill you to the utmost limits of your being with all that you can receive of what He has to give, and bring you in the end, just men made perfect, to the full and open vision of Himself...
>
> *(AMP)* ...that you may be filled [through all your being] unto all the fullness of God [may have the richest measure of the divine Presence, and become a body wholly filled and flooded with God Himself]!
>
> *(Wade)* ...to the end that you may be made complete, up to the full measure of all God's completeness.
>
> *(Bruce)* ...so may you be filled up to the measure of God's own fulness!
>
> *(Weym.)* ...so that you may be made complete in accordance with God's own standard of completeness.

EPHESIANS 3:19 (Dodd.) ...that your expanded hearts, being dilated more and more, may be rendered capable of admitting larger degrees than ever of Divine love, and more ample indwellings of Divine consolation...

(NEB) So may you attain to fullness of being, the fullness of God himself.

(GNB) ...and so be completely filled with the very nature of God.

(Knox) ...May you be filled with all the completion God has to give.

(Phil.) ...May you be filled through all your being with God himself!

(20th C. 1) ...filled to the full with God himself.

(Cony.) ...that you may be filled therewith, even to the measure of the fulness of God.

(Hudson) ...filled with the full content of the divine nature.

(Beck) ...so you will be filled with all that is in God.

(Basic) ...so that you may be made complete as God himself is complete.

(Fenton) ...and to gain an idea how far the love of Christ exceeds our research...

(Cornish) ...and to understand the love of the Christ which goes far beyond all material comprehension...

(Kling.) ...that you might know the erupting knowledge of the love of Christ...

(Godbey) ...and to know the divine love of Christ...

(Authentic) ...filled with the immensity of God.

(Johnson) Experiencing love like this, may you be overwhelmed with the awareness of the presence of God.

See authority of the believer p. 214

EPHESIANS 3:20 Now unto him that is able to do exceeding abundantly above all that we ask or think, according to the power that worketh in us...

(Wade) To Him Who is able to transcend all limits - to do far in excess of all that we request or imagine, in virtue of His Power which is active in us...

(Weym.) Now to Him who, in the exercise of His power that is at work within us, is able to do infinitely beyond all our highest prayers or thoughts...

(Knox) He whose power is at work in us is powerful enough, and more than powerful enough, to carry out his purpose beyond all our hopes and dreams.

(Authentic) Now to him who is supremely powerful to do infinitely more than we can ask or think, in accordance with the power that operates in us.

(Norlie) He who exerts His power within us is able to do in full measure far more than all that we ask for or can think of.

(Mof.) Now to him who by the action of his power within us is able to do all things, aye far more than we can ever ask or imagine...

(Conc.) Now to Him Who is able to do superexcessively above all that we are requesting or apprehending, according to the power that is operating in us...

EPHESIANS 3:20 (Barclay) Now to him who can do for us far more than our lips can ask or our minds conceive through that power of his which is at work in us.

> *(Dist.)* Results beyond our thoughts will arise from these beginnings in which we now participate.
>
> *(NEB)* Now to him who is able to do immeasurably more than all we can ask or conceive...
>
> *(Way)* ...To an extent whose measure is that mighty impulse which thrills us through...
>
> *(Conf.)* Now, to him who is able to accomplish all things in a measure far beyond what we ask or conceive...
>
> *(Jordan)* Now to him who is able, by the power energizing us...
>
> *(TLB)* ...infinitely beyond our highest prayers, desires, thoughts, or hopes.
>
> *(Syriac)* ...by his almighty power...
>
> *(Roth.)* ...According to the power which doth energize itself within us.
>
> *(Roth. 2)* ...according to the power that is inwardly working itself in us...
>
> *(Fenton)* ...by means of His power energizing in us...
>
> *(Johnson)* Now to God, who can do by the power that exists in us greater things than we are able even to imagine or request...
>
> *See authority of the believer p. 215*

EPHESIANS 3:21 Unto him be glory in the church by Christ Jesus throughout all ages, world without end. Amen.

> *(New Life)* May we see His shining greatness in the church...
>
> *See authority of the believer p. 216*

EPHESIANS 6:18 Praying always with all prayer and supplication in the Spirit, and watching thereunto with all perseverance and supplication for all saints.

> *(AMP)* Pray at all times (on every occasion, in every season) in the Spirit, with all (manner of) prayer and entreaty. To that end keep alert and watch with strong purpose and perseverance, interceding in behalf of all the saints (God's consecrated people).
>
> *(Johnson)* Cultivate a continuous attitude of prayer both for yourself and for the God family.
>
> *(Weym.)* Pray with unceasing prayer and entreaty on every fitting occasion in the Spirit, and be always on the alert to seize opportunities for doing so, with unwearied persistence and entreaty on behalf of all God's people.
>
> *(Gspd.)* Use every kind of prayer and entreaty, and at every opportunity pray in the Spirit. Be on the alert about it; devote yourselves constantly to prayer...
>
> *(Deaf)* Pray in the Spirit at all times. Pray with all kinds of prayers and ask for everything you need...
>
> *(Norlie)* Pray much, and at every opportunity. Use every kind of prayer and entreaty. Pray in the Spirit...

EPHESIANS 6:18 (Wms.) Keep on praying in the Spirit, with every kind of prayer and entreaty, at every opportunity...

(Beck) Pray at all times in the Spirit, using every kind of prayer. Be alert and keep at it continually...

(Wuest) ...maintaining a constant alertness in the same...

(Mof.) ...with all manner of prayer and entreaty...

(Knox) Use every kind of prayer and supplication...

(Pl. Eng.) ...with every kind of prayer and petition...

(Fenton) ...and keeping watch in it with steady tenacity.

PHILIPPIANS 4:6 Be careful for nothing, but in everything by prayer and supplication with thanksgiving let your requests be made known unto God.

(Jordan) ...don't fret over anything...

(Noli, Cent.) Do not worry about anything...

(River.) Do not worry...

(Cony.) Let no care trouble you...

(GNB) Don't worry about anything...

(RSV, Gspd.) Have no anxiety about anything...

(Wuest) Stop worrying about even one thing...

(Letters) Don't worry about anything but talk to the Father about everything. Tell Him what you need and keep thanking Him.

(N. Berk., Berk.) Entertain no worry, but under all circumstances let your petitions be made known before God...

(Black.) Do not worry about anything, but in every circumstance...

(Deaf) Don't worry about anything. But pray and ask God for everything you need...

(Knox) Nothing must make you anxious; in every need make your requests known to God...

(Beck) Don't worry about anything, but in everything go to God...

(TLB) Don't worry about anything; instead, pray about everything...

(AMP) Do not fret or have any anxiety about anything, but in everything, by prayer and petition (definite requests), with thanksgiving, continue to make your wants known to God.

(Norlie) So do not worry about anything. No matter what the circumstances, pray to God, entreat Him, and give thanks...

(Way) Let no anxieties fret you: nay, in every matter let the things you would ask be made known by means of prayer - by definite requests - linked with thanksgiving, at God's throne.

(NEB) ...have no anxiety, but in everything make your requests known to God in prayer and petition with thanksgiving...

PHILIPPIANS 4:6 (Jer.) There is no need to worry; but if there is anything you need, pray for it, asking God for it with prayer and thanksgiving.

(New Life) Do not worry. Learn to pray about everything. Give thanks to God as you ask Him for what you need.

(K. & L.) Have no anxiety, but in every concern by prayer and supplication with thanksgiving let your petitions be made known in your communing with God.

(Barclay) Don't worry about anything. In every circumstance of life tell God about the things you want to ask him for in your prayers and your requests to him, and bring him your thanks too.

(NAB) Dismiss all anxiety from your minds. Present your needs to God in every form of prayer and in petitions full of gratitude.

(Basic) Have no cares; but in everything with prayer and praise put your requests before God.

(Weekes) ...let your desires be made known to God.

(Weym.) ...let your requests be unreservedly made known in the presence of God.

See peace p. 354

PHILIPPIANS 4:7 And the peace of God, which passeth all understanding, shall keep your hearts and minds through Christ Jesus.

(AMP) And God's peace (shall be yours, that tranquil state of a soul assured of its salvation through Christ, and so fearing nothing from God and being content with its earthly lot of whatever sort that is, that peace) which transcends all understanding shall garrison and mount guard over your hearts and minds in Christ Jesus.

(Hudson) And God's peace, which excels [and that] any wit [of man can devise], shall, in Christ Jesus, guard your hearts and your thoughts...

(Lovett) God's peace which operates beyond the range of human understanding, will protect your feelings and thought life in Christ.

(Wood) ...peace of God, which surpasses any conception we have...

(Wms.) Then, through your union with Christ Jesus, the peace of God, that surpasses all human thought, will keep guard over your hearts and thoughts.

(Way) And so the peace that God gives, the peace that transcends all conception, shall be the fortress-warder of your hearts, of all your thoughts, in this your life in Messiah Jesus.

See redemption p. 117; peace p. 355

COLOSSIANS 1:9 For this cause we also, since the day we heard it, do not cease to pray for you, and to desire that ye might be filled with the knowledge of his will in all wisdom and spiritual understanding.

(Weym.) ...that you may be filled with a clear knowledge of His will accompanied by thorough wisdom and discernment in spiritual things.

COLOSSIANS 1:9 (Trans.) ...that you may be completely certain of God's will and have the spiritual wisdom to understand it.

(Way) ...that you may have in full measure that perfect knowledge of His will...

(Phil.) ...We are asking God that you may see things, as it were, from his point of view by being given spiritual insight and understanding.

(20th C.R.) ...asking that you may possess that deeper knowledge of the will of God, which comes through all true spiritual wisdom and insight.

(20th C. 1) And that is why we, from the very day that we heard this, have never given up praying for you, and asking that you may be filled with spiritual wisdom and intelligence, and so reach a perfect understanding of God's will.

(Authentic) ...that you may be filled with the knowledge of God's will in all wisdom and spiritual comprehension.

(Johnson) ...that you may grasp God's intention for you both in your head & in your heart...

(Jordan) We are asking that in every scrap of wisdom and spiritual insight you might be loaded up with a clear understanding of what God is up to...

(TLB) ...asking him to make you wise about spiritual things...

(NAB) ...that you may attain full knowledge of his will through perfect wisdom and spiritual insight.

(Basic) ...that you may be full of the knowledge of his purpose...

(Stevens) ...I pray that you may more and more apprehend God's truth.

(AMP) ...that you may be filled with the full (deep and clear) knowledge of His will in all spiritual wisdom [in comprehensive insight into the ways and purposes of God] and in understanding and discernment of spiritual things.

(Estes) ...an exact knowledge of his will...

(Tomanek) ...the exact knowledge...

COLOSSIANS 1:10 That ye might walk worthy of the Lord unto all pleasing, being fruitful in every good work, and increasing in the knowledge of God.

(Black.) ...advancing in this deeper knowledge of God.

(Phil.) We also pray that your outward lives, which men see, may bring credit to your master's name, and that you may bring joy to his heart by bearing genuine Christian fruit, and that your knowledge of God may grow yet deeper.

(20th C.R.) Then you will live lives worthy of the Master and so please God in every way. Your lives will be fruitful in every kind of good action...

(20th C. 1) Then you will live lives that will be worthy of the Master, and you will always please God by good actions of every kind. Your lives will bear fruit, and your characters grow, through a fuller knowledge of God...

COLOSSIANS 1:10 (Johnson) ...so that your lifestyle will please God, your efforts in ministry will be productive, and your understanding of who God is will continually enlarge.

(Jordan) May you...bust out all over with the true understanding of God.

(Fenton) ...successful in every good work...

(GNB) Then you will be able to live as the Lord wants and will always do what pleases him. Your lives will produce all kinds of good deeds, and you will grow in your knowledge of God.

(NAB) Then you will lead a life worthy of the Lord and pleasing to him in every way. You will multiply good works of every sort and grow in the knowledge of God.

(Tomanek) ...growing in the exact knowledge of God...

(ASV) ...strengthened with all power according to the might of his glory...

(Kling.) ...You will produce a crop and increase in the knowledge of God...

COLOSSIANS 1:11 Strengthened with all might, according to his glorious power, unto all patience and long suffering with joyfulness;

(Trans.) We pray that from the resources of his glorious power God may mightily strengthen you...

(Way) I ask Him that with all His strength you may be strengthened, even to the measure of the might of His divine majesty...

(Phil.) As you live this new life, we pray that you will be strengthened from God's boundless resources...

(20th C.R.) ...you will be made strong at all points with a strength worthy of the power manifested in his glory...

(20th C. 1) ...you will be made strong at all points with a strength proportionate to the power displayed in God's majesty - strong to endure with patience, and even with gladness, whatever may befall you...

(Johnson) We want you to become aware of that vast strength which springs out of your relation with God, so that you will have steadiness and be able to endure anything with joy...

(Wand) ...that you may be reinforced with all the strength there is by means of His glorious power...

(Jordan) In everything that demands strength, may you have the energy of his marvelous dynamo to give you all the patience and persistence you need.

(Cony.) ...that you may be strengthened to the uttermost in the strength of his glorious power...

(Wuest) ...by every enabling power being constantly strengthened in proportion to the manifested power of His glory...

(Smith, J. M.) In all power being made able...

COLOSSIANS 1:11 (Berk.) We pray that you be invigorated with complete power in accordance with His glorious strength, for the cheerful exercise of unlimited patience and perseverance...

(GNB) May you be made strong with all the strength which comes from his glorious power...

(TLB) ...that you will be filled with his mighty, glorious strength so that you can keep going no matter what happens - always full of the joy of the Lord...

(NAB) By the might of his glory you will be endowed with the strength needed to stand fast...

(Basic) ...Full of strength in the measure of the great power of his glory...

(Norlie) ...that you may receive strength for every task, drawn from His might and glory...

(Godbey) ...being impowered with all power*... (*Greek - dynamited with all dynamite)

COLOSSIANS 1:12 Giving thanks unto the Father, which hath made us meet to be partakers of the inheritance of the saints in light.

(Weym.) ...who has made us fit to receive our share of the inheritance...

(Trans.) ...fit to take your place...

(Barclay) We pray that you will be ever grateful to the Father who has made you fit to receive a share in the possession which he promised to his dedicated people in the realm of light.

(Wms.) ...who has qualified you to share the lot...

(Noli) ...he enabled us to share the inheritance of the saints who live in the light.

(Gspd.) ...thank the Father who has entitled you to share the lot of God's people in the realm of light.

(Wand) ...who has made it possible for you to claim your share of the inheritance with the Saints in the Kingdom of Light.

(Bruce) ...who has fitted you to receive a share of the heritage which belongs to the people of God in the realm of light.

(Hudson) ...fit for your share of the inheritance which God's people have in the Light...

(Fenton) ...Who brought us into the partnership of the inheritance...

(Berk., N. Berk.) ...who has qualified you for your share in the inheritance of the saints in the Light.

(TLB) ...to share all the wonderful things that belong to those who live in the kingdom of light.

(Douay, Conf., Godbey, Clem.) ...who has made us worthy...

(NAB) ...giving thanks to the Father for having made you worthy to share the lot of the saints in light.

(Lamsa) ...who has enlightened us and made us worthy partakers of the inheritance of the saints.

COLOSSIANS 1:12 (Cent.) ...fit to receive our share of the heritage...
>*(Deaf.)* ...He has made you able to have the things he prepared for you...
>*(Pl. Eng.)* ...who has made us ready to take possession of our portion...
>*(Roth.)* ...the Father that hath made you sufficient for your share...
>*See redemption p. 97; divine healing p. 285*

COLOSSIANS 1:13 Who hath delivered us from the power of darkness, and hath translated us into the kingdom of his dear Son
>*(Weym.)* ...who has delivered us out of the dominion of darkness, and has transferred us into the Kingdom...
>*(Way)* He hath rescued us from the tyranny of darkness, and hath transferred us into the Kingdom of the Son of His love...
>*(Barclay)* It was he who rescued us from the grip of the power of darkness, and transferred us to the Kingdom of his dear Son.
>*(20th C.R.)* For God has rescued us from the tyranny of Darkness, and has removed us into the Kingdom of his Son, who is the embodiment of his love.
>*(Wade)* For God has rescued us from the dominance exercised by the Powers of Spiritual Darkness, and transferred us to the Dominion of His Son - the Object of His love...
>*(Jer.)* ...he has taken us out of the power of darkness and created a place for us in the kingdom of the Son that he loves...
>*(Gspd.)* He has rescued us from the dominion of darkness, and has transferred us into the realm of his dear Son...
>*(Wand)* It was He who rescued us out of the power of darkness and established us as citizens in the Kingdom of His beloved Son...
>*(Jordan)* It was the Father who sprang us from the jailhouse of darkness, and turned us loose in the new world of his beloved Son...
>*(Stevens)* ...who procured our release from our former bondage and made us citizens in the kingdom of his beloved Son.
>*(Cony.)* For He has delivered us from the dominion of darkness, and transplanted us into the kingdom of his beloved Son.
>*(Wuest)* ...who delivered us out of the tyrannical rule of the darkness and transferred us into the kingdom of the Son of His love...
>*(N. Berk.)* He has rescued us from the domain of darkness, and has transferred us into the kingdom of His beloved Son...
>*(TLB)* For he has rescued us out of the darkness and gloom of Satan's kingdom and brought us into the kingdom of his dear Son.
>*(NAB)* He rescued us from the power of darkness and brought us into the kingdom of his beloved.

COLOSSIANS 1:13 (Basic) ...Who has made us free from the power of evil and given us a place in the kingdom of the Son of his love...

    (AMP) [The Father] has delivered and drawn us to Himself out of the control and dominion of darkness and has transferred us into the kingdom of the Son of His love...

    (Cent.) For he has delivered us out of the dominion of the darkness, and transplanted us into the kingdom of his dear Son...

    (Pl. Eng.) He has freed us from the power of darkness and carried us away into the kingdom of his beloved Son...

    (Tomanek) Who delivered us from the authority of darkness and caused a change of sides for the kingdom of the Son of his love...

    (Mof.) ...rescuing us from the power of the Darkness and transferring us to the realm of his beloved Son!

See redemption p. 97; divine healing p. 286

COLOSSIANS 1:14 In whom we have redemption through his blood, even the forgiveness of sins

    (Weym.) ...in whom we have our redemption...

    (Trans.) And the Son forgave our sins and set us free.

    (Way) For in His person we have, through the shedding of blood, the true Redemption...

    (Barclay) It is through this Son that we have received the liberation which comes when sins are forgiven.

See redemption p. 98; divine healing p. 286

COLOSSIANS 3:16 Let the word of Christ dwell in you richly in all wisdom; teaching and admonishing one another in psalms and hymns and spiritual songs, singing with grace in your hearts to the Lord.

    (Gspd.) Let the message of Christ live in your hearts in all its wealth of wisdom...

    (Jer.) Through him, let us offer God an unending sacrifice of praise, a verbal sacrifice...

    (Wuest) The word of Christ, let it be continually at home in you in abundance...

    (Wand) Let the word of Christ have a treasured place in your hearts.

    (Conc.) Let the word of Christ be making its home in you richly...

    (20th C. 1) Let the Message from the Christ dwell in your minds in all its wealth, and make you in every respect wise...

    (Trans.) Let Christ's message in all its richness occupy your hearts...

    (Cent.) Let the word of Christ have its home in you richly, in all wisdom...

    (N. Berk.) Let the enriching message of Christ have ample room in your lives...

    (Phil.) Let Christ's teaching live in your hearts, making you rich in the true wisdom...

    (Black.) Let the word of Christ dwell in you with all its wealth of meaning...

    (Douay) Let the word of Christ dwell in you abundantly...

COLOSSIANS 3:16 (GNB) Christ's message in all its richness must live in your hearts...

(New Life) Let the teaching of Christ and His words keep on living in you. These make your lives rich and full of wisdom...

(Lau.) Be rich in the words of Christ. Let them live in you...

(Hudson) Let the gospel message about Christ...house in your hearts...in no meager measure with full insight...

(Deaf) Let the teaching of Christ live inside you richly...

I TIMOTHY 2:1 I exhort therefore, that first of all, supplication, prayers, intercessions, and giving of thanks, be made for all men;...

(Hudson) Well then, the most important point I urge is...

(Black.) Now, as a matter of first importance...

(Cent.) ...be offered regularly...

I TIMOTHY 2:2 For kings, and for all that are in authority; that we may lead a quiet and peaceable life in all godliness and honesty.

(Black.) ...especially for rulers and all who occupy positions of eminence...

(Knox) ...especially for kings and others in high station...

(Barclay) Pray for kings and for all who hold high office.

(Jordan) ...for heads of state and for all who are in positions of authority...

(NEB) ...for sovereigns and all in high office, that we may lead a tranquil and quiet life in full observance of religion and high standards of morality.

(Roth.) ...In order that an undisturbed and quiet life we may lead, in all godliness and gravity (or dignity).

(New Life) ...so we might live quiet God-like lives in peace.

(Way) ...so that we may live an unharrassed life of inward peace in all reverence for God and in self-respect.

(N. Berk.) ...for kings and all who hold high positions, that with all reverence and dignity we may lead a quiet and undisturbed life.

(Authentic) ...for kings and all holding positions of authority...

(RSV) ...for kings and for all who are in high positions...

(Roth.) ...all those who are in eminent station...

I TIMOTHY 2:3 For this is good and acceptable in the sight of God our Savior...

(Knox) Such prayer is our duty, it is what God, our Savior, expects of us...

(Barclay) Such prayer is a lovely thing. It is the kind of prayer that God our Saviour wants to hear...

(NEB) Such prayer is right, and approved by God our Saviour...

(Conc.) ...for this is ideal and welcome in the sight of our Saviour, God...

I TIMOTHY 2:4 Who will have all men to be saved, and to come unto the knowledge of the truth.

> *(Knox)* Since it is his will that all men should be saved, and be led to recognize the truth...
>
> *(Barclay)* ...for he wants all men to be saved and to arrive at a knowledge of the truth.

I TIMOTHY 2:8 I will therefore that men pray everywhere, lifting up holy hands, without wrath and doubting.

> *(NAB)* ...with blameless hands held aloft...
>
> *(Wuest)* ...without anger or skeptical criticism...
>
> *(Wms.)* ...lifting to heaven holy hands which are kept unstained by anger and dissensions...
>
> *(Weym.)* ...lifting to God holy hands which are unstained with anger or strife...
>
> *(Way)* ...lifting heavenward unsullied hands, nursing the while no secret grudge, harboring no lurking skepticism.

HEBREWS 13:15 By him therefore let us offer the sacrifice of praise to God continually, that is, the fruit of our lips, giving thanks to his name.

> *(Jer.)* Through him, let us offer God an unending sacrifice of praise, a verbal sacrifice...
>
> *(Deaf)* So through Jesus we should never stop offering our sacrifice to God. That sacrifice is our praise, coming from lips that speak his name.
>
> *(Berk.)* Let us then through Him at all times present a praise offering to God, which is the fruit of lips that make confession in His name.
>
> *(Noli)* In his name we always offer a sacrifice of praise to God.
>
> *(River.)* Through him then let us offer to God always the sacrifice of praise, that is, the fruit of lips that make confession in his name.
>
> *(GNB)* Let us, then, always offer praise to God as our sacrifice through Jesus, which is the offering presented by lips that confess him as Lord.
>
> *(Pl. Eng.)* Let us through him, then, offer a sacrifice of praise at all times to God, that is, the fruit of lips making confession of his name.
>
> *(Norlie)* Our constant sacrifice to God should therefore be our songs of praise, the faithful confession of His name with our lips.
>
> *(Cent.)* In his name, then, let us continually offer up a sacrifice of praise to God, that is the fruit of lips that confess his name.
>
> *(N. Berk.)* Through Him, then, let us at all times present a praise offering to God, which is the fruit of lips that confess His name.
>
> *(Cony.)* ...the fruit of our lips, making confession unto His name.

JAMES 1:5-7 If any of you lack wisdom, let him ask of God, that giveth to all men liberally, and upbraideth not, and it shall be given him. But let him ask in faith, nothing wavering. For he that wavereth is like a wave of the sea driven with the wind and tossed. For let not that man think that he shall receive any thing of the Lord.

> *(AMP)* If any of you is deficient in wisdom, let him ask of the giving God [Who gives] to everyone liberally and ungrudgingly, without reproaching or faultfinding, and it will be given him. Only it must be in faith that he asks, with no wavering (no hesitating, no doubting). For the one who wavers (hesitates, doubts) is like the billowing surge out at sea that is blown hither and thither and tossed by the wind. For truly, let not such a person imagine that he will receive anything [he asks for] from the Lord.

> *(TLB)* If you want to know what God wants you to do, ask him, and he will gladly tell you, for he is always ready to give a bountiful supply of wisdom to all who ask him; he will not resent it. But when you ask him, be sure that you really expect him to tell you, for a doubtful mind will be as unsettled as a wave of the sea that is driven and tossed by the wind; And every decision you then make will be uncertain, as you turn first this way, and then that. If you don't ask with faith, don't expect the Lord to give you any solid answer.

> *(Weym.)* ...who gives with open hand...

> *(20th C.R.)* ...with confidence, never doubting.

> *(Gspd.)* Such a man must not expect to get anything from the Lord...

> *See faith p. 169*

JAMES 5:13-18 Is any among you afflicted? let him pray. Is any merry? let him sing psalms. Is any sick among you? let him call for the elders of the church; and let them pray over him, anointing him with oil in the name of the Lord: And the prayer of faith shall save the sick, and the Lord shall raise him up; and if he has committed sins, they shall be forgiven him. Confess your faults one to another, and pray one for another, that ye may be healed. The effectual fervent prayer of a righteous man availeth much. Elias was a man subject to like passions as we are, and he prayed earnestly that it might not rain: and it rained not on the earth by the space of three years and six months. And he prayed again, and the heaven gave rain, and the earth brought forth her fruit.

> *(Gspd.)* ...in trouble, he should pray...

> *(ASV)* ...suffering...

JAMES 5:13-18 (AMP) Is anyone among you afflicted (ill-treated, suffering evil)? He should pray. Is anyone glad at heart? He should sing praise [to God]. Is anyone among you sick? He should call in the church elders (the spiritual guides). And they should pray over him, anointing him with oil in the Lord's name. And the prayer [that is] of faith will save him who is sick, and the Lord will restore him; and if he has committed sins, he will be forgiven. Confess to one another therefore your faults (your slips, your false steps, your offenses, your sins) and pray [also] for one another, that you may be healed and restored [to a spiritual tone of mind and heart]. The earnest (heartfelt, continued) prayer of a righteous man makes tremendous power available [dynamic in its working]. Elijah was a human being with a nature such as we have [with feelings, affections and a constitution like ours]; and he prayed earnestly for it not to rain, and no rain fell on the earth for three years and six months. And [then] he prayed again and the heavens supplied rain and the land produced its crops [as usual].

(NEB) ...He should turn to prayer...

(TLB) ...keep on praying about it...

(Weym.) ...in good spirits...

(Wms.) ...in a happy mood...

(TLB) ...should continually be singing praises to the Lord.

(NIV) ...sing songs of praise.

(TLB) ...they should pray over him and pour a little oil upon him, calling on the Lord to heal him.

(Basic) And by the prayer of faith the man who is ill will be made well, and he will be lifted up by the Lord, and for any sin which he has done he will have forgiveness.

(20th C.R.) The prayer offered in faith will save the man who is sick...

(Gspd.) ...the Lord will restore him to health, and if he has committed sins, he will be forgiven.

(Weym.) ...The heartfelt supplication of a righteous man exerts a mighty influence.

(Trans.) ...The good man's prayer is very powerful because God is at work in it.

(Fenton) ...Very powerfully productive is the prayer of a righteous man.

(TLB) ...The earnest prayer of a righteous man has great power and wonderful results.

(NIV) ...the prayer of a righteous man is powerful and effective.

(Adams) ...The petition of a righteous person has very powerful effects.

(Authentic) ...the heartfelt petition of an upright man has great force.

(Swann) ...The energetic supplications of a righteous one prevails greatly.

(Godbey) ...the inward working prayer of a righteous man avails much.

(Roth. 2) ...Much avails a righteous man's supplication, working inwardly.

(Noli) ...the prayer of a righteous man has tremendous power.

(New Life) ...The prayer from the heart of a man right with God has much power.

(Stevens) ...secures great blessing from God.

(Cress.) ...big things can be done.

JAMES 5:13-18 (Norlie) Think of Elijah, a man with feelings just like ours...

(K. & L.) Elias was a man like us, subject to the same weaknesses...

(Wuest) Elijah was a human being of like nature and constitution to us...

(NAB) Elijah was only a man like us...

(NIV, Trans.) Elijah was a man just like us...

(Jordan) Elijah, for instance, was a human being just like us...

(20th C.R.) Elijah was only a man like ourselves, but, when he prayed fervently that it might not rain, no rain fell upon the land for three years and a half.

(Authentic) Elijah was a human being exactly like ourselves...

(TLB) Then he prayed again, this time that it would rain, and down it poured and the grass turned green and the gardens began to grow again.

(NIV) Again he prayed, and the heavens gave rain, and the earth produced its crops.

(Basic) ...the earth gave her fruit.

I PETER 3:12 For the eyes of the Lord are over the righteous, and his ears are open unto their prayers: but the face of the Lord is against them that do evil.

(Knox) On the upright, the Lord's eye ever looks favorably...

(Wuest) ...the Lord's eyes are directed in a favorable attitude towards the righteous...

See righteousness p. 46

I PETER 5:7 Casting all your cares upon him; for he careth for you.

(N. Berk.) Throw all your anxiety upon Him, for His concern is about you.

(Gspd.) Throw all your anxiety upon him, for he cares for you.

(Noli) Throw all your anxieties upon him, for he cares for you.

(Beck) Throw all your worry on Him because He takes care of you.

(Barclay) Bring all your worries to him to carry for you, for he is always concerned about you.

(Jer.) Unload all your worries on to him, since he is looking after you.

(Wand) Hand over all your anxieties to Him, for you are His care.

(Phil.) You can throw the whole weight of your anxieties upon him, for you are his personal concern.

(AMP) Casting the whole of your care - all your anxieties, all your worries, all your concern, once and for all - on Him; for He cares for you affectionately, and cares about you watchfully...

(Knox) Throw back on him the burden of all your anxiety; he is concerned for you.

(20th C.R.) ...laying all your anxieties upon him, for he makes you his care.

(Wuest) ...having deposited with Him once for all the whole of your worry...

I PETER 5:7 (20th C. 1) Throw all your anxieties upon him, for he makes you his care...

(Wms.) Cast every worry you have upon Him...

(Conc.) ...tossing your entire worry on Him...

(New Life) Give all your worries to Him...

(Lau.) Throw all your cares on Him...

(GNB) Leave all your worries with him...

See peace p. 356

I JOHN 5:14 And this is the confidence that we have in him, that, if we ask anything according to his will, he heareth us:

(Barclay) The reason why we can approach God with complete confidence is that, if we ask for anything that is in accordance with his will, he listens to us.

(Knox) Such familiar confidence we have in him...

(Roth. 2) And this is the freedom of speech which we have towards him...

(K. & L.) This is the extent of our confidence in him: No matter what we ask, provided it is in keeping with his will, he hears us.

(Jer.) We are quite confident that if we ask him for anything, and it is in accordance with his will, he will hear us;...

(NEB) We can approach God with confidence for this reason: if we make requests which accord with his will he listens to us;...

(GNB) We have courage in God's presence, because we are sure that he hears us if we ask him for anything that is according to his will.

(Conc., ASV) ...this is the boldness...

(Weekes) ...if we ask anything agreeable to his will...

(Deaf) We can come to God with no doubts...

(Norlie) Also that we can behold in prayer, feeling sure that He will hear us if we ask for anything according to His will.

(N. Berk.) ...if we petition anything in agreement with His will...

(Berk.) And this is the confidence we have resting on Him, that if we petition anything in agreement with His will, He hears us...

I JOHN 5:15 And if we know that he hears us, whatsoever we ask, we know that we have the petitions that we desired of him.

(Barclay) If we know that he listens to us, whenever we ask him for anything, we know that the things for which we have asked him are already ours.

(Jer.) ...and, knowing that whatever we may ask, he hears us, we know that we have already been granted what we asked of him.

(K. & L.) Now if we know that he hears us in regard to whatever we ask, we know that we have already obtained the requests we have made of him.

I JOHN 5:15 (NEB) ...and if we know that our requests are heard, we know also that the things we ask for are ours.

(GNB) He hears us whenever we ask him...

(AMP) And if (since) we [positively] know that He listens to us in whatever we ask, we also know [with settled and absolute knowledge] that we have [granted us as our present possessions] the requests made of Him.

(Trans.) And if we know that he always listens to us, we know that we possess what we have asked him for.

(River.) And if we know that he hears us when we ask anything...

(Conf.) ...we know that the requests we make of him are granted.

JUDE 20 But ye, beloved, building up yourselves on your most holy faith, praying in the Holy Ghost...

(AMP) But you, beloved, build yourselves up [founded] on your most holy faith [make progress, rise like an edifice higher and higher] praying in the Holy Spirit...

(Cent.) But you, beloved, continually building yourselves up on your most holy faith, and ever praying in the Holy Spirit...

(Jer.) But you, my dear friends, must use your most holy faith as your foundation and build on that, praying in the Holy Spirit...

(NEB) ...fortify yourselves in your most sacred faith...

Notes on Prayer

The
SAME FAITH
that makes you whole
will keep you whole.

Mark Hankins
11:23: THE LANGUAGE OF FAITH

EXODUS

    15:25, 26 269

    23:25 269

DEUTERONOMY

    7:15 269

    28:21-65 270

PSALM

    30:2 272

    42:11 272

    91:1-6, 10 273

    103:2, 3 274

    107:20 274

PROVERBS

    4:20-22 274

    12:18 274

    17:22 274

ISAIAH

    53:3-5 275

JEREMIAH

    30:17 275

    33:6 275

MALACHI

    4:2 276

MATTHEW

    8:2, 3 276

    8:16, 17 276

    9:34, 35 277

MARK

    5:25-34 277

    16:17 278

    16:18 279

LUKE

    1:37 279

    1:38 279

    1:45 279

    5:5 279

    5:15-20 280

    10:19 280

    13:11-13, 16 280

    17:14 281

    17:15 281

JOHN

    4:49, 50 282

    11:40 282

    14:12-14 282

    15:4, 5 282

ACTS

    3:16 283

    9:32-35 283

    10:38 283

    14:7-10 284

ROMANS

    8:2 284

    8:11 284

I CORINTHIANS

    6:13, 15, 19, 20 285

GALATIANS

    2:20 285

    3:13 269

EPHESIANS

    4:27 285

PHILIPPIANS

    2:13 285

COLOSSIANS

    1:12 285

    1:13 286

    1:14 286

HEBREWS

    13:8 277

JAMES

    4:7 286

    5:15, 16 287

I PETER

    2:24 287

    5:8, 9 287

I JOHN

    3:8 288

III JOHN

    2 288

Make sure your
"SPEAKER"
is hooked up
to your
"BELIEVER."

Mark Hankins
11:23: THE LANGUAGE OF FAITH

EXODUS 15:25, 26 And he cried unto the Lord; and the Lord showed him a tree, which when he had cast into the waters, the waters were made sweet: there he made for them a statute and an ordinance, and there he proved them, And said, "If thou wilt diligently hearken to the voice of the Lord thy God, and wilt do that which is right in his sight, and wilt give ear to his commandments, and keep all his statutes, I will put none of these diseases upon thee, which I have brought upon the Egyptians: for I am the Lord that healeth thee."

> *(NEB)* ...I, the Lord, am your healer.
>
> *(Leeser)* ...for I, the Lord, am thy physician.
>
> *(Basic)* ...I am the Lord your life-giver.
>
> *(Roth.)* ...I am Yahweh, thy physician.
>
> *(Young)* ...I, Jehovah, am healing thee.
>
> *(Smith, J.M., Gspd.)* ...for I, the Lord, make you immune to them (diseases).
>
> *(Knox)* ...I, the Lord, will bring thee only health.

EXODUS 23:25 And ye shall serve the Lord your God, and He shall bless thy bread, and thy water; and I will take sickness away from the midst of thee.

> *(Basic)* And give worship to the Lord your God, who will send his blessing on your bread and on your water; and I will take all disease away from among you.
>
> *(Mof., Smith, J.M.)* ...I will free you from disease.
>
> *(Young)* ...I have turned aside sickness from thine heart.
>
> *(Knox)* ...and keep sickness far away from thy company.

DEUTERONOMY 7:15 And the Lord will take away from thee all sickness, and will put none of the evil diseases of Egypt, which thou knowest, upon thee...

> *(AMP)* And the Lord will take away from you all sickness, and none of the evil diseases of Egypt, which you knew, will he put on you...
>
> *(Basic)* And the Lord will take away from you all disease...
>
> *(Mof.)* The Eternal will also free you from all sickness...
>
> *(Smith, J.M.)* The Lord will also free you from all sickness, and none of the malignant diseases...will he inflict on you...

GALATIANS 3:13 Christ hath redeemed us from the curse of the law, being made a curse for us: for it is written, Cursed is every one that hangeth on a tree.

> *(AMP)* Christ purchased our freedom [redeeming us] from the curse (doom) of the Law [and its condemnation], by [Himself] becoming a curse for us, for it is written [in the Scriptures], Cursed is everyone who hangs on a tree (is crucified)...
>
> *(Berk.)* Christ has bought us free from the curse of the Law...
>
> *(Noli)* ...by becoming a curse for us...
>
> *(Black.)* ...by taking the curse upon himself in our behalf...

GALATIANS 3:13 (Deaf) The law put a curse on us. But Christ took away that curse. He changed places with us. Christ put Himself under that curse...

> *(Hayman)* Christ it was who redeemed us from that curse of the Law, by receiving our curse on His own person.
>
> *(Way)* From that curse, which is of the essence of the Law, we have been ransomed only by Messiah.
>
> *(20th C.R.)* Christ ransomed us from the curse pronounced in the Law...
>
> *(Trans.)* Christ ransomed us from the curse of the Law, by taking that curse upon himself for our sakes...
>
> *(Wand)* Now, Christ bought us off the curse of the Law at the cost of being accursed for our sakes...
>
> *(TLB)* But Christ has bought us out from under the doom of that impossible system by taking the curse for our wrong doing upon himself.
>
> *(Knox)* From this curse invoked by the law Christ has ransomed us, by himself becoming, for our sakes, an accursed thing...
>
> *(Weym.)* Christ has purchased our freedom...
>
> *(GNB)* ...the curse that the Law brings...
>
> *(Barclay)* ...by taking the curse upon himself for our sakes...
>
> *(Beck.)* Christ paid the price to free us...
>
> *(Gspd.)* ...by taking our curse upon himself...
>
> *See redemption p. 58; finances p. 309*

Christ has redeemed us from the curse of the law according to Galatians 3:13. The curse of the law is found in Deuteronomy 28. It is the curse for breaking God's law and includes all sickness.

DEUTERONOMY 28:21, 22, 27, 28, 59-61, 65 The Lord shall make the pestilence cleave unto thee, until he has consumed thee from off the land, whither thou goest to possess it. The Lord shall smite thee with a consumption, and with a fever, and with an inflammation, and with an extreme burning, and with the sword, and with blasting, and with mildew; and they shall pursue thee until thou perish...The Lord will smite thee with the botch of Egypt, and with the emerods, and with the scab, and with the itch, whereof thou canst not be healed. The Lord shall smite thee with madness, and blindness, and astonishment of heart...The Lord shall smite thee in the knees, and in the legs, with a sore botch that cannot be healed, from the sole of thy foot unto the top of thy head...Then the Lord will make thy plagues wonderful, and the plagues of thy seed, even great plagues, and of long continuance, and sore sicknesses, and of long continuance. Moreover he will bring upon thee all the diseases of Egypt, which thou wast afraid of; and they shall cleave unto thee. Also every sickness, and every plague, which is not written in the book of this law, them will the Lord bring upon thee, until thou be destroyed...the Lord shall give thee there a trembling heart, and failing of eyes, and sorrow of mind.

DEUTERONOMY 28:21, 22, 27, 28, 59-61, 65

Pestilence	*(GNB, Basic)* = disease after disease
Consumption	*(TLB)* = tuberculosis
	(GNB) = infectious diseases
	(Basic) = wasting disease
Inflammation	*(Sept.)* = cold
	(Mof., Knox) = ague (or malarial fever)
	(TLB) = infections
Extreme burning	*(Smith, J.M.)* = sunstroke
	(Mof.) = erysipelas
Sword	*(Jer., Beck, Berk., Smith, J.M., others)* = drought
Blasting	*(TLB, others)* = blight
Mildew	*(Fenton, Sept.)* = paleness; jaundice
Botch of Egypt	*(Leeser)* = inflammatory disease
	(Fenton, Douay, Young) = ulcer
	(Roth., Smith, J.M.) = sores
Botch of Egypt	*(Jer., GNB, NAB, Berk., Beck, others)* = boils
Emerods	*(Fenton, TLB, Mof., NAB, NIV, NASB, AMP., Berk.)* = tumors
	(Roth., Leeser) = hemorrhoids
	(RSV, Smith, J.M.) = ulcers
	(Knox, Jer.) = swellings in the groin
	(GNB) = sores
Scabs	*(Fenton, TLB, Young, Smith, J.M., Jer., RSV, AMP, others)* = scurvy
	(NAB) = eczema
	(NASB, Berk.) = incurable itch
	(Sept.) = malignant scab
	(NIV) = festering sores
Itch	*(Basic)* = other sorts of skin diseases
Madness	*(Sept.)* = insanity
	(GNB) = lose your mind
	(Knox) = distracted
	(Basic) = your minds diseased
Astonishment of heart	*(Jer.)* = distraction of mind
	(Berk., GNB) = confusion
	(NIV) = confusion of mind
	(Smith, J.M.) = dismay
	(AMP) = dismay of (mind and) heart
	(Knox) = crazed in thy wits

DEUTERONOMY 28:21, 22, 27, 28, 59-61, 65

Astonishment of heart	*(Leeser)* = confusion of heart
	(NAB) = panic
Sore botch	*(Fenton, Young, Douay)* = ulcer
	(Roth., AMP) = boil
	(Jer., GNB, Beck, NASB, NAB, NIV, TLB, RSV) = boils
	(Berk., Smith, J.M.) = sores
	(Basic) = a skin disease
	(Leeser) = a sore inflammation
Plagues	*(Young)* = thy strokes and the strokes of thy seed
	(GNB) = incurable diseases and horrible epidemics
	(NASB) = severe and lasting plagues and chronic sicknesses
	(NAB) = malignant and lasting maladies
	(Basic) = cruel diseases stretching on through long years
	(AMP) = extraordinary strokes and blows
	(NIV) = ...every kind of sickness and disaster not recorded in this Book of the Law
	(NAB, Conf.) = ...any kind of sickness or calamity not mentioned in this book of the law
Trembling heart	*(NIV)* = an anxious mind
	(Jer.) = a quaking heart
	(Basic) = a shaking heart
Failing of eyes	*(Jer.)* = weary eyes
Sorrow of mind	*(NIV)* = a despairing heart

PSALM 30:2 O Lord my God, I cried unto thee and thou hast healed me.

PSALMS 42:11 Why art thou cast down, O my soul? And why art thou disquieted within me? Hope thou in God: for I shall yet praise Him, who is the health of my countenance, and my God.

> *(TLB)* But O my soul, don't be discouraged. Don't be upset. Expect God to act! For I know that I shall again have plenty of reason to praise him for all that he will do. He is my help! He is my God!

PSALM 91:1-6, 10 He that dwelleth in the secret place of the Most High shall abide under the shadow of the Almighty. I will say of the Lord, He is my refuge and my fortress: my God; in Him will I trust. Surely He shall deliver thee from the snare of the fowler, and from the noisome pestilence. He shall cover thee with His feathers, and under His wings shalt thou trust; His truth shall be thy shield and buckler. Thou shalt not be afraid for the terror by night; nor for the arrow that flieth by day; Nor for the pestilence that walketh in darkness; nor for the destruction that wasteth at noonday. There shall no evil befall thee, neither shall any plague come nigh thy dwelling.

(AMP) He who dwells in the secret place of the Most High shall remain stable and fixed under the shadow of the Almighty (Whose power no foe can withstand).

(RSV) He who dwells in the shelter of the Most High, who abides in the shadow of the Almighty, will say to the Lord, "My refuge and my fortress; my God, in whom I trust."

(Young) He who is dwelling in the secret place of the Most High, in the shade of the Mighty lodgeth habitually, He is saying of Jehovah...

(Basic) Happy is he whose resting-place is in the secret of the Lord, and under the shade of the wings of the Most High; Who says of the Lord, He is my safe place and my tower of strength: He is my God...He will take you out of the bird-net, and keep you safe from wasting disease...You will have no fear of the evil things of the night... Or of the disease which takes men in the dark...

(Smith, J.M.) He who dwells...Says of the Lord...No disaster will befall you, nor calamity come near your tent.

(Leeser) He who sitteth under the secret protection of the Most High, shall rest under the shadow of the Almighty.

(Knox) He who lives under the protection of the Most High, under his heavenly care content to abide, can say to the Lord, Thou art my support and my stronghold, my God, in whom I trust. It is He that rescues me from every treacherous snare, from every whisper of harm. Sheltered under His arms, under His wings nestling, thou art safe: His faithfulness will throw a shield about thee. Nothing shalt thou have to fear from nightly terrors...from the assault of man or fiend under the noon. There is no harm that can befall thee...

(TLB) ...His faithful promises are your armor.

(GNB) He will keep you safe from all hidden dangers and from all deadly diseases... and so no disaster will strike you, no violence will come near your home.

(Beck) ...and from the deadly plague...the plague ravaging at noon.

(NAB) ...nor the devastating plague at noon.

(Leeser) ...nor of the deadly disease that wasteth at noonday.

(NEB) ...or the plague raging at noonday...No disaster shall befall you, no calamity shall come upon your home.

PSALM 91:1-6, 10 (NIV) ...nor the plague that destroys at midday.

   (Fenton) So sickness will not approach you, contagion not enter your Rest.

PSALM 103:2, 3 Bless the Lord, O my soul, and forget not all His benefits: Who forgiveth all thine iniquities; Who healeth all thy diseases.

   (NEB) He pardons all my guilt and heals all my suffering.

   (Basic) ...he takes away all your diseases.

   (Young) ...Who is healing all thy diseases.

PSALM 107:20 He sent His Word, and healed them, and delivered them from their destruction.

   (Mof.) ...he sent his Word to heal them and preserve their life.

   (Leeser) ...and delivereth them from their graves.

   (Fenton) He sent out His word, and it healed, and from their corruptions it freed!

PROVERBS 4:20-22 My son, attend to my words; incline thine ear unto my sayings. Let them not depart from thine eyes; keep them in the midst of thine heart. For they are life unto those that find them, and health to all their flesh.

   (TLB) ...let them penetrate deep within your heart...

   (Knox) ...let a man master them, they will bring life and healing to his whole being.

   (Leeser) ...and to all his body a healing.

   (Roth.) ...to every part of one's flesh they bring healing.

   See faith p. 138

PROVERBS 12:18 There is that speaketh like the piercings of a sword: but the tongue of the wise is health.

   (Mof.) A reckless tongue wounds like a sword, but there's healing power in thoughtful words.

   (GNB) Thoughtless words can wound as deeply as any sword, but wisely spoken words can heal.

   (Basic) There are some whose uncontrolled talk is like the wounds of a sword, but the tongue of the wise makes one well again.

   See faith p. 139

PROVERBS 17:22 A merry heart doeth good like a medicine: but a broken spirit drieth the bones.

   (GNB) Being cheerful keeps you healthy...

   (Smith, J.M.) A happy heart is a healing medicine...

   (Basic) A glad heart makes a healthy body...

   (Mof.) A glad heart helps and heals...

   (Jer.) A glad heart is excellent medicine, a spirit depressed wastes the bones away.

PROVERBS 17:22 (Knox) A cheerful heart makes a quick recovery; it is crushed spirits that waste a man's frame.

(Fenton) The best medicine is a cheerful heart...

(Roth.) A joyful heart worketh an excellent cure...

(TLB) ...a broken spirit makes one sick.

JEREMIAH 30:17 For I will restore health unto thee, and I will heal thee of thy wounds, saith the Lord; because they called thee an Outcast, saying, This is Zion, whom no man seeketh after.

(AMP) For I will restore health to you, and I will heal your wounds, says the Lord...

(TLB) I will give you back your health again and heal your wounds.

(Message) As for you, I'll come with healing, curing the incurable...

JEREMIAH 33:6 Behold, I will bring it health and cure, and I will cure them, and will reveal unto them the abundance of peace and truth.

(AMP) Behold, [in the future restored Jerusalem] I will lay upon it health and healing, and I will cure them and will reveal to them the abundance of peace (prosperity, security, stability and truth.

(TLB) Nevertheless the time will come when I will heal Jerusalem's damage and give her prosperity and peace.

(Message) But now take another look. I'm going to give this city a thorough renovation, working a true healing inside and out. I'm going to show them life whole, life brimming with blessings.

ISAIAH 53:3-5 He is despised and rejected of men; a man of sorrows, and acquainted with grief: and we hid as it were our faces from Him; He was despised, and we esteemed Him not. Surely He hath borne our griefs, and carried our sorrows: yet we did esteem Him stricken, smitten of God, and afflicted. But He was wounded for our transgressions, He was bruised for our iniquities: the chastisement of our peace was upon Him; and with His stripes we are healed.

(Leeser, Masoretic O.T.) ...a man of pains, and acquainted with disease...

(Basic) ...he was a man of sorrows, marked by disease...

(Roth.) ...Man of pains and familiar with sickness...

(Leeser) But only our diseases did He bear Himself, and our pains He carried.

(Basic) But it was our pain he took, and our diseases were put on him: while to us he seemed as one diseased, on whom God's punishment had come.

(Masoretic O.T.) Surely our disease He did bear, and our pains He carried...

(Roth) Yet surely our sicknesses he carried, and as for our pains he bare the burden of them...

(Smith, J.M.) Yet it was our sicknesses that He bore, our pains that He carried.

(Leeser) ...through His bruises was healing granted to us.

ISAIAH 53:3-5 (Roth.) ...by his stripes there is healing for us.

(Mof.) ...the blows that fell to him have brought us healing.

(GNB) ...We are healed by the punishment he suffered, made whole by the blows he received.

(Young) ...by his bruise there is healing to us.

(AMP) ...the chastisement needful to obtain peace and well-being for us was upon Him, and with the stripes that wounded Him, we are healed and made whole.

See redemption p. 53

MALACHI 4:2 But unto you that fear My name shall the Son of Righteousness arise with healing in His wings; and ye shall go forth, and grow up as calves of the stall.

(Berk.) But for you, who revere My name, the sun of righteousness will arise with healing in its beams, and you will go forth and leap like calves from the stall.

(Sept.) ...and you shall go forth and leap for joy like young bullocks loosed from yokes.

See righteousness p. 49

MATTHEW 8:2, 3 And, behold, there came a leper and worshipped Him, saying, Lord, if thou wilt, thou canst make me clean. And Jesus put forth His hand, and touched him, saying, I will; be thou clean. And immediately his leprosy was cleansed.

(Jer.) A leper now came up and bowed low in front of him. "Sir," he said, "If you want to, you can cure me." Jesus stretched out his hand, touched him and said, "Of course I want to! Be cured!" And his leprosy was cured at once.

(Wade) ...if you have the will, you have the power, to cleanse me. (Jesus said)...I have the will; be cleansed.

(Jordan) ...Sir, if you really wanted to, you could heal me. (Jesus said)...I do want to. Be healed.

(Phil.) ...if you want to, you can make me clean.. (Jesus said) Of course I want to. Be clean!

(Basic) ...Lord, if it is your pleasure, you have power to make me clean. And he put his hand on him, saying, It is my pleasure; be clean.

(Rieu) ...I will it. Be cleansed.

(Knox) ...It is my will...

(Fenton, Weym., 20th C. 1) ...I am willing...

(Wuest) ...I am desiring it from all my heart. Be cleansed at once.

(Authentic) ...I do will it...

MATTHEW 8:16, 17 When the even was come, they brought unto Him many that were possessed with devils: and He cast out the spirits with His word, and healed all that were sick: That it might be fulfilled which was spoken by Esaias, the prophet, saying, "Himself took our infirmities, and bare our sicknesses."

(Norlie) ...He took our infirmities upon Himself, and took away our diseases.

MATTHEW 8:16, 17 (AMP) ...He, Himself, took (in order to carry away) our weaknesses and infirmities and bore away our diseases.

(NEB) He took away our illnesses and lifted our diseases from us.

(Trans.) ...He took away our illnesses and carried away our diseases.

(Jer.) He took our sicknesses away and carried our diseases for us.

(Mof.) ...He took away our sicknesses and our diseases he removed.

(New Life) ...He took on Himself our sickness and carried away our diseases.

(Wuest, Berk.) ...carried off our diseases.

MATTHEW 9:34, 35 But the Pharisees said, He casteth out devils through the prince of the devils. And Jesus went about all the cities and villages, teaching in their synagogues, and preaching the gospel of the kingdom, and healing every sickness and every disease among the people.

(TLB) ...And wherever he went he healed people of every sort of illness.

(AMP) But the Pharisees said, He drives out demons through and with the help of the prince of demons. And Jesus went about all the cities and villages, teaching in their synagogues and proclaiming the good news (the Gospel) of the kingdom, and curing all kinds of disease and every weakness and infirmity.

(NIV) ...preaching the good news of the kingdom and healing every disease and sickness.

(Basic) ...making well all sorts of disease and pain.

(Gspd.) ...proclaiming the good news of the kingdom, and curing every disease and illness.

(ASV) ...healing all manner of disease and all manner of sickness.

HEBREWS 13:8 Jesus Christ the same yesterday, and to day, and for ever.

(AMP) Jesus Christ, (the Messiah) is [always] the same, yesterday, today, [yes,] and forever (to the ages).

(Knox) What Jesus Christ was yesterday, and is today, he remains forever.

(Mof.) Jesus Christ is always the same...

MARK 5:25-34 And a certain woman, which had an issue of blood twelve years, And had suffered many things of many physicians, and had spent all that she had, and was nothing bettered, but rather grew worse, When she had heard of Jesus, came in the press behind, and touched his garment. For she said, If I may touch but His clothes, I shall be whole. And straightway the fountain of her blood was dried up; and she felt in her body that she was healed of that plague. And Jesus, immediately knowing in himself that virtue had gone out of him, turned him about in the press, and said, Who touched my clothes? And his disciples said unto him, Thou seest the multitude thronging thee, and sayest thou, Who touched me? And he looked round about to see her that had done this thing. But the woman fearing and trembling, knowing what was done in her, came and fell down before him, and told him all the truth. And he said unto her, Daughter, thy faith hath made thee whole; go in peace, and be whole of thy plague.

MARK 5:25-34 (AMP) For she kept saying, If I only touch His garments, I shall be restored to health.

> *(Wms.)* ...for she kept saying, If I can only touch His clothes, I shall get well.
> *(Wuest)* ...for she kept saying, If I touch even His garments, I shall be made whole.
> *(Phil.)* ...she kept saying...
> *(Authentic)* Jesus also was immediately aware that power had been drawn from Him...
> *(Wade)* ...Jesus, becoming conscious that the healing Power within Him had been in active operation...
> *(Smith, J.M.)* Jesus instantly perceived that healing power had passed from him...
> *(20th C. 1)* Jesus instantly became conscious that there had been a demand upon his powers...
> *(AMP)* Still He kept looking to see her who had done it.
> *(Johnson)* Jesus studied the faces in the crowd to see who had made contact with him.
> *(20th C. 1)* ...your own faith has made you well...
> *(Barclay)* ...Go and enjoy your new health, free from the trouble that was your scourge.
> *(Phil.)* ...it is your faith that has healed you.
> *(AMP)* ...your faith (your trust and confidence in Me, springing from faith in God) has restored you to health. Go in (into) peace and be continually healed and freed from your [distressing bodily] disease.
> *(NEB)* ...Go in peace, free forever from this trouble.
> *See faith p. 147*

MARK 16:17 And these signs shall follow them that believe; In my name shall they cast out devils; they shall speak with new tongues...

> *(New Life)* These special powerful works will be done by those who have put their trust in Me. In My name they will put out demons. They will speak with languages they have never learned.
> *(NEB)* Faith will bring with it these miracles: believers will cast out devils in my name...
> *(Wms.)* ...By using my name they will drive out demons...
> *(Knox)* Where believers go, these signs shall go with them...
> *(Phil.)* ...they will drive out evil spirits in my name...
> *(Gspd.)* ...with my name they will drive out demons...
> *(Weym.)* ...making use of my name, they shall expel demons.
> *(Trans.)* Wherever men believe, these signs will be found...
> *(Wade)* ...By the use of my Name they will expel demons; they will speak rapturously in strange languages...
> *(Wuest)* And these attesting miracles will accompany those who believe...
> *See authority of the believer p. 199; signs and wonders p. 409*

MARK 16:18 They shall take up serpents; and if they drink any deadly thing, it shall not hurt them; they shall lay hands on the sick, and they shall recover.

>*(Knox)* ...they will lay their hands upon the sick and make them recover.
>
>*(Fenton)* ...they shall lay their hands upon the sick, and fully restore them to strength.
>
>*(Norlie)* ...they will lay their hands on the sick and make them well again.
>
>*(Wade)* ...they will place their hands upon invalids, and they will be restored to health.
>
>*See authority of the believer p. 200; signs and wonders p. 409*

LUKE 1:37 For with God nothing shall be impossible.

>*(ASV)* For no word from God shall be void of power.
>
>*(Weym.)* For no promise from God will be impossible of fulfilment.
>
>*(Phil.)* For no promise of God can fail to be fulfilled.
>
>*(Cent.)* For no word of God shall be void of power.
>
>*(Roth.)* Because no declaration from God shall be void of power.
>
>*(Syriac)* Because nothing is difficult for God.
>
>*(20th C.R.)* No promise from God shall fail to be fulfilled.
>
>*(River.)* For no word that comes from God will fail.
>
>*(20th C. 1)* For not one word from God will prove powerless!

LUKE 1:38 And Mary said, Behold the handmaid of the Lord; be it unto me according to thy word. And the angel departed from her.

>*(Barclay)* Mary said: "I am the Lord's servant. Whatever you say, I accept."
>
>*(K. & L.)* ...May all that you have said be fulfilled in me!...

LUKE 1:45 And blessed is she that believed: for there shall be a performance of those things which were told her from the Lord.

>*(Roth.)* And happy is she who hath believed that there shall be a perfecting of the things which have been spoken to her from the Lord!
>
>*(Berk.)* And blessed is she who believed that the things told her by the Lord shall be accomplished.
>
>*(TLB)* You believed that God would do what he said; that is why he has given you this wonderful blessing!

LUKE 5:5 And Simon answering said unto him, Master, we have toiled all the night, and have taken nothing: nevertheless at thy word I will let down the net.

>*(Rieu)* "Master," replied Peter, "we toiled away all night and caught nothing. However, I will take your word for it and lower the nets."
>
>*(AMP)* ...on the ground of Your word, I will lower the nets [again].

LUKE 5:5 (Weekes) ...yet on thy word I will let down the nets.

Luke 5:15-20 But so much the more went there a fame abroad of him: and great multitudes came together to hear, and to be healed by him of their infirmities. And he withdrew himself into the wilderness, and prayed. And it came to pass on a certain day, as he was teaching, that there were Pharisees and doctors of the law sitting by, which were come out of every town of Galilee, and Judea, and Jerusalem: and the power of the Lord was present to heal them. And, behold, men brought in a bed a man which was taken with a palsy: and they sought means to bring him in, and to lay him before him. And when they could not find by what way they might bring him in because of the multitude, they went upon the housetop, and let him down through the tiling with his couch into the midst before Jesus. And when he saw their faith, he said unto him, Man, thy sins are forgiven thee.

 (Basic) ...to give hearing to his words and to be made well from their diseases.

 (Berk.) ...to listen and to be healed of their diseases.

 (Message) The healing power of God was on him...Impressed by their bold belief, he said, "Friend, I forgive your sins."

 (AMP) And when He saw [their confidence in Him, springing from] their faith...

 (TLB) Seeing their faith, Jesus said to the man, "My friend, your sins are forgiven!"

 (Conc.) ...And, perceiving their faith,...

LUKE 10:19 Behold, I give unto you power to tread on serpents and scorpions, and over all the power of the enemy: and nothing shall by any means hurt you.

 (Norlie) I have given you authority to trample on serpents and scorpions and all the might of the satanic foe, and nothing will harm you in any way.

 (Knox) ...I have given you the right to...

 (AMP) Behold! I have given you authority and power to trample upon serpents and scorpions, and (physical and mental strength and ability) over all the power that the enemy (possesses), and nothing shall in any way harm you.

 (Condon) Yes, I have given you power to trample every evil under foot, to counter all the might of the enemy; nothing whatever shall harm you.

 (Authentic) I have indeed invested you with power to stamp on snakes and scorpions...

 See authority of the believer p. 200

LUKE 13:11-13, 16 And, behold, there was a woman which had a spirit of infirmity eighteen years, and was bowed together, and could in no wise lift up herself. And when Jesus saw her, He called her to Him, and said unto her, Woman, thou art loosed from thine infirmity. And He laid His hands on her; and immediately she was made straight, and glorified God. And ought not this woman, being a daughter of Abraham, whom Satan hath bound, lo, these eighteen years, be loosed from this bond on the Sabbath day?

LUKE 13:11-13, 16 (AMP) ...an infirmity caused by a spirit (a demon of sickness).

> *(Pl. Eng.)* ...had a disease caused by an evil spirit; she was bent double and altogether unable to hold herself up.
>
> *(Gspd., Conf., NASB)* ...a sickness caused by a spirit.
>
> *(Wuest)* A woman had a spirit that caused an infirmity eighteen years and was completely bent together by a curvature of the spine, and was not able to raise herself up at all.
>
> *(Douay)* ...thou art delivered...
>
> *(NASB)* ...you are freed from your sickness...
>
> *(Mar.)* ...thou hast been loosed...
>
> *(Basic)* ...you are made free from your disease.
>
> *(NIV)* ...you are set free from your infirmity.
>
> *(Norlie)* ...you are now rid of your infirmity.
>
> *(Pl. Eng.)* ...you are freed from your disease.
>
> *(Jordan)* ...Lady, you have been freed from your weakness.
>
> *(Worrell)* ...Woman, you have been loosed from your infirmity.
>
> *(Condon)* ...Your bondage is at an end.
>
> *(Wms.)* ...at once she straightened herself up and burst into praising God.
>
> *(Roth.)* ...was there not a needs-be that she be loosed...
>
> *(Wade)* And ought not this woman, a descendant of Abraham as she is, whose power of movement Satan has fettered actually for seventeen years, to have been released from such fetters on the day of the Sabbath?
>
> *(Barclay)* ...For eighteen years Satan has fettered her. Is it not right that she should be liberated from her fetters?
>
> *(Basic)* And is it not right for this daughter of Abraham, who has been in the power of Satan for eighteen years, to be made free on the Sabbath?
>
> *(Norlie)* But this woman, a daughter of Abraham, who has been in the bondage of Satan— think of it!—for eighteen years, should not have the right to be released from her bonds because it is the Sabbath?

LUKE 17:14 And when he saw them, he said unto them, Go show yourselves unto the priests. And it came to pass, that, as they went, they were cleansed.

> *(Berk.)* ...and as they went they were being cleansed.
>
> *(Young)* ...and it came to pass, in their going, they were cleansed.

LUKE 17:15 And one of them, when he saw that he was healed, turned back, and with a loud voice glorified God...

> *(Barclay)* One of them (lepers), when he saw he was cured, turned back praising God at the top of his voice.

JOHN 4:49, 50 The nobleman saith unto him, Sir, come down ere my child die. Jesus saith unto him, Go thy way; thy son liveth. And the man believed the word that Jesus had spoken unto him, and he went his way.

> *(Beck)* "Go," Jesus told him, "your boy is well."
> *(Rieu)* "You can go back"' said Jesus. "Your son is living." And the man set out, convinced that he had heard the truth from Jesus.
> *(NIV)* ...the man took Jesus at his word and departed.
> *(Knox)* And the man began his journey home, putting his trust in the words Jesus had spoken to him.
> *(TLB)* ...the man believed Jesus and started home.
> *(AMP)* ...the man put his trust in what Jesus said...

JOHN 11:40 Jesus saith unto her, Said I not unto thee, that, if thou wouldest believe, thou shouldest see the glory of God?

> *(Knox)* ...thou wilt see God glorified?
> *(TLB)* "But didn't I tell you that you will see a wonderful miracle from God if you believe?"

JOHN 14:12-14 Verily, Verily, I say unto you, He that believeth on me, the works that I do shall he do also; and greater works than these shall he do; because I go unto my Father. And whatsoever ye shall ask in My name, that will I do, that the Father may be glorified in the Son. If ye shall ask anything in My name, I will do it.

> *(Authentic)* I tell you for a positive fact...
> *(Tomanek)* ...and more of these he shall do...

JOHN 15:4, 5 Abide in Me, and I in you. As the branch cannot bear fruit of itself, except it abide in the vine; no more can ye, except ye abide in Me. I am the vine, ye are the branches: He that abideth in Me, and I in him, the same bringeth forth much fruit: for without Me, ye can do nothing.

> *(New Life)* Get your life from Me and I will live in you. No branch can give fruit by itself. It has to get life from the vine. You are able to give fruit only when you have life from Me. I am the Vine and you are the branches. Get your life from Me...
> *(Phil.)* You must go on growing in me and I will grow in you. For just as the branch cannot bear any fruit unless it shares the life of the vine, so you can produce nothing unless you go on growing in me. I am the vine itself; you are the branches. It is the man who shares my life and whose life I share, who proves fruitful. For the plain fact is that apart from me you can do nothing at all...

> *See redemption p. 120*

ACTS 3:16 And His name, through faith in His name, hath made this man strong, whom ye see and know; yea, the faith which is by Him hath given him this perfect soundness in the presence of you all.

(Weym.) It is His name - faith in that name being the condition - which has strengthened this man...

(Knox) Here is a man you all know by sight, who has put his faith in that name, and that name has brought him strength...

(NEB) And the name of Jesus, by awakening faith, has strengthened this man, whom you see and know.

ACTS 9:32-35 And it came to pass, as Peter passed throughout all quarters, he came down also to the saints which dwelt at Lydda. And there he found a certain man named Aeneas, which had kept his bed eight years, and was sick of the palsy. And Peter said unto him, Aeneas, Jesus Christ maketh thee whole: arise, and make thy bed. And he arose immediately. And all that dwelt at Lydda and Saron saw him, and turned to the Lord.

(AMP) ...Jesus Christ (the Messiah) [now] makes you whole. Get up and make your bed! And immediately [Aeneas] stood up.

(TLB) ...Jesus Christ has healed you! Get up and make your bed. And he was healed instantly.

(Message) Peter said, "Aeneas, Jesus Christ heals you. Get up and make your bed!" And he did it – jumped right out of bed.

ACTS 10:38 How God anointed Jesus of Nazareth with the Holy Ghost and with power: who went about doing good, and healing all that were oppressed of the devil; for God was with him.

(Mof.) ...all who were harassed by the devil...

(NIV, Pl. Eng.) ...healing all who were under the power of the devil...

(Rieu) ...healing everyone in the devil's clutches...

(Barclay) ...curing all those who were under the tyranny of the devil...

(N. Berk.) ...healing all that were overpowered by the devil...

(Weym.) ...curing all who were continually oppressed by the devil...

(Jordan) ...God equipped him with the Holy Spirit and power, who passed through our midst acting nobly and healing all those who were lorded over by the devil...

(Phil.) ...healing all who suffered from the devil's power...

(Conc.) ...Who passed through as a benefactor and healer of all those who are tyrannized over by the Adversary...

(AMP) ...harassed and oppressed by [the power of] the devil...

ACTS 14:7-10 And there they preached the gospel. And there sat a certain man at Lystra, impotent in his feet, being a cripple from his mother's womb, who never had walked: The same heard Paul speak: who stedfastly beholding him, and perceiving that he had faith to be healed, Said with a loud voice, Stand upright on thy feet. And he leaped and walked.

(AMP) And there they continued to preach the glad tidings (Gospel). Now at Lystra a man sat who found it impossible to use his feet, for he was a cripple from birth and had never walked. He was listening to Paul as he talked, and [Paul] gazing intently at him and observing that he had faith to be healed, Shouted at him, saying, Stand erect on your feet! And he leaped up and walked.

(TLB) …and preaching the Good News there. While they were at Lystra, they came upon a man with crippled feet who had been that way from birth, so he had never walked. He was listening as Paul preached, and Paul noticed him and realized he had faith to be healed. So Paul called to him, "Stand up!" and the man leaped to his feet and started walking!

(Message) There was a man in Lystra who couldn't walk. He sat there, crippled since the day of his birth. He heard Paul talking, and Paul, looking him in the eye, saw that he was ripe for God's work, ready to believe. So he said, loud enough for everyone to hear, "Up on your feet!" The man was up in a flash—jumped up and walked around as if he'd been walking all his life.

ROMANS 8:2 For the law of the Spirit of life in Christ Jesus hath made me free from the law of sin and death.

(Knox) The spiritual principle of life has set me free, in Christ Jesus, from the principle of sin and death.

(Trans.) For the principle of spiritual life in Christ Jesus has liberated me from the principle of sin and death.

(AMP) …[the law of our new being]…

See redemption p. 93; eternal life p. 380

ROMANS 8:11 But if the Spirit of Him that raised up Jesus from the dead dwells in you, He that raised up Christ from the dead shall also quicken your mortal bodies by His Spirit that dwelleth in you.

(Way) If the Spirit of God, of Him who raised Jesus from the dead, has its home in you, then He who raised the Messiah Jesus from the dead will thrill with a new life your very bodies— those mortal bodies of yours—by the agency of His own Spirit, which now has its home in you.

(Gspd.) If the Spirit of him who raised Jesus from the dead has taken possession of you, he who raised Christ Jesus from the dead will also give your mortal bodies life through his Spirit that has taken possession of you.

ROMANS 8:11 (Godbey) ...will also create life in your mortal bodies...

See Holy Spirit p. 186; eternal life p. 381

I CORINTHIANS 6:13, 15, 19, 20 Meats for the belly and the belly for meats: but God shall destroy both it and them. Now the body is not for fornication, but for the Lord; and the Lord for the body...Know ye not that your bodies are the members of Christ? Shall I then take the members of Christ, and make them the members of an harlot? God forbid. What? Know ye not that your body is the temple of the Holy Ghost, which is in you, which ye have of God, and ye are not your own? For ye are bought with a price: therefore glorify God in your body, and in your spirit, which are God's.

GALATIANS 2:20 I am crucified with Christ: nevertheless, I live; yet not I, but Christ, liveth in me: and the life which I now live in the flesh, I live by the faith of the Son of God, who loved me and gave Himself for me.

> *(Lau.)* ...Christ took me to the cross with Him, and I died there with Him
> *(ASV, NASB, RSV, NEB, NIV)* I have been crucified with Christ.

See redemption p. 75; eternal life p. 385

EPHESIANS 4:27 Neither give place to the devil.

> *(Wms.)* ...stop giving the devil a chance.
> *(Barclay)* Give the devil no place or opportunity in your life.
> *(Trans.)* ...and do not give the devil a chance.
> *(Jordan)* ...don't give in one inch to the Devil.

See authority of the believer p. 216

PHILIPPIANS 2:13 For it is God which worketh in you, both to will and to do of His good pleasure.

> *(Weym.)* For it is God Himself whose power creates within you the desire to do His gracious will.
> *(Beck)* ...who makes you willing and gives you the energy to do what He wants.
> *(Gspd.)* For it is God who in his good-will is at work in your hearts, inspiring your will and your action.

See Holy Spirit p. 193

COLOSSIANS 1:12 Giving thanks unto the Father, which hath made us meet to be partakers of the inheritance of the saints in light.

> *(Gdsp.)* ...thank the Father, Who has entitled you to share the lot of God's people in the realm of light.

COLOSSIANS 1:12(N. Berk.) ...Who has qualified you for your share in the inheritance of the saints in the light.

> **(Roth.)** ...the Father that hath made you sufficient for your share...
>
> **(Godbey)** ...who has made us worthy...
>
> **(Noli)** ...He enabled us to share the inheritance of the saints who live in the light.
>
> **(TLB)** ...to share all the wonderful things that belong to those who live in the kingdom of light.
>
> *See redemption p. 97; prayer p. 255*

COLOSSIANS 1:13 Who hath delivered us from the power of darkness, and hath translated us into the kingdom of his dear Son.

> **(Gspd.)** He has rescued us from the dominion of darkness, and has transferred us into the realm of His dear Son.
>
> **(Pl. Eng.)** He has freed us from the power of darkness and carried us away into the kingdom of his beloved Son.
>
> **(Cony.)** For He has delivered us from the dominion of darkness and transplanted us into the kingdom of his beloved Son.
>
> **(Wade)** For God has rescued us from the dominance exercised by the powers of Spiritual Darkness, and transferred us to the Dominion of His Son—the Object of His love.
>
> **(TLB)** For he has rescued us out of the darkness and gloom of Satan's kingdom and brought us into the kingdom of his dear Son.
>
> *See redemption p. 97; prayer p. 256*

COLOSSIANS 1:14 In whom we have redemption through His blood, even the forgiveness of sins.

> **(Gspd.)** ...by whom we have been ransomed from captivity...
>
> **(Cony.)** ...in Whom we have our redemption...
>
> **(Way)** ...in whom we have our ransoming, the remission of our sins.
>
> *See redemption p. 98; prayer p. 257*

JAMES 4:7 Submit yourselves therefore to God. Resist the devil, and he will flee from you.

> **(Barclay)** So then, accept the authority of God. Take a stand against the devil, and he will run away from you.
>
> **(NEB)** Stand up to the devil and he will turn and run.
>
> **(Wuest)** Stand immovable against the onset of the devil and he will flee from you.
>
> **(Basic)** ...be ruled by God; but make war on the Evil One, and he will be put to flight before you.
>
> *See authority of the believer p. 222*

JAMES 5:15, 16 And the prayer of faith shall save the sick, and the Lord shall raise him up; and if he has committed sins, they shall be forgiven him. Confess your faults one to another and pray one for another, that ye may be healed. The effectual fervent prayer of a righteous man availeth much.

(Basic) And by the prayer of faith, the man who is ill will be made well...

(Wade) And the prayer offered in faith will restore the sufferer to health, and the Lord will raise him from the sick-bed.

I PETER 2:24 Who His own self bare our sins in His own body on the tree, that we, being dead to sins, should live unto righteousness: by Whose stripes ye were healed.

(AMP) He personally bore our sins in His [own] body to the tree [as to an altar and offered Himself on it], that we might die (cease to exist) to sin and live to righteousness. By His wounds you have been healed.

(Phil.) It was the suffering that he bore which has healed you.

(Adams) ...so that by dying to sins we might live to righteousness...

(NEB) In his own person he carried our sins...

(Pl. Eng.) ...that we might die to sins and live again in righteousness...

(Mof.) ...that we might break with sin and live the good life...

(Basic) ...might have a new life in righteousness, and by his wounds we have been made well.

(20th C.R.) ...His bruising was your healing...

(Wuest) ...by means of whose bleeding stripe (singular), you were healed.

(FSB, Godbey, Alf.) ...stripe...by whose stripes ye are healed.

(TLB) For his wounds have healed ours!

(NIV) ...by his wounds you have been healed.

See redemption p. 59; eternal life p. 395

I PETER 5:8, 9 Be sober, be vigilant; because your adversary the devil, as a roaring lion, walketh about, seeking whom he may devour: whom resist steadfast in the faith, knowing that the same afflictions are accomplished in your brethren that are in the world.

(Barclay) You must resist him with a rock-like faith...

(Wuest) Stand immovable against his onset, solid as a rock in your faith...

(AMP) ...be firm in faith (against his onset)—rooted, established, strong, immovable and determined...

See authority of the believer p. 223

I JOHN 3:8 He that committeth sin is of the devil, for the devil sinneth from the beginning. For this purpose the Son of God was manifested, that he might destroy the works of the devil.

(AMP) The reason the Son of God was made manifest (visible) was to undo (destroy, loosen and dissolve) the works the devil (has done).

(Young) ...that he may break up the works of the devil.

(Basic) And the Son of God was seen on earth, so that he might put an end to the works of the Evil One.

(Wand) ...that He might neutralize what the Devil had done.

(Wuest) ...that He might bring to naught the works of the devil.

(Jordan) ...that he might break up the Devil's doings.

(Jer.) ...to lead a sinful life is to belong to the devil, since the devil was a sinner from the beginning. It was to undo all that the devil has done that the Son of God appeared.

(Phil.) Now the Son of God came to earth with the express purpose of liquidating the devil's activities.

(Conc.) ...that He should be annulling the acts of the Adversary.

III JOHN 2 Beloved, I wish above all things that thou mayest prosper and be in health, even as thy soul prospereth.

(20th C. 1) Dear friend, I pray that all may go well with you and that you may have good health...

(Weym.) Dearly loved one, I pray that you may in all respects prosper and enjoy good health...

(Message) ...for good fortune in everything you do, and for your good health - that your everyday affairs prosper, as well as your soul!

(Wuest) ...you will be prospering, and that you will be continually having good health just as your soul is prospering.

(RSV) ...that all may go well with you and that you may be in health...

(Gspd.) ...that everything is going well with you and that you are well; I know it is well with your soul.

(Letters) ...to make your body as strong and healthy as your spirit is.

(TLB) ...that your body is as healthy as I know your soul is.

See finances p. 313

Notes on Divine Healing

FAITH
will work for
ANYONE
and will work on
ANYTHING.

Mark Hankins
11:23 : THE LANGUAGE OF FAITH

GENESIS
2:8 293
2:10 293
2:12 293
8:22 293
13:2 293
DEUTERONOMY
8:18 293
14:22 293
14:23 293
26:8, 9 294
JOSHUA
1:8 294
I CHRONICLES
29:3 294
29:12 295
29:26 295
29:28 295
II CHRONICLES
9:20 295
9:27 295
20:20 295
26:5 296
JOB
8:6 296
8:7 296
36:11 296
PSALM
23:1 296
34:9 297
34:10 297
35:27 297
66:12 297
105:37 297
112:2 298
112:3 298
115:14 298
115:15 298
147:14 298
PROVERBS
3:9, 10 298
8:20 298
8:21 298
10:22 299
11:24, 25 299

13:22 299
15:6 300
22:4 300
ECCLESIASTES
11:1-6 300
ISAIAH
1:19 300
32:20 301
60:17 301
61:7 301
MALACHI
3:10 301
MATTHEW
6:32 302
6:33 302
7:11 303
23:23 303
LUKE
6:38 304
12:31-32 304
16:9-12 304
II CORINTHIANS
8:9 304
9:6 305
9:7 305
9:8 306
9:9 307
9:10 307
9:11 308
GALATIANS
3:9 308
3:13 309
3:14 309
6:7-10 310
PHILIPPIANS
4:15 310
4:16 310
4:17 310
4:18 311
4:19 311
I TIMOTHY
4:8 312
6:17-19 312
HEBREWS
7:2 312

7:5 313
7:8 313
III JOHN
2 313

God wants to
**BLESS YOU SO
ABUNDANTLY**
so He can use you as
**ADVERTISEMENT ON
HOW WELL**
He treats His children.

Mark Hankins

GENESIS 2:8 And the Lord God planted a garden eastward in Eden; and there he put the man whom he had formed.

> *(Douay)* And the Lord God had planted a paradise of pleasure from the beginning; wherein he placed man whom he had formed.
>
> *(Knox)* God had planted a garden of delight, in which he now placed the man...

GENESIS 2:10 And a river went out of Eden to water the garden; and from thence it was parted, and became into four heads.

> *(Douay)* And a river went out of the place of pleasure to water paradise...
>
> *(Mof.)* ...streams...

GENESIS 2:12 And the gold of that land is good: there is bdellium and the onyx stone.

> *(TLB)* ...where nuggets of pure gold are found...

GENESIS 8:22 While the earth remaineth, seedtime and harvest, and cold and heat, and summer and winter, and day and night shall not cease.

GENESIS 13:2 And Abram was very rich in cattle, in silver, and in gold.

> *(AMP)* ...Abram was extremely rich...
>
> *(Douay)* And he was very rich in possession of gold and silver.
>
> *(Young)* ...exceedingly wealthy...
>
> *(Knox)* Abram was by now the master of rich possessions, with abundance of gold and silver.

DEUTERONOMY 8:18 But thou shalt remember the Lord thy God: for it is he that giveth thee power to get wealth, that he may establish his covenant which he sware unto thy fathers, as it is this day.

> *(TLB)* Always remember that it is the Lord your God who gives you power to become rich, and he does it to fulfill his promise to your ancestors.

DEUTERONOMY 14:22 Thou shalt truly tithe all the increase of thy seed, that the field bringeth forth year by year.

> *(Basic)* Put on one side a tenth of all the increase of your seed, produced year by year.
>
> *(Jer.)* Every year you must take a tithe of all that your sowing yields on the land...

DEUTERONOMY 14:23 And thou shalt eat before the Lord thy God, in the place which he shall choose to place his name there, the tithe of thy corn, of thy wine, and of thine oil, and the firstlings of thy herds and of thy flocks; that thou mayest learn to fear the Lord thy God always.

> *(TLB)* ...The purpose of tithing is to teach you always to put God first in your lives.

DEUTERONOMY 14:23 (Torah) ...so that you may learn to revere the Lord your God forever.

DEUTERONOMY 26:8, 9 And the Lord brought us forth out of Egypt with a mighty hand, and with an outstretched arm, and with great terribleness, and with signs, and with wonders: And he hath brought us into this place, and hath given us this land, even a land that floweth with milk and honey.
>   *(NAB)* ...with terrifying power...
>   *(Torah)* ...awesome power...
>   *(Mof.)* ...with signal acts...
>   *(Knox)* ...and brought us here, where he has given us a land that is all milk and honey.

JOSHUA 1:8 This book of the law shall not depart out of thy mouth; but thou shalt meditate therein day and night, that thou mayest observe to do according to all that is written therein: for then thou shalt make thy way prosperous, and then thou shalt have good success.
>   *(Mof.)* This law-book you shall never cease to have on your lips; you must pore over it day and night, that you may be mindful to carry out all that is written in it, for so shall you make your way prosperous, so shall you succeed.
>   *(Roth.)* ...then thou must talk to thyself therein day and night...
>   *(NAB)* ... Recite it by day and by night...
>   *(Knox)* The law thou hast in writing must govern every utterance of thine; night and day thou must ponder over it, so as to carry out all the terms of it faithfully; so wilt thou guide thy steps truly and prosper.
>   *(Young)* ...then thou dost cause thy way to prosper, and then thou dost act wisely.
>   *(AMP)* ...then you shall deal wisely and have good success.
>   *(Jer.)* Have the book of this Law always on your lips...
>   *(Basic)* Let this book of the law be ever on your lips and in your thoughts day and night, so that you may keep with care everything in it; then a blessing will be on all your way, and you will do well.

See faith p. 135

I CHRONICLES 29:3 Moreover, because I have set my affection to the house of my God, I have of mine own proper good, of gold and silver, which I have given to the house of my God, over and above all that I have prepared for the holy house...
>   *(NEB)* Further, because I delight in the house of my God, I give my own private store of gold and silver for the house of my God - over and above all the store which I have collected for the sanctuary.
>   *(Berk.)* Furthermore, because of my deep interest in my God's temple, I have, over and beyond all I have provided for the sacred temple, a private treasure of gold and silver, which I have designated for the temple...

I CHRONICLES 29:12 Both riches and honour come of thee, and thou reignest over all; and in thine hand is power and might; and in thine hand it is to make great, and to give strength unto all.

> ***(Knox)*** Riches and honour come from thee; all things obey thy will; from thee power comes and dominion; only thy hand exalts, only thy hand makes strong.

I CHRONICLES 29:26 Thus David the son of Jesse reigned over all Israel.

I CHRONICLES 29:28 And he died in a good old age, full of days, riches, and honour: and Solomon his son reigned in his stead.

> ***(Young)*** ...satisfied with days, riches, and honour...
>
> **(NEB)** He died in ripe old age, full of years, wealth, and honour...
>
> ***(Knox)*** And he died grown old in comfort, neither length of days nor riches nor honours wanting to him...

II CHRONICLES 9:20 And all the drinking vessels of King Solomon were of gold, and all the vessels of the house of the forest of Lebanon were of pure gold: none were of silver; it was not any thing accounted of in the days of Solomon.

> ***(TLB)*** ...Silver was too cheap to count for much in those days!
>
> ***(NAB)*** ...silver was not considered of value in Solomon's time.

II CHRONICLES 9:27 And the king made silver in Jerusalem as stones, and cedar trees made he as the sycamore trees that are in the low plains in abundance.

> ***(TLB)*** He made silver become as plentiful in Jerusalem as stones in the road!
>
> **(NEB)** He made silver as common in Jerusalem as stones, and cedar as plentiful as sycamorefig in the Shephelah.

II CHRONICLES 20:20 And they rose early in the morning, and went forth into the wilderness of Tekoa: and as they went forth, Jehoshaphat stood and said, Hear me, O Judah, and ye inhabitants of Jerusalem; Believe in the Lord your God, so shall ye be established; believe his prophets, so shall ye prosper.

> ***(AMP)*** ...Believe in the Lord your God and you shall be established; believe and remain steadfast to His prophets and you shall prosper.
>
> ***(TLB)*** ...Believe in the Lord your God, and you shall have success! Believe his prophets, and everything will be all right!
>
> ***(Message)*** ...Believe firmly in God, your God, and your lives will be firm! Believe in your prophets and you'll come out on top!

II CHRONICLES 26:5 And he sought God in the days of Zechariah, who had understanding in the visions of God: and as long as he sought the Lord, God made him to prosper.

>**(AMP)** ...as long as he sought (inquired of, yearned for) the Lord, God made him prosper.
>**(TLB)** ...always eager to please God.
>**(Message)** ...lived a godly life. And God prospered him.

JOB 8:6 If thou wert pure and upright; surely now he would awake for thee, and make the habitation of thy righteousness prosperous.

>**(AMP)** Then, if you are pure and upright, surely He will bestir Himself for you and make your righteous dwelling prosperous again.

JOB 8:7 Though thy beginning was small, yet thy latter end should greatly increase.

>**(AMP)** And though your beginning was small, yet your latter end would greatly increase.
>**(Jer.)** Your former state will seem to you as nothing beside your new prosperity.
>**(Knox)** A poor thing thy old prosperity will seem, matched with the abundance he gives thee now.
>**(NIV)** Your beginnings will seem humble, so prosperous will your future be.
>**(TLB)** And though you started with little, you would end with much.
>**(Mof.)** ...small though your start may be, amply he will enrich you in the end.

JOB 36:11 If they obey and serve him, they shall spend their days in prosperity, and their years in pleasures.

>**(Jer.)** If they listen and do as he says, their days end in happiness, and their closing years are full of ease.
>**(NEB)** If they listen to him, they spend their days in prosperity and their years in comfort.
>**(TLB)** If they listen and obey him, then they will be blessed with prosperity throughout their lives.
>**(Mof.)** If they will hear him and submit, they spend a life of prosperous days, and pleasant years.

PSALM 23:1 The Lord is my shepherd; I shall not want.

>**(TLB)** Because the Lord is my Shepherd, I have everything I need!
>**(Mof.)** The Eternal shepherds me, I lack for nothing...
>**(Basic)** The Lord takes care of me as his sheep; I will not be without any good thing.
>**(Norlie)** The Lord shepherds me, I shall never be in need.
>**(Young)** Jehovah is my shepherd, I do not lack.
>**(Knox)** The Lord is my shepherd; how can I lack anything?
>**(Beck, GNB)** ...I have everything I need.

PSALM 23:1 (AMP) ...I shall not lack.

 (Jer.) Yahweh is my shepherd, I lack nothing.

PSALM 34:9 O fear the Lord, ye his saints: for there is no want to them that fear him.

 (TLB) If you belong to the Lord, reverence him; for everyone who does this has everything he needs.

PSALM 34:10 The young lions do lack, and suffer hunger: but they that seek the Lord shall not want any good thing.

 (TLB) ...those of us who reverence the Lord will never lack any good thing.

 (Douay) ...they that seek the Lord shall not be deprived of any good.

 (Jer.) ...but those who seek Yahweh lack nothing good.

 (AMP) ...they who seek (inquire of and require) the Lord [by right of their need and on authority of His Word], none of them shall lack any beneficial thing.

 (Basic) ...those who are looking to the Lord will have every good thing.

 (GNB) ...those who obey the Lord lack nothing good.

PSALM 35:27 Let them shout for joy, and be glad, that favour my righteous cause: yea, let them say continually, Let the Lord be magnified, which hath pleasure in the prosperity of his servant.

 (Mof.) ...All hail to the Eternal, who loves to see his servant prospering!

 (Beck) ...shout and be glad and keep on saying...

 (GNB) ...shout for joy and say again and again...

PSALM 66:12 Thou hast caused men to ride over our heads; we went through fire and through water: but thou broughtest us out into a wealthy place.

 (AMP) ...You brought us out into a broad, moist place [to abundance and refreshment and the open air].

 (TLB) ...But in the end, you brought us into wealth and great abundance.

 (Message) ...took us to hell and back; Finally he brought us to this well-watered place.

PSALM 105:37 He brought them forth also with silver and gold: and there was not one feeble person among their tribes.

 (Norlie) ...loaded with silver and gold...

 (NEB) ...laden with silver and gold...

 (GNB) ...they carried silver and gold, and all of them were healthy and strong.

 (TLB) [He] brought his people safely out from Egypt, loaded with silver and gold; there were no sick and feeble folk among them.

PSALM 112:2 His seed shall be mighty upon earth: the generation of the upright shall be blessed.
(TLB) His children shall be honored everywhere, for good men's sons have a special heritage.

PSALM 112:3 Wealth and riches shall be in his house: and his righteousness endureth for ever.
(Basic) A store of wealth will be in his house...
(TLB) He himself shall be wealthy...
(Knox) There is affluence and prosperity in his household...

PSALM 115:14 The Lord shall increase you more and more, you and your children.
(Smith, J.M.) May the Lord give you increase, both you and your children.
(Har.) May the Lord give you continual prosperity...

PSALM 115:15 Ye are blessed of the Lord which made heaven and earth.
(Har.) May you be blessed by the Lord who formed heaven and earth.

PSALM 147:14 He maketh peace in thy borders, and filleth thee with the finest of the wheat.
(TLB) ...[He] fills your barns with plenty of the finest wheat.
(Young) ...With the fat of wheat He satisfieth Thee.

PROVERBS 3:9, 10 Honour the Lord with thy substance, and with the firstfruits of all thine increase: So shall thy barns be filled with plenty, and thy presses shall burst out with new wine.
(AMP) Honor the Lord with your capital and sufficiency [from righteous labors] and with the firstfruits of all your income; So shall your storage places be filled with plenty, and your vats shall be overflowing with new wine.
(TLB) Honor the Lord by giving him the first part of all your income, and he will fill your barns with wheat and barley and overflow your wine vats with the finest wines.
(Spur.) Glorify Jehovah with thy wealth, And with the best of all thine increase...
(Young) ...from the beginning of all thine increase...
(NASB) ...from your wealth...
(Roth.) So shall thy storehouses be filled with plenty, and with new wine shall thy vats overflow.

PROVERBS 8:20 I lead in the way of righteousness, in the midst of the paths of judgment...

PROVERBS 8:21 That I may cause those that love me to inherit substance; and I will fill their treasures.
(TLB) Those who love and follow me are indeed wealthy. I fill their treasuries.
(GNB) ...giving wealth to those who love me, filling their houses with treasures.

PROVERBS 8:21 (Young) To cause my lovers to inherit substance…

> *(Knox)* …to enrich the souls that love me with abundant store.
>
> *(NEB)* I endow with riches those who love me and I will fill their treasuries.
>
> *(Basic)* So that I may give my lovers wealth for their heritage, making their store-houses full.

PROVERBS 10:22 The blessing of the Lord, it maketh rich, and he addeth no sorrow with it.

> *(Mof.)* 'Tis the Eternal's blessing that brings wealth, and never does it bring trouble as well.
>
> *(Knox)* Of the Lord's gift comes wealth without drudgery.
>
> *(Jer.)* The blessing of Yahweh is what brings riches, to this hard toil has nothing to add.
>
> *(NAB)* It is the Lord's blessing that brings wealth, and no effort can substitute for it.

PROVERBS 11:24, 25 There is that scattereth, and yet increaseth; and there is that withholdeth more than is meet, but it tendeth to poverty. The liberal soul shall be made fat: and he that watereth shall be watered also himself.

> *(Mof.)* One gives away, and still he grows the richer: another keeps what he should give, and is the poorer. A liberal soul will be enriched, and he who waters will himself be watered.
>
> *(TLB)* It is possible to give away and become richer! It is also possible to hold on too tightly and lose everything. Yes, the liberal man shall be rich! By watering others, he waters himself.
>
> *(Masoretic O.T.)* …And he that satisfieth abundantly shall be satisfied also himself.
>
> *(RSV)* One man gives freely, yet grows all the richer; another withholds what he should give, and only suffers want.
>
> *(NAB)* He who confers benefits will be amply enriched, and he who refreshes others will himself be refreshed.
>
> *(Smith, J.M.)* …The generous man will be enriched…

PROVERBS 13:22 A good man leaveth an inheritance to his children's children: and the wealth of the sinner is laid up for the just.

> *(AMP)* A good man leaves an inheritance [of moral stability and goodness] to his children's children, and the wealth of the sinner [finds its way eventually] into the hands of the righteous, for whom it was laid up.
>
> *(ABPS)* But the sinner's wealth is laid up for the righteous.
>
> *(Sept.)* …but the wealth of the wicked is treasured up for the righteous.
>
> *(NEB)* A good man leaves an inheritance to his descendants, but the sinner's hoard passes to the righteous.

PROVERBS 15:6 In the house of the righteous is much treasure: but in the revenues of the wicked is trouble.

> *(Basic)* In the house of the upright man there is a great store of wealth...
>
> *(NEB)* In the righteous man's house there is ample wealth; the gains of the wicked bring trouble.

PROVERBS 22:4 By humility and the fear of the Lord are riches, and honour, and life.

> *(GNB)* Obey the Lord, be humble, and you will get riches, honor, and a long life.
>
> *(TLB)* True humility and respect for the Lord lead a man to riches, honor and a long life.
>
> *(Mof.)* The humble and the reverent are rewarded with wealth and honour and long life.

ECCLESIASTES 11:1-6 Cast thy bread upon the waters: for thou shalt find it after many days. Give a portion to seven, and also to eight; for thou knowest not what evil shall be upon the earth. If the clouds be full of rain, they empty themselves upon the earth; and if the tree fall toward the south, or toward the north, in the place where the tree falleth, there it shall be. He that observeth the wind shall not sow; and he that regardeth the clouds shall not reap. As thou knowest not what is the way of the spirit, nor how the bones do grow in the womb of her that is with child: even so thou knowest not the works of God who maketh all. In the morning sow thy seed, and in the evening withhold not thine hand: for thou knowest not whether shall prosper, either this or that, or whether they both shall be alike good.

> *(AMP)* 1Cast your bread upon the waters, for you will find it after many days...6In the morning sow your seed, and in the evening withhold not your hands, for you know not which shall prosper, whether this or that, or whether both alike will be good.
>
> *(TLB)* 1Give generously, for your gifts will return to you later...6Keep on sowing your seed, for you never know which will grow—perhaps it all will.
>
> *(Message)* 1Be generous: Invest in acts of charity. Charity yields high returns...6Go to work in the morning and stick to it until evening without watching the clock. You never know from moment to moment how your work will turn out in the end.

ISAIAH 1:19 If ye be willing and obedient, ye shall eat the good of the land...

> *(NEB)* Obey with a will, and you shall eat the best that earth yields.
>
> *(Basic)* If you will give ear to my word and do it, the good things of the land shall be yours...
>
> *(Leeser)* ...the best of the land shall ye eat.
>
> *(TLB)* If you will only let me help you, if you will only obey, then I will make you rich!
>
> *(Beck)* ...you will eat the good things of the land.

ISAIAH 32:20 Blessed are ye that sow beside all waters, that send forth thither the feet of the ox and the ass.

(AMP) Happy and fortunate are you who cast your seed upon all waters [when the river overflows its banks; for the seed will sink into the mud and when the waters subside, the plant will spring up; you will find it after many days and reap an abundant harvest]…

(TLB) And God will greatly bless his people. Wherever they plant, bountiful crops will spring up…

(Message) But you will enjoy a blessed life…

ISAIAH 60:17 For brass I will bring gold, and for iron I will bring silver, and for wood brass, and for stones iron: I will also make thy officers peace, and thine exactors righteousness.

(Roth.) Instead of bronze I will bring in gold, and instead of iron I will bring in silver, and instead of wood bronze, and instead of stones iron, - and I will appoint the oversight of thee to Prosperity, and the setting of thy tasks to Righteousness.

ISAIAH 61:7 For your shame ye shall have double; and for confusion they shall rejoice in their portion: therefore in their land they shall possess the double: everlasting joy shall be unto them.

(TLB) Instead of shame and dishonor, you shall have a double portion of prosperity and everlasting joy.

(NIV) Instead of their shame my people will receive a double portion, and instead of disgrace they will rejoice in their inheritance; and so they will inherit a double portion in their land, and everlasting joy will be theirs.

(AMP) Instead of your [former] shame you shall have a twofold recompense…they shall possess double [what they had forfeited]: everlasting joy shall be theirs.

(Smith, J.M.) …therefore in their land shall they inherit a double measure…

(Roth.) Instead of your shame - double! and instead of disgrace they shall shout in triumph over their portion - therefore in their own land shall they possess double…

(NEB) …they shall receive in their own land a double measure of wealth, and everlasting joy shall be theirs.

MALACHI 3:10 Bring ye all the tithes into the storehouse, that there may be meat in mine house, and prove me now herewith, saith the Lord of hosts, if I will not open you the windows of heaven, and pour you out a blessing, that there shall not be room enough to receive it.

(Beck) …and pour out a blessing for you till there is more than enough.

(Basic) …and put me to the test by doing so…and see if I do not make the windows of heaven open and send down such a blessing on you that there is no room for it.

MALACHI 3:10 (GNB) ...and pour out on you in abundance all kinds of good things.

(Masoretic O.T.) ...That there shall be more than sufficiency.

(Knox) ...rain down blessing to your heart's content!

(Smith, J.M.) ...and pour out for you a blessing until there is no more need.

(Mof.) ...see if I will not then open the very sluices of heaven to pour a blessing down for you, a harvest more than enough.

(Leeser) ...until it be more than enough.

MATTHEW 6:32 (For after all these things do the Gentiles seek:) for your heavenly Father knoweth that ye have need of all these things.

(Johnson) All this continuous quest for more and more of the physical necessities occupies the full attention of those who are unaware of God's presence. I assure you that your Father, the source of your being, is aware of all your physical needs.

See peace p. 351

MATTHEW 6:33 But seek ye first the kingdom of God, and his righteousness; and all these things shall be added unto you.

(Jordan) Then set your heart on the God Movement and its kind of life, and all these things will come as a matter of course.

(Crickmer) But be-going-on-petitioning-always-for first-of all The Kingdom of-your God and that His Righteousness, and-then things-of-this-kind the whole-of them shall-go-on-being-added as covenant blessing to-you.

(Johnson) You are to give first priority to the Spirit dimension and to setting all your relationships right. When you get a proper perspective, these other things will take care of themselves.

(20th C. 1) But first be eager about his Kingdom, and about what he thinks right, and then all these things will be given you in addition.

(TLB) ... And he will give them to you if you give him first place in your life and live as he wants you to.

(Mof.) Seek God's Realm and his goodness, and all that will be yours over and above.

(Phil.) Set your heart on his kingdom and his goodness, and all these things will come to you as a matter of course.

(Barclay) Make the Kingdom of God, and life in loyalty to him, the object of all your endeavor, and you will get all these other things as well.

(Wade) But make your first aim His Dominion and His Righteousness, and all these things will be granted to you in addition.

(Weym.) But make His Kingdom and righteousness your chief aim, and then these things shall be given you in addition.

MATTHEW 6:33 (NEB) Set your mind on God's kingdom and his justice before everything else...
See peace p. 351

MATTHEW 7:11 If ye then, being evil, know how to give good gifts unto your children, how much more shall your Father which is in heaven give good things to them that ask him?

(Barclay) ...how much more can you depend on your Father in heaven to give good things...

(Phil.) If you then, for all your evil, quite naturally give good things to your children, how much more likely is it that your Heavenly Father will give good things to those who ask him?

(Wade) ...how much more readily will your Father that is in the Heavens give what is good to those who ask Him?

(N. Berk.) ...how much more surely...

(TLB) And if you hardhearted, sinful men know how to give good gifts to your children, won't your Father in heaven even more certainly give good gifts to those who ask him for them?

(Knox) Why then, if you, evil as you are, know well enough how to give your children what is good for them, is not your Father in heaven much more ready to give wholesome gifts to those who ask him?

(Johnson) If you, then, being human respond to the legitimate desires and needs of your children, do you not know that to a greater extent, your Father, the source of all being, will give you the true needs and desires of your life?

(Gspd.) So if you, bad as you are, know enough to give your children what is good, how much more surely will your Father in heaven give what is good to those who ask him for it!

See prayer p. 229

MATTHEW 23:23 Woe unto you, scribes and Pharisees, hypocrites! for ye pay tithe of mint and anise and cummin, and have omitted the weightier matters of the law, judgment, mercy, and faith: these ought ye to have done, and not to leave the other undone.

(TLB) ...For you tithe down to the last mint leaf in your garden, but ignore the important things...

(Knox) ..forgotten...

(NEB) ...overlooked the weightier demands...

(Knox) ...mercy, and honour...

(NASB) ...and faithfulness...

(Gspd.) ...and integrity...

(NEB) ...It is these you should have practiced, without neglecting the others.

LUKE 6:38 Give, and it shall be given unto you; good measure, pressed down, and shaken together, and running over, shall men give into your bosom. For with the same measure that ye mete withal it shall be measured to you again.

(New Life) ...You will have more than enough. It can be pushed down and shaken together and it will still run over as it is given to you...

(Jordan) ...it will be measured out to you in your own measuring basket.

(Trans.) ...good measure, pressing it down and shaking it together until it runs over...

(Barclay) You will get in exactly the same proportion as you give.

(TLB) For if you give, you will get!

(Godbey) ...good measure, heaped up, and shaken down, and running over...

LUKE 12:31, 32 But rather seek ye the kingdom of God; and all these things shall be added unto you...it is your Father's good pleasure to give you the kingdom.

(AMP) ...and all these things shall be supplied to you also. Do not be seized with alarm and struck with fear...it is your Father's good pleasure to give you the kingdom!

(TLB) He will always give you all you need from day to day if you will make the Kingdom of God your primary concern...don't be afraid...it gives your Father great happiness to give you the Kingdom.

(Message) Steep yourself in God-reality, God-initiative, God-provisions. You'll find all your everyday human concerns will be met. Don't be afraid of missing out. You're my dearest friends! The Father wants to give you the very kingdom itself.

LUKE 16:9-12 And I say unto you, Make to yourselves friends of the mammon of unrighteousness; that, when ye fail, they may receive you into everlasting habitations. He that is faithful also in that which is least is faithful also in much: and he that is unjust in the least is unjust also in much. If therefore ye have not been faithful in the unrighteous mammon, who will commit to your trust the true riches? And if ye have not been faithful in that which is another man's, who shall give you that which is your own?

(AMP) ...make friends for yourselves by means of unrighteous mammon (deceitful riches, money, possessions), so that when it fails, they [those you have favored] may receive and welcome you into the everlasting habitations (dwellings).

II CORINTHIANS 8:9 For ye know the grace of our Lord Jesus Christ, that though he was rich, yet for your sakes he became poor, that ye through his poverty might be rich.

(Johnson) You know the unconditional love of our Lord Jesus Christ; he had all the wealth of God and he became a pauper so that through his poverty we could become wealthy.

(Cress.) ...Because he became poor, you can become rich.

(Wood) ...we might gain riches through His poverty.

II CORINTHIANS 8:9 (Weekes) For ye know the generosity...

(*Weym.*) ...the condescending goodness...

(*Basic*) ...though he had wealth, he became poor on your account, so that through his need you might have wealth.

(*Wuest*) ...by means of His poverty you might be made wealthy.

(*AMP*) ...enriched (abundantly supplied).

See redemption p. 59

II CORINTHIANS 9:6 But this I say, He which soweth sparingly shall reap also sparingly; and he which soweth bountifully shall reap also bountifully.

(*Barclay*) ...meager sowing means meager reaping...

(*Jordan*) ...A stingy sower gathers a stingy harvest...

(*Weym.*) But do not forget that he who sows with a niggardly hand will also reap a niggardly crop...

(*20th C.R.*) Remember the saying - Scanty sowing brings scanty harvest, plentiful sowing plentiful harvest.

(*Way*) Bear in mind the saying, Grudging sowing makes grudging harvest, and bounteous sowing makes bounteous harvest.

(*Phil.*) ...poor sowing means a poor harvest, & generous sowing means a generous harvest.

(*Jer.*) Do not forget: thin sowing means thin reaping; the more you sow, the more you reap.

(*Basic*) ...He who puts in only a small number of seeds, will get in the same; and he who puts them in from a full hand, will have produce in full measure from them.

(*GNB*) Remember that the person who plants few seeds will have a small crop; the one who plants many seeds will have a large crop.

II CORINTHIANS 9:7 Every man according as he purposeth in his heart, so let him give: not grudgingly, or of necessity: for God loveth a cheerful giver.

(*NEB*) ...there should be no reluctance, no sense of compulsion...

(*Fenton*) ...as each is incited by his heart, not as though grudgingly, or as if compelled...

(*GNB*) ...not with regret or out of a sense of duty...

(*Basic*) ...not giving with grief, or by force...

(*Jer.*) Each one should give what he has decided in his own mind, not grudgingly or because he is made to, for God loves a cheerful giver.

(*Phil.*) Let everyone give as his heart tells him...

(*Way*) Let each man give according to his heart's choice, not regretting his gift, as if it were wrung from him, for 'It is the cheerful giver that God loves.'

(*New Life*) ...He should not give, wishing he could keep it. Or he should not give if he feels he has to give. God loves a man who gives because he wants to give.

II CORINTHIANS 9:7 (Jordan) Let each person follow the dictates of his conscience...

(Barclay) ...for God loves a man who enjoys giving.

(Godbey) ...God loves the hilarious giver.* (*Greek: the laughing giver)

(Weekes) ...for God loveth a joyful (hilarious) giver.

II CORINTHIANS 9:8 And God is able to make all grace abound toward you; that ye, always having all sufficiency in all things, may abound to every good work...

(Weekes) And God is able to make all blessing overflow to you, so that, having all sufficiency in everything and always, ye may overflow to every good work...

(Barclay) God can give you more than enough of every good gift, enough for you to have plenty for yourselves always and in any circumstances, and to have enough left over to contribute to every good cause.

(Way) Ay, and God is able to lavish every gracious gift upon you, so that you, always possessing abundance of everything, may lavishly contribute to every good undertaking.

(New Life) God can give you all you need. He will give you more than enough. You will have everything you need for yourselves. And you will have enough left over to give when there is a need.

(20th C.R.) God has power to shower all kinds of blessings upon you, so that, having, under all circumstances and on all occasions, all that you can need, you may be able to shower all kinds of benefits on others.

(Cony.) And God is able to give you an overflowing measure of all good gifts, that all your wants of every kind may be supplied at all times, and you may give of your abundance to every good work.

(Wade) And God can enable every gracious favour to be yours in abundant measure, in order that you, having in every respect at all times enough for your own emergencies, may be abundantly supplied with means for promoting every kind service...

(Wand) And He is able to provide amply for your every need, so that you may not only have enough to satisfy every possible want of your own, but also may have plenty for any kind act to another.

(Phil.) After all, God can give you everything that you need, so that you may always have sufficient both for yourselves and for giving away to other people.

(Jer.) And there is no limit to the blessings which God can send you - he will make sure that you will always have all you need for yourselves in every possible circumstance, and still have something to spare for all sorts of good works.

(GNB) And God is able to give you more than you need, so that you will always have all you need for yourselves and more than enough for every good cause.

(Tomanek) Powerful is God to make every favor abound to you...

(Gspd.) God is able to provide you with every blessing in abundance so that you will always have enough for every situation, & ample means for every good enterprise.

II CORINTHIANS 9:8 (Mof.) God is able to bless you with ample means, so that you may always have quite enough for any emergency of your own & ample besides for any kind act to others...

(Noli) God has the power to supply you abundantly with every blessing. Thus you will always have enough for every situation, and you will be able to provide abundantly for every good work.

(Lau.) ...God is able to bless you with more than you need. He will give you so much that you will always be able to give to every good cause.

(Weym.) And God is able to bestow every blessing on you in abundance, so that richly enjoying all sufficiency at all times, you may have ample means for all good works.

(AMP) And God is able to make all grace (every favor and earthly blessing) come to you in abundance, so that you may always and under all circumstances and whatever the need be selfsufficient [possessing enough to require no aid or support and furnished in abundance for every good work & charitable donation].

(NEB) ...thus you will have ample means in yourselves to meet each and every situation, with enough and to spare for every good cause.

(Cent.) ...so that all your wants of every kind may be supplied at all times, and you may give of your abundance to every good work...

(Roth.) Moreover God is able to cause every gracious gift to superabound unto you...

II CORINTHIANS 9:9 As it is written, He hath dispersed abroad; he hath given to the poor: his righteousness remaineth for ever.

(AMP) As it is written, He [the benevolent person] scatters abroad; He gives to the poor; His deeds of justice and goodness and kindness and benevolence will go on and endure forever!

(NEB) Scripture says of such a man: He has lavished his gifts on the needy, his benevolence stands fast for ever.

(20th C. 1) ...he gave to the poor; His goodness continues for ever.

(TLB) ...His good deeds will be an honor to him forever.

II CORINTHIANS 9:10 Now he that ministereth seed to the sower both minister bread for your food, and multiply your seed sown, and increase the fruits of your righteousness.

(AMP) And [God] Who provides seed for the sower and bread for the eating will also provide and multiply your [resources for] sowing and increase the fruits of your righteousness [which manifests itself in active goodness, kindness, and charity].

(Wuest) Now, He, who supplies seed to the sower and bread for food, shall also supply and multiply your seed [your means of giving]...

(Noli) ...supply and multiply your resources and increase the harvest of your charity.

(Phil.) ...will give you the seed of generosity to sow and, for harvest, the satisfying bread of good deeds done.

II CORINTHIANS 9:10 (Weym.) ...will supply you with seed and multiply it...
(TLB) ...so that you can give away more and more fruit from your harvest.

II CORINTHIANS 9:11 Being enriched in every thing to all bountifulness, which causeth through us thanksgiving to God.
(Lau.) God will make you rich in all things: rich enough for you to be a great blessing to the poor.
(Jer.) ...and made richer in every way, you will be able to do all the generous things which, through us, are the cause of thanksgiving to God.
(Pl. Eng.) You will grow rich in every way, rich enough for every kind of generosity...
(Gspd.) You will grow rich in every way...
(Barclay) He will always make you rich enough to be generous to every claim on you...
(NEB) ...you will always be rich enough to be generous.
(AMP) Thus you will be enriched in all things and in every way, so that you can be generous...
(Weym.) May you be abundantly enriched so as to show all liberality...
(Trans.) He will make you abundantly rich so that you may be generous in every way.
(GNB) He will always make you rich enough to be generous at all times...
(Phil.) The more you are enriched by God, the more scope will there be for generous giving...
(Wms.) In every way you will grow richer and richer so as to give with perfect liberality...
(20th C.R.) growing rich in all things, you will be prepared to show all kinds of generosity...
(NIV) You will be made rich in every way so that you can be generous on every occasion.

GALATIANS 3:9 So then they which be of faith are blessed with faithful Abraham.
(Basic) So then those who are of faith have a part in the blessing of Abraham who was full of faith
(Noli) All men of faith are blessed with faithful Abraham.
(Gspd.) So the men of faith share the blessing of Abraham and his faith.
(Knox) It is those, then, who take their stand on faith that share the blessing Abraham's faithfulness won.
(NEB) Thus it is the men of faith who share the blessing with faithful Abraham.
(Jer.) Those therefore who rely on faith receive the same blessing as Abraham, the man of faith.
(Syriac) Believers, therefore, it is, who are blessed with believing Abraham.
(NIV) So those who have faith are blessed along with Abraham, the man of faith.
(Way) ...those who rely on faith shall share the blessing of Abraham, the Man of Faith.
(Wms.) So the men of faith are blessed as partners with trusting Abraham.
(20th C.R.) And, therefore, those whose lives are based on faith, share the blessings bestowed upon the faith of Abraham.

GALATIANS 3:9 (20th C. 1) And so people whose lives are based on faith share the blessings of Abraham and his faith.

> *(Lau.)* All men who have faith receive the same blessing that Abraham received.
>
> *(Trans.)* So it is that all who believe share in a common blessing with Abraham who believed.
>
> *(Phil.)* All men of faith share the blessing of Abraham who "believed God."
>
> *(GNB)* ...all who believe are blessed as he was.
>
> *(Barclay)* So then, all who rely on faith are blessed along with Abraham the man of faith.
>
> *(TLB)* And so it is: all who trust in Christ share the same blessing Abraham received.
>
> *(Cunn.)* So then they that rest on faith are blessed along with the faithful Abraham.
>
> *(Weym.)* ...believing Abraham.
>
> *(NASB)* ...Abraham, the believer.

GALATIANS 3:13 Christ hath redeemed us from the curse of the law, being made a curse for us: for it is written, Cursed is every one that hangeth on a tree...

> *(Berk.)* Christ has bought us free from the curse of the Law...
>
> *(Noli)* ...by becoming a curse for us...
>
> *(Black.)* ...by taking the curse upon Himself in our behalf...
>
> *(Deaf)* The law put a curse on us. But Christ took away that curse. He changed places with us. Christ put Himself under that curse...
>
> *(Hayman)* Christ it was who redeemed us from that curse of the Law, by receiving our curse on His own person...
>
> *(Way)* From that curse, which is of the essence of the Law, we Jews have been ransomed only by Messiah...
>
> *(Trans.)* Christ ransomed us from the curse of the Law by taking that curse upon Himself for our sakes...
>
> *(Wand)* Now, Christ bought us off the curse of the Law at the cost of being accursed for our sakes.
>
> *(Weym.)* Christ has purchased our freedom...
>
> *(20th C.R.)* Christ ransomed us from the curse pronounced in the Law...
>
> *(GNB)* ...the curse that the Law brings...
>
> *(Barclay)* ...by taking the curse upon himself for our sakes...
>
> *(Beck)* Christ paid the price to free us...
>
> *(Gspd.)* ...by taking our curse upon himself...
>
> *See redemption p. 58; divine healing p. 269*

GALATIANS 3:14 That the blessing of Abraham might come on the Gentiles through Jesus Christ; that we might receive the promise of the Spirit through faith.

> *(Way)* He so ransomed us in order that to the Gentiles might come, by their acceptance of Messiah Jesus, the blessing pronounced on Abraham, and in order that we through the exercise of faith may receive the realization of the promise of the Spirit.

GALATIANS 3:14 (NIV) He redeemed us in order that the blessing given to Abraham might come to the Gentiles through Christ Jesus...

(20th C.R.) And this he did that the blessing given to Abraham might be extended to the Gentiles through their union with Jesus Christ...

(Lau.) So Jesus Christ by dying on the tree gave you Gentiles the blessing which God promised Abraham that you should have...

(GNB) ...that the blessing which God promised to Abraham might be given to the Gentiles by means of Christ Jesus...

(TLB) Now God can bless the Gentiles, too, with this same blessing he promised to Abraham...

(Weym.) Our freedom has been thus purchased in order that in Christ Jesus the blessing belonging to Abraham may come upon the nations...

(New Life) Because of the price Christ Jesus paid, the good things that came to Abraham might come to the people who are not Jews...

GALATIANS 6:7-10 Be not deceived; God is not mocked: for whatsoever a man soweth, that shall he also reap. For he that soweth to his flesh shall of the flesh reap corruption; but he that soweth to the Spirit shall of the Spirit reap life everlasting. And let us not be weary in well doing: for in due season we shall reap, if we faint not. As we have therefore opportunity, let us do good unto all men, especially unto them who are of the household of faith.

(AMP) And let us not lose heart and grow weary and faint in acting nobly and doing right, for in due season we shall reap, if we do not loosen and relax our courage and faint.

(TLB) And let us not get tired of doing what is right, for after a while we will reap a harvest of blessing if we don't get discouraged and give up.

(Message) So let's not allow ourselves to get fatigued doing good. At the right time we will harvest a good crop if we don't give up, or quit.

PHILIPPIANS 4:15 Now ye Phillipians know also, that in the beginning of the gospel, when I departed from Macedonia, no church communicated with me as concerning giving and receiving, but ye only.

(Gspd.) ...no church but yours went into partnership and opened an account with me.

(Wms.) ...no church but yours went into partnership with me to open an account of credits and debits.

PHILIPPIANS 4:16 For even in Thessalonica ye sent once and again unto my necessity.

(20th C.R.) ...you sent more than once to relieve my wants.

PHILIPPIANS 4:17 Not because I desire a gift: but I desire fruit that may abound to your account.

(Mof.) It is not the money I am anxious for...

PHILIPPIANS 4:17 (20th C.R.) ...but I am anxious to see the abundant return that will be placed to your account.

(Knox) ...I set store by the rich increase that stands to your credit.

(AMP) ...but I do seek and am eager for the fruit which increases to your credit [the harvest of blessing that is accumulating to your account].

PHILIPPIANS 4:18 But I have all, and abound: I am full, having received of Epaphroditus the things which were sent from you, an odour of a sweet smell, a sacrifice acceptable, wellpleasing to God.

(Gspd.) You have paid me in full, and more too. It is like fragrant incense, just such a sacrifice as God welcomes and approves.

(Cony.) ...I am fully supplied...

(Phil.) ...Your generosity is like a lovely fragrance, a sacrifice that pleases the very heart of God.

PHILIPPIANS 4:19 But my God shall supply all your need according to his riches in glory by Christ Jesus.

(Hudson) And my God, on the scale of his wealth, will fully supply in Christ Jesus your every need in [heaven's] glory.

(Lovett) ...out of the fantastic treasures amassed in Christ.

(Jer.) In return my God will fulfill all your needs, in Christ Jesus, as lavishly as only God can.

(N. Berk.) And my God will fully supply all your needs according to His abundant wealth so glorious in Christ Jesus.

(Wade) And every need of yours my God will satisfy in Glory through Christ Jesus (as His inexhaustible resources enable Him to do).

(TLB) And it is he who will supply all your needs from his riches in glory, because of what Christ Jesus has done for us.

(Way) And God, my God, shall fill up the measure of all your need, with an abundance limited only by His own riches, shall supply it by His glorious presence in the person of Messiah Jesus.

(20th C. R.) ...fully satisfy your every need, through your union with Christ Jesus.

(NEB) And my God will supply all your wants out of the magnificence of his riches in Christ Jesus.

(AMP) ...will liberally supply (fill to the full) your every need...

See redemption p. 110

I TIMOTHY 4:8 For bodily exercise profiteth little: but godliness is profitable unto all things, having promise of the life that now is, and of that which is to come.

(New Life) Growing strong in body is all right but growing in God-like living is more important. It will not only help you in this life now but in the next life also.

(Jer.) Physical exercises are useful enough, but the usefulness of spirituality is unlimited, since it holds out the reward of life here and now and of the future life as well.

(Jordan) Physical fitness is quite valuable, but spiritual fitness is worth more than anything...

(Beck) ...life here and hereafter...

(GNB) Physical exercise has some value, but spiritual exercise is valuable in every way...

(20th C.1) ...carrying with it, as it does, a promise of Life both here and hereafter.

(Barclay) Physical training has a limited usefulness, but to live the life whose goal is God has an unlimited usefulness...

(Wade) ...godliness is beneficial in every way, carrying with it a promise for the present life and for that which is to be hereafter.

(Noli) Physical training is profitable to a certain extent. But piety is profitable in every way. It promises blessedness in the present life and also in the life to come.

(Weym.) Train yourself in godliness. Exercise for the body is not useless, but godliness is useful in every respect, possessing, as it does, the promise of Life now and of the Life which is soon coming.

I TIMOTHY 6:17-19 Charge them that are rich in this world, that they be not highminded, nor trust in uncertain riches, but in the living God, who giveth us richly all things to enjoy; that they do good, that they be rich in good works, ready to distribute, willing to communicate; laying up in store for themselves a good foundation against the time to come, that they may lay hold on eternal life.

(AMP) ...nor to set their hopes on uncertain riches, but on God, Who richly and ceaselessly provides us with everything for [our] enjoyment...

(TLB) ...but their pride and trust should be in the living God who always richly gives us all we need for our enjoyment.

(Message) ...Tell them to go after God, who piles on all the riches we could ever manage —to do good, to be rich in helping others, to be extravagantly generous. If they do that, they'll build a treasury that will last, gaining life that is truly life.

HEBREWS 7:2 To whom also Abraham gave a tenth part of all, first being by interpretation King of righteousness and after that also King of Salem, which is King of peace.

(AMP) And Abraham gave to him a tenth portion of all the spoil...

(NEB) ...a tithe of everything.

(Weym.) ...presented a tenth part of all...

(Wms.) ...contributed a tenth of all his spoils...

HEBREWS 7:5 And verily they that are of the sons of Levi, who receive the office of the priesthood, have a commandment to take tithes of the people...

> *(20th C. 1)* ...are directed to collect tithes...
>
> *(Wms.)* ...are authorized by the law to collect a tenth...
>
> *(Phil.)* ...have the right to demand a "tenth" from the people...

HEBREWS 7:8 And here men that die receive tithes; but there he receiveth them, of whom it is witnessed that he liveth.

> *(NIV)* In the one case, the tenth is collected by men who die; but in the other case, by him who is declared to be living.
>
> *(AMP)* ...that he lives [perpetually].
>
> *(20th C.R.)* ...that his life still continues.

III JOHN 2 Beloved, I wish above all things that thou mayest prosper and be in health, even as thy soul prospereth.

> *(20th C. 1)* Dear friend, I pray that all may go well with you and that you may have good health.
>
> *(Weym.)* My dear friend, I pray that you may in all respects prosper and enjoy good health...
>
> *(Message)* ...for good fortune in everything you do, and for your good health - that your everyday affairs prosper, as well as your soul!
>
> *(Wuest)* ...you will be prospering, and that you will be continually having good health just as your soul is prospering.
>
> *(RSV)* ...that all may go well with you and that you may be in health...
>
> *(Gspd.)* ...that everything is going well with you and that you are well; I know it is well with your soul.
>
> *(Stevens)* May God who has so richly prospered you in your spiritual life, grant you a full measure of all temporal blessing.
>
> *(Young)* Concerning all things I desire thee to prosper...

See divine healing p. 288

Your enemy, the devil, does not have any of the **FRUIT OF THE SPIRIT.** Develop the fruit of the spirit and **YOU WILL OVERCOME!**

Mark Hankins
11:23: THE LANGUAGE OF FAITH

JOHN
13:34 317
13:35 317
17:23 317

ROMANS
5:5 318
12:9, 10 319
13:10 319

I CORINTHIANS
13:4-8 320
14:1 322

GALATIANS
5:6 322
5:22 322
5:23 323
5:24 323

EPHESIANS
4:31 323
4:32 324

COLOSSIANS
3:14 324

I THESSALONIANS
3:12 325
4:9 326
4:10 326

II TIMOTHY
2:24 327
2:25 327
2:26 329

I PETER
3:8-12 329
4:8 331

I JOHN
2:10 331
3:18 331
4:7 332
4:8 332
4:16 332

JUDE
21 333

The **LOVE TALK**
is a lot easier than
the **LOVE WALK.**

Mark Hankins

JOHN 13:34 A new commandment I give unto you, That ye love one another; as I have loved you, that ye also love one another.

> *(Crickmer)* ...That ye be divinely Loving one another, exactly as I went and divinely loved you that-so also ye-be divinely-loving one-another.
>
> *(Fenton)* I give you a new command, that you love one another: just as I have loved you, in the same way you ought also to love one another.
>
> *(Godbey)* I give unto you a new commandment, That you must love one another with divine love; as I have loved you with divine love, that you must also love one another with divine love.
>
> *(Knox)* I have a new commandment to give you, that you are to love one another; that your love for one another is to be like the love I have borne you.
>
> *(20th C. 1)* ...love one another just as I have loved you.
>
> *(NAB)* I give you a new commandment: Love one another. Such as my love has been for you, so must your love be for each other.

JOHN 13:35 By this shall all men know that ye are my disciples, if ye also have love one to another.

> *(Crickmer)* ...divine-Love...
>
> *(Godbey)* ...in this shall all know that you are my disciples, if you may have divine love one with another.
>
> *(Knox)* The mark by which all men will know you for my disciples will be the love you bear one another.
>
> *(20th C. 1)* It is by this that every one will recognize you as my disciples...
>
> *(Basic)* By this it will be clear to all men that you are my disciples...
>
> *(Weym.)* ...if you cherish mutual love.
>
> *(Wms.)* ...if you keep on showing love for one another.
>
> *(TLB)* Your strong love for each other will prove to the world that you are my disciples.

JOHN 17:23 I in them, and thou in me, that they may be made perfect in one; and that the world may know that thou hast sent me, and hast loved them, as thou hast loved me.

> *(TLB)* I in them and you in me, all being perfected into one - so that the world will know you sent me & will understand that you love them as much as you love me.
>
> *(Wade)* (I united to them and Thou united to me), that they may be brought to perfect union in one, in order that the world may recognize that Thou hast sent me on a mission, and hast loved them just as Thou hast loved me.
>
> *(Gspd.)* I in union with them and you with me, so that they may be perfectly unified, and the world may recognize that you sent me and that you love them just as you loved me.

JOHN 17:23 (Crickmer) I in organic oneness with them, and Thou in organic oneness with Me, that they may have been absolutely blended homogeneous oneness ward...and that Thou didst get to divinely Love them, with the same kind of love with which Me Thou didst go and divinely Love.

(Jer.) With me in them and you in me, may they be so completely one that the world will realize that it was you who sent me...

(NASB, Conf.) ...that they may be perfected in unity...

(20th C.R.) I in union with them and thou with me - so that they may be perfected in their union.

(Weym.) ...and hast loved them with the same love as that with which Thou hast loved me.

(Knox) ...and that thou hast bestowed thy love upon them, as thou hast bestowed it upon me.

ROMANS 5:5 And hope maketh not ashamed; because the love of God is shed abroad in our hearts by the Holy Ghost which is given unto us.

(Way) This hope is no delusive one, as is proved by the fact that the brimming river of God's love has already overflowed into our hearts, on-drawn by His Holy Spirit, which He has given to us.

(Berk.) ...for God's love is poured out into our hearts by means of the Holy Spirit which is given us.

(Knox) ...the love of God has been poured out in our hearts by the Holy Spirit, whom we have received.

(Cent.) ...For through the Holy Spirit who has been given to us, the "brimming river of the love of God" has overflowed in our hearts.

(20th C. R.) For the love of God has filled our hearts...

(Gspd.) ...God's love has flooded our hearts.

(Beck) ...the Holy Spirit, who has been given to us, poured God's love into our hearts.

(N. Berk.) ...for God's love is poured out into our hearts by means of the Holy Spirit.

(Johnson) ...God's love fills our inner being through his Holy Spirit whom he has given us.

(Black.) ...God's love has been poured forth into and continues inundating our hearts...

(Jordan) ...For God has given us a love transfusion by the Holy Spirit he provided for us.

(NIV) ...God has poured out his love into our hearts by the Holy Spirit...

(Trans.) ...God's love has been poured into our hearts...

(Wuest) ...because the love of God has been poured out in our hearts and still floods them...

(Lau.) ...God's love has been poured into our hearts by the Holy Spirit...

(Syriac) ...the love of God is diffused in our hearts...

ROMANS 5:5 (20th C. l) For the love of God has, through the Holy Spirit which was given us, flooded our hearts...

(Basic) ...our hearts are full of the love of God through the Holy Spirit which is given to us.

(TLB) ...we are able to hold our heads high no matter what happens and know that all is well...because God has given us the Holy Spirit to fill our hearts with his love.

ROMANS 12:9, 10 Let love be without dissimulation. Abhor that which is evil; cleave to that which is good. Be kindly affectioned one to another with brotherly love; in honour preferring one another.

(AMP) [Let your] love be sincere (a real thing); hate what is evil [loathe all ungodliness, turn in horror from wickedness], but hold fast to that which is good. Love one another with brotherly affection [as members of one family], giving precedence and showing honor to one another.

(TLB) Don't just pretend that you love others: really love them. Hate what is wrong. Stand on the side of the good. Love each other with brotherly affection and take delight in honoring each other.

(Message) Love from the center of who you are; don't fake it. Run for dear life from evil; hold on for dear life to good. Be good friends who love deeply; practice playing second fiddle.

ROMANS 13:10 Love worketh no ill to his neighbour: therefore love is the fulfilling of the law.

(Pl. Eng.) Love does no evil to a neighbour: therefore love is the sum-total of the law.

(Black.) This purposive good will does not work any harm to its neighbor.

(Johnson) So love fulfills the intent of the rule because it wills positive good to the neighbor.

(20th C.R. & l) Love never wrongs a neighbour. Therefore Love fully satisfies the Law.

(Knox) Love of our neighbour refrains from doing harm of any kind; that is why it fulfills all the demands of the law.

(Godbey) Divine love works no evil to its neighbor: for divine love is the fulfilling of the law.

(Weym.) Love avoids doing any wrong to one's fellow man...

(GNB) If you love someone, you will never do him wrong...

(Authentic) ...so love is the sum total of law.

(Berk.) ...so love meets all the Law's requirements.

I CORINTHIANS 13:4-8 Charity suffereth long, and is kind; charity envieth not; charity vaunteth not itself, is not puffed up, Doth not behave itself unseemly, seeketh not her own, is not easily provoked, thinketh no evil; Rejoiceth not in iniquity, but rejoiceth in the truth; Beareth all things, believeth all things, hopeth all things, endureth all things. Charity never faileth...

(AMP) Love endures long and is patient and kind; love never is envious nor boils over with jealousy; is not boastful or vainglorious, does not display itself haughtily. It is not conceited (arrogant and inflated with pride); it is not rude (unmannerly) and does not act unbecomingly. Love (God's love in us) does not insist on its own rights or its own way, for it is not selfseeking; it is not touchy or fretful or resentful; it takes no account of the evil done to it [it pays no attention to a suffered wrong]. It does not rejoice at injustice and unrighteousness, but rejoices when right and truth prevail. Love bears up under anything and everything that comes, is ever ready to believe the best of every person, its hopes are fadeless under all circumstances, and it endures everything [without weakening]. Love never fails [never fades out or becomes obsolete or comes to an end].

(Hayford) Love suffers long, having patience with imperfect people. Love is kind, and active in doing good. Love does not envy; since it is non-possessive and noncompetitive, it actually wants others to get ahead. Hence it does not parade itself. Love has a self-effacing quality; it is not ostentatious. Love is not puffed up, treating others arrogantly; it does not behave rudely, but displays good manners and courtesy. Love does not seek its own, insisting on its own rights and demanding precedence; rather, it is unselfish. Love is not provoked; it is not irritable or touchy, rough or hostile, but is graceful under pressure. Love thinks no evil; it does not keep an account of wrongs done to it; instead it erases resentments. Love does not rejoice in iniquity, finding satisfaction in the shortcomings of others and spreading an evil report; rather, it rejoices in the truth, aggressively advertising the good. Love bears all things, defending and holding other people up. Love believes the best about others, credits them with good intentions, and is not suspicious. Love hopes all things, never giving up on people, but affirming their future. Love endures all things, persevering and remaining loyal to the end.

(Godbey) Divine love suffers long; divine love is kind; divine love envies not;...Divine love never falls...

(Phil.) This love of which I speak is slow to lose patience - it looks for a way of being constructive. It is not possessive: it is neither anxious to impress nor does it cherish inflated ideas of its own importance. Love has good manners and does not pursue selfish advantage. It is not touchy. It does not keep account of evil or gloat over the wickedness of other people. Love knows no limit to its endurance, no end to its trust, no fading of its hope; it can outlast anything. It is, in fact, the one thing that still stands when all else has fallen.

I CORINTHIANS 13:4-8 (Wms.) Love is so patient and so kind; Love never boils with jealousy; It never boasts, is never puffed with pride; It does not act with rudeness, or insist upon its rights; It never gets provoked, it never harbors evil thoughts; Is never glad when wrong is done, But always glad when truth prevails; It bears up under anything, It exercises faith in everything, It keeps up hope in everything, It gives us power to endure in anything.

(Cent.) ...Love bears no malice.

(Way) ...Love does not parade her gifts, swells not with self-conceit, she flouts not decency: She grasps not at her rights, refuses to take offense, has no memory for injuries.

(Jordan) ...Love is not envious, nor does it strut and brag. It does not act up, nor try to get things for itself. It pitches no tantrums, keeps no books on insults or injuries, sees no fun in wickedness, but rejoices when truth prevails. Love is all-embracing, all-trusting, all-hoping, allenduring. Love never quits...

(Wand) [Love] never lacks courtesy, never pursues its own selfish interest, never shows bitterness or resentment, never takes pleasure in wickedness but only in the truth. Love keeps its own counsel, shows a ready trust, is full of hope and sturdy perseverance. Love never falls down on its task...

(New Life) Love does not give up...Love does not put itself up as being important. Love has no pride.

(GNB) ...love does not keep record of wrongs...Love is eternal.

(Lau.) Love does not look down upon others;...It does not insist upon having its own will. It does not get angry at little things; It does not nurse hurt feelings. Love is not glad when others go wrong. It is glad when they do right. Love stands true through every trouble, believes the best always, always hopes for the best, is always patient.

(Pl. Eng.) ...love has no loud words in her mouth...Love always forgives...Love never dies...

(Wuest) Love meekly and patiently bears ill treatment from others. Love is kind, gentle, benign, pervading and penetrating the whole nature, mellowing all which would have been harsh and austere...Love does not brag, nor does it show itself off...does not have an inflated ego...is not irritated, provoked, exasperated, aroused to anger...

(Barclay) Love is patient with people; love is kind...Love never does the graceless thing; never insists on its rights, never irritably loses its temper; never nurses its wrath to keep it warm. Love finds nothing to be glad about when someone goes wrong...Love can stand any kind of treatment; love's first instinct is to believe in people; love never regards anyone or anything as hopeless; nothing can happen that can break love's spirit. Love lasts for ever.

(NEB) ...Love is never boastful, nor conceited, nor rude; never selfish, not quick to take offense. Love keeps no score of wrongs; does not gloat over other men's sins...

(Mof.) ...love makes no parade, gives itself no airs, is never rude, never selfish, never irritated, (never resentful)...always slow to expose, always eager to believe the best...Love never disappears.

I CORINTHIANS 13:4-8 (Gspd.) It does not put on airs. It is not rude. It does not insist on its rights...

> *(TLB)* ...Love does not demand its own way. It is not irritable or touchy. It does not hold grudges and will hardly even notice when others do it wrong. It is never glad about injustice, but rejoices whenever truth wins out. If you love someone you will be loyal to him no matter what the cost. You will always believe in him, always expect the best of him, and always stand your ground in defending him.
>
> *(Authentic)* ...Love is never jealous, self-assertive, blustering or inconsiderate. It never seeks its own ends, is never irritable, keeps no score of wrongs...Love is ever protective, ever trustful, ever hopeful, ever constant.
>
> *(Knox)* ...[love] cannot be provoked, does not brood over an injury.
>
> *(Weym.)* She knows how to be silent (can overlook faults). She is full of trust, full of hope, full of patient endurance.
>
> *(Johnson)* Let me describe love. Love stays in difficult relationships with kindness. Love does not play "one-up-man-ship," nor does it react to those who do. Love is not rude or grasping or overly sensitive, nor does love search for imperfections and faults in others. Love is the most enduring quality of human existence. It keeps on keeping on; it trusts in God in every situation and expects God to act in all circumstances. Nothing can destroy love.
>
> *(Bruce)* Love puts on no airs, never acts dishonourably, never places her own interests first...Love never imputes evil motives...Love conceals the faults of others, always believes the best, never despairs, and remains steadfast to the end.
>
> *(K. & L.)* ...it takes no note of injury...Always it is ready to make allowances...

I CORINTHIANS 14:1 Follow after charity, & desire spiritual gifts, but rather that ye may prophesy.

> *(AMP)* Eagerly pursue and seek to acquire [this] love [make it your aim, your great quest]: and earnestly desire and cultivate the spiritual endowments (gifts), especially that you may prophesy (interpret the divine will and purpose in inspired preaching and teaching).

GALATIANS 5:6 For in Jesus Christ neither circumcision availeth anything, nor uncircumcision; but faith which worketh by love.

> *(AMP)* ...but only faith activated and energized and expressed and working through love.
>
> *(TLB)* ...for all we need is faith working through love.
>
> *(NIV)* ...The only thing that counts is faith expressing itself through love.
>
> *(Mof.)* ...but only faith active in love.

GALATIANS 5:22 But the fruit of the Spirit is love, joy, peace, longsuffering, gentleness, goodness, faith...

> *(Godbey)* ...divine love...

GALATIANS 5:22 (NAB) In contrast, the fruit of the spirit is ...

(New Life) ...love, joy, peace, not giving up...

(Knox) Whereas the spirit yields a harvest of love, joy, peace...

GALATIANS 5:23 Meekness, temperance: against such there is no law.

(Knox) ...No law can touch lives such as these.

(New Life) ...being gentle, and being the boss over our own desires...

(Way) ...It was not to curb such qualities as these that the Law was instituted.

(Noli) ...The law is not needed by men who practice these virtues.

(Basic) ...control over desires...

GALATIANS 5:24 And they that are Christ's have crucified the flesh with the affections and lusts.

(New Life) Those of us who belong to Christ have nailed our sinful old selves on His cross. Our sinful desires are now dead.

(Way) They who belong to Messiah Jesus have, by sharing in His death, thereby slain upon His cross their sensual nature, with its passions and its cravings.

(Roth.) ...with its susceptibilities and covetings.

(Phil.) Those who belong to Christ Jesus have crucified their old nature with all that it loved and lusted for.

(Conc.) Now those of Christ Jesus crucify the flesh together with its passions and lusts.

(Cunn.) ...the flesh together with its emotions and desires.

EPHESIANS 4:31 Let all bitterness, and wrath, and anger, and clamour, and evil speaking, be put away from you, with all malice...

(Jordan) Let every scrap of bitterness and resentment and anger and loud talk and running down of others be put away from you, along with all other evil.

(Wms.) You must remove all bitterness, rage, anger, loud threats, and insults, and all malice.

(NEB) Have done with spite and passion, all angry shouting and cursing, and bad feeling of every kind.

(Mof.) ...drop all bitter feeling and passion and anger and clamouring and insults, together with all malice...

(Knox) There must be no trace of bitterness among you, of passion, resentment, quarreling, insulting talk, or spite of any kind.

(Beck) Get rid of all bitter feelings, temper, anger, yelling, slander, and every way of hurting one another.

(Lau.) Throw away bitter words and quarrels and anger. Avoid loud talk or any talk at all that hurts other people. Throw away all ill will.

EPHESIANS 4:31 (Basic) Let all bitter, sharp and angry feeling, and noise, and evil words, be put away from you, with all unkind acts...

> *(Fenton)* ...be expelled from you...
> *(Weym.)* ...all anger and loud insulting language...
> *(Noli)* ...cast away from you...

EPHESIANS 4:32 And be ye kind one to another, tenderhearted, forgiving one another, even as God for Christ's sake hath forgiven you.

> *(Jordan)* Deal gently with one another and maintain a good attitude. Show goodwill toward each other as God showed toward you in Christ.
> *(Wms.)* You must practice being kind to one another...
> *(Fenton)* ...and become useful to one another...

COLOSSIANS 3:14 And above all these things put on charity, which is the bond of perfectness.

> *(Weym.)* And over all these put on love, which is the perfect bond of union...
> *(Barclay)* And, to crown all, you must clothe yourselves in love, which holds all the other qualities together and completes them.
> *(Basic)* ...And more than all, have love; the only way in which you may be completely joined together.
> *(Trans.)* Above all there must be love, for it is love which binds everything together in perfect unity.
> *(Wuest)* ...put on divine and self-sacrificial love which is a binding factor of completeness.
> *(N. Berk.)* But crown it all with love, which is the perfect bond of union.
> *(GNB)* And to all these qualities add love, which binds all things together in perfect unity.
> *(TLB)* Most of all, let love guide your life, for then the whole church will stay together in perfect harmony.
> *(Norlie)* And on top of all these place love, which binds you together in perfect harmony.
> *(NEB)* To crown all, there must be love, to bind all together and complete the whole.
> *(Jordan)* Over all these things wear love, which is the robe of maturity.
> *(Johnson)* As the most important piece of new clothing, be sure to wear love, because love is the evidence of maturity.
> *(Gspd.)* And over all these put on love, which completes them and fastens them all together.
> *(Way)* And, over all these, with love enfold yourselves—love, the all-clasping bond, the mark of perfectness.
> *(Roth.)* And over all these things love, which is a uniting-bond of completeness.
> *(Berk.)* But cap it all with love, which is the perfect bond of union.
> *(Godbey)* ...divine love...
> *(Wms.)* ...which is the tie of perfection that binds us together.

COLOSSIANS 3:14 (New Life) ...Love holds everything and everybody together...

(Phil.) ...love is the golden chain of all the virtues.

I THESSALONIANS 3:12 And the Lord make you to increase and abound in love one toward another, and toward all men, even as we do toward you...

(Way) And you - may the Lord fill you more and more - ay, till you overflow - with love to one another and to all men, even as my heart is full of love toward you!

(Trans.) May the Lord help you to love one another and all men with an overflowing abundance, as we love you.

(Beck) The Lord make you grow in love and overflow with it for one another and for everybody, just as we love you...

(N. Berk., Berk.) May the Lord make your love for one another and for everyone abundant and running over, just as ours is for you...

(Barclay) It is our prayer that the Lord may make your love for each other and for all men to grow until it overflows, just as ours for you...

(Basic) ...And the Lord give you increase of love in fullest measure to one another and to all men, even as our love to you...

(Knox) ...may the Lord give you a rich and an ever richer love for one another and for all men, like ours for you.

(20th C. 1) ...may the Lord fill your hearts to overflowing with love for one another and for everybody...

(Gspd.) May the Lord make your love for one another and for all men wide and full like my love for you...

(Johnson) And may the Lord teach you the meaning of love and how to express it to each other as I express love to you.

(Wuest) ...the Lord cause you to increase and superabound in your divine and self-sacrificial love for one another and toward all...

(Lau.) And may the Lord help your love to grow big for one another and for all people...

(Weym.) ...may the Lord teach you to love one another and all men, with a growing and a glowing love...

(Tomanek) But the Lord will cause you to be full and to overflow with the love to each other...

(Jordan) May the Lord load you up and run you over with love for one another and for everybody else too...

(Godbey) ...and the Lord fill you and cause you to superabound in divine love toward one another...

(Fenton) And may the Lord fill you to overflowing with love to one another, and to all...

(Jer.) ...one another and the whole human race...

I THESSALONIANS 3:12 (NIV, Weekes, Wms.) ...increase and overflow...
> *(Phil.)* ...increasing and overflowing love...
> *(River.)* ...abound and overflow in love...
> *(Black.)* ...to increase and abound in purposive concern for one another...
> *(NEB)* ...may the Lord make your love mount and overflow...
> *(Mof.)* ...the Lord make you increase and excel in love...

I THESSALONIANS 4:9 But as touching brotherly love ye need not that I write unto you: for ye yourselves are taught of God to love one another.
> *(Wuest)* ...loving one another with a love that impels you to deny yourselves for the benefit of the one whom you love...
> *(Berk.)* ...for you have been personally taught of God to love one another,...
> *(Black.)* ...you yourselves are God-taught to continue demonstrating purposive good will to one another.
> *(Fenton)* ...Divinely instructed...
> *(Roth., Young)* (lit.) ...God-taught... (marg.) ...divinely instructed...
> *(Godbey)* ...to love one another with divine love...

I THESSALONIANS 4:10 And indeed ye do it toward all the brethren which are in all Macedonia: but we beseech you, brethren, that ye increase more and more...
> *(Fenton)* ...But we beg you, brethren, to progress still further.
> *(Berk.)* ...and you are actually practicing it toward all the brothers throughout Macedonia. But we appeal to you, brothers, to keep advancing in it...
> *(Noli)* Indeed, you do practice this love toward all the brethren who live all over Macedonia. But I entreat you, brethren, to progress still more.
> *(Trans.)* ...We would beg you, brothers, to go even further...
> *(Lau.)* ...I want you, brothers, to show more and more of this love.
> *(Jer.)* ...However, we do urge you, brothers, to go on making even greater progress...
> *(Jordan)* ...But we are encouraging you to grow even more in this respect...
> *(Beck)* ...But we urge you, my fellow Christians, grow more and more...
> *(N. Berk.)* ...But we appeal to you, brothers, to keep advancing in it...
> *(Way)* ...So I do but exhort you, my brothers, to rise to high heights still.
> *(Wade)* ...And we appeal to you, Brothers, to rise to higher levels still...
> *(Fenton)* ...to progress still further.
> *(NASB)* ...But we urge you, brethren, to excel still more.
> *(Roth. 2)* ...But we are exhorting you, brethren, to be overflowing yet more...

II TIMOTHY 2:24 And the servant of the Lord must not strive; but be gentle unto all men, apt to teach, patient...

> *(Black.)* And the Lord's servant must not be contentious but courteous to everyone, skillful in teaching, bearing adverse treatment without resentment.
>
> *(Hudson)* ...but the Lord's servant must not quarrel but be mild to all, a skillful teacher, forbearing...
>
> *(Weym.)* ...a bond servant of the Lord must not quarrel, but must be inoffensive towards all men, a skillful teacher, and patient under wrongs.
>
> *(Knox)* A servant of the Lord has no business with quarreling; he must be kindly towards all men, persuasive and tolerant...
>
> *(Barclay)* The Lord's servant must not be quarrelsome; he must be characteristically kindly. He must be a good teacher. He must have a mind above resentment.
>
> *(Jer.)* ...a servant of the Lord is not to engage in quarrels...
>
> *(Berk.)* But a servant of the Lord must not quarrel; instead, he must be affable toward everyone, skilled in teaching, willing to suffer wrong.
>
> *(Noli)* A servant of the Lord must not be quarrelsome, He must be kindly, persuasive, and tolerant toward all.
>
> *(Syriac)* And a servant of our Lord ought not to contend, but to be mild towards everyone, and instructive, and patient;...
>
> *(Phil.)* ...he must have patience...
>
> *(NASB)* ...patient when wronged...
>
> *(Roth.)* ...ready to endure malice...
>
> *(Jordan)* ...not easily riled up...
>
> *(New Life)* ...He must be willing to suffer when hurt for doing good.
>
> *(Basic)* ...putting up with wrong.
>
> *(N. Berk.)* ...willing to suffer wrong.
>
> *(Mof.)* ...a man who will not resent injuries...
>
> *(Wms.)* ...not resentful under injuries.
>
> *(Wand)* ...slow to take offense...
>
> *(Norlie)* ...he should be kind to everyone, ready to teach them and ready to overlook grievances.
>
> *(Gspd.)* ...he must be persuasive and unresentful...

II TIMOTHY 2:25 In meekness instructing those that oppose themselves; if God peradventure will give them repentance to the acknowledging of the truth...

> *(Black.)* He should correct opponents with meekness, in the hope that God may grant them repentance that leads to full knowledge of the truth...

II TIMOTHY 2:25 (Hudson) ...gentle in correcting the opponents in the hope that God may lead them to change their mind and recognize the truth...

(*Weym.*) He must speak in a gentle tone when correcting the errors of opponents, in the hope that God will at last give them repentance, for them to come to a full knowledge of the truth...

(*Knox*) ...with a gentle hand for correcting those who are obstinate in their errors. It may be that God will enable them to repent, and acknowledge the truth...

(*Barclay*) When he has to exercise discipline upon those who oppose him, he must do so in the strength of gentleness, for it may be that God will lead them to repentance and to a knowledge of the truth.

(*Jer.*) He has to be gentle when he corrects people who dispute what he says, never forgetting that God may give them a change of mind so that they recognize the truth...

(*Berk.*) In a gentle way he must discipline those who put themselves in opposition...

(*Noli*) He must correct his opponents with gentleness...

(*Syriac*) ...that with mildness he may enlighten those who dispute against him...

(*Phil.*) ...the ability gently to correct those who oppose his message. He must always bear in mind the possibility that God will give them a different outlook, and that they may come to know the truth.

(*NASB*) ...with gentleness correcting those who are in opposition...

(*Roth.*) In meekness bringing under discipline them that oppose themselves...

(*Jordan*) ...one who puts his point across to his opponents with genuine humility, hoping that God might give his opponents a change of mind so as to understand the truth.

(*New Life*) Be gentle when you try to teach those who are against what you say...

(*Basic*) Gently guiding those who go against the teaching...

(*N. Berk.*) In a gentle way he must correct those who put themselves in opposition to him...

(*TLB*) Be humble when you are trying to teach those who are mixed up concerning the truth. For if you talk meekly and courteously to them they are more likely, with God's help, to turn away from their wrong ideas and believe what is true.

(*Norlie*) He should discipline the unruly with gentleness...

(*Way*) ...that God may some day grant them a better frame of mind, which may lead to recognition of the truth, and that so from their drunken slumber amid the toils of the devil, where, trapped by him, they have lain, they may start up, to do the will of God.

(*Roth. 2*) ...in meekness bringing under discipline those that oppose themselves, lest at any time God give them repentance for gaining full knowledge of truth...

(*GNB*) ...who is gentle as he corrects his opponents...

(*Wade*) ...gently correcting those who take up an attitude of opposition...

(*Pl. Eng.*) ...gentle in correcting those of opposite opinion...

(*Conc.*) ...with meekness training those who are antagonizing...

II TIMOTHY 2:25 (Cunn.) ...in meekness correcting them that contend with him...

(20th C.R.) ...for, possibly, God may give them a repentance that will lead to a fuller knowledge of Truth...

(Conf.) ...gently admonishing those who resist.

(Authentic) ...quietly correcting antagonists...

(NAB) ...gently correcting those who contradict him...

II TIMOTHY 2:26 And that they may recover themselves out of the snare of the devil, who are taken captive by him at his will.

(Black.) ...and that they may return to their senses [and so escape] from the devil who has held them captive to do *his will. (*Lit., "to do the will of that one." The latter part of the verse could be rendered, and so escape from the devil's captivity to do his [God's] will.)

(Weym.) ...and recover sober-mindedness and freedom from the Devil's snare, though they are now entrapped by him to do his will.

(Knox) ...so they will recover their senses, and shake off the snare by which the devil, till now, has held them prisoners to his will.

(Barclay) True, they were captured alive by the Devil, but it may be that they will come to their senses and escape from his trap, and end up by accepting God's will.

(Jer.) ...and come to their senses, once out of the trap where the devil caught them and kept them enslaved.

(Jordan) And when they do understand, they'll wise up to the fact that the Devil has had them in the palm of his hand all along, and they'll bust out of his trap.

(New Life) Then they will know they had been held in a trap by the devil to do what he wanted them to do. But now they are able to get out of it.

(Fenton) ...and on awakening, they may disentangle themselves from the net of the Devil, escaping from under it into His freedom.

I PETER 3:8-12 Finally, be ye all of one mind, having compassion one of another, love as brethren, be pitiful, be courteous: Not rendering evil for evil, or railing for railing: but contrariwise blessing; knowing that ye are thereunto called, that ye should inherit a blessing. For he that will love life, and see good days, let him refrain his tongue from evil, and his lips that they speak no guile: Let him eschew evil, and do good; let him seek peace, and ensue it. For the eyes of the Lord are over the righteous, and his ears are open unto their prayers: but the face of the Lord is against them that do evil.

(NEB) Finally, be ye all of one mind, having compassion one of another, love as brethren, be pitiful, be courteous: To sum up: be one in thought and feeling all of you; be full of brotherly affection, kindly and humble-minded.

I PETER 3:8-12 (ASV) Finally, be ye all likeminded, compassionate, loving as brethren, tenderhearted,humbleminded...not rendering evil for evil, reviling for reviling (railing for railing)...let him seek peace, and ensue it...and pursue it.

(AMP) Finally all [of you] should be of one and the same mind (united in spirit), sympathizing [with one another], loving [each other] as brethren [of one household], compassionate and courteous (tenderhearted and humble). Never return evil for evil or insult for insult (scolding, tongue-lashing, berating), but on the contrary blessing [praying for their welfare, happiness, and protection, and truly pitying and loving them]. For know that to this you have been called, that you may yourselves inherit a blessing [from God - that you may obtain a blessing as heirs, bringing welfare and happiness and protection]. For let him who wants to enjoy life and see good days [good - whether apparent or not] keep his tongue free from evil and his lips from guile (treachery, deceit). Let him turn away from wickedness and shun it, and let him do right. Let him search for peace (harmony; undisturbedness from fears, agitating passions, and moral conflicts) and seek it eagerly. [Do not merely desire peaceful relations with God, with your fellowmen, and with yourself, but pursue, go after them!] For the eyes of the Lord are upon the righteous (those who are upright and in right standing with God), and His ears are attentive to their prayer. But the face of the Lord is against those who practice evil [to oppose them, to frustrate, and defeat them].

(TLB) And now this word to all of you...

(20th C.R.) Lastly, you should all be united, sympathetic, full of brotherly love, kind-hearted, humble-minded; never returning evil for evil, or abuse for abuse, but, on the contrary, blessing. It was to this that you were called – to obtain a blessing! He who would enjoy life and see happy days – Let him keep his tongue from evil And his lips from deceitful words, Let him turn from evil and do good, Let him seek for peace and follow after it; For the eyes of the Lord are on the righteous, And his ears are attentive to their prayers, But the face of the Lord is set against those who do wrong.

(Phil.) ...an insult with another insult...

(Knox) ...hard words with hard words...

(Basic) ...curse for curse...

(Alf.) ...reproach for reproach...

(Mof.) ...but on the contrary blessing. For this is your vocation, to bless and to inherit a blessing...

(Mof.) ...let him shun wrong and do right...let him seek peace, making peace his aim.

(Basic) ...searching for peace and going after it with all his heart.

(TLB) ...Try to live in peace even if you must run after it to catch and hold it.

(Wms.) Because the eyes of the Lord are on upright men, And His ears listen to their pleading cries.

I PETER 4:8 And above all things have fervent charity among yourselves: for charity shall cover the multitude of sins.

(AMP) Above all things have intense and unfailing love for one another, for love covers a multitude of sins [forgives and disregards the offenses of others].

(TLB) Most important of all, continue to show deep love for each other, for love makes up for many of your faults.

(Message) Most of all, love each other as if your life depended on it. Love makes up for practically anything.

I JOHN 2:10 He that loveth his brother abideth in the light, and there is none occasion of stumbling in him.

(Knox) It is the man who loves his brother that lives in light; no fear of stumbling haunts him.

(Jer.) But anyone who loves his brother is living in the light and need not be afraid of stumbling.

(Beck) If you love your brother, you live in the light, and there's nothing in you to offend anyone.

(Mof.) He who loves his brother remains in the light - and in the light there is no pitfall.

(Authentic) He who loves his brother continues in the light, and in it there is no pitfall.

(Weym.) ...and his life puts no stumbling block in the way of others.

(Berk.) ...is continually in the light and there is nothing within him to occasion stumbling.

(Jordan) But the brother-hater is in the dark and moves in the dark...

(Godbey) The one loving his brother with divine love...

(Cent.) ...and in it there is no cause of stumbling.

I JOHN 3:18 My little children, let us not love in word, neither in tongue; but in deed and in truth.

(20th C. R.) My children, do not let your love be mere words, or end in talk; let it be true and show itself in acts.

(Phil.) My children, let us love not merely in theory or in words — let us love in sincerity and in practice!

(GNB) My children, our love should not be just words and talk; it must be true love, which shows itself in action.

(TLB) Little children, let us stop just saying we love people; let us really love them, and show it by our actions.

(NEB) My children, love must not be a matter of words or talk; it must be genuine, and show itself in action.

(Noli) My children, we must not love merely in words and in theory, but in deeds and in reality.

I JOHN 3:18 (Beck) Children, let us not love only in words or in talk, but let us put our love into action and make it real.

> *(Barclay)* Dear children, our love must not be a thing of words and of fine talk; it must be a thing of action and of sincerity.
>
> *(Jer.)* My children, our love is not to be just words or mere talk, but something real and active...
>
> *(Knox)* My little children, let us shew our love by the true test of action, not by taking phrases on our lips.
>
> *(AMP)* Little children, let us not love [merely] in theory or in speech but in deed and in truth (in practice and in sincerity).
>
> *(Godbey)* ...let us love with divine love...
>
> *(NAB)* ...let us love in deed and in truth and not merely talk about it.
>
> *(Fenton)* ...let us not love in pretense, nor with the tongue; but in act and truth.

I JOHN 4:7 Beloved, let us love one another: for love is of God; and every one that loveth is born of God, and knoweth God.

> *(20th C. 1)* ...Love comes from God; and all who love have derived their Life from God and are learning to know him.
>
> *(Roth.)* ...whosoever loveth of God hath been born and is getting to understand God...
>
> *(Jordan)* ...every lover has been fathered by God and is sensitive to God.
>
> *See eternal life p. 399*

I JOHN 4:8 He that loveth not knoweth not God; for God is love.

> *(Roth.)* He that doth not love doth not understand God, Because God is love.
>
> *(Godbey)* The one not loving with divine love does not know God; because God is divine love.
>
> *(Jordan)* The nonlover is not sensitive to God because God is love.

I JOHN 4:16 And we have known and believed the love that God hath to us. God is love; and he that dwelleth in love dwelleth in God, and God in him.

> *(Weym.)* And, as for us, we know the love which God has for us, and we confide in it. God is love, and he who continues to love continues in union with God, and God continues in union with him.
>
> *(Godbey)* And we have known and we have believed the divine love which God has in us. God is divine love; and the one abiding in divine love abides in God, and God abides in him.
>
> *(20th C. R.)* ...we have learnt to know, and have accepted as a fact, the love which God has for us. God is love; and he who lives in love lives in God, and God in him.

I JOHN 4:16 (Berk.) We both know and put faith in the love which God cherishes in us...

(Wms.) ...God is love, and whoever continues to love continues in union with God and God in union with him.

(Noli) ...Everyone who practices love can be sure that he abides in God, and God in him.

(Jordan) So we have both experienced, and based our lives on, the love that God has put in us...

(Weekes) And we have come to understand and to trust in the love that God hath to us.

(Jer.) We ourselves have known and put our faith in God's love toward ourselves...

(Knox) We have learned to recognize the love God has in our regard, to recognize it, and to make it our belief...

(Trans.) We know the love which God has for us, and have put our trust in it...

(Roth.) And we have come to understand and to trust the love which God hath in us...

(20th C. 1) ...all who are living in a spirit of love are living in union with God, and God with them.

(Fenton) And we realize and rely upon the love which God has for us...

JUDE 21 Keep yourselves in the love of God, looking for the mercy of our Lord Jesus Christ unto eternal life.

(TLB) Stay always within the boundaries where God's love can reach and bless you.

(AMP) Guard and keep yourselves in the love of God...

(Pl. Eng.) ...keeping yourselves safe in the love of God...

(Weym.) ...keep yourselves safe in the love of God...

JOY is the bridge between BELIEVING & RECEIVING.

Mark Hankins
THE SECRET POWER OF JOY

GENESIS
21:6 337

II SAMUEL
6:14 339

NEHEMIAH
8:10 339

JOB
5:22 337
8:21 339

PSALM
2:4 337
4:7 340
5:11, 12 338
32:11 338
68:3, 4 339
89:15, 16 340
119:162 338
126:1-3 340

PROVERBS
15:15 341
15:23 341
17:22 341

ISAIAH
12:3 341

JEREMIAH
15:16 338

HABAKKUK
3:17-19 337

JOHN
16:24 341

ACTS
13:52 341

ROMANS
14:17 342
14:18 342

PHILIPPIANS
1:25 342
4:4 342

HEBREWS
1:9 343
11:11 343

JAMES
1:2 343
1:3 344

I PETER
1:8 344

FAITH
laughs at
IMPOSSIBILITIES.

Smith Wigglesworth

GENESIS 21:6 And Sarah said, God hath made me to laugh, so that all that hear will laugh with me.

(AMP) And Sarah said, God has made me to laugh; all who hear will laugh with me.

(TLB) And Sarah declared, God has brought me to laughter! All who hear about this shall rejoice with me.

(Message) Sarah said, God has blessed me with laughter and all who get the news will laugh with me!

JOB 5:22 At destruction and famine thou shalt laugh: neither shalt thou be afraid of the beasts of the earth.

(AMP) At destruction and famine you shall laugh, neither shall you be afraid of the living creatures of the earth.

(TLB) You shall laugh at war and famine...

(Message) You'll shrug off disaster and famine...

(NEB) You will laugh at violence and starvation...

PSALM 2:4 He that sitteth in the heavens shall laugh: the Lord shall have them in derision.

(AMP) He Who sits in the heavens laughs...

(Message) Heaven-throned God breaks out laughing.

(TLB) But God in heaven merely laughs! He is amused by all their puny plans.

(Knox) He who dwells in heaven is laughing at their threats.

HABAKKUK 3:17-19 Although the fig tree shall not blossom, neither shall fruit be in the vines; the labour of the olive shall fail, and the fields shall yield no meat; the flock shall be cut off from the fold, and there shall be no herd in the stalls: yet I will rejoice in the Lord, I will joy in the God of my salvation. The Lord God is my strength, and he will make my feet like hinds' feet, and he will make me to walk upon mine high places.

(AMP) Yet I will rejoice in the Lord; I will exult in the [victorious] God of my salvation! The Lord God is my Strength, my personal bravery, and my invincible army; He makes my feet like hinds' feet and will make me to walk [not to stand still in terror, but to walk] and make [spiritual] progress upon my high places [of trouble, suffering, or responsibility]!

(TLB) Even though the fig trees are all destroyed, and there is neither blossom left nor fruit, and though the olive crops all fail, and the fields lie barren; even if the flocks die in the fields and the cattle barns are empty, yet I will rejoice in the Lord; I will be happy in the God of my salvation. The Lord God is my Strength, and he will give me the speed of a deer and bring me safely over the mountains.

HABAKKUK 3:17-19 (Message) I'm singing joyful praise to God. I'm turning cartwheels of joy to my Savior God. Counting on God's Rule to prevail, I take heart and gain strength. I run like a deer. I feel like I'm king of the mountain!

JEREMIAH 15:16 Thy words were found, and I did eat them; and thy word was unto me the joy and rejoicing of mine heart: for I am called by thy name, O Lord God of hosts.

(*AMP*) Your words were found, and I ate them; and Your words were to me a joy and the rejoicing of my heart…

(*TLB*) Your words are what sustain me; they are food to my hungry soul. They bring joy to my sorrowing heart and delight me.

(*Message*) When your words showed up, I ate them—swallowed them whole. What a feast! What delight I took in being yours…

PSALM 119:162 I rejoice at thy word, as one that findeth great spoil.

(*AMP*) I rejoice at Your word as one who finds great spoil.

(*TLB*) I rejoice in your laws like one who finds a great treasure.

(*Message*) I'm ecstatic over what you say, like one who strikes it rich.

PSALM 5:11, 12 But let all those that put their trust in thee rejoice: let them ever shout for joy, because thou defendest them: let them also that love thy name be joyful in thee. For thou, Lord, wilt bless the righteous; with favour wilt thou compass him as with a shield.

(*AMP*) But let all those who take refuge and put their trust in You rejoice; let them ever sing and shout for joy, because You make a covering over them and defend them; let those also who love Your name be joyful in You and be in high spirits. For You, Lord, will bless the [uncompromisingly] righteous [him who is upright and in right standing with You]; as with a shield You will surround him with goodwill (pleasure and favor).

(*TLB*) But make everyone rejoice who puts his trust in you. Keep them shouting for joy because you are defending them. Fill all who love you with your happiness. For you bless the godly man, O Lord; you protect him with your shield of love.

(*Message*) But you'll welcome us with open arms when we run for cover to you. Let the party last all night! Stand guard over our celebration. You are famous, God, for welcoming God-seekers, for decking us out in delight.

(*Smith, J.M.*) That all who take refuge in thee may rejoice and shout for joy forever.

PSALM 32:11 Be glad in the Lord, and rejoice, ye righteous: and shout for joy, all ye that are upright in heart.

(*AMP*) Be glad in the Lord and rejoice, you [uncompromisingly] righteous [you who are upright and in right standing with Him]; shout for joy, all you upright in heart!

PSALM 32:11 (TLB) So rejoice in him, all those who are his, and shout for joy, all those who try to obey him.

> (*Message*) Celebrate God. Sing together - everyone! All you honest hearts, raise the roof!

PSALM 68:3, 4 But let the righteous be glad; let them rejoice before God: yea, let them exceedingly rejoice. Sing unto God, sing praises to his name: extol him that rideth upon the heavens by his name JAH, and rejoice before him.

> (*AMP*) But let the [uncompromisingly] righteous be glad; let them be in high spirits and glory before God, yes, let them [jubilantly] rejoice! Sing to God, sing praises to His name, cast up a highway for Him Who rides through the deserts—His name is the Lord—be in high spirits and glory before Him!

> (*TLB*) But may the godly man exult. May he rejoice and be merry. Sing praises to the Lord! Raise your voice in song to him who rides upon the clouds! Jehovah is his name—oh, rejoice in his presence.

> (*Message*) When the righteous see God in action they'll laugh, they'll sing, they'll laugh and sing for joy. Sing hymns to God; all heaven, sing out; clear the way for the coming of Cloud- Rider. Enjoy God, cheer when you see him!

II SAMUEL 6:14 And David danced before the Lord with all his might; and David was girded with a linen ephod.

> (*Mof.*) David whirled before the Eternal with all his might in the dance...

> (*GNB*) ...danced with all his might to honor the Lord.

> (*Roth.*) And David was dancing with all boldness before Yahweh...

> (*Jer.*) And David danced whirling around before Yahweh with all his might...

> (*Smith, J.M.*) David was whirling in a dance with all his might...

> (*NEB*) David, wearing a linen ephod, danced without restraint before the Lord.

NEHEMIAH 8:10 ...for the joy of the Lord is your strength.

> (*Smith, J.M.*) ...for the joy of the Lord is your refuge.

> (*NEB*) ...for joy in the Lord is your strength.

> (*TLB*) ...for the joy of the Lord is your strength. You must not be dejected and sad.

> (*AMP*) ...for the joy of the Lord is your strength and stronghold.

> (*Mof.*) ...to rejoice in the Eternal is your strength.

JOB 8:21 Till he fill thy mouth with laughing, and thy lips with rejoicing.

> (*TLB*) He will yet fill your mouth with laughter and your lips with shouts of joy.

> (*Roth.*) At length he shall fill with laughter thy mouth, and thy lips with a shout of triumph.

PSALM 4:7 Thou hast put gladness in my heart, more than in the time that their corn and their wine increased.

>**(Knox)** Never did rich harvest of corn and wine bring gladness like the gladness thou puttest into my heart.

PSALM 89:15, 16 Blessed is the people that know the joyful sound: they shall walk, O Lord, in the light of thy countenance. In thy name shall they rejoice all the day: and in thy righteousness shall they be exalted.

>**(Mof.)** Happy the people who know thy festal songs, who live within the sunshine of thy favour!
>
>**(Knox)** Happy is the people that knows well the shout of praise, that lives, Lord, in the smile of thy protection!
>
>**(Young)** O the happiness of the people knowing the shout, O Jehovah, in the light of Thy face they walk habitually.
>
>**(Mar.)** ...the joyful shout...
>
>**(GNB)** How happy are the people who worship you with songs...
>
>**(Norlie)** ...who go about radiant with Your presence.
>
>**(Fenton)** In Your Name they can laugh all the day...
>
>**(NEB)** ...thy righteousness shall lift them up.
>
>*See righteousness p. 46-47*

PSALM 126:1-3 When the Lord turned again the captivity of Zion, we were like them that dream. Then was our mouth filled with laughter, and our tongue with singing: then said they among the heathen, The Lord hath done great things for them. The Lord hath done great things for us; whereof we are glad.

>**(Har.)** When the Lord restores the fortunes of captive Zion, it will be like being in a dream.
>
>**(AMP)** ...we were like those who dream [it seemed so unreal]. Then were our mouths filled with laughter, and our tongues with singing...The Lord has done great things for us! We are glad!
>
>**(TLB)** How we laughed and sang for joy. And the other nations said, What amazing things the Lord has done for them. Yes, glorious things! What wonder! What joy!
>
>**(Basic)** Then our mouths were full of laughing, and our tongues gave a glad cry...
>
>**(McFadyen)** Then we broke into shouts of happy laughter.
>
>**(Message)** We laughed, we sang, we couldn't believe our good fortune.
>
>**(NIV)** ...we are filled with joy.
>
>**(Roth.)** ...We are full of joy!

PROVERBS 15:15 All the days of the afflicted are evil: but he that is of a merry heart hath a continual feast.

(AMP) All the days of the desponding and afflicted are made evil [by anxious thoughts and forebodings], but he who has a glad heart has a continual feast [regardless of circumstances].

PROVERBS 15:23 A man hath joy by the answer of his mouth: and a word spoken in due season, how good is it!

See faith p. 140

PROVERBS 17:22 A merry heart doeth good like a medicine: but a broken spirit drieth the bones.

(TLB) A cheerful heart does good like medicine, but a broken spirit makes one sick.

(Young) A rejoicing heart doth good to the body...

(Roth.) A joyful heart worketh an excellent cure...

(AMP) A happy heart is good medicine and a cheerful mind works healing...

(Message) A cheerful disposition is good for your health...

ISAIAH 12:3 Therefore with joy shall ye draw water out of the wells of salvation.

(TLB) Oh, the joy of drinking deeply from the Fountain of Salvation!

(Mof.) Joyfully then shall you draw upon the fountains of deliverance...

(Roth) Therefore shall ye draw water with rejoicing...

(Knox) So, rejoicing, you shall drink deep from the fountain of deliverance.

JOHN 16:24 Hitherto have ye asked nothing in my name: ask, and ye shall receive, that your joy may be full.

(TLB) You haven't tried this before, [but begin now]. Ask, using my name, and you will receive, and your cup of joy will overflow.

(Knox) Until now, you have not been making any requests in my name; make them, and they will be granted, to bring you gladness in full measure.

(Wms.) Up to this time you have not asked for anything as bearers of my name, but now you must keep on asking, and you will receive, that your cup of joy may be full to the brim.

See prayer p. 232

ACTS 13:52 And the disciples were filled with joy, and with the Holy Ghost.

(NASB) And the disciples were continually filled with joy and with the Holy Spirit.

(Jordan) And the Lord's learners were just bubbling over with joy and Holy Spirit.

(Wms.) ...and the disciples continued to be full of joy and the Holy Spirit.

ACTS 13:52 (Weym.) ...and as for the disciples, they were more and more filled with joy and with the Holy Spirit.

> *See Holy Spirit p. 185*

ROMANS 14:17 For the kingdom of God is not meat and drink; but righteousness, and peace, and joy in the Holy Ghost.

> *(Way)* ...it is righteousness, heart-peace, and joy in the presence of the Holy Spirit.
>
> *(Knox)* The kingdom of God is not a matter of eating or drinking this or that; it means rightness of heart, finding our peace and our joy in the Holy Spirit.
>
> *See righteousness p. 39*

ROMANS 14:18 For he that in these things serveth Christ is acceptable to God, and approved of men.

> *(Way)* He who in this respect surrenders his own freedom to Messiah is acceptable in God's sight; in men's he is of tested worth.
>
> *(Weym.)* ...and whoever in this way devotedly serves Christ, God takes pleasure in him, and men highly commend him.
>
> *(Cony.)* ...and he who lives in these things as Christ's bondsman is well-pleasing to God, and cannot be condemned by men.

PHILIPPIANS 1:25 And having this confidence, I know that I shall abide and continue with you all for your furtherance and joy of faith...

> *(Norlie)* ...to help all of you advance in Christian living, as well as in the joy that comes from faith.
>
> *(Wuest)* ...for your pioneer advance [in the Christian life] and your joy in the Faith...
>
> *(Barclay)* ...to help you to make still further progress, and to have still more joy in the faith.
>
> *(N. Berk.)* ...that you may progress and have the joy that comes with faith...
>
> *(Gspd.)* ...to help you develop and to be glad in your faith.
>
> *(Roth. 2)* ...for your faith's advancement and joy...

PHILIPPIANS 4:4 Rejoice in the Lord always: and again I say, Rejoice.

> *(Phil.)* Delight yourselves in the Lord; yes, find your joy in him at all times.
>
> *(Wade)* Rejoice at all times, united as you are to the Lord: I repeat it, Rejoice.
>
> *(New Life)* Be full of joy always because you belong to the Lord. Again I say, be full of joy!
>
> *(Wms.)* By the help of the Lord always keep up the glad spirit; yes, I will repeat it, keep up the glad spirit.
>
> *(Barclay)* Never lose your Christian joy. Let me say it again! Never lose it!
>
> *(20th C. R.)* All joy be yours at all times in your union with the Lord. Again I repeat—All joy be yours.
>
> *(TLB)* Always be full of joy in the Lord...

HEBREWS 1:9 Thou hast loved righteousness, and hated iniquity; therefore God, even thy God, hath anointed thee with the oil of gladness above thy fellows.

(AMP) You have loved righteousness [You have delighted in integrity, virtue and uprightness in purpose, thought and action] and You have hated lawlessness (injustice and iniquity). Therefore God, [even] Your God (Godhead), has anointed You with the oil of exultant joy and gladness above and beyond Your companions.

(TLB) You love right and hate wrong; so God, even your God, has poured out more gladness upon you than on anyone else.

(NIV) ...has set you above your companions by anointing you with the oil of joy.

(Roth.) ...with the oil of exultation beyond thy partners.

(Mof.) ...with the oil of rejoicing...

HEBREWS 11:11 Through faith also Sara herself received strength to conceive seed, and was delivered of a child when she was past age, because she judged him faithful who had promised.

(AMP) Because of faith also Sarah herself received physical power to conceive a child, even when she was long past the age for it, because she considered [God] Who had given her the promise to be reliable and trustworthy and true to His word.

(TLB) Sarah, too, had faith, and because of this she was able to become a mother in spite of her old age, for she realized that God, who gave her his promise, would certainly do what he said.

(Message) By faith, barren Sarah was able to become pregnant, old woman as she was at the time, because she believed the One who made a promise would do what he said. That's how it happened that from one man's dead and shriveled loins there are now people numbering into the millions.

JAMES 1:2 My brethren, count it all joy when ye fall into divers temptations...

(Beck) When you're tested in different ways, my fellow Christians, consider it a pure joy...

(Wuest) Be constantly rejoicing. Consider it a matter for unadulterated joy [without and admixture of sorrow] whenever you fall into the midst of variegated trials which surround you.

(Noli) You must be deeply gratified when you are harassed by fiendish temptations.

(Berk.) Consider it maximum joy, my brothers, when you get involved in all sorts of trials...

(NIV) Consider it pure joy, my brothers, whenever you face trials of many kinds...

(20th C. 1) My Brothers, when you meet with temptations, whatever they are, think of them as a cause for nothing but rejoicing...

(NEB) My brothers, whenever you have to face trials of many kinds, count yourselves supremely happy...

JAMES 1:2 (Weym.) Reckon it nothing but joy, my brethren, whenever you find yourselves hedged in by various trials.

(*20th C. R.*) ...always regard them as a reason for rejoicing.

JAMES 1:3 Knowing this, that the trying of your faith worketh patience.

(*Berk.*) ...well aware that the testing of your faith brings out steadfastness. But let steadfastness have full play, so that you may be completed and rounded out with no defects whatever.

(*Weekes*) ...since ye know that the testing of your faith worketh out constancy. And let constancy...

(*Tomanek*) ...knowing that the proof of your faith works out patience.

I PETER 1:8 Whom having not seen, ye love; in whom, though now ye see him not, yet believing, ye rejoice with joy unspeakable and full of glory...

(*Weym.*) Him you love, though your eyes have never looked on Him. In Him, though at present you cannot see Him, you nevertheless trust, and triumph with a joy which is unspeakable and is crowned with glory...

(*Phil.*) And though you have never seen him, yet I know that you love him. At present you trust him without being able to see him, and even now he brings you a joy that words cannot express and which has in it a hint of the glories of Heaven.

(*Jer.*) ...and still without seeing him, you are already filled with a joy so glorious that it cannot be described, because you believe.

(*Noli*) ...you do not see him even now. But you believe in him, and you experience an ineffable and heavenly joy.

(*TLB*) ...even now you are happy with the inexpressible joy that comes from heaven itself.

(*AMP*) ...and exult and thrill with inexpressible and glorious (triumphant, heavenly) joy.

(*Wms.*) ...you must continue to rejoice with an unutterable and triumphant joy.

(*Conf.*) ...you exult with a joy unspeakable and triumphant.

(*Wade*) ...thrilled with a joy inexpressible and triumphant.

(*Berk.*) ...you exult with inexpressible and heavenly joy.

(*NIV*) ...and are filled with an inexpressible and glorious joy.

(*Gspd.*) ...triumphant, unutterable joy...

(*NEB*) ...you are transported with a joy too great for words, while you reap the harvest of your faith, that is, salvation for your souls.

Notes on Joy

Thou wilt keep him in **PERFECT PEACE,** whose mind is stayed on thee: because he **TRUSTETH** in thee.

Isaiah 26:3(KJV)

PSALM

4:8 349

89:17 349

89:18 349

119:165 349

ISAIAH

26:3 349

28:12 349

32:17 350

48:18 350

53:5 350

54:13 350

MATTHEW

6:25-33 351

JOHN

14:27 352

16:33 353

ROMANS

5:1 353

I CORINTHIANS

14:33 354

PHILIPPIANS

4:6 354

4:7 355

II THESSALONIANS

3:16 356

I PETER

5:7 356

GOD IS ON MY SIDE,

for the blood has been applied.
Every need shall be supplied.

NOTHING SHALL BE DENIED.

So I enter into rest,
I know that I am blessed.
I have passed the test.

I WILL GET GOD'S BEST!

Trina Hankins

PSALM 4:8 I will both lay me down in peace, and sleep: for thou, Lord, only makest me dwell in safety.

> *(Roth.)* In peace will I lay me down and at once sleep...
>
> *(Jer.)* In peace I lie down, and fall asleep at once, since you alone, Yahweh, make me rest secure.
>
> *(Mof.)* So quietly I lay me down to sleep, for even alone, thanks to thee, I am secure.
>
> (Fides) I lie down and at once sleep in peace...

PSALM 89:17 For thou art the glory of their strength: & in thy favour our horn shall be exalted.

> *(Mof.)* ...and, thanks to thy favour, our honour is high.
>
> *(GNB)* You give us great victories; in your love you make us triumphant.
>
> *(Knox)* What else but thy glory inspires their strength? What else but thy favor bids us lift our heads?
>
> *(NEB)* Thou art thyself the strength in which they glory; through thy favour we hold our heads high.

PSALM 89:18 For the Lord is our defense; and the Holy One of Israel is our king.

> *(Knox)* From the Lord, the Holy One of Israel, that royal protection comes which is our shield.

PSALM 119:165 Great peace have they which love thy law: and nothing shall offend them.

> *(Norlie)* Those who love Your law experience great peace; no obstacle can cause them to stumble.
>
> *(Beck)* ...and nothing can make them fall.
>
> *(Roth.)* Blessing in abundance have the lovers of thy law...
>
> *(Leeser)* ...and there is nothing that causeth them to stumble.
>
> *(Smith, J.M.)* Great prosperity have they who love thy law...
>
> *(Fides)* ...nothing can make them stumble.

ISAIAH 26:3 Thou wilt keep him in perfect peace, whose mind is stayed on thee: because he trusteth in thee.

> *(Mof.)* Thou dost protect and prosper steadfast souls, for they rely on thee.
>
> *(Knox)* Our thoughts wayward no longer, thou wilt maintain us in peace, peace that comes surely to those who trust in thee.
>
> *(Smith, J.M.)* The steadfast mind thou keepest in perfect peace, for it trusts in thee.

ISAIAH 28:12 To whom he said, This is the rest wherewith ye may cause the weary to rest; and this is the refreshing: yet they would not hear.

ISAIAH 28:12 (AMP) To these [complaining Jews the Lord] had said, This is the true rest [the way to true comfort and happiness] that you shall give to the weary, and, This is the [true] refreshing - yet they would not listen [to His teaching].

(Basic) ...and by this you may get new strength...

See prayer p. 227

**Peace is translated "prosperity" in some translations.*

ISAIAH 32:17 And the work of righteousness shall be peace; and the effect of righteousness quietness and assurance for ever.

(AMP) And the effect of righteousness will be peace [internal and external], and the result of righteousness will be quietness and confident trust forever.

(Mof.) ...and justice brings us welfare, honesty renders us secure...

(TLB) And out of justice, peace. Quietness and confidence will reign forever more.

(Jer.) ...integrity will bring peace, justice give lasting security.

(Basic) ...and the effect of an upright rule will be to take away fear for ever.

See righteousness p. 48

ISAIAH 48:18 O that thou hadst hearkened to my commandments! Then had thy peace been as a river, and thy righteousness as the waves of the sea.

(AMP) ...Then your peace and prosperity would have been like a flowing river, and your righteousness...like the [abundant] waves of the sea.

(TLB) ...Then you would have had peace flowing like a gentle river...

(Knox) ...Then had a flowing stream of peace been with thee, a full tide of the Lord's favour.

(Phil.) ...your peace like brooks.

(NEB) If only you had listened to my commands, your prosperity would have rolled on like a river in flood...

ISAIAH 53:5 ...the chastisement of our peace was upon him.

(AMP) ...the chastisement needful to obtain peace and well-being for us was upon Him.

(TLB) ...He was chastised that we might have peace.

(Knox) ...on him the punishment fell that brought us peace.

(NAB) ...the chastisement that makes us whole.

ISAIAH 54:13 And all thy children shall be taught of the Lord; and great shall be the peace of thy children.

(AMP) ...great shall be the peace and undisturbed composure of your children.

(TLB) ...their prosperity shall be great.

(Knox) ...blessed how abundantly with peace!

(NEB) ...your sons shall enjoy great prosperity.

MATTHEW 6:25-33 Therefore I say unto you, Take no thought for your life, what ye shall eat, or what ye shall drink; nor yet for your body, what ye shall put on. Is not the life more than meat, and the body than raiment? Behold the fowls of the air: for they sow not, neither do they reap, nor gather into barns; yet your heavenly Father feedeth them. Are ye not much better than they? Which of you by taking thought can add one cubit unto his stature? And why take ye thought for raiment? Consider the lilies of the field, how they grow; they toil not, neither do they spin: And yet I say unto you, That even Solomon in all his glory was not arrayed like one of these. Wherefore, if God so clothe the grass of the field, which to day is, and to morrow is cast into the oven, shall he not much more clothe you, O ye of little faith? Therefore take no thought, saying, What shall we eat? or, What shall we drink? or, Wherewithal shall we be clothed? (For after all these things do the Gentiles seek:) for your heavenly Father knoweth that ye have need of all these things. But seek ye first the kingdom of God, and his righteousness; and all these things shall be added unto you.

(AMP) Therefore I tell you, stop being perpetually uneasy (anxious and worried) about your life, what you shall eat or what you shall drink; or about your body, what you shall put on. Is not life greater [in quality] than food, and the body [far above and more excellent] than clothing? Look at the birds of the air; they neither sow nor reap nor gather into barns, and yet your heavenly Father keeps feeding them. Are you not worth much more than they? And who of you by worrying and being anxious can add one unit of measure (cubit) to his stature or to the span of his life? And why should you be anxious about clothes? Consider the lilies of the field and learn thoroughly how they grow; they neither toil nor spin. Yet I tell you, even Solomon in all his magnificence (excellence, dignity, and grace) was not arrayed like one of these. But if God so clothes the grass of the field, which today is alive and green and tomorrow is tossed into the furnace, will He not much more surely clothe you, O you of little faith? Therefore do not worry and be anxious, saying. What are we going to have to eat? or, What are we going to have to drink? or, What are we going to have to wear? For the Gentiles (heathen) wish for and crave and diligently seek all these things, and your heavenly Father knows well that you need them all. But seek (aim at and strive after) first of all His kingdom and His righteousness (His way of doing and being right), and then all these things taken together will be given you besides.

(Johnson) All this continuous quest for more and more of the physical necessities occupies the full attention of those who are unaware of God's presence. I assure you that your Father, the source of your being, is aware of all your physical needs. You are to give first priority to the Spirit dimension and to setting all your relationships right. When you get a proper perspective, these other things will take care of themselves.

MATTHEW 6:25-33 (Jordan) Then set your heart on the God Movement and its kind of life, and all these things will come as a matter of course.

(Crickmer) But be-going-on-petitioning-always-for first-of all The Kingdom of-your God and that His Righteousness, and-then things-of-this-kind the whole-of them shall-go-on-being added as covenant blessing to-you.

(20th C. 1) But first be eager about his Kingdom, and about what he thinks is right, and then all these things will be given you in addition.

(TLB) ...And he will give them to you if you give him first place in your life and live as he wants you to.

(Mof.) Seek God's Realm and his goodness, and all that will be yours over and above.

(Phil.) Set your heart on his kingdom and his goodness, and all these things will come to you as a matter of course.

(Barclay) Make the Kingdom of God, and life in loyalty to him, the object of all your endeavour, and you will get all these other things as well.

(Wade) But make your first aim His Dominion and His Righteousness and all these things will be granted to you in addition.

(Weym.) But make His Kingdom and righteousness your chief aim, and then these things shall be given you in addition.

(NEB) Set your mind on God's kingdom and his justice before everything else...

JOHN 14:27 Peace I leave with you, my peace I give unto you: not as the world giveth, give I unto you. Let not your heart be troubled, neither let it be afraid.

(Jer.) Peace I bequeath to you, my own peace I give you, a peace the world cannot give, this is my gift to you...

(AMP) ...[Stop allowing yourselves to be agitated and disturbed; and do not permit yourselves to be fearful and intimidated and cowardly and unsettled.]

(Berk.) Peace I bequeath to you;...Do not allow your hearts to be unsettled or intimidated.

(GNB) ...Do not be worried and upset; do not be afraid.

(NEB) Peace is my parting gift to you, my own peace, such as the world cannot give. Set your troubled hearts at rest, and banish your fears.

(Knox) ...Do not let your hearts be distressed...

(TLB) I am leaving you with a gift—peace of mind and heart! And the peace I give isn't fragile like the peace the world gives...

(Condon) Let no anxiety, no fear, trouble your hearts.

JOHN 16:33 These things I have spoken unto you, that in me ye might have peace. In the world ye shall have tribulation: but be of good cheer; I have overcome the world.

> *(Noli)* I am giving all these assurances, so that you may have peace in me. You will have tribulation in the world. But take courage, I have conquered the world.

> *(NEB)* I have told you all this so that in me you may find peace. In the world you will have trouble. But courage! The victory is mine; I have conquered the world.

> *(Fenton)* All this I have told you, so that you might enjoy perfect confidence in Me. In the world you have distress; but take courage! I have conquered the world.

> *(AMP)* I have told you these things, so that in Me you may have [perfect] peace and confidence. In the world you have tribulation and trials and distress and frustration; but be of good cheer [take courage; be confident, certain, undaunted]! For I have overcome the world [I have deprived it of power to harm you and have conquered it for you.]

> *(Douay)* ...In the world you shall have distress: but have confidence, I have overcome the world.

> *(Wuest)* I have come off victorious over the world with a permanent victory.

> *(Syriac)* ...In the world ye will have trouble: but, take courage, I have vanquished the world.

> *(Weym.)* ...But keep up your courage: I have won the victory over the world.

> *(Jer.)* ...In the world you will have trouble, but be brave: I have conquered the world.

> *(Wade)* ...that, through union with me, you may have peace...

> *(Berk.)* ...In the world you are under pressure; but be confident! I have overcome the world.

> *(Mof.)* ...in the world you have trouble, but courage! I have conquered the world.

> *(GNB)* ...that you will have peace by being united to me...I have defeated the world!

> *(Godbey)* ...but take courage; I have conquered the world.

> *(Gspd.)* ...I have conquered the world.

> *(Wms.)* ...that you through union with me may have peace...

> *(Crickmer)* ...in-organic oneness with Me peaceful-tranquillity ye-may-be-enjoying...

ROMANS 5:1 Therefore being justified by faith, we have peace with God through our Lord Jesus Christ.

> *(Berk.)* Since, then, we are made righteous through faith, let us enjoy peace with God through our Lord Jesus Christ.

> *(Hudson)* ...let us enjoy the peace with God which is ours through our Lord Jesus Christ.

> *(20th C. R.)* Therefore, having been pronounced righteous as the result of faith, let us enjoy peace with God, through Jesus Christ, our Lord.

> *(Wms.)* Since we have been given right standing with God through faith, let us continue enjoying peace with God...

> *(Young)* Having been declared righteous, then, by faith...

ROMANS 5:1 (Weekes) Being therefore made righteous from faith...

    (GNB) Now that we have been put right with God through faith...

    (Lau.) We are made right with God by our faith...

    (Mof.) ...let us enjoy the peace we have with God...

    (Cent.) ...let us continue to enjoy the peace we have with God...

    (AMP) Therefore, since we are justified (acquitted, declared righteous, and given a right standing with God) through faith, let us [grasp the fact that we] have [the peace of reconciliation to hold and to enjoy] peace with God through our Lord Jesus Christ, the Messiah, the Anointed One.

I CORINTHIANS 14:33 For God is not the author of confusion, but of peace, as in all churches of the saints.

    (TLB) God is not one who likes things to be disorderly and upset. He likes harmony...

    (Authentic) God is a God of order, not of chaos...

    (Basic) For God is not a God whose ways are without order, but a God of peace...

    (20th C. R., Beck, Weym., Jer., Gspd.) God is not a God of disorder but of peace...

    (Phil.) God is not a God of disorder but of harmony...

    (GNB) ...because God does not want us to be in disorder but in harmony and peace...

    (Young) ...for God is not a God of tumult...

    (Wms.) For God is not a God of disorder but of order...

    (Conc.) For God is not for turbulence, but peace...

PHILIPPIANS 4:6 Be careful for nothing; but in everything by prayer and supplication with thanksgiving let your requests be made known unto God.

    (Jordan) ...don't fret over anything...

    (Noli, Cent.) Do not worry about anything...

    (River.) Do not worry...

    (Cony.) Let no care trouble you...

    (GNB) Don't worry about anything...

    (RSV, Gspd.) Have no anxiety about anything...

    (Wuest) Stop worrying about even one thing...

    (Letters) Don't worry about anything but talk to the Father about everything. Tell Him what you need and keep thanking Him.

    (N. Berk., Berk) Entertain no worry, but under all circumstances let your petitions be made known before God...

    (Black.) Do not worry about anything, but in every circumstance...

    (Deaf) Don't worry about anything. But pray and ask God for everything you need...

    (Knox) Nothing must make you anxious; in every need make your requests known to God...

PHILIPPIANS 4:6 (Beck) Don't worry about anything, but in everything go to God...

(TLB) Don't worry about anything; instead, pray about everything...

(AMP) Do not fret or have any anxiety about anything, but in every circumstance and in everything, by prayer and petition (definite requests), with thanksgiving, continue to make your wants known to God.

(Norlie) So do not worry about anything. No matter what the circumstances, pray to God, entreat Him, and give thanks...

(Way) Let no anxieties fret you: nay, in every matter let the things you would ask be made known by means of prayer - by definite requests - linked with thanksgiving, at God's throne.

(NEB) Have no anxiety, but in everything make your requests known to God in prayer and petition with thanksgiving.

(Jer.) There is no need to worry; but if there is anything you need, pray for it, asking God for it with prayer and thanksgiving.

(New Life) Do not worry. Learn to pray about everything. Give thanks to God as you ask Him for what you need.

(K. & L.) Have no anxiety, but in every concern by prayer and supplication with thanksgiving let your petitions be made known in your communing with God.

(Barclay) Don't worry about anything. In every circumstance of life tell God about the things you want to ask Him for in your prayers and your requests to him, and bring him your thanks too.

(NAB) Dismiss all anxiety from your minds. Present your needs to God in every form of prayer and in petitions full of gratitude.

(Basic) Have no cares; but in everything with prayer and praise put your requests before God.

(Weekes) ...let your desires be made known to God.

(Weym.) ...let your requests be unreservedly made known in the presence of God.

See prayer p. 251

PHILIPPIANS 4:7 And the peace of God, which passeth all understanding, shall keep your hearts and minds through Christ Jesus.

(AMP) And God's peace [shall be yours, that tranquil state of a soul assured of its salvation through Christ, and so fearing nothing from God and being content with its earthly lot of whatever sort that is, that peace] which transcends all understanding shall garrison and mount guard over your hearts and minds in Christ Jesus.

(Hudson) And God's peace, which excels [any that] any wit [of man can devise], shall, in Christ Jesus, guard your hearts and your thoughts...

PHILIPPIANS 4:7 (Lovett) God's peace which operates beyond the range of human understanding, will protect your feelings and thought life in Christ.

(Wood) ...peace of God, which surpasses any conception we have...

(Hayman) So shall His peace, which transcends all power to understand it...

(Wms.) Then, through your union with Christ Jesus, the peace of God, that surpasses all human thought, will keep guard over your hearts and thoughts.

(Way) And so the peace that God gives, the peace that transcends all conception, shall be the fortress-warder of your hearts, of all your thoughts, in this your life in Messiah Jesus.

See redemption p. 117; prayer p. 252

II THESSALONIANS 3:16 Now the Lord of peace himself give you peace always by all means. The Lord be with you all.

(Way) And may the Lord Himself, the author of peace, bestow on you peace, always, under all conditions...

(Berk.) May the Lord of peace Himself grant you peace at all times under all circumstances...

(Phil.) ...personally give you his peace at all times and in all ways...

(Wade) ...the Lord Himself, the Source of Peace, give you peace at all times and in all circumstances...

(Mof.) May the Lord of peace himself grant you peace continually, whatever comes.

(Wms.) And may the Lord who gives us peace give you peace in whatever circumstances you may be...

(AMP) ...grant you His peace...at all times and in all ways - under all circumstances and conditions, whatever comes...

(GNB) ...who is our source of peace...

I PETER 5:7 Casting all your care upon him; for he careth for you.

(N. Berk.) Throw all your anxiety upon Him, for His concern is about you.

(Beck) Throw all your worry on Him because He takes care of you.

(Barclay) Bring all your worries to him to carry for you, for he is always concerned about you.

(Jer.) Unload all your worries on to him, since he is looking after you.

(Wand) Hand over all your anxieties to Him, for you are His care.

(AMP) Casting the whole of your care [all your anxieties, all your worries, all your concerns, once and for all] on Him, for He cares for you affectionately and cares about you watchfully.

(Conc.) ...tossing your entire worry on Him...

See prayer p. 262

Notes on Love, Joy, and Peace

IN CHRIST

you are not just a different person, you are a

NEW KIND

of person **IN HIM.** You are a new kind of creature that never existed before.

Mark Hankins
TAKING YOUR PLACE IN CHRIST

JOHN

1:4 361
3:15 361
3:16 361
3:36 361
4:10 362
4:14 362
5:21 363
5:24 363
5:25 364
5:26 364
5:39 364
5:40 364
6:33 365
6:35 365
6:40 365
6:47 365
6:48 365
6:51 366
6:53 366
6:54 366
6:56 366
6:57 367
6:63 367
6:68 367
7:38 367
8:12 368
10:10 368
10:28 369
11:25 369
12:50 369
14:6 369
14:19 370
14:20 370
17:2 370
17:3 370
20:30, 31 370

ACTS

2:28 371
3:15 371
5:20 371
11:18 372
13:46 372
13:48 373
17:25 373

ROMANS

1:17 373
4:17 373
5:10 373
5:11 374
5:17 375
5:18 376
5:21 377
6:4 377
6:8 378
6:11 379
6:23 380
7:9 380
7:10 380
8:2 380
8:6 381
8:10 381
8:11 381
8:13 382

I CORINTHIANS

15:45 382

II CORINTHIANS

2:16 383
3:6 383
4:10 383
4:11 383
4:12 384
5:4 384
13:4 384

GALATIANS

2:19 385
2:20 385
3:21 385
5:25 385
6:8 385

EPHESIANS

2:1 386
2:4, 5 386
4:18 387

PHILIPPIANS

1:21 387
2:16 387

COLOSSIANS

1:18 388
2:13 388

3:4 388

I THESSALONIANS

5:10 389

I TIMOTHY

1:16 389
6:12 389
6:13 389
6:19 390

II TIMOTHY

1:1 390
1:10 391

TITUS

1:2 391
3:7 392

HEBREWS

4:12 392
10:20 393
10:38 393
12:9 393

I PETER

1:3 393
1:23 394
2:24 395
3:7 395
3:18 395
4:6 396

II PETER

1:4 396

I JOHN

1:1 396
1:2 397
3:9 397
3:14 398
3:15 398
4:7 399
4:9 399
5:1 399
5:4 399
5:11, 12 400
5:13 400
5:18 401
5:20 401

REVELATION

1:5 401

REVELATION

1:18 401
2:7 401
3:5 402
7:17 402
13:8 402
17:8 402
20:12 402
20:15 403
21:6 403
21:27 403
22:1 403
22:2 404
22:14 404
22:17 404
22:19 404

JOHN 1:4 In him was life; and the life was the light of men.

    (TLB) Eternal life is in him, and this life gives light to all mankind.

    (GNB) The Word was the source of life, and this life brought light to mankind.

    (Rieu) ...Life was the Light of mankind.

    (Jordan) ...the life was humanity's light.

    (Crickmer) Eternally energizing in This-Being Life was-essentially, and The Life was essentially the light of-human-kind.

JOHN 3:15 That whosoever believeth in him should not perish, but have eternal life.

    (20th C. 1) ...enduring Life.

    (Weym.) ...so must the Son of Man be lifted up, in order that every one who trusts in Him may have the Life of the Ages.

    (Jordan) ...that all who trust him might have spiritual life.

    (Roth.) ...life age-abiding.

    (Wade) ...in order that everyone who believes in Him may in Him have Eternal Life.

    (NEB) ...that everyone who has faith in him may in him possess eternal life.

JOHN 3:16 For God so loved the world, that he gave his only begotten Son, that whosoever believeth in him should not perish, but have everlasting life.

    (Weym.) ...the Life of the Ages.

    (Jordan) ...have spiritual life.

    (Roth.) ...life age-abiding.

JOHN 3:36 He that believeth on the Son hath everlasting life: and he that believeth not the Son shall not see life; but the wrath of God abideth on him.

    (Knox) ...possesses eternal life...

    (Barclay) To believe in the Son is to enjoy the experience of eternal life; to refuse to believe in the Son is to deprive oneself of the experience of life.

    (Crickmer) ...is-now-in-actual possession-of life eternal...

    (Wade) He who believes on the Son has Eternal Life; he who disobeys the Son will have no experience of true Life, but God's wrath remains upon him.

    (Roth.) ...life age-abiding...

    (NIV) Whoever believes in the Son has eternal life, but whoever rejects the Son will not see life, for God's Wrath remains on him.

    (Wms.) Whoever trusts in the Son possesses eternal life, but whoever refuses to trust in the Son will not see life...

    (Jordan) When one lives by the Son, one has spiritual life...

    (Condon) Any man who has faith in the Son already possesses eternal life...

JOHN 3:36 (Conc.) ...he who is stubborn as to the Son shall not be seeing life, but the indignation of God is remaining on him.

    (Weym.) ...the Life of the Ages...

    (20th C. 1) ...enduring Life...

    (Noli) Whoever believes in the Son possesses everlasting life...

JOHN 4:10 Jesus answered and said unto her, If thou knewest the gift of God, and who it is that saith to thee, Give me to drink; thou wouldest have asked of him, and he would have given thee living water.

    (Wuest) ...water which is alive.

    (GNB) ...life-giving water.

JOHN 4:14 But whosoever drinketh of the water that I shall give him shall never thirst; but the water that I shall give him shall be in him a well of water springing up into everlasting life.

    (Noli) The water I will give him will be a fountain of water leaping up to eternal life.

    (Weym.) ...But the water that I shall give him will become a fountain within him of water springing up for the Life of the Ages.

    (20th C.R.) ...the water that I will give him shall become a spring welling up within him-a source of Immortal Life.

    (20th C. 1) ...enduring Life.

    (Basic) ...the water I give him will become in him a fountain of eternal life.

    (Jordan) ...the water I give someone becomes an inner-flowing spring, bubbling over with spiritual life.

    (Beck) ...the water I'll give him will be in him a spring of water bubbling up to everlasting life.

    (Norlie) ...the water that I will give him will become within him a well bubbling up into everlasting life.

    (Wms.) ...the water that I will give him will become a spring of water that keeps on bubbling (Greek – leaping) up within him for eternal life.

    (Gspd.) ...a spring of water within him, bubbling up for eternal life.

    (Cent.) ...a living spring of water within him, welling up into eternal life.

    (TLB) ...a perpetual spring within them, watering them forever with eternal life.

    (Barclay) ...a spring of water inside him, always welling up to give him eternal life.

    (NEB) ...an inner spring always welling up for eternal life.

    (Knox) ...a spring of water within him, that flows continually to bring him everlasting life.

    (Cunn.) ...a spring of water leaping up into eternal life.

    (Roth.) ...life age-abiding.

    (Berk.) ...a well of water within him that bubbles up for eternal life.

JOHN 5:21 ...For as the Father raiseth up the dead, and quickeneth them; even so the Son quickeneth whom he will.

> *(Barclay)* As the Father raises the dead and gives them life, so the Son gives life to those to whom he wishes.
>
> *(Gspd.)* For just as the Father awakens the dead and brings them to life, the Son brings anyone he chooses to life.
>
> *(Wms.)* ...possesses eternal life...
>
> *(Basic)* ...as the Father gives life to the dead, even so the Son gives life to those to whom he is pleased to give it...
>
> *(20th C. R.)* For, just as the Father raises the dead and gives them Life, so also the Son gives Life to whom he pleases.

JOHN 5:24 Verily, verily, I say unto you, He that heareth my word, and believeth on him that sent me, hath everlasting life, and shall not come into condemnation; but is passed from death unto life.

> *(Deaf)* ...He has already left death and has entered into life.
>
> *(Barclay)* I tell you, and it is true, if a man listens to my message and believes in him who sent me, he already has eternal life. He is no longer on the way to judgment; he has already crossed the boundary between death and life.
>
> *(Basic)* ...The man whose ears are open to my word and who has faith in him who sent me, has eternal life.
>
> *(Gspd.)* ...possesses eternal life, and will not come to judgment, but has already passed out of death into life.
>
> *(Jordan)* ...has spiritual life...has transferred from the death region to the life region.
>
> *(20th C. R.)* ...has already passed out of Death into Life.
>
> *(20th C. 1)* ...have enduring Life...have already passed out of Death into Life.
>
> *(Weym.)* ...has the Life of the Ages...but has passed over out of death into Life.
>
> *(Knox)* ...enjoys eternal life...he has passed over already from death to life.
>
> *(Mof.)* ...he has already passed from death across to life.
>
> *(Wade)* ...has Eternal Life...has already passed over from spiritual Death into spiritual Life.
>
> *(NIV)* ...he has crossed from death to life.
>
> *(Young)* ...out of the death to the life.
>
> *(Roth.)* ...life age-abiding...
>
> *(NEB)* ...has hold of eternal life.

See redemption p. 94

JOHN 5:25 Verily, verily, I say unto you, The hour is coming, and now is, when the dead shall hear the voice of the Son of God: and they that hear shall live.

(Jordan) I'm telling you, the time is coming—it's here already—when the lifeless ones will tune in to the voice of God's Son and, having heard him, will come alive.

JOHN 5:26 For as the Father hath life in himself; so hath he given to the Son to have life in himself...

(Barclay) As the Father himself is the source of life, so he has given the Son power to be the source of life.

(Jordan) For as the Father is a life-bearer, so he has made the Son a life-bearer.

(20th C. R.) For, just as the Father has Life within himself, so also he has granted to the Son to have Life within himself.

(20th C. 1) For just as the Father has Life within himself, so he has given his Son Life, that he too may have it within himself.

(Crickmer) For even-as the Father possesses Life eternally energizing-in Himself, just-so did-He get-to-impart also, to-His Son the possession-of Life eternally energizing-in Himself.

(GNB) Just as the Father is himself the source of life, in the same way he has made his Son to be the source of life.

(Wade) For as the Father has Life centered in Himself as its original Source, so He has also enabled the Son to have Life centered in Himself, as its mediate Source.

(Fenton) For as the Father possesses life within Himself, so He has conferred upon the Son the possession of life within Himself.

(Trans.) For as the Father is himself the source of life, so he has granted to the Son also to be the source of life.

(Rieu) For the Father, being as He is the source of Life, has made the Son the source of Life.

(Knox) As the Father has within him the gift of life, so he has granted to the Son that he too should have within him the gift of life.

JOHN 5:39 Search the scriptures; for in them ye think ye have eternal life: and they are they which testify of me.

(Roth.) ...life age-abiding...

(Mof.) You search the scriptures, imagining you possess eternal life in their pages...

(Weym.) ...the Life of the Ages...

JOHN 5:40 And ye will not come to me, that ye might have life.

(Roth.) ...life age-abiding...

(Weym.) ...the Life...

(Wms.) ...but you refuse to come to me to get possession of life.

JOHN 6:33 For the bread of God is he which cometh down from heaven, and giveth life unto the world.

> *(Wade)* For the Bread of God is that which not only descends out of Heaven but also imparts true Life to the world.
>
> *(Berk.)* ...for what comes down from heaven & furnishes life to the world that is the Bread of God.

JOHN 6:35 And Jesus said unto them, I am the bread of life: he that cometh to me shall never hunger; and he that believeth on me shall never thirst.

> *(20th C. R.)* I am the Life-giving Bread...
>
> *(20th C. 1)* I myself am the Life-giving Bread...
>
> *(Wade)* It is I that am the Life-sustaining Bread...
>
> *(Wms.)* ...I am the bread that gives life...
>
> *(Young)* ...I am the bread of the life...

JOHN 6:40 And this is the will of him that sent me, that every one which seeth the Son, and believeth on him, may have everlasting life: and I will raise him up at the last day.

> *(20th C. 1)* ...enduring Life...
>
> *(Knox)* ...all those who believe in the Son when they see him should enjoy eternal life...
>
> *(Weym.)* ...the Life of the Ages...
>
> *(Roth.)* ...life age-abiding...
>
> *(Jordan)* ...have spiritual life...
>
> *(Crickmer)* ...may-be-being-in-actual-possession-of life eternal...

JOHN 6:47 Verily, verily, I say unto you, He that believeth on me hath everlasting life.

> *(20th C. 1)* ...enduring Life.
>
> *(Knox)* ...the man who has faith in me enjoys eternal life...
>
> *(Condon)* Believe me, whoever has faith already has eternal life.
>
> *(Wms.)* ...possesses eternal life.
>
> *(Weym.)* ...the Life of the Ages.
>
> *(Mof., Berk.)* ...the believer has eternal life.
>
> *(Roth.)* ...life age-abiding.
>
> *(NEB)* ...the believer possesses eternal life.
>
> *(Barclay)* I tell you, and it is true, to believe is to have eternal life.
>
> *(Jordan)* ...has spiritual life.
>
> *(Crickmer)* ...is-in-actual present-possession-now already-of life eternal.

JOHN 6:48 I am that bread of life.

> *(20th C.R.)* I am the Life-giving Bread...

JOHN 6:48 (20th C. 1) I myself am the Life-giving Bread.

(Wms.) I am the bread that gives life.

(Young) ...I am the bread of the life.

JOHN 6:51 I am the living bread which came down from heaven: if any man eat of this bread, he shall live for ever: and the bread that I will give is my flesh, which I will give for the life of the world.

(Wade) It is I Who am the Living and Life-imparting Bread that descended out of Heaven...And the Bread which I shall give is my flesh, given to sustain the Life of the world.

(Rieu) ...the Bread which I will give, to bring the world to Life, is my flesh.

JOHN 6:53 Then Jesus said unto them, "Verily, Verily, I say unto you, Except ye eat the flesh of the Son of Man, and drink His blood, ye have no life in you."

(Deaf) ...you don't have real life in you.

(Berk.) ...you have no inner life.

(TLB) ...Unless you eat the flesh of the Messiah and drink his blood, you cannot have eternal life within you.

(Wade) ...you lack within you true Life.

(Fenton) ...you do not possess life in yourselves.

(Mof.) ...you have no life within you.

(Jordan) ...you'll have no inner life.

See redemption p. 95

JOHN 6:54 Whoso eateth my flesh, and drinketh my blood, hath eternal life; and I will raise him up at the last day.

(AMP) ...has (possesses now) eternal life...

(Wms.) ...already possesses eternal life...

(Knox) ...enjoys eternal life.

(Weym.) ...the Life of the Ages...

(Mof., NEB, Barclay) ...possesses eternal life...

(Roth.) ...life age-abiding...

(Jordan) ...had spiritual life...

(20th C. 1) ...enduring Life...

See redemption p. 95

JOHN 6:56 He that eateth my flesh, and drinketh my blood, dwelleth in Me, and I in Him.

(20th C. 1) Those who take my flesh for their food, and drink my blood, are always in union with me, and I with them.

JOHN 6:56 (Wade) He that feeds on my Flesh and drinks my Blood remains in union with me and I in union with him.

> *(Phil.)* The man who eats my body and drinks my blood shares my life and I share his.
>
> *(Wms.)* Whoever continues to eat my flesh and drink my blood continues to live in union with me and I in union with him.
>
> *(Weym.)* ...remains in union with me, and I remain in union with him.
>
> *See redemption p. 96*

JOHN 6:57 As the living Father hath sent me, and I live by the Father: so he that eateth me, even he shall live by me.

> *(Jer.)* As I, who am sent by the living Father, myself draw life from the Father, so whoever eats me will draw life from me.
>
> *(Pl. Eng.)* As the living Father sent me, and I have life because of the Father, so he that eats me shall have life because of me.
>
> *(N. Berk.)* ...the life-giving Father...
>
> *(Basic)* As the living Father has sent me, and I have life because of the Father, even so he who takes me for his food will have life because of me.
>
> *(Weym.)* As the ever-living Father has sent me...

JOHN 6:63 It is the spirit that quickeneth; the flesh profiteth nothing: the words that I speak unto you, they are spirit, and they are life.

> *(Wade)* It is the Spirit that creates true Life; mere flesh is of no avail. The words that I have spoken to you are Spiritual in their meaning, and Life-giving in their effects.
>
> *(Berk.)* The Spirit is the life-giver...

JOHN 6:68 Then Simon Peter answered him, Lord, to whom shall we go? thou hast the words of eternal life.

> *(Weym.)* ...Your teachings tell us of the Life of the Ages.
>
> *(Roth.)* ...life age-abiding.
>
> *(Jordan)* ...the words of spiritual life.
>
> *(Wade)* ...You have at your command words that impart Eternal Life.
>
> *(TLB)* You alone have the words that give eternal life.
>
> *(Noli)* ...You preach eternal life.
>
> *(Gspd.)* ...you have a message of eternal life.

JOHN 7:38 He that believeth on me, as the scripture hath said, out of his belly shall flow rivers of living water.

> *(Norlie)* Out of the heart...

JOHN 7:38 (AMP) ...From his innermost being shall flow [continuously]...

(Jordan) From the heart of the man who lives, my life will flow, as the Bible says, floods of life-giving water.

(Authentic) ...from his interior streams of living water will flow...

(Wade) ...From His breast there will flow streams of Life-imparting water.

(Conc.) ...shall gush rivers of living water.

(Knox) ...Fountains of living water shall flow...

(GNB) ...streams of life-giving water will pour out from his heart.

(Crickmer) ...rivers out-from his inward-parts-shall-be-flowing of-Water,-all-Alive-as it is.

(NEB) 'Streams of living water shall flow out from within him.'

See Holy Spirit p. 179

JOHN 8:12 Then spake Jesus again unto them, saying, I am the light of the world: he that followeth me shall not walk in darkness, but shall have the light of life.

(Syriac) ...he that cometh to me, will not walk in darkness; but will find for himself the light of life.

(Knox) ...he will possess the light which is life.

(Wade) He who follows me will never have to pursue his course in spiritual Darkness, but will have the Light that proceeds from Him Who is the Life.

(Godbey, Young) ...the light of the life.

(Berk.) ...My follower shall not walk around in darkness, but has the Light of life.

(Crickmer) ...he that is following Me, shall be kept from ever transacting daily affairs in the Darkness, but so far from that shall be in possession of The Light of The Life.

JOHN 10:10 The thief cometh not, but for to steal, and to kill, and to destroy: I am come that they might have life, and that they might have it more abundantly.

(Wade) ...I, on the contrary, have come that they may have Life, and have it in fullest measure.

(Roth.) ...I came that life they might have, and above measure might have.

(Weym.) ...I have come that they may have Life, and may have it in abundance.

(Wms.) ...I have come for people to have life and have it till it overflows.

(20th C. 1) ...that they may have Life, and may have it in abundance.

(Barclay) I have come that they may have life and overflowing life.

(Mof.) ...that they may have life and have it to the full.

(Fenton) ...in order that they may enjoy life, and have it in abundance.

(20th C.R.) ...that they may have Life, and may have it in greater fulness.

(Trans.) ...that men may have life, and have it in overflowing measure.

(Syriac) ...that they may have life, and may have that which is excellent.

JOHN 10:10 (Wuest) I alone came in order that they might be possessing life, and that they might be possessing it in superabundance.

> *(Weekes)* ...and may have it more and more.
> *(Beck)* ...I came so that they will have life and have it overflowing in them.
> *(Crickmer)* ...and ever-more-and-more possessing.
> *(Norlie)* The thief comes only to steal and kill and destroy. I come so that they may have life, and have an abundance of it.
> *(Berk.)* The thief's only purpose in coming is to steal, to butcher and to spoil...

JOHN 10:28 And I give unto them eternal life; and they shall never perish, neither shall any man pluck them out of my hand.

> *(Weym.)* ...the Life of the Ages...
> *(Roth.)* ...life age-abiding...

JOHN 11:25 Jesus said unto her, I am the resurrection, and the life: he that believeth in me, though he were dead, yet shall he live...

> *(Wade)* He that believes on me, even if he has died, shall live; and everyone who spiritually lives and believes on me shall never die.
> *(Trans.)* ...He who believes in me will live even if he dies.

JOHN 12:50 And I know that his commandment is life everlasting: whatsoever I speak therefore, even as the Father said unto me, so I speak.

> *(GNB)* ...his command brings eternal life.
> *(Weym.)* ...the Life of the Ages...
> *(Roth.)* ...life age-abiding...
> *(TLB)* And I know his instructions lead to eternal life; so whatever he tells me to say, I say.
> *(Berk.)* ...His bidding means eternal life...

JOHN 14:6 Jesus saith unto him, I am the way, the truth, and the life: no man cometh unto the Father, but by me.

> *(Basic)* ...I am the true and living way: no one comes to the Father but by me.
> *(Message)* ...I am the Road, also the Truth, also the Life. No one gets to the Father apart from me.
> *(Phil.)* "I myself am the road," replied Jesus, "and the truth and the life."
> *(Mof.)* ...I am the real and living way.
> *(NEB)* ...I am the way; I am the truth and I am life.
> *(Dist.)* ...The road to Heaven is Truth—the light that gives life. I am all this for you.

JOHN 14:19 Yet a little while, and the world seeth me no more; but ye see me: because I live, ye shall live also.

> *(Rieu)* ...because I have Life and you too shall have Life.
>
> *(Wade)* ...because I am in possession of Life, you will possess It also.

JOHN 14:20 At that day ye shall know that I am in my Father, and ye in me, and I in you.

> *(AMP)* At that time [when that day comes] you will know [for yourselves] that I am in My Father, and you [are] in Me, and I [am] in you.
>
> *(Basic)* At that time it will be clear to you that I am in my Father, and you are in me, and I in you.
>
> *(Wuest)* In that day you shall know experientially that I am in my Father and you in me and I in you.
>
> *(Wade)* In that day you will come to know that I am united to the Father, and you are united to me, and I am united to you.

JOHN 17:2 As thou hast given him power over all flesh, that he should give eternal life to as many as thou hast given him.

> *(Wade)* ...so He on all whom Thou hast given to Him may bestow Eternal Life.
>
> *(Roth.)* ...life age-abiding.
>
> *(Weym.)* ...Thou hast given Him authority over all mankind, so that on all whom Thou hast given Him He may bestow the Life of the Ages.
>
> *(20th C. 1)* ...enduring Life...

JOHN 17:3 And this is life eternal, that they might know thee the only true God, and Jesus Christ, whom thou hast sent.

> *(Wade)* That Eternal Life consists in this—in their learning to know Thee, the only Real God...
>
> *(TLB)* And this is the way to have eternal life—by knowing you, the only true God, and Jesus Christ, the one you sent to earth!
>
> *(Roth.)* ...age-abiding life...
>
> *(Weym.)* And in this consists the Life of the Ages—in knowing Thee the only true God and Jesus Christ whom Thou hast sent.
>
> *(20th C. 1)* ...enduring Life...
>
> *(Authentic)* Eternal life consists in knowing Thee...

JOHN 20:30, 31 And many other signs truly did Jesus in the presence of his disciples, which are not written in this book: But these are written, that ye might believe that Jesus is the Christ, the Son of God; and that believing ye might have life through his name.

> *(Syriac)* ...and that when ye believe, ye may have life eternal by his name.

JOHN 20:30, 31 (Fenton) ...and believing, that you might become possessed of life by means of His power.

    (NEB) ...that through this faith you may possess life by his name.

    (Godbey) ...through His name.

ACTS 2:28 Thou hast made known to me the ways of life; thou shalt make me full of joy with thy countenance;

    (Wuest) You made known to me the courses of thought, feeling, and action of life [that life, the eternal life given a believer in salvation].

ACTS 3:15 And killed the Prince of life, whom God hath raised from the dead; whereof we are witnesses.

    (Conc.) ...the Inaugurator of Life...

    (Authentic) ...the Fount of Life...

    (Roth.) ...the Princely Leader of Life...

    (Trans.) ...and you killed the one from whom life comes...

    (Norlie) ...the Lord of Life...

    (Beck) ...the Author of life.

    (Mof.) ...the pioneer of Life.

    (Barclay) You killed the man who blazed the way that leads to life...

    (Young) ...the Prince of the Life...

    (Gspd.) ...the very source of life.

    (Cunn.) ...the Captain of life...

    (NIV) ...the author of life...

    (Cent.) The Pioneer of Life...

    (AMP) ...you killed the very Source (the Author) of life. Whom God raised from the dead...

    (Crickmer) ...The Fountain-lord of-The Life...

ACTS 5:20 Go, stand and speak in the temple to the people all the words of this life.

    (New Life) ...Keep on telling the people about this new life.

    (AMP) Go, take your stand in the temple courts and declare to the people the whole doctrine concerning this Life (the eternal life which Christ revealed).

    (NIV) "Go, stand in the temple courts," he said, "and tell the people the full message of this new life."

    (Basic) ...Go, take your place in the Temple and give the people all the teaching about this Life.

    (Gspd., Barclay, Trans., GNB, Berk.) ...tell the people all about this new life.

    (Wms.) ...continue to tell the people the message of this new life.

ACTS 5:20 (20th C.R.) ...tell the people the whole Message of this new life.

(20th C. 1) ...tell the people all you have to say about the new Life.

(Beck) ...keep on telling the people everything about this life.

(Nodie) ...teach the people all about this life.

(Wade) ...tell the People all the facts concerning this—the True—Life.

(NEB) ...tell them about this new life and all it means.

(Jordan) ...explain to the people all the matters concerning this kind of life.

(Crickmer) ...the-whole-of the overflowings of-The Life, This-of God in the New Creation.

ACTS 11:18 When they heard these things, they held their peace, and glorified God, saying, Then hath God also to the Gentiles granted repentance unto life.

(TLB) "God has given to the Gentiles, too, the privilege of turning to him and receiving eternal life!"

(Wade) ...To the Gentiles, also, it seems, God has granted the repentance needful for the attainment of true Life.

(20th C.R.) ...God has granted the repentance which leads to Life!

(Berk.) ...the repentance that leads to life.

(New Life) "Thus God has given life also to the people who are not Jews. They have this new life by being sorry for their sins and turning from them."

(Fenton) ...conversion into life.

(Wuest) ...repentance to the Gentiles resulting in life.

ACTS 13:46 Then Paul and Barnabas waxed bold, and said, It was necessary that the word of God should first have been spoken to you: but seeing ye put it from you, and judge yourselves unworthy of everlasting life, lo, we turn to the Gentiles.

(Basic) ...because you will have nothing to do with it, and have no desire for eternal life, it will now be offered to the Gentiles.

(Syriac) ...To you first, ought the word of God to be spoken; but because ye repel it from you, and decide, against yourselves, that ye are not worthy of life eternal...

(20th C. 1) ...Enduring Life...

(Wade) ...deem yourselves undeserving of the Life that is eternal...

(Roth.) ...the age-abiding life...

(Weym.) ...the Life of the Ages...

(Jordan) ...since you cast it aside and don't consider yourselves candidates for spiritual life, we're going over to the outsiders...

ACTS 13:48 And when the Gentiles heard this, they were glad, and glorified the word of the Lord: and as many as were ordained to eternal life believed.

(Roth.) ...life age-abiding...

(Weym.) ...the Life of the Ages...

ACTS 17:25 Neither is worshipped with men's hands, as though he needed anything, seeing he giveth to all life, and breath, and all things...

(Syriac) Nor is he ministered to by human hands, neither hath he any wants...

(Berk.) ...He, the Giver of life and breath and all things to every one.

ROMANS 1:17 For therein is the righteousness of God revealed from faith to faith: as it is written, The just shall live by faith.

(Black.) For in it is revealed God's kind of righteousness—[the righteousness] which is entirely by faith...

(20th C.R.) ...Through faith the Righteous man shall find Life.

(20th C. 1) ...Those who stand right with God will find Life as the result of faith.

(Barclay) ...It is the man who is right with God through faith who will find life.

ROMANS 4:17 (As it is written, I have made thee a father of many nations,) before him whom he believed, even God, who quickeneth the dead, and calleth those things which be not as though they were:

(Tomanek) ...calling the things not being, as being.

(Berk.) ...and calls into existence what has no being.

(Authentic) ...he relied on God the "Giver of life to the dead," and the Namer of things as existing which as yet are non-existent.

(20th C. 1) ...who gives life to the dead, and speaks of what does not yet exist as if it did...

(Godbey) ...calls things which are not as really existing.

(Mof.) ...a God...who calls into being what does not exist.

See faith p. 157

ROMANS 5:10 For if, when we were enemies, we were reconciled to God by the death of His Son; much more, being reconciled, we shall be saved by His life.

(Johnson) If Christ through his death created a truce between us and God when we were acting like God's enemies, now that we are at peace won't he make us whole through his life?

(Cress.) ...his life will save us.

(Richert) ...by restoring life to His Son, He assures us we are safe and sound...

ROMANS 5:10 (Wood) If His death reconciled us to God while we were still His enemies, much more will His life in us save us now that we are reconciled.

(Barclay) It was the death of his Son which restored us to friendship with God, even when we were hostile to him. And if that is so, now that we are God's friends, how much surer we can be that we will be saved by his continuing life!

(Way) ...for, if, while we were still God's enemies, peace was made between us and Him by means of the death of His Son, much more may we expect, now that this peace has been made, that in the life of His Son we shall find shelter from all future wrath.

(Jordan) For if, while we were rebels, we were won over to God through his Son's death, how much more, having been won over, shall we be saved in his life.

(Knox) ...reconciled to him, we are surer than ever of finding salvation in His Son's life.

(AMP) ...we shall be saved (daily delivered from sin's dominion) through His [resurrection] life.

(20th C.R.) ...shall we be saved by virtue of Christ's life.

(Syriac) ...how much more shall we, in his reconciliation, live (or, be saved) by his life?

(Cony.) ...being already reconciled, shall we be saved by sharing in His life.

(20th C. 1) ...by sharing Christ's Life.

(Gspd.) ...through sharing in his life!

(Wade) ...through sharing His Life!

(Cent.) ...saved in his life.

(Wuest) ...by the life He possesses.

(Norlie) ...by His life in us.

(Young) ...saved in his life.

(Weekes) ...by means of His life.

(Conq.) ...by His being raised from the dead.

See redemption p. 100

ROMANS 5:11 And not only so, but we also joy in God through our Lord Jesus Christ, by whom we have now received the atonement.

(N. Berk.) ...we also exult in God through our Lord Jesus Christ...

(Barclay) And this is not merely a future hope. Here and now, we can take a legitimate and joyful pride in our relationship with God, made possible through the work of our Lord Jesus Christ, for by him we have been made friends with God.

(Way) Nay, we have more than a sense of security: we even exult in a new life in God, which has come through our Lord Jesus the Messiah, from whose hands we have received this our charter of peace.

(Jordan) And on top of all this, we get "status" with God through our Lord Jesus Christ, by whom we have now been won over.

ROMANS 5:11 (Mof.) Not only so, but we triumph in God through our Lord Jesus Christ, by whom we now enjoy our reconciliation.

(Roth.) ...even boasting in God...

(Black.) ...we are jubilant continually...

(Johnson) So we are not only glad about the future, but at this very moment we are happy because God has made us one with himself through Jesus Christ.

(Conq.) ...by His being raised from the dead.

(Hayman) Nay, our state is not one of bare safety, but of positive triumph in God through Jesus Christ.

See redemption p. 101

ROMANS 5:17 For if by one man's offence death reigned by one; much more they which receive abundance of grace and of the gift of righteousness shall reign in life by one, Jesus Christ.

(Weym.) For if, through the transgression of the one individual, Death made use of the one individual to seize the sovereignty, all the more shall those who receive God's overflowing grace and gift of righteousness reign as kings in Life through the one individual, Jesus Christ.

(Way) If, in consequence of that single first transgression, death became king of men's lives, through the one man's demerit, all this will be far more compensated when those who receive the measureless wealth of God's grace and God's gift of righteousness shall be kings in the New Life, through the merit of the One, Jesus the Messiah.

(Beck) If one man by his sin made death a king, we, on whom God has poured His love and His gift of righteousness, are all the more certain the one Jesus Christ makes us live and be kings.

(Wand) If then by one man's transgression all became the subjects of death, much more shall those who receive the bounty of God and the gift of righteousness through the Unique Person Jesus Christ become the lords of life.

(Lau.) That one man, Adam, when he sinned, put all men under the rule of death. But that other Man, Jesus Christ, makes men right with God so that they shall live and rule like kings. This He does for all who accept God's rich forgiving love and His free gift.

(AMP) ...those who receive [God's] overflowing grace (unmerited favor) and the free gift of righteousness [putting them into right standing with Himself] reign as kings in life...

See redemption p. 102; authority of the believer p. 201; righteousness p. 34

ROMANS 5:18 Therefore as by the offence of one judgment came upon all men to condemnation; even so by the righteousness of one the free gift came upon all men unto justification of life.

(*Beck*) Now then, as by one sin all people were condemned, so by one righteous work all people were judged to be righteous and alive.

(*Young*) So, then, as through one offence to all men it is to condemnation, so also through one declaration of "Righteous" it is to all men to justification of life.

(*Gspd.*) So as one offense meant condemnation for all men, just so one righteous act means acquittal and life for all men.

(*Wade*) Therefore, it seems, just as through a single transgression the consequences extended to all men, resulting in a sentence of Doom upon them, so through a single act of righteousness the consequences have extended to all men, resulting in God's setting them right with Himself, and bestowing upon them Life.

(*Jordan*) Well, then, just as the result of one disobedient act was banishment for the whole human race, even so the result of one God-pleasing act was the restoration to life for the whole human race.

(*New Life*) Through Adam's sin, death and hell came to all men. But another Man, Christ, by His right act makes men free and gives them life.

(*GNB*) So then, as the one sin condemned all mankind, in the same way the one righteous act sets all mankind free and gives them life.

(*Trans.*) So then as one man's wrong act brought doom to all men, one man's right act brings all men life and gives them freedom.

(*NIV*) Consequently, just as the result of one trespass was condemnation for all men, so also the result of one act of righteousness was justification that brings life for all men.

(*Noli*) Therefore, as through the sin of one man all men were condemned, so through the righteousness of one man, all men were justified and brought back to life.

(*Lau.*) Well, then! One man's sin led all men to be sentenced to death. The other man's right act sets all men free and gives them life.

(*Pl. Eng.*) ...through one man's righteous acts comes deliverance and life for all.

(*Way*) ...an acquittal that bestows life upon all men now.

(*20th C.R.*) ...a single decree of righteousness resulted for all mankind in that declaration of righteousness which brings Life.

(*20th C. 1*) ...a single decree setting man right with God resulted for all mankind in righteousness and Life.

(*Roth.*) ...So also through one recovery of righteousness the decree of favour is unto all men for a righteous acquittal unto life.

ROMANS 5:21 That as sin hath reigned unto death, even so might grace reign through righteousness unto eternal life by Jesus Christ our Lord.

(*Black.*) ...So that just as sin reigned by death, even so grace might reign by means of righteousness resulting in life eternal through Jesus Christ our Lord.

(*Berk.*) ...so grace might reign through Jesus Christ our Lord with righteousness that issues in eternal life.

(*Way*) The consequence is, that, just as sin once wielded kingly power in inflicting death, so grace shall henceforth wield kingly power in bestowing that righteousness which issues in eternal life for humanity—life attained through Jesus, through the Messiah, through our Lord—ours!

(*Phil.*) ...sin used to be the master of men and in the end handed them over to death; now grace is the ruling factor, with righteousness as its purpose and its end the bringing of men to the eternal Life of God through Jesus Christ our Lord.

(*NIV*) ...so that, just as sin reigned in death, so also grace might reign through righteousness to bring eternal life through Jesus Christ our Lord.

(*Wade*) ...in order that, as Sin exercised dominion, occasioning universal Death, so Divine Favour might exercise dominion through the establishment of a right relation to God, resulting in eternal Life through Jesus Christ our Lord.

(*Weym.*) ...in order that as sin has exercised kingly sway inflicting death, so grace, too, may exercise kingly sway in bestowing a righteousness which results in the Life of the Ages through Jesus Christ our Lord.

(*Wand*) So just when sin and death seemed to be the reigning powers grace took possession of the throne, and that by means of a righteousness that opened the way to eternal life though Jesus Christ our Lord.

(*20th C. 1*) ...so, too, Mercy might reign through righteousness, and result in enduring Life, through Jesus Christ, our Lord.

(*Barclay*) ...which was made possible through the work of Jesus Christ our Lord.

(*Cony.*) ...by the work of Jesus Christ our Lord.

(*Syriac*) ...by means of our Lord Jesus Messiah.

(*Young*) ...the death...

ROMANS 6:4 Therefore we are buried with him by baptism into death: that like as Christ was raised up from the dead by the glory of the Father, even so we also should walk in newness of life.

(*Hudson*) ...so we also might [be raised from a life of sin now dead and buried and] have our being in a new realm of life.

(*Roth.*) In our baptism, we have indeed laid in His grave with Him...regulate our conduct by a new principle of life.

ROMANS 6:4 (Cress.) So we were buried when he was buried because we were baptized into his death.

(Letters) Aren't you hip to the fact that when the Spirit identified us with Jesus the Messiah, He identified us with His death?

(Mof.) Our baptism in his death made us share his burial, so that, as Christ was raised from the dead by the glory of the Father, we too might live and move in the new sphere of Life.

(TLB) Your old sin-loving nature was buried with him by baptism when he died, and when God the Father, with glorious power, brought him back to life again, you were given his wonderful new life to enjoy.

(Wade) Therefore we, sharing His Death through our baptismal immersion, were with Him laid in the grave, in order that, as Christ was raised to Life from among the dead, through His Father's glorious Power, we, too, might pursue our course in the possession of fresh Life.

(Jer.) ...in other words, when we were baptized we went into the tomb with him and joined him in death...

(Lau.) ...just as He was raised from the dead through the Father's glory, we too are to live a new kind of life like His.

(Wuest) ...thus also we by means of a new life imparted may order our behavior.

(20th C.R.) ...so we also may live a new Life.

(Trans.) ...his being raised from the dead by the Father's glorious act means a new way of life for us. (Note: The primary meaning of the word ôdoxaö is brightness, radiance, splendor in a physical sense. Thus "glory" in the New Testament signifies God's active and radiant presence in all His majesty, splendor and sublimity.)

(Carpenter) ...it was a descent with Christ into His grave.

(Hayman) So then, through this reception into His death by baptism, we were with Him buried; in order that, as Christ was through the Majesty Eternal raised from out of the dead, so our course also should lie in newness of life.

See redemption p. 87

ROMANS 6:8 Now if we be dead with Christ, we believe that we shall also live with him.

(Black.) Now in view of the fact that we died with Christ...

(Johnson) ...and since we have died (as it were) with Christ, we believe that we have also come alive through the new principle of life he revealed.

(Way 1) ...put to death along with Messiah...

(Way) Well, if we have died along with Messiah (and have so been accounted righteous), we have a right to believe that we shall also share His new life.

(Weym.) But, seeing that we have died with Christ, we believe that we shall also live with Him.

ROMANS 6:8 (20th C.R.) And our belief is, that, as we have shared Christ's Death, we shall also share His Life.

(Phil.) And if we were dead men with him we can believe that we shall also be men newly alive with him.

(TLB) And since your old sin-loving nature "died" with Christ, we know that you will share his new life.

(Cony.) Now, if we have shared the death of Christ, we believe that we shall also share His life.

(Mof.) We believe that as we have died with Christ...

(AMP) Now if we have died with Christ...

See redemption p. 91

ROMANS 6:11 Likewise reckon ye also yourselves to be dead indeed unto sin, but alive unto God through Jesus Christ our Lord.

(Deaf) 10...he died to defeat the power of sin one time—enough for all time...11In the same way, you should see yourselves dead to the power of sin. And see yourselves as being alive for God through Christ Jesus.

(Richert) Because you are vitally connected to Jesus, God's appointed Minister who now directs our lives in all dimensions.

(Way) 10In respect of His death, He passed by dying, once for all, out of the sphere of sin; but, in respect of His new life, He is in living relation to God. 11In the same manner you also are to account yourselves to be, in relation to sin, dead men; but in relation to God, living men, whose life is absorbed in the life of the Messiah, Jesus.

(Weym.) In the same way you also must regard yourselves as dead in relation to sin, but as alive in relation to God, because you are in Christ Jesus.

(Wade) So you, too, must count yourselves dead men who have finished with Sin, yet fully alive to serve God in union with Christ Jesus.

(N. Berk) Similarly let us consider ourselves as actually dead to sin...

(Authentic) And so you no less can count yourselves dead so far as sin is concerned but alive to God in Christ Jesus.

(New Life) ...Think of yourselves as dead to the power of sin. But now you have new life because of Jesus Christ our Lord...

(Basic) Even so see yourselves as dead to sin...

(Knox) And you, too, must think of yourselves as...

(Wuest) ...be constantly counting upon the fact...

(Norlie) ...you have been restored to life again...

(Gspd.) ...through union with Christ Jesus...

(NASB) ...in Christ Jesus.

See redemption p. 91

ROMANS 6:23 For the wages of sin is death; but the gift of God is eternal life through Jesus Christ our Lord.

(Noli) Death is the penalty of sin. Everlasting life in Jesus Christ our Lord is the free gift of God.

(20th C.R.) ...the gift of God is Immortal Life, through union with Christ Jesus, our Lord.

(20th C. 1) ...the gift God gives is enduring Life through union with Christ Jesus, our Lord.

(Way) ...but the lavish bounty of God is life eternal, involved in your union with the Messiah, with Jesus our Lord—ours!

(Wms.) ...the gracious gift of God is eternal life through union with Christ Jesus our Lord.

(Weym.) ...but God's free gift is the Life of the Ages bestowed upon us in Christ Jesus our Lord.

(NEB) ...but God gives freely, and his gift is eternal life, in union with Christ Jesus our Lord.

(Roth.) ...God's gift of favour is life age-abiding...

(NASB) ...in Christ Jesus our Lord.

(Jordan) ...spiritual life...

(Barclay) ...in union with Christ Jesus our Lord.

ROMANS 7:9 For I was alive without the law once: but when the commandment came, sin revived, and I died.

(Johnson) In a period of innocence I was alive but unaware of the rules. Then I heard the rules which awakened me to the contradiction in my being, and I felt my estrangement.

ROMANS 7:10 And the commandment, which was ordained to life, I found to be unto death.

(Way) Thus I found that that legal ordinance, which was designed to point the way to life, actually thrust me down to death.

(20th C.R. & 1) The very Commandment that should have meant Life I found to result in Death!

ROMANS 8:2 For the law of the Spirit of life in Christ Jesus hath made me free from the law of sin and death.

(Knox) The spiritual principle of life has set me free, in Christ Jesus, from the principle of sin and death.

(Trans.) For the principle of spiritual life in Christ Jesus has liberated me from the principle of sin and death.

(AMP) ...(the law of our new being)...

See redemption p. 93; divine healing p. 284

ROMANS 8:6 For to be carnally minded is death; but to be spiritually minded is life and peace.

(Johnson) To be captive to one's own impulses results in meaninglessness and despair, but to live spontaneously out of the Spirit means real life through the unity of your being.

(Wade) ...For the bent of the mind induced by the fleshly impulses involves Death; but the bent of mind induced by Spiritual influences results in Life and Peace.

(Weym.) Because for the mind to be given up to earthly things means death; but for it to be given up to spiritual things means Life and peace.

ROMANS 8:10 And if Christ be in you, the body is dead because of sin; but the Spirit is life because of righteousness.

(Black.) ...death is inevitable for the body because of sin...

(Hudson) ...[your] spirit...is a living thing because of [being integrated into Christ's] righteousness.

(Johnson) ...your spirit is truly free to direct your life.

(Roth.) ...the spirit is life by reason of righteousness...

(Richert) Your old evil-oriented self is now defunct and the living Spirit within sensitizes you to what is right and good.

(Wms.) But if Christ lives in you, although your bodies must die because of sin, your spirits are now enjoying life because of right standing with God.

(20th C. 1) ...but if Christ is within you, then, though the body is dead as a consequence of sin, the spirit is full of Life as a consequence of righteousness.

(Weym.) ...though your body must die because of sin, yet your spirit has Life because of righteousness.

(Wade) ...though your body is no better than a corpse on account of the infection of Sin, your Spirit is endued with Life because of the power of Righteousness.

(Cony.) ...yet your spirit is life, because of righteousness [which dwells within it]...

(Cent.) ...your spirit is full of life because of righteousness.

(Trans.) ...your spirit is alive because you have been made right with God.

(Pl. Eng.) ...your spirit is a living thing because of righteousness.

(Beck) ...your spirits are alive because you are righteous.

(Way) ...your spirit is instinct with life through the power of righteousness.

See redemption p. 94

ROMANS 8:11 But if the Spirit of Him that raised up Jesus from the dead dwells in you, He that raised up Christ from the dead shall also quicken your mortal bodies by His Spirit that dwelleth in you.

ROMANS 8:11 (Way) If the Spirit of God, of Him who raised Jesus from the dead, has its home in you, then He who raised the Messiah Jesus from the dead will thrill with a new life your very bodies— those mortal bodies of yours-by the agency of His own Spirit, which now has its home in you.

> *(Gspd.)* If the Spirit of him who raised Jesus from the dead has taken possession of you, he who raised Christ Jesus from the dead will also give your mortal bodies life through his Spirit that has taken possession of you.
>
> *(Godbey)* ...will also create life in your mortal bodies...
>
> *See Holy Spirit p. 186; divine healing p. 284*

ROMANS 8:13 For if we live after the flesh, ye shall die: but if ye through the Spirit do mortify the deeds of the body, ye shall live.

> *(Black.)* ...But if by the Spirit you keep putting to death the [improper] deeds of the body, you will continue to live.
>
> *(Wade)* For if you live as the flesh would have you live, you are destined to die. But if by the help of spiritual influences, you deal a death-blow to the activities that originate with the body, you will live.
>
> *(Basic)* ...For if you go in the way of the flesh, death will come on you; but if by the Spirit you put to death the works of the body, you will have life.
>
> *(20th C. l)* ...if, by the power of the Spirit, you put the bad habits of the body to death, you will live.

I CORINTHIANS 15:45 And it is written, the first man Adam was made a living soul; the last Adam was made a quickening spirit.

> *(Berk.)* ...the last Adam became an alive-making Spirit.
>
> *(Way)* The first man, Adam, came into being as a living existence, The last Adam as a lifegiving spirit.
>
> *(Barclay)* ...The first man Adam became a life-having person. The last Adam became a lifegiving spirit.
>
> *(20th C.R.)* The last Adam became a Life-giving spirit.
>
> *(Cent.)* ...The first man, Adam, became a living being, the last Adam, a life-giving Spirit.
>
> *(NIV)* ...The first man Adam became a living being...
>
> *(Wade)* ...the last Adam became a Spirit imparting spiritual Life.
>
> *(Godbey)* ...a life-creating spirit.
>
> *(Wms.)* ...a living creature...a life-giving Spirit.
>
> *(Trans.)* ...The first man, Adam, became a living being, the last Adam has become a lifegiving spirit.

II CORINTHIANS 2:16 To the one we are the savour of death unto death; and to the other the savour of life unto life. And who is sufficient for these things?

(20th C.R.) ...to the former an odour which arises from life and tells of Life.

(Wade) ...the latter finding in the Good News which they reject an Odour emanating from Death and conducing to Death, and the former finding in the same Good News, through acceptance of it, an Odour emanating from Life and conducing to fuller Life.

(TLB) To those who know Christ we are a life-giving perfume.

(Way) ...to the former, the fragrance of life; it ushers them on to life.

II CORINTHIANS 3:6 Who also hath made us able ministers of the new testament; not of the letter, but of the spirit: for the letter killeth, but the spirit giveth life.

(Way) ...The written ordinance denounces a death-penalty; but the Spirit thrills with a new life.

(TLB) He is the one who has helped us tell others about his new agreement to save them. We do not tell them that they must obey every law of God or die; but we tell them there is life for them from the Holy Spirit. The old way, trying to be saved by keeping the Ten Commandments, ends in death; in the new way, the Holy Spirit gives them life.

(Godbey) ...the spirit creates life.

(Black.) ...the Spirit imparts life.

(Trans.) ...who gave us all we need when he made us ministers of a new covenant which is spiritual, not just a written code; for the written code brings death, but the Spirit gives life.

II CORINTHIANS 4:10 Always bearing about in the body the dying of the Lord Jesus, that the life also of Jesus might be made manifest in our body.

(Johnson) These negative experiences remind me that I am daily sharing the death of Christ while the inner resources which these experiences call forth manifest my participation in the resurrection.

(AMP) ...that the (resurrection) life of Jesus...

II CORINTHIANS 4:11 For we which live are always delivered unto death for Jesus' sake, that the life also of Jesus might be made manifest in our mortal flesh.

(Johnson) During our life we constantly experience different kinds of death for Jesus' sake so that new dimensions of the life he revealed may be expressed through us.

(Cony.) ...that in my dying flesh the life whereby Jesus conquered death might show forth its power.

II CORINTHIANS 4:12 So then death worketh in us, but life in you.

> *(TLB)* Because of our preaching we face death, but it has resulted in eternal life for you.
>
> *(Lau.)* Death works in me so that Christ can pour His life into you.
>
> *(Weym.)* Thus we are constantly dying, while you are in full enjoyment of Life.
>
> *(Wade)* ...while Death is active in us, Life is active in you.
>
> *(Way)* So then while death is wearing down my frame, a new life is animating you.

II CORINTHIANS 5:4 For we that are in this tabernacle do groan, being burdened: not for that we would be unclothed, but clothed upon that mortality might be swallowed up of life.

> *(TLB)* We want to slip into our new bodies so that these dying bodies will, as it were, be swallowed up by everlasting life.
>
> *(Syriac)* For while we are here in this house, we groan under its burden; yet we desire, not to throw it off, but to be clothed over it, so that its mortality may be absorbed in life.
>
> *(20th C.R.)* For we who are in this 'tent' sigh under our burden, unwilling to take it off, yet wishing to put our heavenly body over it, so that all that is mortal may be absorbed in Life.
>
> *(Way)* ...that mortality may be drowned in the sea of Life.
>
> *(Barclay)* ...then our mortality will be engulfed in the ocean of life.

II CORINTHIANS 13:4 For though he was crucified through weakness, yet he liveth by the power of God. For we also are weak in him, but we shall live with him by the power of God toward you.

> *(Barclay)* ...the source of our life, as it is with his life, is the power of God.
>
> *(Way)* ...I shall also share in His life, through the manifestation of God's power...
>
> *(Johnson)* It is true that his crucifixion evidences Christ's weakness, but his resurrection evidences the energy of God giving him life. I share his weakness and I also experience the divine energy as I deal with you.
>
> *(Berk.)* For while He was crucified out of weakness, yet He lives through divine power, and we, too, are weak as joined in Him, but we shall live with Him through the power of God that flows into you.
>
> *(Black.)* It is true that he was crucified due to [his assumption of our] weakness, yet he lives by the power of God. So it is with us: We are weak in relation to him, but we shall share in his life, through [the expression of] God's power.
>
> *(Wand)* In His new life He now reveals the power of God. I share His weakness, but I shall also share His life in the power of God towards you.
>
> *(Mof.)* ...you will find I am alive as he is alive by the power of God.

GALATIANS 2:19 For I through the law am dead to the law, that I might live unto God.

> (*Knox*) Through the law my old self has become dead to the law, so that I might live to God.

GALATIANS 2:20 I am crucified with Christ: nevertheless, I live; yet not I, but Christ, liveth in me: and the life which I now live in the flesh I live by the faith of the Son of God, who loved me, and gave himself for me.

> (*Message*) ...The life you see me living is not "mine," but it is lived by faith in the Son of God, who loved me and gave himself for me.
>
> (*Weym.*) ...the life which I now live in the body I live through faith in the Son of God who loved me and gave Himself up to death on my behalf.
>
> (*Lau.*) ...Christ took me to the cross with Him, and I died there with Him.
>
> (*ASV, NASB, RSV, NEB, NIV*) I have been crucified with Christ.
>
> (*Way*) ...it is Messiah whose life is in me...
>
> *See redemption p.75; divine healing p. 285*

GALATIANS 3:21 Is the law then against the promises of God? God forbid: for if there had been a law given which could have given life, verily righteousness should have been by the law.

> (*Way*) ...if there had been given a Law such as could avail to make the dead live, then in very truth would righteousness have had its foundation in that Law.
>
> (*Knox*) ...if a law had been given that was capable of imparting life to us...
>
> (*Wms.*) For if a law had been given that was able to impart life, surely then right standing would have come through law.
>
> (*Cunn.*) ...that could impart life...
>
> (*20th C. 1*) ...capable of bestowing Life...
>
> (*Wade*) ...capable of imparting Spiritual Life...

GALATIANS 5:25 If we live in the Spirit, let us also walk in the Spirit.

> (*Weekes*) Since we are alive by the Spirit, by the Spirit also let us go forward.
>
> (*Trans.*) If the Spirit has given us our new life, let us follow the leading of the Spirit.
>
> (*20th C. 1*) Since our Life is due to the Spirit...

GALATIANS 6:8 For he that soweth to his flesh shall of the flesh reap corruption; but he that soweth to the Spirit shall of the Spirit reap life everlasting.

> (*Johnson*) For example, if you cultivate the nonproductive patterns in your life, you will experience emptiness, meaninglessness, and eventually spiritual decay; but if you continue to live in union with the Spirit, not only will you experience real life here and now, you will have life forever.

GALATIANS 6:8 (Gspd.) The man who sows to gratify his physical cravings will reap destruction from them, and the man who sows to benefit the spirit will reap eternal life from the Spirit.

(Wade) ...he who sows in the field of his fleshly nature will, from his fleshly nature, reap only corruption; whilst he who sows in the field of his spiritual nature will, from his spiritual nature, reap Eternal Life.

(20th C. R) ...he who sows the field of the spirit will from that spirit reap Immortal Life.

(20th C. 1) ...those who sow the field of the spirit will from it reap enduring Life.

(Jer.) ...if he sows in the field of the Spirit he will get from it a harvest of eternal life.

(Knox) ...if his seed-ground is the spirit, it will give him a harvest of eternal life.

(Weym.) ...the Life of the Ages.

EPHESIANS 2:1 And you hath he quickened, who were dead in trespasses and sins...

(Weym.) ...to you God has given Life.

(Wade) ...He has made us spiritually alive together with the Christ. You were spiritually dead through your trespasses and sins...

(Way) Yea, to you also has God given life from the dead—for dead you were, slain by your trespasses and sins.

(Phil., Black.) ...spiritually dead...

EPHESIANS 2:4, 5 But God, who is rich in mercy, for his great love wherewith he loved us, Even when we were dead in sins, hath quickened us together with Christ, (by grace ye are saved.)

(Knox) Our sins had made dead men of us, and he, in giving life to Christ, gave life to us too...

(20th C. R.) Yet God, in his abundant compassion, and because of the great love with which he loved us, even though we were dead because of our offenses, gave Life to us in giving Life to the Christ.

(GNB) But God's mercy is so abundant, and his love for us is so great, that while we were spiritually dead in our disobedience he brought us to life with Christ...

(K. & L.) ...was moved by the intense love with which he loved us,...he made us live with the life of Christ,...

(Jordan) ...God in his overflowing sympathy and great love breathed the same new life into us as into Christ.

(Noli) ...out of his excessive love for us.

(AMP) ...Because of and in order to satisfy the great and wonderful and intense love with which He loved us...[He gave us the very life of Christ Himself, the same new life with which He quickened Him...]

(Way) Even when in trespasses we lay dead, thrilled us with the same new life wherewith He quickened our Messiah.—By free grace alone have ye obtained salvation!

EPHESIANS 2:4, 5 (Cony.) ...called us to share the life of Christ...

(Godbey) ...created life in us in Christ...

(Weekes, Basic, Phil.) ...gave us life together with Christ...

(Wade) ...spiritually dead...spiritually alive...

(Mar., Young) ...(by grace ye are having been saved.)

(Lau., Wand) ...we have been saved.

(Cunn., Weym., NASB, NIV, Conf., Wade, 20th C. R., Godbey, Wms., Norlie, Pl. Eng., N. Berk., Trans., Mof., GNB, Jer., Gspd., RSV) ...you have been saved.

(ASV) ...have ye been saved.

See redemption p. 82; authority of the believer p.210

EPHESIANS 4:18 Having the understanding darkened, being alienated from the life of God through the ignorance that is in them, because of the blindness of their heart:...

(Knox) Their minds are clouded with darkness; the hardness of their hearts breeds in them an ignorance, which estranges them from the divine life.

(Way) ...as the Gentiles live, in the folly of their soul, with their intellect benighted, self-banished from the life God gives.

(Beck) ...Their ignorance and their closed minds have made them strangers to the life God gives.

(GNB) ...They have no part in the life that God gives...

(NEB) ...they are strangers to the life that is in God...

(Basic) ...to whom the life of God is strange...

(Berk.) Their understanding is in the dark. Because of their complete inner ignorance and the obstinacy of their hearts, they have grown estranged from the life divine.

(Black.) ...they are in a state of alienation from the life of God...

(Book) ...rendered aliens from the life that is in God...

(Syriac) ...and are alienated from the life of God, because there is not in them knowledge...

(Weym.) ...having...no share in the Life which God gives.

(20th C.R. & 1) ...cut off from the Life of God.

PHILIPPIANS 1:21 For to me to live is Christ, and to die is gain.

(Syriac) For my life is, the Messiah; and if I die, it is gain to me.

PHILIPPIANS 2:16 Holding forth the word of life; that I may rejoice in the day of Christ, that I have not run in vain, neither laboured in vain.

(Noli) Proclaim the life-giving Gospel.

(Knox) ...upholding the message of life.

(20th C.R. & 1) ...offering to men the Message of Life...

PHILIPPIANS 2:16 (Weym.) ...holding out to them a Message of Life...
(Gspd.) ...offering men the message of life...
(Trans.) ...and, as you offer them the message of life, you will shine among them in the world like stars...
(Book) ...among whom do you shine as light-bearers in the world...
(Wade) ...holding out to it a Message of Life.
(Authentic) ...in which shine out like luminaries in a dark universe, radiating a message of Life.
(Syriac) ...so that ye may be to them in place of life...

COLOSSIANS 1:18 And he is the head of the body, the church: who is the beginning, the firstborn from the dead; that in all things he might have the preeminence.
(Black.) ...He is the Primary Source, the Ideal Representative...
(Knox) He too is that head whose body is the Church; it begins with him, since his was the first birth out of death...
(20th C. 1) Being the first to be born again from the dead, he is the source of its Life...
(Johnson) He is also the Church's head—the whole fellowship of Christpersons in his body. He is the first example of real life through his victory over death, a victory which gives him authority over all creation.

COLOSSIANS 2:13 And you, being dead in your sins and the uncircumcision of your flesh, hath he quickened together with him, having forgiven you all trespasses.
(Berk.) ...you He made to live jointly with Himself...
(Wood) ...God gave you life with Christ.
(Phil.) You, who were spiritually dead because of your sins and your uncircumcision (that is, the fact that you were outside the Law), God has now made to share in the very life of Christ!
(Knox) And in giving life to him, he gave life to you too, when you lay dead in your sins...
(Way) ...you God thrilled with that same new life of Jesus.
(GNB) You were at one time spiritually dead...
(20th C.R.) ...to you, God gave Life in giving Life to Christ!
(Cony.) ...and you also...God raised to share His life.
(Mar.) ...he co-quickened you with him...
(FSB) God has given Life in giving it to Him.
  See redemption p. 80

COLOSSIANS 3:4 When Christ, who is our life, shall appear, then shall ye also appear with him in glory.
(Johnson) ...Christ, the source of our life...

I THESSALONIANS 5:10 Who died for us, that, whether we wake or sleep, we should live together with him.

(Black.) ...who died in our behalf so that whether we live or die we might have life with him.

(Basic) ...Who was put to death for us, so that, awake or sleeping, we may have a part in his life.

(Weym.) ...who died on our behalf, so that whether we are awake or are sleeping we may share His Life.

(Knox) ...that we, waking or sleeping, may find life with him.

(Way) ...who died for us, to this end, that, whether in life we yet keep vigil, or sleep in death, sharing His life we may live.

(Phil.) He died for us, so that whether we are "awake" or "asleep" we share his life.

I TIMOTHY 1:16 Howbeit for this cause I obtained mercy, that in me first Jesus Christ might shew forth all longsuffering, for a pattern to them which should hereafter believe on him to life everlasting.

(Black.) ...for these who would later receive eternal life by believing on him.

(NIV) But for that very reason I was shown mercy so that in me, the worst of sinners, Christ Jesus might display his unlimited patience as an example of those who would believe on him and receive eternal life.

(Jordan) ...spiritual life.

(Weym.) ...the Life of the Ages.

(Trans.) ...He wanted to make me a pattern for those who would come to have the faith in him which leads to eternal life.

(20th C.1) ...enduring Life.

(TLB) ...so that others will realize that they, too, can have everlasting life.

I TIMOTHY 6:12 Fight the good fight of faith, lay hold on eternal life, whereunto thou art also called, and hast professed a good profession before many witnesses.

(Knox) Fight the good fight of faith, lay thy grasp on eternal life, that life thou wert called to, when thou didst assert the great claim before so many witnesses.

(Weym.) ...the Life of the Ages.

See faith p. 162

I TIMOTHY 6:13 I give thee charge in the sight of God, who quickeneth all things, and before Christ Jesus, who before Pontius Pilate witnessed a good confession...

(Godbey) ...who creates life in all things...

(Way) ...God who keeps all things in life...

(Fenton) ...the life-giving God of all...

I TIMOTHY 6:13 (Knox) ...God who gives life to all things...

(*20th C.R. & 1*) ...in the sight of God, the source of all life...

(*Authentic*) ...the Source of all life...

(*Barclay*) ...God, the universal giver of life...

(*Beck*) ...God, from whom comes all life...

(*Wand*) ...God, the author of all life...

(*Weekes*) ...who giveth life to all things...

(*Phil.*) ...God who gives us life...

(*Noli*) ...God, who gives life to all creation...

I TIMOTHY 6:19 Laying up in store for themselves a good foundation against the time to come, that they may lay hold on eternal life.

(*Way*) ...that they may grasp the prize of the life that is life indeed.

(*Trans.*) ...and take hold of that life which is true life.

(*Gspd.*) ...so as to grasp the life that is life indeed.

(*Weym.*) ...that they may lay hold of the Life which is life indeed.

(*Barclay*) ...Thus they will grasp the life which is real life.

II TIMOTHY 1:1 Paul, an apostle of Jesus Christ by the will of God, according to the promise of life which is in Christ Jesus...

(*Berk.*) ...for the announcing of the life that is in fellowship with Christ Jesus.

(*Gspd.*) Paul, by God's will an apostle of Christ Jesus in fulfillment of the promise of that life which is found in union with Christ Jesus...

(*Trans.*) This letter is from Paul, whom God willed to be an apostle of Christ Jesus and to proclaim the life that is promised in union with Christ Jesus, to his dear son Timothy.

(*Wand*) To Timothy from Paul, one of the Apostles of Christ Jesus, commissioned by God to proclaim that new life which He has promised in Christ Jesus.

(*20th C. 1*) ...an Apostle of Christ Jesus to proclaim the Life that is found in union with Christ Jesus.

(*20th C. R*) From Paul who, by the will of God, is an Apostle of Christ Jesus, charged to proclaim the Life that comes from union with Christ Jesus.

(*Cony.*) ...sent forth to proclaim the promise of the life which is in Christ Jesus.

(*GNB*) From Paul, an apostle of Christ Jesus by God's will, sent to proclaim the promised life which we have in union with Christ Jesus.

(*Lau.*) God chose me to tell men about his promise. This promise was that they might have life through Christ Jesus.

(*TLB*) From: Paul, Jesus Christ's missionary, sent out by God to tell men and women everywhere about the eternal life he has promised them through faith in Jesus Christ.

II TIMOTHY 1:10 But is now made manifest by the appearing of our Saviour Jesus Christ, who hath abolished death, and hath brought life and immortality to light through the gospel:...

> *(Black.)* ...who has rendered death ineffective [in all its aspects and consequences]...

> *(Book)* ...who did away with death...

> *(Berk.)* ...who on the one hand rendered death ineffectual and on the other brought life and immortality to light through the Gospel...

> *(Jordan)* It was he who deactivated death and, through the great story, brought to light life and health.

> *(Authentic)* ...now tangibly expressed through the visible appearance of Christ Jesus our Deliverer, who has put Death out of action and brought Life and imperishability into operation...

> *(Wand)* He has annihilated death and poured a flood of new light on life and immortality by means of the Gospel.

> *(Gspd.)* ...He has taken away the power of death and brought life and immortality to light through the good news...

> *(Godbey)* ...the one having indeed destroyed death, and lighted up life and immortality through the gospel.

> *(Knox)* ...he has annulled death, now he has shed abroad the rays of life and immortality...

> *(20th C. R.)* ...who has made an end of Death, and has brought Life and Immortality to light by that Good News...

> *(Weekes)* ...who both made death of no account, and brought to light life and incorruptibility through the Good-tidings.

> *(Wms.)* ...our Savior Christ Jesus, who through the good news has put a stop to the power of death...

> *(Cent.)* ...our Savior Christ Jesus, who has put an end to death...

> *(AMP)* ...Who annulled death and made it of no effect...

> *(Basic)* ...who put an end to death...

> *(Noli)* ...He annihilated death...

> *(Trans.)* ...He has put an end to death...

> *(N. Berk.)* ...rendered death ineffectual...

> *(River.)* ...who has defeated death...

> *(Syriac)* ...our Vivifier (or, Saviour)...

TITUS 1:2 In hope of eternal life, which God, that cannot lie, promised before the world began...

> *(TLB)* I have been sent to bring faith to those God has chosen and to teach them to know God's truth—the kind of truth that changes lives—so that they can have eternal life, which God promised them before the world began—and he cannot lie.

TITUS 1:2 (Jordan) My business is the faith of God's special people and their understanding of the truth, so that they may have a genuine devotion based on confidence in spiritual life. Before the age of time, the ever truthful God was pregnant with this life. And in his own good time, he brought it forth in the great story which, by orders of our Savior-God, was entrusted to me.

> *(Roth.)* ...life age-abiding...
>
> *(Weym.)* ...the Life of the Ages...

TITUS 3:7 That being justified by his grace, we should be made heirs according to the hope of eternal life.

> *(Jordan)* This means that we have been set right by his undeserved favor and have become participants in a spiritual life that has purpose.
>
> *(Gspd.)* ...so that we might be made upright in his mercy and become possessors of eternal life in fulfilment of our hope.
>
> *(20th C. R.)* That, having been pronounced righteous through his loving-kindness, we might enter on our inheritance with the hope of Immortal Life.
>
> *(Wms.)* ...so that we might come into right standing with God through His unmerited favor and become heirs of eternal life in accordance with our hope.
>
> *(Roth.)* ...life age-abiding...
>
> *(Weym.)* ...in order that having been declared righteous through His grace we might become heirs to the Life of the Ages in fulfillment of our hopes.
>
> *(20th C. 1)* For his intention was that, when by his gracious help we should stand right with him, we should, in the fulfillment of our hopes, become possessors of enduring Life.

HEBREWS 4:12 For the word of God is quick, and powerful, and sharper than any two edged sword, piercing even to the dividing asunder of soul and spirit, and of the joints and marrow, and is a discerner of the thoughts and intents of the heart.

> *(Jordan)* For God's Word is alive with energy, and sharper than any double-edged sword you ever saw; so sharp, in fact, that it can draw a line between the mental and the spiritual, like separating bones from marrow, and discern all our inner emotions and drives.
>
> *(Knox)* God's word to us is something alive, full of energy; it can penetrate deeper than any two-edged sword...
>
> *(Mof.)* For the Logos of God is a living thing, active and more cutting than any sword with double edge...
>
> *(20th C. 1)* God's Message is a living and active power...piercing its way till it penetrates soul and spirit—not the joints only but the very marrow...

HEBREWS 4:12 (Weym.) For God's Message is full of life and power...

    (Syriac) For the word of God is living, and all-efficient...

    (Wms.) For God's message is alive and full of power in action...

    (20th C. R.) God's Message is a living and active power...

    (Noli) For the message of God is a living and active force...

    (Fenton, Weekes) For the word of God is living, and energetic...

HEBREWS 10:20 By a new and living way, which he hath consecrated for us, through the veil, that is to say, his flesh...

    (Syriac) ...by the blood Jesus, and by a way of life.

    (TLB) This is the fresh, new, life-giving way which Christ has opened up for us by tearing the curtain—His human body—to let us into the holy presence of God.

    (Wade) ...an entry which He has opened up for us, by a Way newly made and conducting to Life...

HEBREWS 10:38 Now the just shall live by faith: but if any man draw back, my soul shall have no pleasure in him.

    (Knox) It is faith that brings life to the man whom I accept as justified...

    (20th C.R.) ...through faith the righteous man shall find his Life.

    (Gspd.) And he whom I accept as righteous will find life through his faith...

HEBREWS 12:9 Furthermore we have had fathers of our flesh which corrected us, and we gave them reverence: shall we not much rather be in subjection unto the Father of spirits, and live?

    (Berk.) ...shall we not far rather submit to our spiritual Father and enjoy life?

    (Way) ...shall we not all the more cheerfully submit our wills to the Father of Spirits, and gain life through union with Him?

    (Lau.) ...Shall we not be much more willing to submit to the discipline of the Father of our spirits, and so have life?

    (Wade) Moreover, in our earthly fathers we have had disciplinarians, and we paid them respect; and shall we not far more cheerfully show subordination to the Father of Spirits, and so live the true Life?

    (Mof., Authentic, Cony., Roth.) ...the Father of our spirits...

    (Pl. Eng.) ...and have life?

    (Knox) ...and draw life from him?

I PETER 1:3 Blessed be the God and Father of our Lord Jesus Christ, which according to his abundant mercy hath begotten us again unto a lively hope by the resurrection of Jesus Christ from the dead...

I PETER 1:3 (Jordan) Three cheers for the Father-God of our Lord Jesus Christ! By his overflowing mercy he has refathered us into a life of hope, based on the raising of Jesus Christ from the dead.

> *(Beck)* Let us praise the God and Father of our Lord Jesus Christ, who by raising Jesus Christ from the dead has in His great mercy given us a new birth so that we live and hope 4 for an inheritance that isn't destroyed or defiled and never fades away, as it is kept for you in heaven.

> *(GNB)* ...Because of his great mercy he gave us new life by raising Jesus Christ from death. This fills us with a living hope.

> *(Trans.)* May the God and Father of our Lord Jesus Christ be praised! By raising Jesus Christ from death, in his great mercy he gave us new life and set before us a living hope.

> *(Wade)* ...regenerated us through the Resurrection of Jesus Christ from among the dead...

I PETER 1:23 Being born again, not of corruptible seed, but of incorruptible, by the word of God, which liveth and abideth for ever.

> *(Wade)* ...for you have been regenerated not from a corruptible, but from an incorruptible, germ of Life, through God's Living and Lasting Message.

> *(Authentic)* ...born anew not from perishable life-germ but an imperishable, through the Message of the Living and Everlasting God.

> *(20th C. R.)* Since your new Life has come, not from perishable, but imperishable seed, through the Message of the Ever-living God.

> *(20th C. 1)* Your new Life came from an imperishable, not a perishable, source, at the word of the Ever-living God.

> *(Weym.)* For you have been begotten again by God's ever-living and enduring word from a germ not of perishable, but of imperishable life.

> *(Basic)* Because you have had a new birth, not from the seed of man, but from eternal seed, through the word of a living and unchanging God.

> *(Phil.)* For you are sons of God now; the live, permanent Word of the living God has given you his own indestructible heredity.

> *(Beck)* You were born again, not by a seed that perishes but one that cannot perish, God's ever-living Word.

> *(New Life)* You have been given a new birth. It was from a seed that cannot die. This new life is from the Word of God which lives forever.

> *(Jordan)* For you all have been refathered, not by a mortal man, but by the immortal word of a living and abiding God.

I PETER 2:24 Who his own self bare our sins in his own body on the tree, that we, being dead to sins, should live unto righteousness: by whose stripes ye were healed.

(AMP) He personally bore our sins in His [own] body on the tree [as on an altar and offered Himself on it], that we might die (cease to exist) to sin and live to righteousness. By His wounds you have been healed.

(Message) He used his servant body to carry our sins to the Cross so we could be rid of sin, free to live the right way.

(Phil.) It was the suffering that he bore which has healed you.

(Adams) ...so that by dying to sins we might live to righteousness.

(Mof.) ...that we might break with sin and live the good life...

(Basic) ...might have a new life in righteousness, and by his wounds we have been made well.

See redemption p. 59; divine healing p. 287

I PETER 3:7 Likewise, ye husbands, dwell with them according to knowledge, giving honour unto the wife, as unto the weaker vessel, and as being heirs together of the grace of life; that your prayers be not hindered.

(20th C. R.) ...they share with you in the gift of Life.

(Weym.) ...you are heirs with them of God's free gift of Life...

(Trans.) ...they share with you God's free gift of life...

(NEB) ...you share together in the grace of God which gives you life.

I PETER 3:18 For Christ also hath once suffered for sins, the just for the unjust, that he might bring us to God, being put to death in the flesh, but quickened by the Spirit.

(Barclay) ...he died to open the way to God for you. He underwent physical death, but in his spirit, he was brought to life.

(Wuest) ...that He might provide you with an entree into the presence of God, having in fact, been put to death with respect to the flesh [His human body], but made alive with respect to the spirit [His human spirit]...

(Mar.) ...being put to death on the one hand in the flesh, quickened on the other in the spirit.

(20th C.R.) ...his body being put to death, but his spirit entering upon new Life.

(Norlie) ...put to death in His body, but He was made alive again in His Spirit.

(Godbey) ...quickened in spirit (His own human spirit).

(Beck) ...made alive in His spirit.

(Jer.) ...In the body he was put to death, in the spirit he was raised to life.

(RSV, ASV, NASB, Alf., Young, Weym., AMP) ...made alive in the spirit.

(Knox) 18...but endowed with fresh life in his spirit, 19and it was in his spirit that he went and preached to the spirits who lay in prison.

(Cress.) ...spirit had new life.

I PETER 3:18 (Hayman) ...but again brought to life in the spirit.
(HT Ander, Bart. & Pet.) ...endued with life in the spirit.
See redemption p. 67

I PETER 4:6 For this cause was the gospel preached also to them that are dead, that they might be judged according to men in the flesh, but live according to God in the spirit.
(NEB) ...although in the body they received the sentence common to men, they might in the spirit be alive with the life of God.
(Phil.) (For that is why the dead also had the gospel preached to them—that it might judge the lives they lived as men and give them also the opportunity to share the eternal life of God in the spirit.)
(Fenton) ...but might live spiritually with God.
(20th C. R.) ...that...they might live in the spirit, as God lives.
(Mof.) ...they may live as God lives in the spirit.

II PETER 1:4 Whereby are given unto us exceeding great and precious promises: that by these ye might be partakers of the divine nature, having escaped the corruption that is in the world through lust.
(New Life) Through His shining greatness and perfect life, He has given us promises. These promises are of great worth and no amount of money can buy them. Through these promises you can have God's own life in you now that you have gotten away from the sinful things of the world which came from wrong desires of the flesh.
(Lau.) ...Through these promises we can escape from the death which follows evil passions. God also gave us His divine nature.
(20th C. R.) ...that through them you might participate in the divine nature...
(NEB) ...come to share in the very being of God.
(Basic) ...by them we might have our part in God's being...
(Syriac) ...the nature of God...

I JOHN 1:1 That which was from the beginning, which we have heard, which we have seen with our eyes, which we have looked upon, and our hands have handled, of the Word of life...
(20th C. R.) ...it is about the Word who is the Life that we are now writing.
(Knox) Our message concerns that Word, who is life;...
(Noli) ...Jesus Christ, the life-giving Word of God who has existed from the beginning...
(Barclay) Our theme is the Word which is life...
(Fenton) ...the Living Word.

I JOHN 1:2 (For the life was manifested, and we have seen it, and bear witness, and shew unto you that eternal life, which was with the Father, and was manifested unto us.)

(Wand) What that Word revealed to us was Life.

(Knox) Yes, life dawned; and it is as eye-witnesses that we give you news of that life, that eternal life, which ever abode with the Father and has dawned, now, on us.

(Noli) Yes, the Life-giver was manifested to us. I testify to him, and proclaim the everlasting Life-giver...

(Wms.) ...that life has been unveiled to us...

(Barclay) ...It is news of this eternal life, which was with the Father, and which was full displayed to us, that we are now bringing to you.

(Fenton) ...for the Life was manifested; and we have been with Him and have given evidence, and proclaim to you the Life Who was eternal, Who existed with the Father, and was manifested to us.

(Weym.) ...we declare unto you the Life of the ages...

(Norlie) He was made to appear before us as Life. We saw it and we bear witness to it as a fact. We preach that the Eternal Life who was with the Father has come down to us.

I JOHN 3:9 Whosoever is born of God doth not commit sin; for his seed remaineth in him: and he cannot sin, because he is born of God.

(TLB) The person who has been born into God's family doesn't make a practice of sinning, because now God's life is in him; so he can't keep on sinning, for this new life has been born into him and controls him—he has been born again.

(Wade) No one who has been Begotten from God habitually sins, because in him there remains a germ of Divine Life; and he cannot sin habitually, because he has been Begotten from God.

(Jordan) Anyone who has been fathered by God doesn't make wrong a habit, because he carries in him his Father's genes. Since God has fathered him he just can't wallow in sin.

(Phil.) The man who is really God's son does not practice sin, for God's nature is in him, for good, and such a heredity is incapable of sin.

(20th C. R.) No one who has received the new Life from God lives sinfully, because the very nature of God dwells within him; and he cannot live in sin, because he has received the new Life from God.

(Trans.) No child of God practices sin, because he has God's nature in him...

(Beck) Everyone who is God's child refuses to sin because God's new life is in him...

(Gspd.) ...God's nature remains in his heart...

(AMP) ...God's nature abides in him, [His principle of life, the divine sperm, remains permanently within him]...

I JOHN 3:9 (GNB) ...God's very nature is in him...

(*Weym.*) ...A God-given germ of life remains in him, and he cannot habitually sin...

(*Fenton*) ...His principle of life continues in him...

(*Wms.*) ...the God-given life-principle continues to live in him...

(*Lau.*) ...God's nature is in Him...

I JOHN 3:14 We know that we have passed from death unto life, because we love the brethren. He that loveth not his brother abideth in death.

(*Berk.*) We know that we have made the transfer out of death into life, because we love the brothers. One who is not loving remains in death.

(*Fenton*) We know that we are transplanted out of death into life, when we love the brotherhood. Whoever does not love remains in death.

(*Weym.*) As for us, we know that we have already passed out of death into Life—because we love our fellow men.

(*GNB*) We know that we have left death and come over into life; we know it because we love our brothers.

(*20th C.R.*) We know that we have passed out of Death into Life, because we love our Brothers. The man who does not love remains in a state of Death.

(*Jordan*) We ourselves are convinced that we have switched from death to life because we love the brothers. The man with no love still lives in death country.

(*Wade*) ...we know we have passed out of a state of spiritual Death into a state of spiritual Life, because we love our Brothers: he who does not love his Brothers remains in a state of spiritual Death.

(*Trans.*) We know that we have passed over from death into life...

(*Young*) ...out of the death to the life...

(*Godbey*) ...out of the death into the life...

(*Barclay*) ...Not to love is to remain in the realm of death.

(*Gspd.*) ...Anyone who does not love is still in death.

I JOHN 3:15 Whosoever hateth his brother is a murderer: and ye know that no murderer hath eternal life abiding in him.

(*Jordan*) The brother-hater is a man-killer, and you know that no man-killer has spiritual life residing in him.

(*Barclay*) To hate one's fellowman is to be a murderer, and you know well that no murderer possesses eternal life as a permanent part of his being.

(*Gspd.*) ...no murderer can have eternal life remain in his heart.

(*Phil.*) ...you will readily see that the eternal life of God cannot live in the heart of a murderer.

(*Fenton*) ...has eternal life existing in him.

I JOHN 3:15 (Weym.) ...no murderer has the Life of the ages continuing in him.
(20th C. R.) ...you know that no murderer has Immortal Life within him.
(Wade) ...no homicide has Eternal Life remaining within him.
(20th C. 1) ...enduring Life within him.
(NEB) ...no murderer, as you know, has eternal life dwelling within him.

I JOHN 4:7 Beloved, let us love one another: for love is of God; and everyone that loveth is born of God, and knoweth God.
(20th C.R.) ...every one who loves has received the new Life from God and knows God.
(Jordan) Loved ones, let's love each other, because love springs from God, and every lover has been fathered by God and is sensitive to God.
See love p. 332

I JOHN 4:9 In this was manifested the love of God toward us, because that God sent his only begotten Son into the world, that we might live through Him.
(Phil.) To us, the greatest demonstration of God's love for us has been his sending his only Son into the world to give us life through him.
(Wade) God's Love manifested itself among us in this way—in His sending His Only Son on a mission into the world, that we might have Life through Him.
(Wms.) ...that we through Him might have life.
(Weekes) ...that we might have life through him.
(Pl. Eng.) ...that we should have life through Christ.
(Jordan) ...so we might start living.
(Gspd.) ...to let us have life through him.
(Weym.) ...so that we may have Life through Him
(20th C. R.) ...that we might find life through him.
(NEB) ...he sent his only Son into the world to bring us life.

I JOHN 5:1 Whosoever believeth that Jesus is the Christ is born of God: and every one that loveth him that begat loveth him also that is begotten of him.
(20th C. R.) Everyone who believes that Jesus is the Christ has received the new Life from God; and every one who loves him who gave that Life loves him who has received it.

I JOHN 5:4 For whatsoever is born of God overcometh the world: and this is the victory that overcometh the world, even our faith.
(AMP) For whatever is born of God is victorious over the world; and this is the victory that conquers the world, even our faith.
(TLB) ...for every child of God can obey him, defeating sin and evil pleasure by trusting Christ to help him.

I JOHN 5:4 (Message) Every God-begotten person conquers the world's ways. The conquering power that brings the world to its knees is our faith. The person who wins out over the world's ways is simply the one who believes Jesus is the Son of God.

I JOHN 5:11, 12 And this is the record, that God hath given to us eternal life, and this life is in his Son. He that hath the Son hath life; and he that hath not the Son of God hath not life.

(Conq.) ...hath this life...

(Fenton) And this is the evidence—that God has granted to us eternal life; and the same life that exists in His Son. The possessor of the Son possesses that life; whoever does not possess the Son of God does not possess that life.

(Wade) ...God has given us Eternal Life, and it is in His Son that this Life is to be found. He who possesses the Son possesses this Life. He who does not possess the Son of God does not possess this Life.

(NEB) ...God has given us eternal life, and that this life is found in his Son. He who possesses the Son has life indeed; he who does not possess the Son of God has not that life.

(Barclay) ...God gave us eternal life, and that his Son is the source of this life.

(Jordan) ...God gave us spiritual life...

(Syriac) Every one that taketh hold of the Son, taketh hold of life...

(Authentic) He who possesses the Son possesses Life. He who does not possess the Son of God does not possess Life.

(Young) ..this—the life—is in His Son...

(Lau.) ...this eternal life...this eternal life.

(Knox) ...he is lifeless, who has no hold of the Son of God.

(AMP, Trans., N. Berk.) ...that life...that life.

See redemption p. 96

I JOHN 5:13 These things have I written unto you that believe on the name of the Son of God; that ye may know that ye have eternal life, and that ye may believe on the name of the Son of God.

(Barclay) My purpose in writing this letter to you is to give you the assurance that you do possess eternal life.

(Fenton) ...that you may recognise that you are the possessors of everlasting life...

(Noli) ...to assure you that you already possess everlasting life...

(Phil.) ...that you may be quite sure that, here and now, you possess eternal life.

(Wade) ...that you may be sure that you possess Eternal Life.

(Authentic) ...that you may be aware that you do possess Eternal Life.

(20th C. 1) ...enduring Life.

I JOHN 5:18 We know that whosoever is born of God sinneth not; but he that is begotten of God keepeth himself, and that wicked one toucheth him not.

> *(Wand)* ...the Son of God preserves him and the Evil One cannot get hold of him.
>
> *(Roth.)* ...the evil one fastens not on him.
>
> *(20th C. R.)* We know that no one who has received the new Life from God lives in sin. No, he who has received the new Life from God keeps the thought of God in his heart, and then the Evil One does not touch him.
>
> *(Jordan)* We are aware that anyone who has been fathered by God does not wallow in sin...
>
> *(Knox)* ...that divine origin protects him, and the evil one cannot touch him.

I JOHN 5:20 And we know that the Son of God is come, and hath given us an understanding, that we may know him that is true, and we are in him that is true, even in his Son Jesus Christ. This is the true God, and eternal life.

> *(Roth.)* We know moreover that the Son of God hath come, And hath given us insight so that we are getting to understand him that is Real, and we are in him that is Real, in his Son Jesus Christ. This is the Real God, and life age-abiding.
>
> *(20th C. 1)* ...enduring Life.
>
> *(Gspd.)* ...we are in union with him who is true...
>
> *(Weym.)* ...He is the true God and the Life of the ages.

REVELATION 1:5 And from Jesus Christ, who is the faithful witness, and the first begotten of the dead, and the prince of the kings of the earth. Unto Him that loved us, and washed us from our sins in His own blood.

> *(Godbey)* ...To the one loving us with divine love.
>
> *(Weym.)* ...the first of the dead to be born to Life...
>
> *(Wade)* ...the First of the dead to be born into renewed Life...
>
> *(Noli)* ...the pioneer of the resurrection...
>
> *(20th C. 1)* ...the First of the Dead to be born again...
>
> *See redemption p. 68*

REVELATION 1:18 I am he that liveth, and was dead; and, behold, I am alive for evermore, Amen; and have the keys of hell and of death.

> *(Barclay)* I am the living one...
>
> *(Weym.)* ...I am...the ever-living One...

REVELATION 2:7 He that hath an ear, let him hear what the Spirit saith unto the churches; To him that overcometh will I give to eat of the tree of life, which is in the midst of the paradise of God.

> *(Mof.)* ...The conqueror I will allow to eat from the tree of Life...

REVELATION 2:7 (Godbey) ...to him who conquers...
(Noli) ...I will reward the victory with the fruit of the tree of life which is in the Paradise of God.

REVELATION 3:5 He that overcometh, the same shall be clothed in white raiment; and I will not blot out his name out of the book of life, but I will confess his name before my Father, and before His angels.
(Young) ...the scroll of the life...
(NEB) ...the roll of the living...
(Godbey) The one conquering...

REVELATION 7:17 For the Lamb which is in the midst of the throne shall feed them, and shall lead them unto living fountains of water: and God shall wipe away all tears from their eyes.
(Godbey) ...the Lamb in the midst of the throne will shepherdize them...
(Wade) ...the Life-Imparting water springs...
(20th C. R.) ...for the Lamb that stands in the space before the throne will be their shepherd, and will lead them to life-giving springs of water...
(Weym.) ...the Lamb...will guide them to water-springs of Life...

REVELATION 13:8 And all that dwell upon the earth shall worship him, whose names are not written in the book of life of the Lamb slain from the foundation of the world.
(Barclay) ...the roll of the living...
(NEB, Young) ...the scroll of the life of the Lamb...
(New Life) ...the book of the life of the Lamb...
(Syriac) ...the book of the life of the Lamb...
(Basic) ...the book of life of the Lamb...

REVELATION 17:8 The beast that thou sawest was, and is not; and shall ascend out of the bottomless pit, and go into perdition: and they that dwell on the earth shall wonder, whose names were not written in the book of life from the foundation of the world, when they behold the beast that was, and is not, and yet is.
(NEB, Barclay) ...the roll of the living...
(Young) ...the scroll of the life...

REVELATION 20:12 And I saw the dead, small and great, stand before God; and the books were opened: and another book was opened, which is the book of life: and the dead were judged out of those things which were written in the books, according to their works.
(Barclay) ...the register of the living.
(NEB) ...the roll of the living...

REVELATION 20:15 And whosoever was not found written in the book of life was cast into the lake of fire.

> *(Young)* ...the scroll of the life...
> *(Barclay)* ...the book of the living...
> *(NEB)* ...the roll of the living.

REVELATION 21:6 And he said unto me, It is done. I am Alpha and Omega, the beginning and the end. I will give unto him that is athirst of the fountain of the water of life freely.

> *(Weekes)* I will give to him that thirsteth, of the fountain of the water of Life, as a free gift.
> *(Wms.)* I myself, without cost, will give to anyone who is thirsty water from the springs of living water.
> *(Wade)* It is I, Who to the thirsty will give a draught from the fountain of Life-imparting water without payment.
> *(Noli)* 6...I will give priceless water to the thirsty from the fountain of life. 7The victors will inherit all these blessings...
> *(Young)* ...the water of the life...

REVELATION 21:27 And there shall in no wise enter into it any thing that defileth, neither whatsoever worketh abomination, or maketh a lie: but they which are written in the Lamb's book of life.

> *(Barclay, NEB)* ...the Lamb's roll of the living...
> *(Wuest)* ...those written in the scroll of the life of the Lamb.

REVELATION 22:1 And he showed me a pure river of water of life, clear as crystal, proceeding out of the throne of God and of the Lamb.

> *(Wuest)* ...a river of water of life, sparkling like crystal...
> *(Roth.)* ...bright as crystal...
> *(Weekes)* And he pointed out to me a river of water of life, brilliant like crystal, coming forth out of the throne of God and of the Lamb, in the midst of the broad street of the city.
> *(Norlie)* Then he showed me the pure river of living water. It was bright as crystal and flowed from the throne of God and of the Lamb...
> *(Trans.)* Then the angel showed me the river of the water of life, shining like crystal, flowing from the throne of God and of the Lamb.
> *(Wms.)* Then he showed me a river of living water, clear as crystal, which continued to flow from the throne of God and of the Lamb.
> *(Noli)* ...the river of living water, transparent as crystal which flowed from the throne of God and of the Lamb...

REVELATION 22:1 (Wade) And he showed me a river of Life-giving Water, bright as crystal, issuing from the Throne of God and of the Little Lamb...

REVELATION 22:2 In the midst of the street of it, and on either side of the river, was there the tree of life, which bare twelve manner of fruits, and yielded her fruit every month: and the leaves of the tree were for the healing of the nations.

    (Basic) ...the leaves of the tree give life to the nations.

    (Wade) ...in the centre of the Square within the city; and on either side of the river is a grove of Life-sustaining Trees...

REVELATION 22:14 Blessed are they that do his commandments, that they may have right to the tree of life, and may enter in through the gates into the city.

    (Wade) ...the grove of Life-sustaining Trees...

    (Young) ...the tree of the life...

REVELATION 22:17 And the Spirit and the bride say, Come. And let him that heareth say, Come. And let him that is athirst come. And whosoever will, let him take the water of life freely.

    (AMP) The [Holy] Spirit and the bride (the church, the true Christians) say, Come! And let him who is listening say, Come! And let everyone come who is thirsty... and whoever [earnestly] desires to do it, let him come, take, appropriate, and drink the water of life without cost.

    (Wms.) Let everyone who wishes come and take the living water without any cost.

    (Trans.) ...Let anyone who wants the water of life take it freely.

    (Wade) ...and he that is athirst should come; and he that wishes to drink of the Life-giving Water can do so without cost.

REVELATION 22:19 And if any man should take away from the words of the book of this prophecy, God shall take away his part out of the book of life, and out of the holy city, and from the things which are written in this book.

    (Wade) ...the Life-sustaining Trees...

    (Young) ...the scroll of the life...

Notes on Eternal Life

Just because you know **HOW FAITH WORKS** doesn't mean you know how God is going to do **YOUR MIRACLE.**

Mark Hankins
11:23: THE LANGUAGE OF FAITH

PSALM

71:7 409

ISAIAH

8:18 409

DANIEL

4:2, 3 409

MARK

16:17, 18 409

JOHN

14:12 409
20:30 410
21:25 410

ACTS

2:22 410
2:43 410
4:29, 30 410
5:12 410
8:5-8. 410
8:13 411
19:11, 12 411

ROMANS

15:19 411

I CORINTHIANS

2:4, 5 411

II CORINTHIANS

12:12 412

GALATIANS

3:5 412

I THESSALONIANS

1:5 412

HEBREWS

2:4 412

The door to the
supernatural has
ONE KNOB,
and it is on **YOUR SIDE**
of the door.

Mark Hankins
11:23: THE LANGUAGE OF FAITH

PSALM 71:7 I am as a wonder unto many; but thou art my strong refuge.
> *(TLB)* My success - at which so many stand amazed - is because you are my mighty protector.
> *(AMP)* I am as a wonder and surprise to many, but You are my strong refuge.

ISAIAH 8:18 Behold, I and the children whom the Lord hath given me are for signs and for wonders in Israel from the Lord of hosts, which dwelleth in mount Zion.

DANIEL 4:2, 3 I thought it good to shew the signs and wonders that the high God hath wrought toward me. How great are his signs! and how mighty are his wonders! his kingdom is an everlasting kingdom, and his dominion is from generation to generation.
> *(Jer.)* It is my pleasure to make known the signs and wonders with which the Most High God has favored me.
> *(Mof.)* It is my royal pleasure to declare the signal acts of the Most High God in dealing with me.
> *(Spur.)* The signs and wonders which the high God hath achieved towards me, it becomes me to declare.

MARK 16:17, 18 And these signs shall follow them that believe; In my name shall they cast out devils; they shall speak with new tongues; They shall take up serpents; and if they drink any deadly thing, it shall not hurt them; they shall lay hands on the sick, and they shall recover.
> *(New Life)* These special powerful works will be done by those who have put their trust in Me. In My name they will put out demons.
> *(NEB)* Faith will bring with it these miracles: believers will cast out devils in my name...
> *(Knox)* Where believers go, these signs shall go with them...they will lay their hands upon the sick and make them recover.
> *(Trans.)* Wherever men believe, these signs will be found...
> *(Fenton)* ...they shall lay their hands upon the sick, and fully restore them to strength.
> *(Wade)* ...they will be restored to health.
> *See authority of the believer p. 199-200; divine healing p. 278-279*

JOHN 14:12 Verily, verily, I say unto you, He that believeth on me, the works that I do shall he do also; and greater works than these shall he do; because I go unto my Father.
> *(Mof.)* ...will do the very deeds I do...
> *(Norlie)* ...will do the very things I am doing...
> *(Knox)* ...will be able to do what I do...
> *(Weym.)* ...can himself do the things that I am doing...
> *(Way)* ...and he shall do greater deeds than these...
> *(Phil.)* ...and he will do even greater things than these...
> *See authority of the believer p. 200; divine healing p. 282*

JOHN 20:30 And many other signs truly did Jesus in the presence of his disciples, which are not written in this book...

    (Beck) His disciples saw Jesus do many other miracles that are not written in this book.

JOHN 21:25 And there are also many other things which Jesus did, the which, if they should be written every one, I suppose that even the world itself could not contain the books that should be written. Amen.

    (AMP) And there are also many other things which Jesus did. If they should be all recorded one by one [in detail], I suppose that even the world itself could not contain (have room for) the books that would be written.

ACTS 2:22 Ye men of Israel, hear these words; Jesus of Nazareth, a man approved of God among you by miracles and wonders and signs, which God did by him in the midst of you, as ye yourselves also know.

    (AMP) ...by the mighty works and [the power of performing] wonders and signs which God worked through Him [right] in your midst...

ACTS 2:43 And fear came upon every soul: and many wonders and signs were done by the apostles.

    (Weym.) ...many marvels...

ACTS 4:29, 30 And now, Lord, behold their threatenings: and grant unto thy servants, that with all boldness they may speak thy word, By stretching forth thine hand to heal; and that signs and wonders may be done by the name of thy holy child Jesus.

    (AMP) While You stretch out Your hand to cure and to perform signs and wonders through the authority and by the power of the name...

      See prayer p. 233

ACTS 5:12 And by the hands of the apostles were many signs and wonders wrought among the people; and they were all with one accord in Solomon's porch.

    (20th C.R.) Many signs and wonders continued to occur among the people...

    (AMP) ...numerous and startling signs and wonders were being performed...

ACTS 8:5-8 Then Philip went down to the city of Samaria, and preached Christ unto them. And the people with one accord gave heed unto those things which Philip spake, hearing and seeing the miracles which he did. For unclean spirits, crying with loud voice, came out of many that were possessed with them: and many taken with palsies, and that were lame, were healed. And there was great joy in that city.

    (Mof.) ...listening to him and watching the miracles...

ACTS 8:5-8 (RSV) ...when they heard him and saw the signs...

(*AMP*) ...they heard him and watched the miracles and wonders which he kept performing [from time to time].

ACTS 8:13 Then Simon himself believed also: and when he was baptized, he continued with Philip, and wondered, beholding the miracles and signs which were done.

(*ASV*) ...and beholding signs and great miracles wrought, he was amazed.

(*AMP*) ...utterly amazed.

(*Mof.*) ...utterly astonished.

(*Phil.*) ...signs and remarkable demonstrations of power which took place, he lived in a state of constant wonder.

ACTS 19:11, 12 And God wrought special miracles by the hands of Paul: So that from his body were brought unto the sick handkerchiefs or aprons, and the diseases departed from them, and the evil spirits went out of them.

(*Gspd.*) God did such extraordinary wonders...

(*AMP*) ...unusual and extraordinary miracles...

(*Wms.*) God also continued to do such wonder-works...

(*Phil.*) God gave most unusual demonstrations of power...

(*Basic*) ...special works of power...

ROMANS 15:19 Through mighty signs and wonders, by the power of the Spirit of God; so that from Jerusalem, and round about unto Illyricum, I have fully preached the gospel of Christ.

(*AMP*) [Even as my preaching has been accompanied] with the power of signs and wonders, [and all of it] by the power of the Holy Spirit.

(*20th C.R.*) ...through the power displayed in signs and marvels, and through the power of the Holy Spirit.

(*SEB*) ...powerful proofs from God, miracles, and the power of the Spirit.

(*Barclay*) ...by the compulsion of miraculous demonstrations of the power of God in action, and by the power which the Holy Spirit gave me.

(*Gspd.*) ...by the force of signs and marvels, and by the power of the Holy Spirit...

(*Wand*) Marvelous signs have been granted to reinforce my words and deeds, and that could only have been by the power of the Holy Spirit.

I CORINTHIANS 2:4, 5 And my speech and my preaching was not with enticing words of man's wisdom, but in demonstration of the Spirit and of power: That your faith should not stand in the wisdom of men, but in the power of God.

(*AMP*) ...in demonstration of the [Holy] Spirit and power [a proof by the Spirit and power of God, operating on me and stirring in the minds of my hearers...]

I CORINTHIANS 2:4, 5 (Wms.) ...they were attended with proof and power given by the Spirit...

> *(Weym.)* ...convincing power of the Spirit.
>
> *(TLB)* ...but the Holy Spirit's power was in my words, proving to those who heard them that the message was from God.

II CORINTHIANS 12:12 Truly the signs of an apostle were wrought among you in all patience, in signs, and wonders, and mighty deeds.

> *(Conc.)* ...in signs and miracles and powerful deeds.

GALATIANS 3:5 He therefore that ministereth to you the Spirit, and worketh miracles among you, doeth he it by the works of the law, or by the hearing of faith?

> *(20th C.R.)* He who supplies you abundantly with his Spirit and endows you with such powers does he do this as the result of obedience to Law? Or as the result of your having listened with faith?
>
> *(Knox)* When God lavishes his Spirit on you and enables you to perform miracles, what is the reason for it? Your observance of the law, or your obedience to the call of faith?
>
> *(AMP)* Then does He Who supplies you with His marvelous [Holy] Spirit, and works powerfully and miraculously among you, do so on [the grounds of your doing] what the Law demands, or because of your believing in and adhering to and trusting in and relying on the message that you heard?

I THESSALONIANS 1:5 For our gospel came not unto you in word only, but also in power, and in the Holy Ghost, and in much assurance; as ye know what manner of men we were among you for your sake.

> *(AMP)* For our [preaching of the] glad tidings (the Gospel) came to you not only in word, but also in (its own inherent) power and in the Holy Spirit, and with great conviction and absolute certainty (on our part)...
>
> *(Conc.)* ...but in power also, and in Holy Spirit...
>
> *(Phil.)* ...a message with power behind it - the effectual power, in fact, of the Holy Spirit...
>
> *(TLB)* ...What we told you produced a powerful effect upon you, for the Holy Spirit gave you great and full assurance that what we said was true.

HEBREWS 2:4 God also bearing them witness, both with signs and wonders, and with divers miracles, and gifts of the Holy Ghost, according to his own will?

> *(AMP)* [Besides this evidence] it was also established and plainly endorsed by God, Who showed His approval of it by signs and wonders and various miraculous manifestations of [His] power and by imparting the gifts of the Holy Spirit [to the believers] according to His own will.

HEBREWS 2:4 (Basic) ...supernatural proofs, wonders, different kinds of miracles.
(*Alf.*) ...distributions of the Holy Spirit, according to his own will.
(*20th C.R.*) ...imparting the Holy Spirit as he saw fit.

The **GOD-KIND** of faith is not an accessory or an option; it is an **ABSOLUTE NECESSITY!**

Mark Hankins
11:23: THE LANGUAGE OF FAITH

ABLE MINISTERS
II Corinthians 3:6 383
BLOOD OF CHRIST
John 6:53-56 . . . . 95, 96, 366
Romans 5:9 60
Ephesians 1:7 99
Colossians 1:14 . . . . 98, 257, 286
Hebrews 9:12 72
Hebrews 10:19 . . . . 44, 115
Revelation 1:5 . . . . 68, 401
Revelation 12:11 173
BOLDNESS
Acts 4:29 . . . . 233, 410
Acts 4:31 . . . . 183, 234
Ephesians 3:12 41
Hebrews 10:19 . . . . 44, 115
Hebrews 13:6 168
I John 4:17 121
CASTING DOWN OF IMAGINATIONS
II Corinthians 10:5 202
CHILDREN
Psalm 112:2 298
Psalm 115:14 298
Proverbs 13:22 299
CONFIDENCE
Philippians 1:25 342
I John 5:14 263
FAITH
Romans 1:17 . . . . 29, 373
Hebrews 3:1 162
Hebrews 4:14 . . . . 128, 163
Hebrews 10:38 393
Hebrews 11:3 166
I Timothy 6:12 . . . . 162, 389
FORGIVENESS
Psalm 103:2, 3 274
James 5:15 287
I John 1:9 46
FRUIT OF THE HOLY SPIRIT
Philippians 1:11 111
Galatians 5:22-24 . . . . 322, 323, 324
GIFTS OF THE HOLY SPIRIT
I Corinthians 1:5, 7 . . . . 105, 106
I Corinthians 12:9-11 191
I Corinthians 14:1 322

GLORY OF GOD
Romans 6:4 . . . . 87, 377
II Corinthians 3:18 191
Ephesians 3:16 . . . . 192, 211, 245
I Peter 1:8 344
GRACE
Romans 3:24 . . . . 31, 84
Romans 5:17 . . . . 34, 102, 201, 375
Romans 5:21 377
Romans 6:14 . . . . 34, 92
II Corinthians 8:9 . . . . 59, 304
II Corinthians 9:8 306
Hebrews 4:16 128
Titus 3:7 392
IDENTIFICATION WITH CHRIST
Romans 6:4 . . . . 87, 377
Romans 6:8 . . . . 91, 378
Romans 6:11 . . . . 91, 379
Galatians 2:20 . . . . 75, 285, 385
Ephesians 2:4, 5 . . . . 82, 210, 386
Ephesians 2:6 . . . . 83, 210
Colossians 2:13 . . . . 80, 388
INTERCESSION
Romans 8:26, 27 . . . . 187, 188, 235
KNOWLEDGE
Colossians 2:3 109
II Peter 1:3, 4 109
LED BY THE SPIRIT
Romans 8:16 . . . . 124, 187
MARRIAGE
I Peter 3:7 395
MERCY
I Timothy 1:16 389
I Peter 1:3 393
NAME OF JESUS
Psalm 89:16 . . . . 47, 340
Mark 16:17, 18 . . . . . 199, 200, 278, 279, 409
Acts 3:16 283
Philippians 2:9, 10 . . . . 219, 220
I John 5:13 400
I John 5:18 401
NEW BIRTH
II Corinthians 5:17 117
Galatians 6:15 76
Ephesians 4:24 . . . . 41, 118

NEW BIRTH
Colossians 3:9, 10 119
I Peter 1:23 394
I John 3:9 397
I John 4:7 . . . . 332, 399
I John 5:1 399

OUR COMFORTER
John 14:16 180

OUR HELPER
Romans 8:26 . . . . 187, 235

OVER & ABOVE GIVING
I Chronicles 29:3 294

POWER OF THE TONGUE
Proverbs 4:24 138
Proverbs 6:2 138
Proverbs 10:11 138
Proverbs 12:6 139
Proverbs 12:13 139
Proverbs 12:14 139
Proverbs 12:18 . . . . 139, 274
Proverbs 13:3 139
Proverbs 14:3 140
Proverbs 15:4 140
Proverbs 15:23 . . . . 140, 341
Proverbs 16:21 140
Proverbs 16:23 140
Proverbs 16:24 140
Proverbs 18:7 140
Proverbs 18:20 141
Proverbs 18:21 141
Proverbs 21:23 141
I Peter 3:10 172

POWER OVER THE ENEMY
Luke 10:19 . . . . 200, 280
Ephesians 4:27 . . . . 216, 285
Ephesians 6:10-16 . . . . 216 - 219
Colossians 1:13 . . . . 97, 256, 286
Colossians 2:15 . . . . 68, 220
Hebrews 2:14, 15 . . . . 70, 221
James 4:7 . . . . 222, 286
I Peter 5:8, 9 . . . . 223, 287
I John 3:8 288
I John 4:4 195

POWER OVER UNFORGIVENESS
Mark 11:25 231

PRAISE & WORSHIP
Psalm 89:15 . . . . 46, 340
Psalm 100:2 227
Psalm 100:4 227
Psalm 138:2 137
Colossians 3:16 257
Hebrews 10:1, 2 . . . . 43, 114
Hebrews 13:15 259

PRAYERS OF PAUL
Ephesians 1:17 . . . . 202, 238
Ephesians 1:18 . . . . 203, 239
Ephesians 1:19-21 . . . . 72, 207, 242
Ephesians 1:21 . . . . 72, 207, 242
Ephesians 1:22 . . . . 208, 243
Ephesians 1:23 . . . . 209, 244
Ephesians 3:14, 15 . . . . 211, 245
Ephesians 3:16 . . . . 192, 211, 245
Ephesians 3:17, 18 . . . . 213, 247
Ephesians 3:19 . . . . 214, 248
Ephesians 3:20 . . . . 215, 249
Ephesians 3:21 . . . . 216, 250
Colossians 1:9-11 . . . . 253, 254
Colossians 1:12 . . . . 97, 255, 285
Colossians 1:13 . . . . 97, 256, 286
Colossians 1:14 . . . . 98, 257, 286

PRESENT DAY MINISTRY OF JESUS
Romans 8:33, 34 36
I Timothy 2:5 127
Hebrews 4:14 . . . . 128, 163
Hebrews 7:25 127
Hebrews 8:6 127
Hebrews 9:24 126
I Peter 2:25 129
I John 2:1 129

PROTECTION
Psalm 91:1-6, 10 273

PULLING DOWN OF STRONGHOLDS
II Corinthians 10:4 201

REDEEMED
Galatians 3:13 . . . . 58, 269, 309
Galatians 4:5 124

REIGNING WITH CHRIST
Romans 5:17 . . . . 34, 102, 201, 375

REIGNING WITH CHRIST
I Peter 2:9 125
Revelation 1:6 126
SLEEP
Psalm 4:8 349
SONS & HEIRS OF GOD
Romans 8:17 125
Galatians 4:5-7 124
SOUND OF MIND
Isaiah 26:3 349
II Timothy 1:7 116
SPIRIT OF TRUTH
John 16:13 180
STRENGTH
Psalm 89:17 349
SUPPLICATION
Ephesians 6:18 250
TITHING
Deuteronomy 14:22 293
Malachi 3:10 301
Hebrews 7:2, 5, 8 312-313
VICTORY
Romans 8:37 122
I Corinthians 15:57 103
II Corinthians 2:14 103

VICTORY OVER...

BITTERNESS & ANGER
Ephesians 4:31 323
CONFUSION
I Corinthians 14:33 354
FEAR
Isaiah 54:14 48
II Timothy 1:7 116
GRIEF & SORROW
Isaiah 53:4, 10 . . . . 53, 54
OFFENSES
Psalm 119:165 349
OPPRESSION
Isaiah 53:7 54
Isaiah 54:14 48
Acts 10:38 283
TEMPTATION
James 1:2, 3 343-344

THE WORLD
John 16:33 353
I John 5:4 . . . . 99, 173, 399
TROUBLES
John 14:27 352
WALK IN THE SPIRIT
Philippians 1:11 111
Galatians 5:22-24 . . . . 322, 323
WISDOM
I Corinthians 1:30 . . . . 39, 107
I Corinthians 2:13 189
Ephesians 1:8 108
Ephesians 1:17 . . . . 202, 238
Colossians 2:3 109
James 1:5 . . . . 169, 260
WORD OF GOD
Joshua 1:8 . . . . 135, 294
Psalm 1:1-3 . . . . 135, 136
Psalm 89:34 136
Psalm 119:130 137
Proverbs 4:20-23 . . . . 138, 274
Isaiah 55:10, 11 142
Jeremiah 1:12 142
Matthew 24:35 146
Luke 1:38 . . . . 150, 279
II Timothy 3:16 162
Hebrews 4:12 392
I Peter 1:23 394
I Peter 1:25 172
WORRY
Philippians 4:6 . . . . 251, 354
Philippians 4:7 . . . . 117, 252, 355
I Peter 5:7 . . . . 262, 356

Scriptures are King James Version, unless otherwise marked. Translations used in the text are identified by the abbreviations as noted below.

Adams   Adams, Jay E. *The New Testament in Everyday English.* Baker Book House, Grand Rapids, Michigan, 1979.

Alf.   Alford, Henry. *The New Testament for English Readers.* Rivingtons, Waterloo Place, London, England, 1863.

ASV.   American Standard Version. Thomas Nelson and Sons, New York, New York, 1901.

AMP   *Amplified Bible.* Zondervan Publishing House, Grand Rapids, Michigan, 1972.

H.T. Anders   Anderson, H.T. *A Translation of the New Testament.* Louisville, Kentucky, 1864.

River.   Ballentine, William. *The Riverside New Testament.* Houghton Mifflin Company, Boston, Massachusetts, 1923.

Barclay   Barclay, William. *The New Testament, A New Translation.* Collins, London, England, 1968.

Bart. & Pet.   Barlett, Edward and Peters, John. *Scriptures Hebrew and Christian.* G.P. Putnam's Sons, New York, New York, 1886.

Barth   Barth, Markus. *Anchor Bible.* Double Day and Company, Inc., Garden City, New York, 1974.

Baxter   Baxter, Richard. *A Paraphrase of the New Testament with Notes.* Parkhureff, London, England 1695.

Beck   Beck, William. *The Holy Bible in the Language of Today.* A.J. Holman Company, New York, New York, 1976.

Bird, R.   Bird, Robert. *Paul of Tarsus.* Charles Scribner's Sons, New York, New York, 1900.

Black.   Blackwelder, Boyce. *Letters from Paul, An Exegetical Translation.* Warner Press, Anderson, Indiana, 1971.

Sept.	Brenton, Charles Lee. *The Septuagint Version of the Old Testament.* Bagster & Sons, London, England, 1944.
Bruce	Bruce, F.F. *The Letters of Paul, An Expanded Paraphrase.* Eerdmans Publishing Company, Grand Rapids, Michigan, 1965.
Campbell	Campbell, Alexander. *The Sacred Writings of the Apostles and Evangelists of Jesus Christ.* Gospel Advocate Company, Nashville, Tennessee, 1974.
Carpenter	Carpenter, S.C. *A Paraphrase of Ephesians.* A.R. Mowbray & Co. Limited, London, England, 1956.
Carpenter	Carpenter, S.C. *Selections from Romans and The Letter to the Philippians.* Spirit to Spirit Publications, 1981.
Clem.	Clementson, Edgar Lewis. *The New Testament, A Translation.* The Pittsburgh Bible Institute Press, Pittsburgh, Pennsylvania, 1920.
Conc.	*Concordant Literal New Testament, Sixth Edition.* Concordant Publishing Concern, 1976.
Condon	Condon, Kevin. *The Alba House New Testament.* The Priest and Brothers of the Society of St. Paul, New York, New York, 1972.
Conf.	*Confraternity Version New Testament.* Catholic Book Publishing Company, New York, New York, 1963.
Conq.	Conquest, J.T. *The Holy Bible Containing the Old and New Testaments.* Longman & Company, London, England, n.d.
Cony.	Conybeare, W.J. *The Epistles of Paul.* Marshall Morgan and Scott, London, England, n.d.
Cornish	Cornish, Gerald Warre. *Saint Paul from the Trenches.* Spirit to Spirit Publications, Tulsa, Oklahoma, 1981.
Cress.	Cressman, A. *Good News for the World.* SOON! Publications, Bombay, India, 1969.
Crickmer	Crickmer, William Burton. *The Greek Testament Englished.* Elliot Stock, London, England, 1881.
Cunn.	Cunnington, E.E. *The New Covenant.* George Routledge & Sons, Limited, London, England, 1914.

Deane Deane, Anthony C. *St. Paul and His Letters.* Hodder and Stoughton, London, England, n.d.

Dodd. Doddridge, P. *The Family Expositor: or a Paraphrase and Version of The New Testament.* C & J Rivington, London, England, 1828.

Douay *Douay Rheims Version of the Holy Bible.* Douay Bible House, New York, New York, 1942.

Eadie Eadie, John. *Translation of Buchanan's Latin Psalms into English Verse.* Muir, Gowans & Company, Glasgow, Scotland, 1836.

Estes Estes, Chester. *The Better Version of The New Testament.* Chester Estes, Muscle Shoals, AL, n.d.

Fenton Fenton, Ferrar. *The Holy Bible in Modern English.* Destiny Publisher, Massachusetts, n.d.

Godbey Godbey, W.B. *Translation of the New Testament.* Newby Bookroom, Indiana, 1973.

GNB *Good News Bible, The Bible in Today's English Version.* American Bible Society, New York, New York, 1976.

Gspd. Goodspeed, Edgar J. *The New Testament, An American Translation.* University of Chicago, Chicago, Illinois, 1923.

Hammond Hammond, H. *A Paraphrase and Annotations Upon All Books of the New Testament, Second Edition.* Flesber and Royston, London, England, 1659.

Hanson Hanson, J.W. *The New Covenant.* Universalist Publishing House, 1886.

Har. Harrison, R.K. *The Psalms for Today: A New Translation from the Hebrew into Current English,* Zondervan Publishing House, Grand Rapids, Michigan, 1961.

Hayford Hayford, Jack W. *Spirit-Filled Life Bible.* Thomas Nelson, Inc., Nashville, Tennessee, 1991.

Hayman Hayman, Henry, D.D. *Romans and Galatians, Vol. 1.* Spirit to Spirit Publications, 1982.

Hayman Hayman, Henry, D.D. *I and II Corinthians, Vol. 2.* Spirit to Spirit Publications, 1982.

Hayman Hayman, Henry, D.D. *Ephesians through Philemon, Vol. 3.* Spirit to Spirit Publications, 1982.

Hayman   Hayman, Henry, D.D. *Hebrews & the General Epistles, Vol. 4.* Spirit to Spirit Publications, 1982.

Hoerber   Hoerber, Robert G. St. *Paul's Shorter Letters.* Fulton, Missouri, 1954.

Hudson   Hudson, James T. *The Pauline Epistles, Their Meaning and Message.* James Clarke and Co., Ltd., London, England, 1958.

Johnson   Johnson, Ben Campbell. *Matthew and Mark, A Rational Paraphrase of the New Testament.* Word Books, Waco, Texas, 1978.

Johnson   Johnson, Ben Campbell. *The Heart of Paul, A Rational Paraphrase of the New Testament.* Word Books, Waco, Texas, 1976.

Jordan   Jordan, Clarence. *The Cotton Patch Version of Paul's Epistles.* Association Press, New York, New York, 1968.

K. & L.   Kleist, James A. and Lilly, Joseph L. *The New Testament Rendered from the Original Greek with Explanatory Notes.* The Bruce Publishing Company, Milwaukee, Wisconsin, 1956.

Kling.   Klingensmith, Don J. *The New Testament in Everyday English.* Kaye's Inc., Fargo, North Dakota, 1974.

Knox   Knox, Ronald. *The Old Testament Newly Translated from the Latin Vulgate.* Burns, Oates and Washbourne, Ltd., London, England, 1949.

Knox   Knox, Ronald. *The New Testament of Our Lord and Savior Jesus Christ, A New Translation.* Sheed and Ward, New York, New York, 1953.

Lamsa   Lamsa, George M. *The Holy Bible from Ancient Eastern Manuscripts.* A.J. Holman Co., Marietta, Georgia, 1961.

Lau.   Laubach, Frank C. *The Inspired Letters in Clearest English.* Thomas Nelson and Sons, New York, New York, 1956.

New Life   Ledyard, Gleason. *The New Life Testament.* Word Books, Waco, Texas, 1970.

Leeser   Leeser, Isaac. *Twenty-Four Books of the Holy Scriptures.* Hebrew Publishing Company, New York, New York, n.d.

Letters   *Letters to Street Christians by Two Brothers from Berkeley.* Zondervan Publishing House, Grand Rapids, Michigan, 1971.

Lovett   Lovett, C.S. *Lovett's Lights on First John.* Personal Christianity, Baldwin Park, California, 1969.

                                                          Mark Hankins Ministries

Lovett   Lovett, C.S. *Lovett's Lights on Galatians, Ephesians, Philippians, Colossians, 1 & 2 Thessalonians with Rephrased Text.* Personal Christianity, Baldwin Park, California, 1969.

MacK.   MacKnight, James. *A New Literal Translation from the Original Greek of All the Apostolical Epistles.* Longman, Hurst, and Others, London, England. 1821.

McFadyen   McFadyen, John Edgar. *The Messages of the Psalmists.* Charles Scribner's Sons, New York, 1904.

Merrick   Merrick, James. A Version or Paraphrase of the Psalms. Thomas Payne and Son, London, England, 1789.

Mof.   Moffat, James. *The Holy Bible Containing the Old and New Testaments.* Double Day and Company, Inc., New York, New York, 1926.

Cent.   Montgomery, Helen Barrett. *Centenary Translation of the New Testament.* The American Baptist Publication Society, Philadelphia, Pennsylvania, 1924.

Syriac   Murdock, James. *The Syriac New Testament Translated into English from The Peshitto Version.* H.L. Hastings, Boston, Massachusetts, 1893.

NAB   *New American Bible.* Thomas Nelson Publishers, New York, New York, 1975.

NASB   *New American Standard Bible.* A.J. Holman, New York, New York, 1971.

NEB   *New English Bible.* Oxford University Press, Oxford, England, 1961.

NEV   *New English Version of the Holy Bible.* Zondervan Bible Publishers, Grand Rapids, Michigan, 1979.

NIV   *New International Version of the Holy Bible.* Zondervan Bible Publishers, Grand Rapids, Michigan, 1979.

Noli   Noli, Fans. S. *The New Testament of Our Lord and Savior Jesus Christ.* Albanian Orthodox Church in America, Boston, Massachusetts, 1961.

Norlie   Norlie, Olaf M. *Norlie's Simplified New Testament in Plain English – For Today's Readers.* Zondervan Bible Publishers, Grand Rapids, Michigan, 1961.

Message   Peterson, Eugene. *The Message//Remix, The Bible in Contemporary Language.* NavPress Publishing Group, Colorado Springs, Colorado, 2003.

Phil.   Phillips, J.B. *The New Testament in Modern English.* The Macmillan Company, New York, New York, 1958.

Mark Hankins Ministries

Bibliography

Pilcher Pilcher, Charles Venn. *The Epistles of St. Paul to the Romans.* Spirit to Spirit Publications, Tulsa, Oklahoma, 1981.

Quaker Purver, Anthony. *Quaker Bible.* 1764.

Fides Regan, Mary Perkins. *The Fides Translation.* Fides Publishers Association, Chicago, Illinois, 1955.

Richert Richert, Ernest L. *Freedom Dynamics.* The Thinker, Big Bear Lake, California, 1977.

Rieu Rieu, E.V. *The Acts of the Apostles.* Penguin Books, London, England, 1957.

Rieu Rieu, E.V. *The Four Gospels.* Penguin Books, London, England, 1953.

RSV *Revised Standard Version.* Thomas Nelson and Sons, New York, New York, 1952.

Roth. Rotherham, J.B. *The Emphasized Bible.* Kregel Publications, Grand Rapids, Michigan, 1976.

Roth. 2 Rotherham, J.B. *The New Testament: Critically Emphasized.* John Wiley and Sons, New York, New York, 1896.

Sanday & Headlam Sanday, William, D.D., L.L.D. and Headlam, Arthur C., B.D. *The Epistle to the Romans.* [England]: n.p., n.d.

Authentic Schonfield, Hugh. *The Authentic New Testament.* Dennis Dobson, Ltd., Great Britain, 1955.

Sharpe Sharpe, Samuel. *The Hebrew Scriptures, Vol. II.* Whitefield, Green, and Son, London, England, 1865.

Sharpe Sharpe, Samuel. *The New Testament, Translated from Griebach's Text.* J. Russell Smith, London, England, 1862.

Shuttle. Shuttleworth, Philip Nicholas. *Paraphrastic Translation of the Apostolical Epistles.* J.G. & F. Rivington, London, England, 1843.

Smith, J.M. Smith, J.M. and Goodspeed, E.J. *The Complete Bible, An American Translation.* University of Chicago Press, Chicago, Illinois, 1935.

Smith, J. Smith, Julia. *The Holy Bible Translated Literally from the Original Tongues.* American Publishing Company, Hartford, Connecticut, 1876.

Spencer Spencer, Francis. *The New Testament of Our Lord and Saviour Jesus Christ.* Macmillian Company, New York, New York, 1946.

Spur.   Spurrell, Helen. *A Translation of the Old Testament Scriptures from the Original Hebrew.* London, England, 1885.

Stanley   Stanley, Arthur. *The Epistles of St. Paul to the Corinthians, Second Edition.* Klock and Klock Christian Publishers, Inc., n.d.

Stevens   Stevens, George Barker. *The Epistles of Paul in Modern English.* Verploegh Editions, Wheaton, Illinois, 1980.

Stevens   Stevens, George Barker. *The Messages of the Apostles.* Charles Scribner's Sons, New York, 1900.

Swann   Swann, George. *New Testament of Our Lord and Savior, Jesus Christ.* George Swann Company, Robards, Kentucky, 1947.

Taylor   Taylor, John. *A Paraphrase with Notes on the Epistles to the Romans.* J. Waugh, London, England, 1754.

TLB   Taylor, Ken. *The Living Bible.* Tyndale House Publishers, Wheaton, Illinois, 1971.

Abbrev. Bible   *The Abbreviated Bible.* Van Nostrand, New York, New York, n.d.

Basic   *The Bible in Basic English.* University Press, Cambridge, England, 1965.

Book   *The Book of Books, A Translation of the New Testament Complete and Unabridged.* The Lutterworth Press, London, England, 1938.

Comp.   *The Companion Bible.* The Lamp Press, Ltd., London, England, n.d.

Dist.   *The Distilled Bible/New Testament.* Paul Benjamin Publishing Company, Stone Mountain, Georgia, 1980.

ABPS   *The Holy Bible Containing the Old and New Testaments: An Improved Edition.* American Baptist Publication Society, Philadelphia, Pennsylvania, n.d.

JSP   *The Holy Scriptures, A New Translation.* The Jewish Publication Society of America, Philadelphia, Pennsylvania, 1917.

Masoretic O.T. *The Holy Scriptures According to the Masoretic Text: A New Translation.* The O.T. Jewish Publication Society of America, Philadelphia, Pennsylvania, 1955.

Jer.   *The Jerusalem Bible.* Double Day and Company, Inc., New York, New York, 1968.

Deaf.   *The New Testament English Version for the Deaf.* Baker Book House, Grand Rapids, Michigan, 1978.

ABV — *The New Testament of Our Lord and Savior, Jesus Christ.* American Bible Union Version. American Baptist Publication Society, Philadelphia, Pennsylvania, n.d.

SEB — *The Simple English Bible.* Upward Productions, Inc., Oklahoma City, Oklahoma, 1978.

Torah — *The Torah: The Five Books of Moses.* The Jewish Publication Society of America, Philadelphia, Pennsylvania, 1955.

Trans. — *The Translator's New Testament.* The British and Foreign Bible Society, London, England, 1977.

20th C. 1 — *The Twentieth Century New Testament.* The Fleming H. Revell Company, New York, New York, 1902.

20th C.R. — *The Twentieth Century New Testament, Revised Edition.* The Fleming H. Revell Company, New York, New York, 1909.

Tomanek — Tomanek, James L. *The New Testament of Our Lord and Savior Jesus Anointed.* Arrowhead Press, Pocatello, Idaho, 1958.

Berk. — Verkuyl, Gerrit. *The Holy Bible, The Berkeley Version in Modern English.* Zondervan Publishing House, Grand Rapids, Michigan, 1959.

N. Berk. — Verkuyl, Gerrit. *The Holy Bible, The New Berkeley Version Revised Edition, in Modern English.* Zondervan Publishing House, Grand Rapids, Michigan, 1969.

Wade — Wade, G.W. *The Documents of the New Testament.* Thomas Burby and Company, London, England, 1934.

Wand — Wand, J.W.C. *The New Testament Letters.* Oxford University Press, Oxford, England, 1946.

Way — Way, Arthur S. *The Letters of St. Paul to the Seven Churches and Three Friends with the Letter to the Hebrews, Sixth Edition.* Macmillian and Company, New York, New York, 1926.

Weekes — Weekes, Robert D. *The New Dispensation Translated from the Greek.* Funk & Wagnall's Company, New York, New York, 1897.

Weym. — Weymouth, Richard Francis. *The New Testament.* James Clark and Company, London, England, 1909.

Wms. — Williams, Charles G. *The New Testament.* Moody Press, Chicago, Illinois, 1978.

Mark Hankins Ministries

Pl. Eng.	Williams, Charles Kingsley. *The New Testament, A New Translation in Plain English.* Longmans, Green, and Co., London, England, 1952.
Wood	Wood, C.T. *The Life, Letters and Religion of St. Paul.* T. & T. Clark, Edinburgh, England, n.d.
Worrell	Worrell, A.S. *The Worrell New Testament.* Gospel Publishing House, Springfield, Missouri, 1980.
Wuest	Wuest, Kenneth S. *The New Testament, An Expanded Translation.* William B. Eerdmans Publishing Company, Grand Rapids, Michigan, 1981.
Young	Young, Arthur. *Young's Literal Translation of the Holy Bible.* Revised Edition. Baker Book House, Grand Rapids, Michigan, 1976.

Mark Hankins Ministries Publications

THE BLOODLINE OF A CHAMPION - THE POWER OF THE BLOOD OF JESUS
The blood of Jesus is the liquid language of love that flows from the heart of God & gives us hope in all circumstances. In this book, you will clearly see what the blood has done FOR US but also what the blood has done IN US as believers.

TAKING YOUR PLACE IN CHRIST
Many Christians talk about what they are trying to be and what they are going to be. This book is about who you are NOW as believers in Christ.

PAUL'S SYSTEM OF TRUTH
Paul's System of Truth reveals man's redemption in Christ, the reality of what happened from the cross to the throne and how it is applied for victory in life through Jesus Christ.

THE SECRET POWER OF JOY
If you only knew what happens in the Spirit when you rejoice, you would rejoice everyday. Joy is one of the great secrets of faith. This book will show you the importance of the joy of the Lord in a believer's life.

11:23 – THE LANGUAGE OF FAITH
Never under-estimate the power of one voice. Over 100 inspirational, mountain-moving quotes to "stir up" the spirit of faith in you.

LET THE GOOD TIMES ROLL
This book focuses on the five key factors to Heaven on earth: The Holy Spirit, Glory, Faith, Joy, and Redemption. The Holy Spirit is a genius. If you will listen to Him, He will make you look smart.

THE POWER OF IDENTIFICATION WITH CHRIST

Learn how God identified us with Christ in His death, burial, resurrection, and seating in Heaven. The same identical life, victory, joy, and blessings that are In Christ are now in you. This is the glory and the mystery of Christianity – the power of the believer's identification with Christ.

REVOLUTIONARY REVELATION

This book provides excellent insight on how the spirit of wisdom and revelation is mandatory for believers to access their call, inheritance, and authority in Christ.

FAITH OPENS THE DOOR TO THE SUPERNATURAL

In this book you will learn how believing and speaking opens the door to the supernatural in your life. God has given every believer a measure of overcoming faith. The spirit of faith will take the victim out of your voice and put victory in your voice. Your faith will never rise above the level of your confession. So get a grip on your lip!

THE SPIRIT OF FAITH

If you only knew what was on the other side of your mountain, you would move it! Having a spirit of faith is necessary to do the will of God and fulfill your destiny. The spirit of faith turns defeat into victory and dreams into reality.

DIVINE APPROVAL

Understanding you have GOD'S DIVINE APPROVAL on your life sets you free from the sense of rejection, inadequacy or inferiority. You are free to receive God's best blessings and to follow His plan for your life. This confidence in God sets you free from constantly seeking approval from others. One of the most misunderstood subjects in the Bible is righteousness. The Gospel of Christ is a revelation of the righteousness of God. The center of the Gospel reveals the righteousness of God. I call righteousness a radical revelation, a revolutionary revelation. It is a reality that is produced for us by the Lord Jesus Christ.

GOD'S HEALING WORD by Trina Hankins

Trina's testimony and a practical guide to receiving healing through meditating on the Word of God. This guide includes: testimonies, practical teaching, Scriptures & confessions, and a CD with Scriptures & confessions (read by Mark Hankins).

Mark Hankins Ministries
PO BOX 12863 ALEXANDRIA, LA 71315

Phone: 318.767.2001   E-mail: contact@markhankins.org
Website: www.markhankins.org

Mark and Trina Hankins travel nationally and internationally preaching the Word of God with the power of the Holy Spirit. Their message centers on the spirit of faith, who the believer is in Christ, and the work of the Holy Spirit.

After over 40 years of pastoral and traveling ministry, Mark and Trina are now ministering full-time in campmeetings, leadership conferences, and church services across the United States and around the world. Their son Aaron and his wife Errin Cody are now the pastors of Christian Worship Center in Alexandria, Louisiana. Their daughter Alicia Moran and her husband Caleb pastor Metro Life Church in Lafayette, Louisiana. Mark and Trina have eight grandchildren.

Mark is the author of several books. For more information on Mark Hankins Ministries, please log on to our website, www.markhankins.org.

Acknowledgements

My wife, Trina.
My son, Aaron, and his wife Errin Cody.
    Their children, Avery Jane, Macy Claire, and Jude Aaron.
My daughter, Alicia, and her husband Caleb.
    Their children, Jaiden Mark, Gavin Luke, Landon James, Dylan Paul, and Hadley Marie.
My parents, Pastor B.B. and Velma Hankins, who are now in Heaven with the Lord.
My wife's parents, Rev. William and Ginger Behrman.